HANDBOOKS

ARUBA

Rosalie Klein

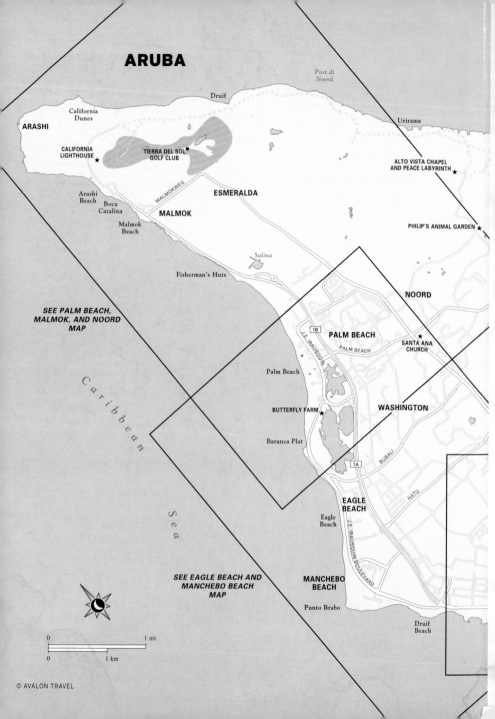

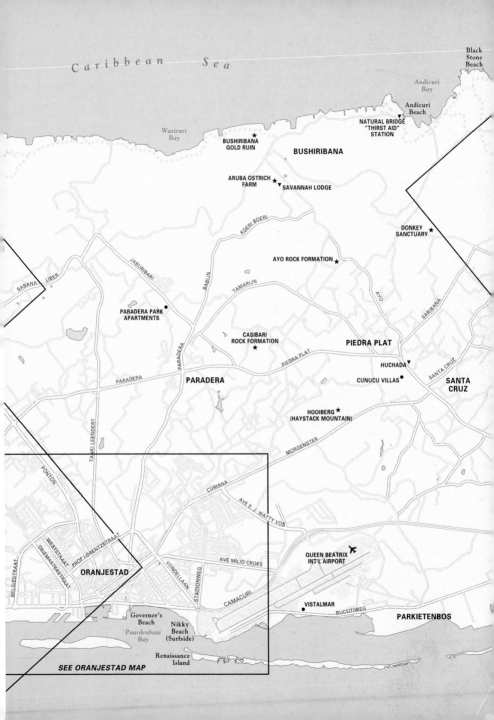

ARUBA (CONTINUED)

SEE
ARIKOK NATIONAL PARK
MAP (P. 90)

Caribbean Sea

★ QUADIKAKIRI CAVES

Rincon Bay

Grapefield Beach

Boca Grande

Bachelor's Beach

SABANA LODO

SERO GRANDI

COSTA RIBA ▼

SEROE COLORADO

WEG FONTEIN

WEG FONTEIN

WEG SEROE BLANCO

BRASIL

PALISAWEG

★ LOURDES GROTTO/
SEROE PRETO CITY OF LIGHTS

ESSO HEIGHTS

FORTHEUVEL STRAAT

LAGO HEIGHTS

LAGOVILLE

CAYA JOSE GEERMAN

ESSOVILLE

SEROE COLORADO

Roger's Beach

Baby Beach

WEG BRASIL

PASTOR HENDRIK STRAAT

▼ CHARLIE'S BAR

RUM REEF BAR ▼

San Nicolas Bay

HENDRIK STRAAT

SAN NICOLAS

■ ROYAL DUTCH MARINE CAMP

Caribbean Sea

0   1 mi

0   1 km

© AVALON TRAVEL

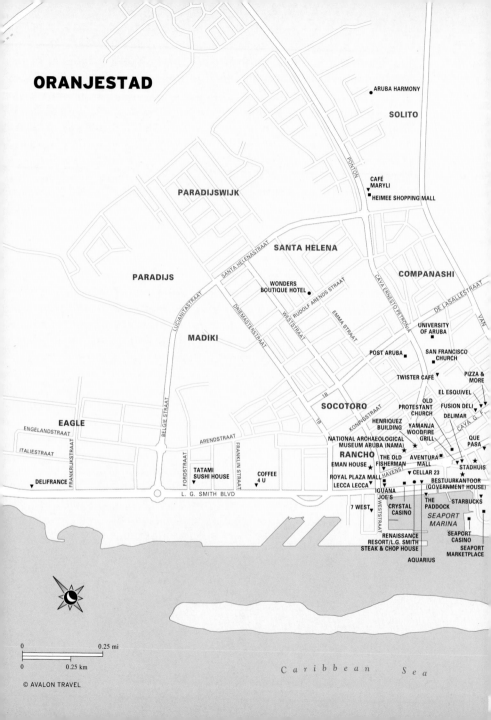

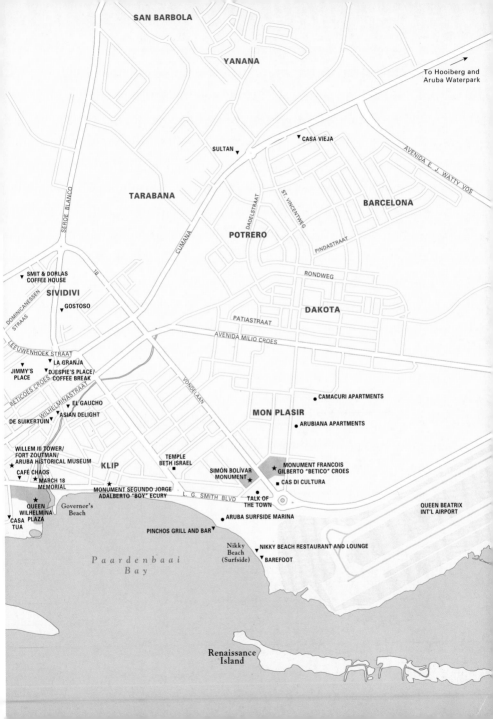

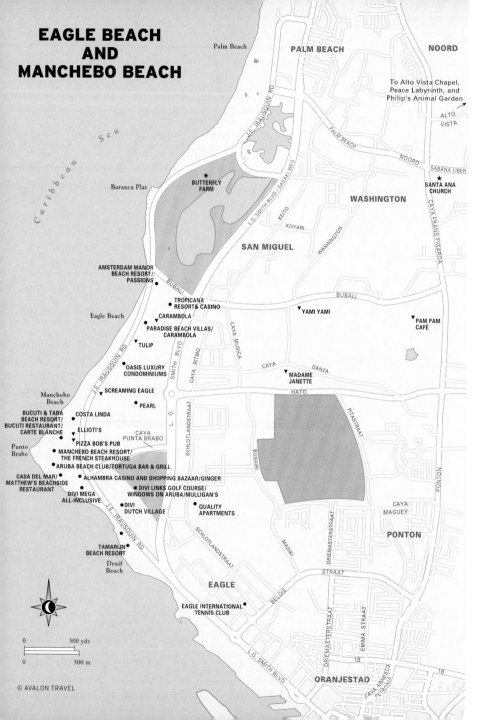

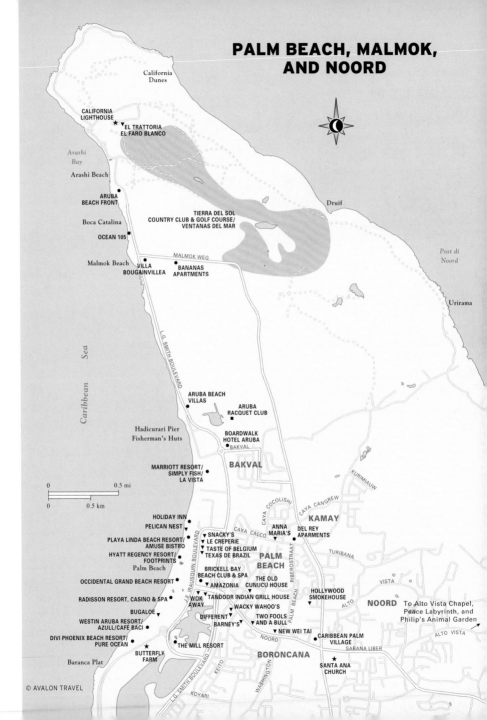

PALM BEACH, MALMOK, AND NOORD

California
Dunes

CALIFORNIA
LIGHTHOUSE
★ EL TRATTORIA
EL FARO BLANCO

Arashi Bay

Arashi Beach

ARUBA
BEACH FRONT

Boca Catalina

OCEAN 105

TIERRA DEL SOL
COUNTRY CLUB & GOLF COURSE/
VENTANAS DEL MAR

Druif

Post di Noord

Malmok Beach

VILLA
BOUGAINVILLEA

MALMOK WEG

BANANAS
APARTMENTS

Urirama

Caribbean Sea

L.G. SMITH BOULEVARD

ARUBA BEACH
VILLAS

ARUBA
RACQUET CLUB

Hadicurari Pier
Fisherman's Huts

BOARDWALK
HOTEL ARUBA

BAKVAL

MARRIOTT RESORT/
SIMPLY FISH/
LA VISTA

BAKVAL

KURIMIAUW

0   0.5 mi
0   0.5 km

HOLIDAY INN
PELICAN NEST

PLAYA LINDA BEACH RESORT/
AMUSE BISTRO

HYATT REGENCY RESORT/
FOOTPRINTS
Palm Beach

OCCIDENTAL GRAND BEACH RESORT

RADISSON RESORT, CASINO & SPA

BUGALOE

WESTIN ARUBA RESORT/
AZULL/CAFÉ BACI

DIVI PHOENIX BEACH RESORT/
PURE OCEAN

Baranca Plat

BUTTERFLY
FARM

THE MILL RESORT

CAYA COCOLISHI

CAYA CANGREW

CAYA CALCO

KAMAY

ANNA
MARIA'S

DEL REY
APARMENTS

▼ SNACKY'S
▼ LE CREPERIE
▼ TASTE OF BELGIUM
TEXAS DE BRAZIL

PALM
BEACH

BRICKELL BAY
BEACH CLUB & SPA

THE OLD
CUNUCU HOUSE
▼ AMAZONIA

TURIBANA

VISTA

WOK
AWAY
TANDOOR INDIAN GRILL HOUSE

HOLLYWOOD
SMOKEHOUSE

ALTO

NOORD   To Alto Vista Chapel,
Peace Labyrinth, and
Philip's Animal Garden

▼ WACKY WAHOO'S

DIFFERENT ▼   TWO FOOLS
BARNEY'S   AND A BULL

CARIBBEAN PALM
VILLAGE

ALTO VISTA

NEW WEI TAI

NOORD

BORONCANA

SANTA ANA
CHURCH

SABANA LIBER

PALM BEACH

RIBEROSTRAAT

KEITO

WASHINGTON

KOYARI

L.G. SMITH BOULEVARD

J.E. IRAUSQUIN BOULEVARD

© AVALON TRAVEL

Contents

DISCOVER
Aruba

Peek out the window when coming in for a landing on Aruba. You'll be struck by the intense blue of the surrounding Caribbean Sea and snowy white beaches. "Aruba is right next door to heaven," is how one long-time visitor describes it.

Aruba is a small island, but rich and varied, fulfilling the vacation needs of families, singles, honeymooners, athletes, adventurers, and those who simply wish to do nothing but relax on the beach.

Some of the most stunning beaches in the Caribbean line the west coast of the island. Their turquoise waters are as calm as a lake. It's where you'll find Palm Beach, a parade of resorts, each at least 10 stories tall, standing side by side over a one-mile length. Turn a corner at the Westpunt going north, and the dramatic contrasts of the island become apparent: It is a lunar landscape of coral rock and pillow basalt, where spume surges high from the crashing waves, carving the rock into fantastical shapes. At Eagle Beach and adjacent Manchebo Beach are smaller, more intimate resorts which stretch to the outskirts of the main town of Oranjestad.

These tourist areas offer a wealth of easily accessible activities, eateries, casinos, and shopping. But a visit to Aruba is not complete

without exploring beyond their limits. Discover Arikok National Park, Conchi (Natural Pool), and the caves, dunes, and *bocas* (coves) of the eastern end near San Nicolas.

In Aruba, there's little divide between island dwellers and tourists. Don't be surprised to find a table of islanders sitting right next to you at a resort restaurant or casino any night of the week. This congenial relationship with vacationers has made Aruba the most popular repeat destination in the Caribbean. It is an extension of the ease among the locals themselves.

Aruba can be a tranquil respite from the hustle and bustle of everyday existence. Each day can be an exciting discovery of nature, island culture, or a new sport on land, sea, or in the air. It is a place where modern luxury and the rugged landscape exist side by side. Your Aruban vacation can embrace either or both—the choice is yours.

Planning Your Trip

Where to Go

Oranjestad

Aruba's capital offers visitors a taste of authentic island life. Playa, as it is also known, boasts quaint side streets interwoven with major shopping avenues. Right next to malls with designer shops, the town residents are still living in homes from the 18th century. Explore Aruba's history and culture here in museums such as the National Archaeological Museum Aruba (NAMA) or the Aruba Historical Museum. Then enjoy superb dining, shopping, and casino play.

Oranjestad also features a harbor filled with deep sea fishing boats; the major resort, the Renaissance Resort; and many attractive guesthouses. Some local beaches like Nikky and Druif Beaches are practically deserted during the week but fill up with islanders on weekends.

Eagle Beach and Manchebo Beach

This resort area offers a tranquil, secluded getaway. Miles of beaches are shadowed by large copses of sea grape. There are many spots where a visitor can settle down, look around, and not see a soul.

The apartment-style resorts here are well suited to families. Divi Links golf course is surrounded by a beautiful resort where golfers can roll out of bed to an early tee time. Organized resort activities, such as arts and crafts, scavenger hunts, pool games, and contests for kids keep the rest of the family happy. Close proximity to Oranjestad allows history buffs and shoppers easy access to museums and designer stores.

Palm Beach, Malmok, and Noord

Palm Beach is the best place on the island

Manchebo Beach

Turk's Cap cactus, known as *bushi* in Papiamento

for lounging on the beach and for night-life. Restaurants, casinos, and clubs are next door to glamorous resorts. It is the center of every water activity imaginable. Sailing, snorkeling, scuba diving off the *Antilla* shipwreck, tubing, deep sea fishing, para-sailing, windsurfing, and *Seaworld Explorer* are all here. Close by is the exhilarating Butterfly Farm and Philip's Animal Garden for family fun.

North Coast

The dramatic, craggy north coast sharply con-trasts with Aruba's tranquil western shores. The Tierra Del Sol Country Club and Golf Course, featuring one of the most challeng-ing courses in the world, borders the coastal road. A beacon to the northwest point, the California Lighthouse can be visited on moun-tain-bike tours.

Follow the spectacular coast trail via 4x4 or ATV to find secluded coves for surf-ing. Off-road adventurers enjoy traversing the Aruban outback for a trip back in time. Horseback tours provided by stables such as Rancho Daimari, weave through the dramatic coastal formations. Befriend a giant bird at the Aruba Ostrich Farm or do some rock climbing at Ayo and explore the Bushiribana Gold Ruin.

Santa Cruz, Paradera, and Piedra Plat

Aruba's inland residential areas of Santa Cruz, Paradera, and Piedra Plat have inter-esting rock formations, native architecture, and inexpensive guesthouses that allow visitors to be immersed in authentic island life. Santa Cruz borders Aruba's national park, where indigenous flora and fauna are protected.

Hikers enjoy the trails of Arikok National Park. Make the trek to the park's high-est point, Seroe Jamanota; or visit Conchi (Natural Pool) within its confines. Conchi is the best example of the dramatic lava rock formations on Aruba. This is horseback rid-ing and ATV country. Spelunking is easy at Quadikakiri and Fontein Caves on the far side of the park. Meet local fauna at the Donkey Sanctuary or go rock climbing among for-mations at Casibari. Collectors enjoy sift-ing through antiques at Rococo Plaza in Paradera.

San Nicolas, Savaneta, and Pos Chiquito

The unspoiled and secluded coves of Aruba's eastern end are favorite spots with kitesurfers, sunbathers, and snorkelers. The south side is known for pristine beaches with stunning turquoise seas. A barrier reef following the coast is home to the island's best scuba spots.

Meet and interact with islanders at authentic local fish restaurants along the shore. The weekly Carubbian Festival is a multi-cultural mix of regional food, entertainment, and authentic handicrafts, all rolled into a lively street fair in San Nicolas. On the outskirts of the town is the atmospheric and spiritual Lourdes Grotto.

When to Go

Unlike many resort destinations at more northern latitudes, Aruba has the advantage of eternal summer with little changes in the seasons. The most expensive peak travel season is December 15-April 15. This is also when the island is the most crowded.

In September and early October room rates are lowest. Visitors can waltz into any restaurant without a reservation and enjoy a deserted beach. Other surprisingly quiet times to escape the cold and the crowds are the 10 days before Christmas and the week after New Year's.

The spectacular pageantry of Carnival dominates Aruba from the first weekend in January until Ash Wednesday. The last two weeks in particular are filled with parades and musical events.

Before You Go

Passports, Visas, and Vaccinations

Valid, current passports are required for visitors from the United States and Canada. Aruban immigration requires that officials see a return ticket upon arrival. An Entry-Departure form, or ED-Card, is issued while on the plane, prior to arrival, to fill in and give to Aruban immigration. A section of this remains with you during your stay; be sure to have it ready to return to local immigration officials when you depart.

Nationals of most countries are required to have a visa to enter Aruba. Exemptions are made for the United States, Canada, the European Union and territories (the Schengen Territory), United Kingdom, Ireland, and Colombian and Jamaican nationals coming from the United States with valid residence permits or U.S. visas.

Transportation

Aruba's Reina Beatrix International Airport receives regular commercial flights daily from the United States and Canada. Several cruise ship lines include Oranjestad Harbor on their agenda.

Once on the island, visitors find ample taxis, which are pricey. It is easy to rent mopeds, cars, and jeeps, or rent or arrange mini-buses to be chauffeured around for large groups. Some are equipped for people with disabilities. A bus system services major resorts and all residential areas. They stop frequently to take visitors to Oranjestad. For touring, ATVs, 4x4s, and Harley-Davidson motorcycles are readily available. Major holiday weeks require car rentals to be made well in advance of the trip.

The Best of Aruba

Aruba's principal attractions are the gorgeous beaches and azure waters. But it is worth it to travel beyond the beaches to explore the culture and unique topography of the island. Main tourist areas offer a myriad of choices for dining and nightlife. Though free musical entertainment is offered at several venues, the most stunning show is the daily gorgeous, colorful sunset along Aruba's western shore. Hotel beach bars and independent lounges provide happy hour prices to enjoy this spectacle, which can segue into a romantic dinner right on the beach.

Day 1

On your first evening run down to the beach to savor the sunset and take advantage of happy hour. Look for 2-for-1 cocktails at most hotel bars and cafés like Bugaloe at the end of the De Palm Pier. Stay for dinner and enjoy a fresh fish meal at Pelican Nest.

After hours, take in some free live music at Palm Beach's Arawak Gardens, Fusion Wine and Piano Bar in the Alhambra Shopping Bazaar, or at the bandstand by the water at the Renaissance Marketplace in Oranjestad. If it's a weekend, find a great band and fun crowd at Café Chaos across the street from Renaissance Marketplace.

Day 2

If it is a Sunday, check out the luxurious Sunday brunch at Windows on Aruba at the Divi Links. Enjoy an exhilarating morning jog along the paths parallel to Eagle Beach, or following the shore from Marriott to Malmok. Or, if you prefer, refresh your chi with some yoga on the beach at the Manchebo Beach Resort. For a true introduction to pampering and relaxation, Okeanos Spa will take you out to Renaissance Island for a treatment in their private cove.

Head over to the Butterfly Farm in Palm Beach for your first real outing; it won't be your last visit. Butterflies are most active in the mornings.

sunset at Eagle Beach

Those eager to learn to snorkel or dive should join a sailing and snorkeling tour. Dive operators like Unique Sports of Aruba will have you exploring under the water in a few short hours. Quick morning courses allow novices to dive at one of the easier, shallower dive sites around the west coast, or snorkelers can enjoy a trip to the *Antilla* shipwreck and Arashi Beach.

Enjoy a romantic dinner on the beach at Passions by the Amsterdam Manor Beach Resort. Afterwards, stroll along the Palm Beach promenade for some souvenir shopping. Stay until late to party at Señor Frog's.

Day 3

Catch a bus to Oranjestad for the day. Explore the landmark buildings that house the National Archeological Museum Aruba (NAMA) and the Aruba Historical Museum located within Fort Zoutman.

A charming lunch spot with a view of the harbor is The Paddock. Or meet island movers and shakers at their favorite power lunch restaurant Aquarius. For dessert, try some fresh-made gelato at Lecca Lecca. Break up the day with a half-hour exploring Aruba from the air with HeliTours, or indulge in an underwater adventure on *Atlantis* Submarine.

Enjoy dinner at celebrated L.G. Smith's Steak & Chop House or romantic Pinchos Grill and Bar.

Day 4

Today, get away from the beach and towns and do some touring with Madi's Magical Tours, a highly personalized, unique safari tour with a dawn trip to Conchi (Natural Pool) on the north coast. From there, Madi can take you on an outback adventure lasting all or part of a day.

Or rent a 4x4 to tour on your own: Start the day by watching the sun rise from the California Lighthouse. From there you can head down the north coast road or make your way back to Noord and take in such sights as Alto Vista Chapel, Philip's Animal Garden, and Santa Ana Church. If venturing farther along the coast in a four-wheel drive, follow

Aruba Ostrich Farm

the gravel road to the Bushiribana Gold Ruin, and the Aruba Ostrich Farm. The Ostrich Farm is a nice spot for lunch, followed by scrambling around the Ayo Rock Formation. Next to the Ostrich Farm is Gold Mine Ranch, where you can schedule an exploration of the area on horseback.

Unwind from an exhausting day of touring with a sunset "toes in the sand" dinner at Footprints at the Hyatt.

Day 5

Enjoy a day of hiking or horseback riding at Arikok National Park and the caves and coves beyond. A light breakfast can be had at Huchada in Santa Cruz, on the way to the park, if you wish to get an early start. Paved roads allow exploration by car, or park rangers will guide you through various hiking paths, such as Cunucu Arikok Trail, or to the summit of Seroe Jamanota, or to Conchi (Natural Pool), which will take up a morning or nearly the entire day. Enjoy a lunch of authentic Aruban cuisine at Urataka Center on the road leading to the park. Call Rancho Daimari if you prefer to take the tour on horseback.

Enjoy a gourmet dinner at Carte Blanche, in the Bucuti & Tara Beach resort, for a long, full, and entertaining evening of socializing with the chefs while watching them prepare dinner.

Day 6

Try one of Oranjestad's many early morning eateries, such as Smit & Dorlas Coffee House. A drive to San Nicolas will allow you to enjoy the scenery of "Sunrise City." Take a dip at Baby Beach or Roger's Beach, two of the most beautiful inlets on Aruba. You can also set up diving or snorkeling in this area with Jad's Dive Shop.

Heading back from San Nicolas, stop at Zeerover in Savaneta for fresh fish, island style. B-55, next to the old drive-in theater, on the main highway, has great BBQ and a beautiful view. From either of these eateries you can easily stop at Mangel Halto beach for a relaxing swim.

For a full day of water fun, families also enjoy the Aruba Waterpark off the Oranjestad-Santa Cruz road, which also has a great kitchen for lunch.

Returning from the waterpark takes you directly past Casa Vieja restaurant, which offers a dinner stop of authentic Middle Eastern or regional cuisine at bargain prices.

Day 7

Dig into gourmet crepes for breakfast at Le Creperie in Palm Beach to fuel up for learning windsurfing or kitesurfing with Aruba Active Vacations. For a real thrill, try Skydive Aruba in the field across the road from the wind-surfing center. Scuba is a no-no less than 24 hours before departure, but sailing and snor-keling are always an option. Try something really different by exploring the south shore with Aruba Kayak Adventures, which in-cludes lunch, or a customized surfing tour with Aruba Surf School.

In the evening hours you can pick up some last-minute souvenirs and explore the hot spots at Arawak Gardens. It is a good time to give in and buy that necklace or earrings that caught your fancy at Kristie's Jewels or at the Caribbean Queen shop in Palm Beach Plaza. Combine shopping with some island history and culture while enjoying the *Waltzing Waters* at Paseo Herencia Shopping Mall. Finish the day at Sky Lounge where you can while away the night and count the stars.

Try tandem skydiving for a safe and thrilling experience.

Best Water Sports

Sailing and Snorkeling Cruises
OCTOPUS CRUISES (PAGE 52)
With the only boat in Aruba without a motor, Octopus offers a true sailing experience! Cruises start at easy, placid sites, where the fish flock to snorkelers in search of snacks. One of the most impressive wrecks in all the Caribbean, the Antilla, is also seen while snorkeling or diving on this tour.

TRANQUILO (PAGE 53)
Enjoy "toes in the water" sailing on the beautiful ketch *Tranquilo,* which tours Aruba's south side snorkel sites. This is one of the few boats that offers all-day trips—and the only one to offer the personal expertise of Captain Anthony and his family.

Scuba Diving
UNIQUE SPORTS OF ARUBA (PAGE 55)
Unique Sports of Aruba offers daily morning lessons for complete novices and regularly scheduled tours for experienced, certified divers. The instructors and divemasters are friendly and capable.

DIVE ARUBA (PAGE 55)
Personal service, customized to experience and ability, is the Dive Aruba trademark. A veteran divemaster takes experienced, certified divers to out-of-the-way sites.

Windsurfing, Kitesurfing, and Surfing
ARUBA ACTIVE VACATIONS (PAGE 59)
Develop a windsurfing obsession with the congenial instructors at Aruba Active Vacations, one of the best outfitters on the island. Located at Fisherman's Huts, just north of the Ritz-Carlton Resort in Palm Beach, they have a large inventory of equipment designed for surfers of all abilities.

ARUBA SURF SCHOOL (PAGE 59)
Instructor Dennis Martinez is passionate about surfing. He also customizes his lessons at Aruba Surf School to his students' ability and experience and scouts out the best surf on any given day.

Parasailing, Tubing, Banana Boats, and Waverunners
NATIVE DIVERS WATERSPORTS (PAGE 59)
Native Divers Watersports pays strong attention to safety while providing a fun time for

kitesurfing

Enjoy an all-day snorkeling cruise with the entire family.

windsurfing at sunset

the whole family. It's easy to arrange the water activity of your choice, from banana boats to parasailing.

FUN FOR EVERYONE (PAGE 60)
Conveniently located in front of the Riu Palace Resort, Fun For Everyone has four boats for tubing, parasailing, and banana boat rides. They take banana passengers on a complete tour of the northwest coastline, all the way to the Westpunt.

Deep Sea Fishing
Principal departure points for fishing boats are Oranjestad Harbor and Hadicurari Pier, at the north end of Palm Beach. Crews clean your catch and take it to a recommended restaurant to have it prepared for your dinner.

DRIFTWOOD FISHING CHARTERS (PAGE 57)
Driftwood is named after the owner's popular seafood restaurant, where they happily cook up your catch. Captain Herby has a passion for the sport. He's highly motivated to find the fish—he has to provide the catch of the day for the restaurant's dinner menu!

MELINA CHARTERS (PAGE 58)
Melina departs from Hadicurari Pier, conveniently located close to the Palm Beach resorts. Captain Piet is a very congenial host, with a love of the sport and a keen knowledge of the best fishing grounds.

snorkeling

Romantic Rendezvous

Aruba has a wealth of ways for honeymooners, or honeymooners-at-heart, to make the most of their special time together on the island.

Spas

Several island spas had couples in mind when they designed their treatment rooms. Not only do they have dual tables, but elegant sunken baths for two, and specialized packages featuring champagne and snacks.

OKEANOS SPA (PAGE 70)

Ease tired muscles and relieve stress with a massage at the Okeanos annex on Renaissance Island. Couples can have a full morning or afternoon session in their private cove, with a stunning view of the sea and absolute privacy.

ZOIA (PAGE 71)

Located within the Hyatt Regency Resort in Palm Beach, ZoiA has a special room for couples with a giant bath and a private terrace with a beautiful view.

Cruises

RED SAIL SPORTS DINNER CRUISE (PAGE 57)

Enjoy an elegant dinner with wine and a champagne toast, while cruising the coast and watching the sun set.

MONSOON (PAGE 53)

This luxurious sailing vessel even sports a giant tub. Private sunset dinner cruises can be arranged with gourmet meals catered by Twister Café.

TRANQUILO (PAGE 53)

Aside from day trips, the *Tranquilo* offers a catered dinner with champagne for two on a sunset trip.

Sunsets

Aruba's glorious sunsets can be enjoyed while dining at a perfectly situated restaurant or during a private dinner for two on the beach.

RADISSON RESORT, CASINO & SPA (PAGE 182)

With one of the longest stretches of beach in Palm Beach, the Radisson has plenty of room to offer a tranquil, private spot. This is the most reasonably priced of all the private beach dinners.

Aruba is a popular wedding destination.

walking with flamingos at Okeanos Spa

Pinchos Grill and Bar at sunset

BARANCA PLAT (PAGE 41)

Only a five-minute walk south from the Divi Phoenix Beach Resort in Palm Beach, this quiet inlet allows couples to escape the audience that lines up on Palm Beach nightly to watch the sunset.

Eats

If there is one thing island restaurateurs and resorts understand, it is the appeal of dining alfresco. It is possible to eat in lovely gardens or with spectacular views nearly every night.

LA TRATTORIA EL FARO BLANCO (PAGE 124)

Next to the California Lighthouse, La Trattoria El Faro Blanco offers the most spectacular sunset view from their charming terrace, overlooking the entire northwest coast.

PINCHOS GRILL AND BAR (PAGE 96)

Sitting right on the water at Nikky Beach, Pinchos was specifically designed to stoke romantic embers. Couches and hammocks for two are just made for cuddling while savoring the sunset and a delectable meal.

PASSIONS (PAGE 107)

An excellent menu and ideal location in Eagle Beach makes the aptly named Passions restaurant one of the most charming and romantic dining spots on Aruba. Tables are placed with enough distance to feel as if you have the beach to yourself.

Miles of pristine beaches are perfect for long, romantic walks.

sunset dinner cruise

Explore the Outback

Exploring Aruba's wilds is an interesting proposition, especially when trying to follow directions or looking for road signs, which are in short supply. Make the days easier and filled with all the must-see sights by taking a tour with an enthusiastic and knowledgeable guide.

Safari Tours

MADI'S MAGICAL TOURS (PAGE 62)

One of the most unique ways to tour Aruba's outback is with guide extraordinaire Madi. She leads small, personal, and customized trips infused with her native charm.

MADAGASCAR ARUBA ADVENTURE (PAGE 63)

Madagascar is also a small tour operator with a very friendly guide. Tours usually end up longer than scheduled, as host and guide Alfredo does not hurry passengers past the most interesting sights just to meet a schedule.

Motorcycle, All-Terrain Vehicle, and Trike Tours

Fun and funky modes of transport make getting to the tour sights as exciting as the destinations themselves.

BIG TWIN HARLEY-DAVIDSON (PAGE 63)

The thrill of zipping along island roads on these giant motor bikes from the Harley-Davidson franchise in Oranjestad, as well as the ability they have to traverse some of the worst trails, provides one of the best touring experiences.

WATAPANA ATV TOURS (PAGE 63)

Another ideal mode for traveling over tough, outback roads, Watapana ATV Tours take visitors to Conchi and through Arikok National Park. Difficult terrain is easy and fun to navigate on all-terrain vehicles, which are easy to learn to drive.

TRIKES (PAGE 63)

The ultimate car-motorcycle-ATV hybrid, Trikes allow passengers and drivers complete comfort while touring in style. Trikes can access tough terrain, and heads will turn wherever you go.

Horseback Tours

Aruba's principal mode of transport from colonial times is still one of the best ways to explore off the beaten track.

a panoramic view from Seroe Jamanota, Aruba's highest point

horseback tour

on the Cunucu Arikok Trail

RANCHO DAIMARI (PAGE 64)

Ideally located on the north shore, close to some of the most dramatic coastal trails, Rancho Daimari picks up and return guests to their resort. Two-hour trips focus on Daimari Beach, Dos Playa, and Conchi (Natural Pool).

GOLD MINE RANCH (PAGE 64)

Riding enthusiasts encounter alternate trails and sights within Arikok National Park on the menu of Gold Mine Ranch. Guides take riders to sites along the coast or inland.

Hiking Trails

Arikok National Park is Aruba's hiking center, where trails have been groomed, timed, and measured for degree of difficulty. Rangers are on hand to lead groups for a nominal fee.

CUNUCU ARIKOK TRAIL (PAGE 66)

This popular trail is about two hours round-trip from the park visitor center. It offers a chance to study endemic flora and fauna along with a genuinely restored landmark farmhouse.

NATURAL POOL TRAIL (PAGE 67)

The all-day journey of the Natural Pool Trail takes hikers directly to Conchi and past Dos Playa beach on the way back. Find forest trails, dramatic rock formations along the coastline, and secluded beaches for a cooling swim.

SEROE JAMANOTA TRAIL (PAGE 66)

Aruba's highest point, Seroe Jamanota, offers two access routes: Reaching the summit can be a relaxing morning stroll or a hardcore adventure. Either way, the reward is stunning vistas.

wild donkey in Aruba's outback

Local Culture

Islanders love to share their culture and traditions with visitors, particularly around holidays and during Carnival season.

Museums

NATIONAL ARCHAEOLOGICAL MUSEUM ARUBA (PAGE 77)

A number of archaeological digs have resulted in a huge collection of ceramics and artifacts linked to the inhabitants of Aruba from prehistoric times. The museum mixes original colonial architecture with a new, special environment, housing exhibits that are entertaining and very hands-on.

ARUBA HISTORICAL MUSEUM (PAGE 77)

Situated in the landmark Fort Zoutman, the museum provides an overview of the cultural development of the island from prehistoric through colonial and modern times. Antiques and artifacts recreate landmark moments in colonial history and the ways islanders survived by fishing and producing aloe.

Festivals and Events

CARNIVAL (PAGE 140)

Considered the premier manifestation of Aruban artistry and creativity, Carnival season includes spectacular parades and original music. Lasting 5-9 weeks, it takes place early January-Ash Wednesday and is island culture at its loudest and most jubilant.

CARUBBIAN FESTIVAL (PAGE 140)

If you can't be on Aruba for Carnival, the weekly Carubbian Festival, every Thursday in San Nicolas, is the next best thing. Tickets include transportation from resorts to the east end of Aruba and come with vouchers for the festival's authentic island and regional cooking.

BON BINI FESTIVAL (PAGE 139)

Conducted every Tuesday evening within Fort Zoutman in Oranjestad, the Bon Bini Festival provides a taste of Carnival, with a focus on folkloric dance, music, and traditions.

CARIBBEAN SEA JAZZ FESTIVAL (PAGE 144)

Columbus Day weekend means two nights of local, regional, and international artists performing innovative, interpretive music. Concert tickets are a bargain, and audience numbers are a fraction of those in

Lynette do Nacimento, 58th Grand Carnival Queen

folkloric dance performance at the Bon Bini Festival

Carnival float

mega-stadiums, resulting in an intimate musical experience.

ARUBA INTERNATIONAL PIANO FESTIVAL (PAGE 142)

Some of the finest classical musicians in the world travel to Aruba to give a week of concerts at the Cas di Cultura. Tickets are inordinately cheap for this smorgasbord of music by the greatest composers of all time, performed for the love of the art.

PASEO HERENCIA SHOPPING MALL CULTURAL SHOWS (PAGE 138)

Every Monday evening, Paseo Herencia in Palm Beach hosts a free cultural show beginning at 8pm. Showcasing local folkloric dance and music, it is a charming introduction to island traditions, conveniently situated to all resorts.

BETICO DAY (PAGE 141)

January 25 is the birthday of one of Aruba's most celebrated statesmen, Gilberto Francois "Betico" Croes. A lengthy show in Plaza Betico Croes behind the Cas di Cultura is accompanied by food and handicrafts.

HIMNO Y BANDERA DAY (PAGE 141)

Celebrating Aruban independence means a flurry of festivities, often for days prior to the actual date, March 18. There is a street fair, national show, and wonderful handicrafts for sale.

traditional ribbon dance at the Carubbian Festival

Best Bets for the Budget-Conscious

An island escape to relieve stress can be a necessity, even when it stresses the wallet. Fortunately, Aruba offers a wealth of affordable options for attractive accommodations, excellent dining, and an authentic cultural experiences.

Accommodations

VILLA BOUGAINVILLEA (PAGE 180)

Three charming, quirky apartments with individual terraces are attached to the home of the friendly hostess. There is a small pool, lovely gardens, lots of rescued dogs, and Boca Catalina beach is a short walk away.

ARUBA HARMONY (PAGE 168)

Located on the outskirts of Oranjestad, this small complex is close to shopping, inexpensive restaurants, and all the island's cultural sights. It has a nice little pool deck and an in-house spa where treatments are customized to your Chinese horoscope sign.

PEARL (PAGE 173)

Pearl, close to Eagle Beach, offers high-end duplex condominiums at reasonable rates. It's only a short walk away from one of Aruba's prettiest beaches and it features two swimming pools, a fitness room, and helpful concierge services.

ARUBA BEACH CHALETS (PAGE 184)

With its own patch of beach in Savaneta, Aruba Beach Chalets are privately-owned condos rented out by the week. The duplex apartments have amazing views, right on the water, and can sleep six very comfortably.

Restaurants

Cuminda criollo (local cuisine) is admittedly a bit heavy on the starches and fried foods, but you will always leave full, without walloping your wallet. A safe bet for health-conscious, affordable dining is to stick to fresh-caught local fish and stews.

CASA VIEJA (PAGE 101)

The most authentic of Colombian restaurants on Aruba, Casa Vieja, located on the eastern outskirts of Oranjestad, serves up huge mixed-meat platters. Eat and drink like royalty for pennies.

ZEEROVER (PAGE 127)

Everyone's favorite place for fresh fish and

beachfront at Aruba Beach Chalets

Colombian restaurant Casa Vieja

waterfront dining at Zeerover

shrimp, Zeerover is basically a glorified fish shack right on the water in Savaneta. Dine on the dock or under the canopy with ice-cold beers, pool tables, and TVs showing the latest soccer matches.

PIZZA & MORE (PAGE 102)

This tiny Italian place in the middle of Oranjestad's main shopping street has a dedicated clientele for a good reason: charming hosts and some of the best pizza and lasagna on Aruba at rock-bottom prices.

YAMI YAMI (PAGE 107)

Yami Yami, in Bubali near Eagle Beach, is the suburban outlet of Oranjestad's Asian Delight. It is named after its iconic, very satisfying, and bargain-price two-course meal.

Entertainment

Aruba has a number of shopping centers with bandstands where talented musicians and singers perform free of charge nightly.

RENAISSANCE MARKETPLACE (PAGE 152)

The bandstand located at the waterside of Renaissance Marketplace in Oranjestad features various bands. Enjoy classic rock, folk, pop, latin, reggae, mellow, or metal, depending on who's playing.

ARAWAK GARDENS (PAGE 138)

Arawak Gardens in Palm Beach has singers and musicians that take to the stage in a centralized gazebo. Five different restaurant terraces allow patrons to linger over dinner or drinks in this amiable alfresco setting.

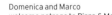

Domenica and Marco welcome patrons to Pizza & More.

Villa Bougainvillea

Family Fun

WALTZING WATERS (PAGE 138)

In the Paseo Herencia Shopping Mall, the free *Waltzing Waters* show has four shows nightly on the half-hour, 7:30pm-10:30pm.

DREAM BOWL (PAGE 136)

At the Palm Beach Plaza Mall, Dream Bowl offers six lanes with neon-glowing gutters and balls, complemented by arcade games, air hockey, and foosball tables.

BUTTERFLY FARM (PAGE 80)

The Butterfly Farm amazes kids with an entertaining introduction to the beautiful world of these exotic insects.

DONKEY SANCTUARY (PAGE 88)

Enjoy a hands-on session with the residents of Aruba's wild donkey population in Santa Lucia. The staff allows children to share in the animals' care.

ARUBA OSTRICH FARM (PAGE 87)

An encounter with the world's largest birds at the Ostrich Farm in Matividiri is informative, fun, and always suprising.

PHILIP'S ANIMAL GARDEN (PAGE 84)

Get acquainted with the exotic animals that have been saved from neglect.

NIKKY BEACH (PAGE 36)

With a shoreline sheltered by a barrier reef, Nikky Beach has extremely quiet, shallow waters. The adjacent restaurant has a kiddie pool and provides service on the beach.

BABY BEACH (PAGE 46)

The breakwaters at Baby Beach create a tranquil lagoon rimmed with a circle of soft sand. Public palapas are scattered along the shore for shade. Vendors rent beach chairs and sell snacks.

PALM BEACH (PAGE 41)

Wave action is negligible and the shallow seas are ideal for youngsters. It's also close to all the resorts, beach toys, refreshments, and bathrooms.

ARUBA WATERPARK (PAGE 57)

Eminently affordable, this collection of slides ranges from kiddy to killer. It also has a great place for lunch and a playground.

Aruba Waterpark

BEACHES

Caribbean islands are usually synonymous with beautiful beaches, but veteran travelers will tell you that Aruba's beaches are exceptional. Aruba has been hailed as one of the top beach destinations in the world. The soft, snowy white sands (a composition of coral and shells crushed into a fine powder over eons) and the breathtaking blue waters make sunbathing, beachcombing, and swimming popular pastimes here. And though the temperature is consistently warm, Aruba's beaches are never too hot for a barefoot stroll even at noon.

Palm Beach and Eagle Beach are the most raved about beaches on the island, with fine accommodations along their shores. The long, uninterrupted miles of sand are the main attraction for both visitors and developers. Unquestionably, the nature of Aruba's beaches has dictated the degree of development of resort areas, as well as their character. It was long ago decided that Palm Beach offered the "best beachfront." Though, of course, vacationers who return to Manchebo Beach and Eagle Beach year after year are confident that they're staying at the best.

Along Palm Beach the shallow water extends almost a half mile from the shore with negligible wave action. Many consider this ideal for families with very young children. The extremely shallow, still water is perfect for a baby's first encounter with the sea. Swimming areas are well-marked, patrolled, and maintained.

Eagle Beach is not quite as maintained and patrolled as Palm Beach, but all the resorts in Aruba take responsibility for the safety of their beachfront. The government is working

© ROSALIE KLEIN

BEACHES

HIGHLIGHTS

LOOK FOR (€ TO FIND RECOMMENDED BEACHES.

(€ **Renaissance Island:** A private island for the guests of the Renaissance Resort, this tranquil enclave offers a choice of family fun or adults only beaches. It also has nice snorkeling, a spa, restaurant, and friendly flamingoes (page 37).

(€ **Eagle Beach:** Eagle Beach is one of the top-rated beaches on the island with many of the same offerings as Palm Beach; the difference here is that there are fewer people and slightly bigger waves (page 40).

(€ **Palm Beach:** Aruba's principal playground has every manner of amenity and activity available within a few steps from your beach lounge. Traditionally, it has the quietest waters of the long beachfronts (page 41).

(€ **Baranca Plat:** You'll encounter quiet waters and snowy white sands at this cozy little cove, a short walk from the big resorts. Shade trees and few people provide that feeling of having a special place in the sun all to yourself (page 41).

(€ **Fisherman's Huts:** At this windsurfing beach, relax among the dunes and take in the colorful sails and parachute kites speeding across the water (page 42).

(€ **California Dunes:** This expansive area is great for a long walk, a day exploring the dunes, or finding a private dune for some topless sunbathing (page 43).

(€ **Andicuri Beach:** Dramatic terraces of limestone formations surround this secluded beach. The wave action here is perfect for body surfing (page 43).

(€ **Black Stone Beach:** Rock formations create multiple natural bridges and beautiful photo-ops. The beach is named for the lava stones that litter the shore (page 43).

(€ **Baby Beach and Roger's Beach:** Two of Aruba's most beautiful beaches are within the remains of the old Lago Colony. Calm, clear waters are found within the breakwaters, surrounded by long stretches of white sands, bordered by greenery and carved stone cliffs (page 46).

on a program to establish lifeguards at crucial areas. As more resorts crop up along Eagle Beach, more cordoned-off swim sections can be expected.

There is more wave action at Eagle Beach, and particularly Manchebo Beach, due to the bottom suddenly dropping off very close to shore. The current action at Punto Brabo, where the southern shore meets west and various currents collide, also contributes to bigger waves. This makes it very popular with surfers and bodyboarders. Other great spots popular for bodyboarding or wave boarding are Andicuri, Dos Playa, and Urirama, all on Aruba's north coast, where heavy winds from the northeast cause strong wave action.

© ROSALIE KLEIN

the western shore

Oranjestad

Oranjestad's beaches are artificially-constructed, carved out from the harbor and created by dumping sand. This was done in the early 1950s. Prior to then, it was a harbor area. Jetties have created some very calm coves and small stretches of beachfront.

DRUIF BEACH
This relatively wide public beach (J. E. Irausquin Blvd. at the western outskirts of the town) is an extension of the beachfront from the Tamarijn Beach Hotel. There is a great deal of greenery and shade trees and areas cleared for small campfires or setting up BBQs. You will most likely find islanders here on the weekends making a day of it with their families. The water is very shallow and very quiet, which makes it a nice spot for small children to play in the waves. A minor cautionary note: If you are planning to lay out a towel on the

grass, please check for and avoid some patches of plants with rather nasty and tenacious thistles that are common during the dry season.

Directly across the road from the beach is the complex of Aruba's major supermarkets, with bathrooms and snack and drink options.

GOVERNOR'S BEACH
Just past the Renaissance complex is a bridge over a lagoon that divides Oranjestad's commercial area from the residential neighborhoods. This headland is informally named Governor's Beach (L. G. Smith Blvd. by Lagoonweg, on the east side of Wilhelmina Park) because it sits directly across from what has traditionally been the residence of Aruba's governor. It has some thatched palapas for shade and a brand new boardwalk plus a snack concession and bathrooms. The area marks the beginning of a long stretch of narrow beach

FREE USE OF ALL BEACHES

By law, all of Aruba's beaches are public beaches within 20 meters (65 ft) of the waterline. This includes all beaches running along Palm Beach and Eagle Beach, no matter what resort is situated there. Blue pillars signal the demarcation point. This rule was reaffirmed by Aruba's Ministers of Tourism and Infrastructure in 2010.

No resort personnel can prevent anyone from sitting on the public beach of their choice, though they can ask you not to use lounges belonging to the resorts. These are reserved for guests. Interlopers are usually detected by their towels. The palapas or "chikies," the little thatched huts placed along the shore for shade, however, are another matter, about which there is some debate.

Thatched palapas are built on the beach and maintained by the resorts. According to law, if they are on the public section of the beach, then technically they are available to anyone, without fee for usage. Anyone can place a beach towel on the sand to bask in the sun, or under a palapa for shade, as long as they are within 20 meters of the waterline.

Exceptions are De Palm Island and Renaissance Island; the owners do have the right to limit access. Homes that are situated on the water, such as in Malmok or Savaneta, have to abide by the same 20-meter rule. Homeowners cannot claim the entire shorefront as their own.

This practice insures Aruba's beaches belong to the Aruban people and all island guests. It is only fair that islanders should not be prohibited from enjoying the island's natural assets, which are their heritage. Beaches are a way of life for Aruban people, accessible at all hours. They do not have opening and closing times. Beaches also do not require beach tags or usage fees, they are always free for all to enjoy.

---

extending all the way east along L. G. Smith Boulevard to Surfside, ending at the beginning of the airport runways. This is interspersed with limestone terraces.

All of this L. G. Smith beachfront is exceptionally quiet and shallow, which is good for little ones. It is interrupted by some rocky outcroppings. There are lots of shade trees along the shore with areas masked from L. G. Smith Boulevard and its busy traffic. Many locals also come to this beach to set out on their boats or Jet Skis.

NIKKY BEACH (SURFSIDE)

Across from the Talk of the Town Resort is the main plaza of the longest linear park (entrance behind the Plaza Turismo at the east end of L. G. Smith Blvd.) in the Caribbean. The miles of dirt paths bordering L. G. Smith Boulevard have been manicured with jogging and biking lanes, gardens, and periodically placed bathrooms and open-air showers. This area, and its beachfront, has had a number of incarnations. Older residents still think of it by its original name, Surfside, though presently it is called Nikky Beach. The area has now taken that name and a certain ambiance associated with it.

The beach is a wide curving cove with lovely white sand and very quiet waters. This is often where sailboats go for safe harbor when the western shore turns rough. Since this beach is popular with the local European crowd, you may encounter some topless sunbathers.

This area offers all the conveniences you will need for a luxurious day at the beach: nice restaurant, bar, small pool on the terrace, and superb service at your beach lounge.

The chic **Nikky Beach Restaurant and Lounge** (L. G. Smith Blvd. 1A, 297/582-0153, www.nikkybeacharuba.com, 9am-10pm daily for meals, bar stays open until 4am daily) features a sunny terrace and shaded interior dining room that opens out to the sea. They also offer food and drink service to sunbathers.

© ROSALIE KLEIN

adults-only Flamingo Beach, Renaissance Island

◖ RENAISSANCE ISLAND

Guests at the Renaissance Resort have unlimited access to Renaissance Island (300 meters off Aruba's south shore, just north of the airport, 1/800/421-8188, 297/583-6000, www.marriott.com, access is only by boat, day pass for non-guests $75), one of Aruba's nicest beaches. There are two sections connected by boardwalks, with mangroves and palm trees providing privacy.

Flamingo Beach, on the western side, is adults only. It is secluded, and topless sunbathing is allowed. The flock of flamingoes that gives the adult beach its name keep guests entertained and are quite tame.

The eastern half of Renaissance Island is comprised of a large sweep of beach outfitted for families. It has a tranquil lagoon perfect for introducing toddlers to the sea. There

is a snack bar, volleyball court, and a dock for paddleboats.

Water taxis to the island leave from two locations about every 15 minutes. One departure point is in the lobby of the Marina Tower of the Renaissance Resort, the other is next to the harbor heliport.

Day passes for non-guests include lunch at the very charming Papagayo restaurant, a drink, beach towels, and use of the tennis court. The day pass also allows a choice of one activity: Visitors can snorkel, kayak, or toodle around on a paddleboat.

There is an outlet of the **Okeanos Spa** (297/583-6000, www.okeanosspaaruba.com), adjacent to Flamingo Beach, called The Cove. Purchase of a massage at this spa also includes access to the island, but no other amenities.

Manchebo Beach and Eagle Beach

The combination of these two shore areas that border the southwestern curve of Aruba are renowned as one of the longest uninterrupted beachfronts in the Caribbean. As yet, the beachfront has not been fully developed, and there are many areas that remain deserted throughout the day. Large sections of greenery provide privacy and shade.

This is also an important nesting area for local and visiting sea turtles from early spring through late autumn. During turtle season, there is the distinct possibility of seeing a giant leatherback lay their eggs, or new hatchlings struggling to the sea. These areas are cordoned off and protected by a local foundation, TurtugAruba, and visitors are asked to report to them any turtle activity.

MANCHEBO BEACH

The two-mile wide expanse of Manchebo Beach, on the southwestern point of the island, is lined with small-sized resorts that provide a feeling of solitude for sunbathers. Unlike some of the larger hotels, you will not feel crowded or packed together. Holiday weeks are busy everywhere, but here, one can really enjoy the feeling of an isolated island getaway.

Most of the shorefront resorts are only two stories high. The accommodation options that offer lodging directly on the beach are for the most part exclusively found in this area. The smaller resorts have a well established European clientele, but the timeshare beaches are primarily occupied by visitors from North and Latin America.

© ROSALIE KLEIN

Manchebo Beach, Aruba's widest beach, is never crowded.

WATER SAFETY AROUND THE SHORE

In the past, the easy going, unregulated island life rarely prompted much thought to cordoning off swim areas. Before the advent of the tourism boom, the beach- and shorefronts were vast and the population was small. As the number of resorts grew, each resort personally took on the responsibility of marking a protected area of the sea for the safety of their guests.

A line of buoys placed by the Coast Guard beyond the swim areas in Palm Beach designates a "no wake" zone. Here, fast boat traffic is prohibited. Those crossing the zone while ferrying passengers to larger boats are required to maintain slower speeds, less than would create a large wake. Swimmers and snorkelers should avoid the areas beyond the swim zone because of the frequent boat traffic.

All boat operators are now required to take courses and obtain at least a "Small Boat License." They must learn safety procedures and "rules of the road" to do business. The current government has initiated a program to station trained lifeguards in the towers along the beach, which have stood unoccupied for decades.

Properly cordoning off swim areas, particularly on the busier beaches, is still an issue left to private concerns. Currently, the swim area markers are maintained by a dedicated enterprise contracted by the hotels. Part of that process is to clean the ropes regularly. Soft corals will begin to grow on underwater ropes, which sting and cause a very irritating rash. Swimmers should avoid sitting or clinging to swim barrier ropes at all times. If exposed, try a topical steroid to relieve the pain and itching.

Aruba's offshore breezes are delightfully cooling. It is partially this wind that helps to keep the waters on Palm Beach so quiet. The drawback is that they tend to blow objects out to sea, including beach balls, lightweight floats, and other fun water toys. The wind also tends to create a gentle wave motion at the surface, which is often not noticeable but is steadily moving out to sea, away from shore. Keep a close eye on youngsters in swim rings and lightweight floats.

Take care not to fall asleep on a float; it is not unheard to wake up far from land. Most float and small craft operators keep a small rescue boat handy for just such instances. Even if you don't go anywhere, falling asleep in the middle of the giant sun reflector that is the Caribbean Sea may prove very distressing. It is no fun being stuck in a hotel room with a sunburn.

Scuba divers are trained to never dive alone, but always with a buddy. This common-sense rule is wise for almost anyone indulging in water activities on the sea. Don't go off by yourself to snorkel in areas with which you are unfamiliar. Inform friends or family where you are going and when you expect to be back (within reason). Dive operators and snorkel charters can provide buddies and will keep an eye on patrons. They are experienced in handling distressing situations on the sea. Those indulging in some unusual water activity for the first time are advised to do it in supervised circumstances.

PUNTO BRABO

Huge, old sea grape trees stand sentinel along the shore just where Manchebo and Eagle Beaches meet at Punto Brabo or "Rough Point" (access via the south lane of J. E. Irausquin Blvd.), a very wide beach that fronts the Bucuti and Costa Linda resorts. It is the southwest curve of the island where currents intertwine and the sea bottom drops off close to shore. The beach is a stunning expanse of brilliant white sands.

Those who choose to stay in this area often cite how much they enjoy the great wave action for body surfing and playing in the waves. Care should be taken with very young children here.

The green areas offer shelter and plenty of secluded places to string up a hammock or set up a BBQ, which islanders will frequently do on the weekends. There is ample parking just north of Costa Linda Resort.

Fofoti trees mark the end of Eagle Beach and the start of Palm Beach.

◖ EAGLE BEACH

The sea is quiet on Eagle Beach (J. E. Irausquin Blvd. btwn. La Quinta Beach Resort and the north end of Amsterdam Manor Beach Resort), which is practically deserted for long stretches. The far northern border of Eagle Beach is marked by Aruba's famous twin fofoti trees. These are a rare species and a popular photo site.

Since the resorts along the beach are located across the street, the wide shorefront of soft, white sugar sands is sparsely populated with vacationers. Though, on weekends, it is quite busy with island residents.

Hotels La Cabana and Amsterdam Manor have beach bars for refreshments at the northen end of the beach. Some condominiums along this stretch of sand have set up palapas (small thatched huts) for shade. Since the resorts are all across the road, away from the beach, many guests often prefer to stay around the beautiful pool decks, rather than on the beach itself.

Resorts have placed amenities along the shore for their patrons, such as lounges or structures to provide shade. The casual passerby can often find unused and unattended palapas and lounges on the beach. Snack wagons are set up for business during the day for a bite to eat around the lunch hour.

The scarcity of resorts has unofficially designated Eagle Beach as a traditionally "local" beach, with parking areas along the shore. It is not unusual to find families or groups camping here on the weekends. During Easter vacation, called Semana Santa, the beach is filled from one end to the other with tents and islanders enjoying the holiday.

Palm Beach, Malmok, and Noord

One of the most famous beaches in the world, Aruba's Palm Beach, has lake-like waters and every convenience imaginable. This is the center and departure point for 90 percent of water activities. Except for the all-inclusive resorts of Riu Palace and Occidental Grand, the beach hotels welcome passersby to their beachfront restaurants, shops, and bars. Clean, modern bathrooms are always close at hand.

PALM BEACH

Palm Beach (from south of the Divi Phoenix Resort to the north end of the Holiday Inn) is Aruba's principal playground, which also makes it a busy and often crowded place. This is a perfect spot to make friends and socialize. But for visitors looking for seclusion and privacy, this beach is not ideal.

The waters here are the calmest of all of Aruba's beaches. It is a favorite area for families with little ones, ideal for their first introduction to the sea. Palm Beach is truly one of the "dream beaches" of the world, a seeming endless stretch of soft white sands and gentle, clear surf.

BARANCA PLAT

Just south of Palm Beach (turn off on the water side where the road divider begins on J. E. Irausquin Blvd., just north of the Blue Condo complex) is a small cove called Baranca Plat, "Flat Stone." Here you will find seclusion among the grape trees, with all the conveniences of Palm Beach only a five-minute walk away. It is a tranquil, conveniently located option and a break from the more heavily populated beaches.

Jetties surround it, producing very quiet

© ROSALIE KLEIN

Palm Beach is Aruba's main area for resort accommodations and water activities.

waters and no waves. The water is shallow here, which makes it an excellent spot for little children to splash and play without being buffeted about. The jetties are often filled with pelicans and gulls, which make for an entertaining show.

No signs mark this beach, but there is a platform where waverunners are tethered. It is also within easy walking distance along the shore, just minutes south of the main resorts.

◖ FISHERMAN'S HUTS

North of Palm Beach, beyond the Ritz-Carlton, is the windsurfing and kitesurfing capital of Aruba. This long stretch is called Fisherman's Huts (L. G. Smith Blvd. across from Bakval). There are a number of huts teaching both sports, and places for refreshments and shade.

The beach is named for tiny beachside domiciles passed down by fishing families through the generations. They were removed to make way for the new resort, but the name remains.

The beach is very popular with islanders. You can spend your days watching the colorful sails whipping through the waves and the aerial acrobatics of the kitesurfers.

Beach access is clearly marked with a sign on L. G. Smith Boulevard and there is ample parking.

BOCA CATALINA

Bordered by limestone formations, Boca Catalina (501 L. G. Smith Blvd. and 2a/2b Rd., Malmokweg) offers some very nice snorkeling. The beach area is not large. However, the water is very quiet and ideal for all ages. Boca Catalina is a popular place for larger sailboats to stop during their charter runs.

The road to get here ends at the south end of the final cluster of waterfront homes. There is a wooden stairway entry at the northern point. Though bordered by the luxurious homes of Malmok, the beach is public. Sometimes referred to as Malmok Beach, it has no public facilities.

© ROSALIE KLEIN

Outcroppings bordering Boca Catalina beach provide interesting snorkeling opportunities.

ARASHI BEACH

The last beachfront house of Malmok ends at the start of Arashi Beach (L. G. Smith Blvd., north of the waterfront homes). The area has been tailored to accommodate the public. It is a quiet spot with shallow waters but some wave action. A manicured, spacious parking lot with chemical toilets and shaded tables and benches for picnics is adjacent to the beach. Every day a colorful wagon selling snacks and snowcones sets up for business here.

The beach has several thatched, shade palapas that are maintained by the government. The beach is usually crowded with locals on the weekends; many islanders take advantage of its amenities for birthday parties and events.

The southern section of the cove is quieter than the northern side, where the waves tend to break with more force.

North Coast

Many coves are scattered along Aruba's north shore. Many of them are suitable as a beach break while touring the Aruban outback, though swimming is usually not recommended. Rip tides are rampant here and can pull swimmers out to sea. Body surfing is generally not recommended due to the heavy waves, though some very fit athletes indulge in it. There are no lifeguards, and any help would have to come from far away. Children should be kept out of these waters.

C CALIFORNIA DUNES

A long, rolling area of Sahara-like dunes, generally referred to as the California Dunes (from the turnoff from the west point and paved road follow the start of a gravel road along the north coast to the base of the lighthouse), ends in some rough shores not really suitable for swimming. The dunes follow the coast for about a mile in line with the mount of the lighthouse. In the past it was a popular place for nude sunbathing, and there are still a few isolated areas offering shelter for those that care to indulge. The area is mainly appreciated as a nature walk.

DRUIF AND URIRAMA BEACHES

On the north coast road, which is not named but can be discerned from the surrounding rocks, are Druif and Urirama Beaches (Druif is about 2 km past the California Dunes; Urirama is another 2 km past Druif). Aside from wave boarding, these beaches attract anglers who have built shacks of driftwood on the beach. Here they can clean their fish and seek shelter from the sun. Islanders picnic here, but these are not good swimming spots for the uninitiated. However, the dramatic photo ops of the rugged seas crashing into the shore and the surrounding cliffs are worth the trip.

C ANDICURI BEACH

Andicuri Beach (follow the winding road leading directly to the sea via the left fork from Ayo Rock Formation) is a wide, pristine beach flanked by dramatic limestone formations. It has large waves that are fun for body surfing. Good swimmers will enjoy the surf, but it may be a bit much for children. The scenery around the beach area is quite dramatic, with stark, almost petrified trees.

Andicuri is only accessible with an off-road vehicle. Getting here is a scenic journey.

C BLACK STONE BEACH

From Andicuri Beach a gravel road along the coast leads to Black Stone Beach (1.5 km past Andicuri Beach). A very dramatic rock formation is located at the juncture of two natural bridges that are carved out of the cliffs. Where the sea meets the shore, the land is covered with lava pebbles, for which the beach is named. These were formed millions of years ago from magma bubbling up in deep sea beds; the magma quickly cooled and fragmented. The

© ROSALIE KLEIN

California Dunes has plenty of secluded, private spots.

constant wearing away by waves makes them smooth.

It is a fun climb down to the shoreline and easy enough for youngsters. Waves crash against the shore with great force here; this is definitely not an area for swimming.

DAIMARI BEACH

This is a very large secluded beach area with two separate coves divided by cliffs. One of the best ways to get here is on a horseback riding tour with **Rancho Daimari** (J. E. Irausquin Blvd. 382 A, 297/586-6284, www.arubaranchodaimari.com, 8am and 2pm daily, $78). Their Natural Pool itinerary includes galloping through the coves. The beaches can also be accessed via the Natural Pool Trail in Arikok National Park. Once on the trail, continue north past the Natural Pool for about half a kilometer to Daimari Beach. While parts of the cove have calm waters that little ones can enjoy, most of the beach is better for body surfing.

The entire area is about 100 meters of surf and conditions vary depending on the wind and time of year.

DOS PLAYA

Dos Playa are dual coves divided by rock formations, hence the name. Featuring rolling dunes and nice waves, this is a favorite spot for local bodyboarders, but it is not recommended for children, and care should be taken if you are not a strong swimmer.

Located within Arikok National Park, Dos Playa is also a popular hiking tour destination (Rooi Tambu Trail, length 5.5 km, 2-3 hrs round-trip from park welcome center via Mira Lamar pass).

To get here by car, follow the Mira Lamar pass gravel road and signs pointing to Dos Playa through the park for four kilometers to the crest of a hill, where you will see the beach below. From here it is a five-minute walk to the beach proper.

Big waves at Andicuri Beach make it popular for bodysurfing and bodyboarding.

BOCA PRINS

Boca Prins is an enormous cove with a wide beach, circled by limestone terraces and outcroppings. Quite secluded, it is accessed through Arikok National Park (via Rooi Prins Trail ending at Phantage, 5.5 km from the visitor center), not far from the caves on the eastern end of the island.

By car you can access the beach via Mira Lamar pass. The path, a sand road that parallels the hiking route to the beach, is marked by signs. It is a nice place to take a break and grab a cold drink from the little snack bar across the road.

The sea at Boca Prins is deceptive and there are some treacherous rip tides. Take care not to go out too far from shore if taking a dip.

EASTER WEEK CAMPING ON ARUBA

A time-honored way to celebrate Semana Santa on Aruba is to pack up the family and take to the beach. Islanders set up temporary homes on the shore in anything from pup tents to elaborately outfitted trailers, powered by generators. The latter are frequently air-conditioned, with full-size refrigerators and giant plasma screens. First-time visitors are often under the mistaken impression that this is how islanders live.

Islanders devoted to camping sometimes take to the beach other weeks of the year. During summer vacation, Christmas, or the first week in October (an important school break), camping is popular. However, it is particularly popular during Easter week, when local beaches get very crowded.

This creates traffic snarls at Eagle Beach and Arashi Beach, two favorite campsites on the west side of Aruba. Baby Beach and Roger's Beach are lined with camping tents and trailers. Parking around these areas becomes much more difficult.

Naturally, with more campers there is also more trash. The government places chemical toilets and extra waste bins to reduce the impact on beach areas. Ecologically-minded organizations along with local waste removal company Eco-tech have made inroads on the litter situation. A contest for the cleanest campsite at the end of the week yields great rewards, from cash prizes to weekend stays at major resorts. The community draws together to see that everyone has a fun and clean camping holiday.

San Nicolas, Savaneta, and Pos Chiquito

The eastern and southern coasts feature quiet beaches and are excellent swimming areas for all ages. The southern side has protective sand bars and reefs, assuring calm waters and some very nice snorkeling.

◖ BABY BEACH AND ROGER'S BEACH

Two of Aruba's loveliest beaches are located within the former Lago Colony. A paved road leads through the colony to the island's eastern tip, forking at the Rum Reef Bar. To the left is the entrance to Baby Beach. To the right is Roger's Beach, named for Captain Robert Rogers, who convinced oil company executives to choose Aruba as the place to build their Caribbean refinery.

Baby Beach is considered a prime swimming destination. The manufactured lagoon inside the breakwaters is perfectly still, very shallow, and ideal for young children, hence the name.

There is a long, clean circle of white beach surrounding the water, with cliffs of greenery rising up to the Lago housing above. Though it is popular with a number of tours, it is sufficiently expansive to provide several quiet areas for a more private sunbathing session or swim. It is very popular with islanders on the weekends, and a favorite camping spot during holidays.

The area boasts some stunning reefs beyond the breakwater, but these seas are quite dangerous. The best of the reef is a few hundred yards from shore. Close in, there is a wide barrier of stag and elk horn coral that sometimes breaks the surface. It is easy for the uninitiated snorkeler to get lost and trapped within. Coral scrapes are painful and get easily infected. When snorkeling, be watchful not to drift out past the breakwater. Unfortunately, there is little to see within that limit. It is better to arrange being taken to the reef with **Jad's Dive Shop** (Seroe Colorado 245E, 297/584-6070, http://jadsaruba.com). This is not a place to go far from shore on your own, and warning signs are posted.

Roger's Beach, right next door, is generally ignored by visitors, as it stands in the shadow of the refinery. It is a clean, beautiful beach, with shallow waters and snowy sands. It provides an equally ideal swimming area for little ones, with far less traffic than Baby Beach. A few picturesque native fishing boats are moored at the docks that occupy the eastern end of the cove.

BOCA GRANDE

The name "Large Mouth," tells you something about this large cove off the northeastern shore. Boca Grande is reached along the same route as Baby Beach (drive through San Nicolas heading east past all the settlements and out towards the former Lago Colony). It can be seen from the large red anchor that marks the entry to Lago Colony. On weekends, it is filled with

A path through mangroves leads to a second secluded beach at Mangel Halto.

© ROSALIE KLEIN

kitesurfers whipping across the water, which is somewhat prohibitive for swimmers. It has a very nice semi-circle of soft white sand and is a nice spot for working on a tan while watching the colorful kites as surfers jump the waves and do tricks.

SAVANETA BEACH

A road runs parallel to the main highway between Oranjestad and San Nicolas, which follows the southern shoreline. This allows access to the southside beaches, such as Savaneta Beach. To get to the beaches, visitors must cross little wooden bridges placed periodically over the water pipes from WEB, Aruba's water production plant. Follow the main highway (1A) past the Pos Chiquito rotunda and continue to Savaneta; then turn right at the gas station and head towards the water. Turn at the first right, which is a paved road. At 200 meters past the turn, take a left turn over a cement crossing over the pipes. Along the shore, the area is dotted with dense mangrove formations, limestone outcroppings, and a secluded stretch of snowy, white sand. This beach has quiet, crystal clear waters, nice snorkeling, and is generally ignored, except by the residents of the neighborhood.

MANGEL HALTO

This protected beach in Pos Chiquito features a series of connected coves with a barrier reef not far from shore. For the best swimming experience here, pass through a break in the mangroves at the far right of the main beach to an expansive swimming area. It is very shallow, standing depth, but then suddenly drops into a deep bowl, before going shallow again.

When the waters are low, the mangrove roots actually make a tunnel to some more secluded beaches beyond the main area. This is not always accessible when the tides are high. Since these are thick mangrove areas, make sure to fully coat yourself in mosquito repellent if planning to spend much time here.

Shaded tables and palapas are available for a relaxing beach day.

To get here, turn toward the ocean at the Balashi traffic light on Highway 1A. Go to the end of the road, which ends in a T-intersection and Aruba's water and power plant. Turn left and cross the small bridge over Spaanslagoen. Turn right at the second road past the bridge, where there is a sign for Marina Pirata. Take this to the very end of the road and turn left. The beach entrance is 500 meters along the road bordering the sea, Spaanslagoenweg, and is clearly marked.

RECREATION

Aruba is a playground for all ages. The constant, reliable climate allows visitors to enjoy favorite fair-weather activities and pastimes in any season, under ideal conditions. Clear, tropical waters and a distinctive marine environment is perfect for scuba diving, snorkeling, and every manner of water sport. Resorts and independent venues host excellent and conveniently located facilities for tennis, golf, hiking, and biking.

There are several ways to explore the island on land, sea, and even in the air. Tour companies offer a head-spinning number of options for discovering the Aruba outback and major sights. Entrepreneurial islanders are always on the lookout for original and interesting ways to show off their beloved homeland. In addition to bus and safari tours, there are trikes (motorcycle and car hybrids), Harley-Davidson treks, all-terrain vehicles, helicopters, and horseback riding tours. For those who feel the journey should be as exciting as the destination, try a 4x4 Outback Adventure, with or without a driver. Outback tour guides can provide fascinating and knowledgeable commentary, while assuring arrival at those hard-to-find spots. Much like snorkeling and diving, it is always advisable to explore a new area with an experienced guide in order to get the lay of the land.

Aruba's steady trade winds assure wonderful sailing weather. Experienced sailors can rent Sunfish sailboats and Beachcats for cruising the coast. Charter boats make way for morning or afternoon snorkel trips or sunset sails daily.

Scuba companies start their day with novice

© ROSALIE KLEIN

RECREATION

HIGHLIGHTS

LOOK FOR ◖ TO FIND RECOMMENDED ACTIVITIES.

◖ **Octopus Cruises:** Enjoy smooth sailing and snorkeling on a wide, three-hulled sailboat. The crew is known for their patient instruction, great lunches, and rum punch (page 52).

◖ *Tranquilo:* For sailing fanatics who enjoy the thrill of leaning into the wind, these all-day trips deliver. Travel to a secluded reef on Aruba's south side for excellent snorkeling opportunities (page 53).

◖ **Jad's Dive Shop:** The only dive operator working out of the Baby Beach area, Jad's offers safe diving to one of Aruba's most vibrant reefs. Serious divers interested in the unusual will find it here (page 55).

◖ **Unique Sports of Aruba:** This reliable and respected dive shop in the Palm Beach area offers a diverse menu of water activities (page 55).

◖ **Madi's Magical Tours:** Don't just take a tour, go tripping with Madi! Her friendly personality make her small group tours one of the

best ways to see what Aruba's outback has to offer (page 62).

◖ **Big Twin Harley-Davidson:** Indulge your Easy Rider fantasy safely, with a guided tour on your own Harley (page 63).

◖ **Trikes:** These motorcycle and car hybrids are one of the most popular and fun ways to tour the island (page 63).

◖ **Rancho Daimari:** Outback adventures are even more enjoyable by horseback, one of the best ways to access Conchi and Daimari Beach. Experienced riders can go galloping on the shore (page 64).

◖ **Skydive Aruba:** One of the most thrilling and adventurous ways to see Aruba is through a skydiving trip, in tandem with an experienced instructor (page 69).

◖ **Okeanos Spa:** The only spa that offers access to Renaissance Island is absolutely the most romantic spot for a couple's massage. It's the ultimate island indulgence (page 70).

resort courses that allow students to safely explore the exhilarating underwater landscape in only a few hours. These fully-tested programs are endorsed and standardized by international dive organizations.

Other athletic pastimes to try are windsurfing and kitesurfing. Aruba is considered one of the world's top destinations for both. If there is any way to play in the waves, the island has it, usually within a few steps from most major resorts.

Aruba waters have also been declared "marlin country" by officials of the annual international billfishing tournaments. Deep sea fishing can be done with full- or half-day trips, and boats depart from several convenient locations.

Golfers will be delighted to find two vastly different courses close to the major resort areas. Both have veteran pros and offer helpful clinics.

Aruba's gusty winds are an interesting challenge; when they have a tailwind, some golfers report record drives.

From sumptuous to simple, Aruba's day spas offer a menu of treatments to relax the body and restore the spirit. Vacation time is the right time to sample these services, even if the most strenuous thing you do is walk back and forth from your beach lounge to the beach bar.

A principal reason veteran visitors give for returning annually is "whatever you like to do, day or night, Aruba has it all." Vacationers can spend their time lazing on the beach, or they can be busy from morning to sunset enjoying a favorite activity, or learning a new one. Whether you choose to tour the coastline by sailboat, explore the underwater environment, or visit popular tourist sites, you will find reasonably priced services accommodating individuals and any size family or group.

Snorkeling and Diving

The experience of seeing the tropical marine environment for the first time, whether snorkeling or on a scuba dive, has literally changed lives. It can elicit eco-conservation attitudes or, at the very least, the dedication to an invigorating and fascinating pastime. Snorkeling trips, as well as other water tours, are easily arranged through independent booking agents right on the beaches in front of most resorts.

SNORKEL SITES

Aruban waters offer a large variety of dive and snorkel sites. Aside from reef areas, there are quite a few wrecks, some purposely placed, such as the Jane Sea and the Sonesta Planes. These soon become havens for schools of fish. Some dive operations have mapped out 39 dive spots on Aruba, though many of these are not accessible or appropriate for the casual vacation

diver. The most commonly visited sites are popular for a good reason: Calm waters assure a safe, enjoyable adventure for divers with limited experience. Those with years of diving expertise should look to some of the smaller, private operators for diving beyond the norm. They can provide custom trips to more remote locations. Aruba has a few appealing offshore snorkeling sites along the west coast, not far from Palm Beach.

It is always advisable to snorkel with a buddy, and it's a required practice for scuba divers. Renting an inflatable snorkel vest is also advised when snorkeling on your own.

BOCA CATALINA

Bordering Boca Catalina (north of Palm Beach on the west coast, close to Malmokweg), the coastline is a coral wall rampant with a variety

© ROSALIE KLEIN

Snorkeling in Aruba is a kid-friendly activity.

of sea life. This is a good spot for offshore snorkeling, with no need to swim far to enjoy the schools of grunts, copperheads, and silversides that shelter under the limestone outcroppings along the shoreline. There are two entry points, but the most interesting sea life can be found at the entry where steps have been carved into the stone. This is just where the houses on the water side begin. Swim north or south of this point.

MANGEL HALTO
Aruba's south side has an extensive reef formation bordering the mangrove reefs along Pos Chiquito, the midpoint of the island. The inner lagoon has some sea life, but a sandy bottom. It is enclosed by an extensive outcropping of elkhorn and staghorn coral. The areas facing into the lagoon provide interesting snorkeling. Traveling through the reef to the outer areas and the dropoff reefs are best done with an experienced guide who knows the route, as it requires snaking through sharp coral that skims the surface.

SNORKELING TRIPS
Families and groups with diverse tastes will particularly appreciate the many large catamarans and trimarans common to Aruba. They have a stability that guarantees smooth sailing in heavy winds. Their wider breadth also makes it easier to move about and stretch out. Day trips are geared to pleasing all passengers, with snorkel stops, instruction, equipment, light meals, and beverages included. Guests have the option of exploring the reefs, or simply relaxing on board and working on their tan.

Palm Beach has the greatest concentration of water activities, including sailboat departures. Three large piers provide boarding and debarkation points for most trips. Pier operators are large watersports companies that offer a diversity of services, and they usually operate a few sailboats. They also have contracts with visiting cruise ships, resulting in days when the trips are not available to independent bookings.

An alternative to these larger companies are smaller, owner-operated boats, which provide good value and a dedication to the craft. The love of sailing is often passed down through the generations, and captains who run their own boats, whether sailing or deep sea fishing, are dedicated to the art. The atmosphere on these boat trips can feel like spending a day on the water with friends. They are a very personalized experience, usually with smaller groups as well.

Catamarans and Trimarans
Multi-hulled sailboats are better suited to Aruba's blustering winds, providing less heeling and a more stable ride. Their width also allows passengers to move around more comfortably. This is why so many of these large boats dot the shore. Day trips on all boats include meals or snacks, snorkel equipment and instruction, along with an open bar. Some boats charge extra for beer.

◖ OCTOPUS CRUISES
One of the most experienced sailing outfitters on Aruba, Octopus Cruises (Borancana 12, departs from Playa Linda beach, 297/593-3739, www.octopusaruba.com, 9am-12:30pm Wed.-Fri., 1:30pm-4pm Mon.-Fri., and 5pm-7pm Tues. and Thurs., $35-50) has a 40-foot trimaran sailboat. This is an authentic, tranquil sailing experience with Captain Jethro, one of the few fully certified sailors on the island. It is the only boat on Aruba without a motor, running strictly on sail power. They strictly limit 22 passengers per trip, to assure comfort and personal attention.

Jethro has been sailing Aruba's waters for decades; he loves the sailor's life. His crew is particularly appreciated for their patient and thorough instruction for novice snorkelers. Fish are accustomed to their daily visits and do not shy away from snorkelers.

Morning trips include a continental breakfast with mimosas and two snorkel stops, including the *Antilla* shipwreck. The buffet lunch features a freshly made salad and make-your-own hoagies, with a diverse array of exotic tropical fruits. Shorter afternoon trips are mostly spent snorkeling, and include their famous Dutch cheese baguettes and fresh fruit. Relaxing sunset sails feature cocktails and snacks, but no snorkel stops. An open bar is included on all trips.

Single-Hulled Sailing Charters
🄲 TRANQUILO
The all-day trips on the 43-foot *Tranquilo* (Alto Vista 34K, departs from Renaissance Harbor, 297/594-2173, www.tranquiloaruba.com, 10am-3pm Tues., Thurs., and Fri., $75) have long been a family affair made popular decades ago by Captain Mike, a local sailing legend. His son Anthony has kept up the tradition, and is passing the love of the sea and sailing on to the next generation.

Best known as the only regularly scheduled full-day trips to Aruba's south side, the excursion offers authentic toes-in-the-water moments at some of the windier points along the coast. The single keel affords heeling well into the wind and some adventurous moments on the water.

The snorkel spot is an attractive reef that is part of the Mangle Halto formation, affectionately referred to as "Mike's Reef." A platform on one of the sandbanks facilitates entry and exit. They have a regular clientele who come back each year for the famous Dutch pea soup that Anthony's mom, Celia, makes for lunch. *Tranquilo* also offers a Romantic Dinner for Two tour ($475), which includes champagne toast, wine, and a customized menu arranged in advance, via email.

MONSOON
More than just day trips, *Monsoon* (Nikky Beach, 297/568-4035, www.goldships.com, $175 per hour) is a sailing experience on a 72-foot world-class boat meant for circumnavigating the globe. It is gloriously outfitted with luxurious cabins and even a bathtub. Customs charter trips run along Aruba's shores or for a few days to the Venezuelan coastline. Sandwiches and soft drinks are included; beer and wine can be purchased on board. All special trips are individually priced.

It is possible to rent the boat on its mooring for an overnight romantic interlude in the Captain's Cabin. *Monsoon* also partners with the fine chefs from **Twister Café** (Dominicanessenstraat 10, 297/583-9077, twistercafearuba10@yahoo.com) for dinner cruises. Menus and fees are arranged separately with restaurant staff.

MI DUSHI
The longest running of the historic schooner class is *Mi Dushi* (Noord 128P, 297/586-2010, www.midushi.com, 9:30am-2:30pm and 3:30pm-6:30pm Tues.-Fri., $39-59 adults, $20 children 6-12), "My Sweetheart," departing from the De Palm Pier in Palm Beach.

Aruba Adventures owner Marcus Wiggins began running *Mi Dushi* decades ago, but now leaves that to his capable young crew. The original boat was sunk to become a new dive site. The "new" schooner, an historic 80-foot wooden ship built in Sweden in 1925, has a distinctive charm. The size allows for their famous rope swing, a fun way to get wet. Morning trips include a premium brand bar, BBQ chicken lunch, snorkel equipment, and fresh fruit. Afternoon trips feature snacks and drinks. *Mi Dushi* is one of the few sailing trips to combine snorkeling with a sunset sail.

JOLLY PIRATES
A name like Jolly Pirates (J. E. Irausquin Blvd. 230, 297/586-8107, www.jolly-pirates.com, 9:30am-1pm and 2:30pm-5:30pm daily, 5pm-7pm Mon. and Fri., $30-75) already sets the mood for these popular trips. Captain Harold and his lively crew have a reputation for doing their best to deliver on the expectations. The ships are also famous for their rope swing.

Trips depart from the Hadicurari Pier by MooMba Beach, where they maintain their headquarters and logo shop. Jolly Pirates runs two of these stylish ships, each taking a maximum of 65 passengers. Morning trips include snorkeling, BBQ lunch, a bar, and fresh fruit, which they also serve on their sunset dinner cruises.

RECREATION

TAKE PRECAUTIONS: DRINK WATER, COVER UP, AND DON'T LOSE YOUR WEDDING RING!

Underwater activities such as scuba diving that place unique stresses on the body are not the only activities that require some precautions to insure full enjoyment. Aruba's intense sun and temperatures can be extremely taxing, even for the very fit. Continual re-hydration, whether playing beach volleyball or just lying on the beach, is necessary. Any strenuous activity should be accompanied by bottles of cool water or frequent stops for refreshments.

When touring in open vehicles, especially mopeds, don't make the mistake of wearing skimpy clothing. Not only does this invite severe sunburn, but Aruba's roads can accumulate blown sand. This is like driving over ice, particularly on a curve. If you crash, aside from road rash, you will likely run into the foliage. You can expect it to be cactus with long, sharp thorns. Dress as you would dress for riding a motorcycle at home: protective jeans, shirts with sleeves, and lots of sun block on exposed areas. Be sure to use the helmet provided.

Tropical temperatures also pose the threat of heatstroke or exhaustion when engaging in physical activity, particularly if it is not part of a regular routine. The chronically inactive should think twice about biking far distances in mid-day, or trying any physically demanding activity to which they are unaccustomed. A completely new sport, or hiking off into some dry, deserted part of the landscape, should not be done alone or without supervision.

Lastly, perhaps due to fingers slicked up by sun lotion, there isn't a week that goes by without a story of some newlywed losing their shiny new wedding ring in the sea. It might happen while snorkeling on a boat, or just swimming off shore. Crews on pleasure boats have gotten pretty good at finding lost rings since they get quite a bit of practice. Beach boxes will contain wedding rings nicely, or lock them away. It is nice to show off the newly married status, but this happens too often to take a chance.

DIVING

Snorkeling is an easy and quick way to explore the marine environment. But in order to really study the minutiae of reef and wrecks, visitors should learn how to scuba dive.

Dive Operators

PADI-certified (Professional Association of Diving Instructors) dive shops are plentiful on Aruba, with most located along the Palm Beach boardwalk. Some offer more than SCUBA (Self Contained Underwater Breathing Apparatus) lessons, but also sailing trips with SNUBA (Surface Nexus Underwater Breathing Apparatus). With scuba, each diver has their own breathing unit. SNUBA deploys what is known in the diving community as a "hookah." Four divers are attached to one tank, which floats on the surface. This allows them to submerge to about 20 feet under the water at the very maximum. Since four are sharing a tank

of air, the time underwater is also quite limited. SNUBA divers do have to take some instruction and learn a few scuba techniques.

Resort courses, devised and approved by PADI, provide enough background information and preliminary training for novices to perform a shallow, heavily supervised dive. The actual doing of scuba is not very complicated or difficult to learn. Becoming a fully certified diver involves training to plan and perform dives without supervision, which requires much more background knowledge. One can learn enough in a resort course to get a taste of the sport. The ideal conditions of Aruba's tropical marine environment is the perfect place for an introduction to what may become a lifelong diversion.

Full certification courses are offered by all certified dive shops. They are an intense four days of classes, pool sessions, and dives, which meet PADI requirements. It is essential to contact a dive shop prior to your trip to arrange taking a class. All the lectures, pool work, tests, and dives that would normally be conducted over a five-week period are done in a few days. Be prepared to commit nearly an entire day, each day, to complete the course.

Certifying organizations also allow the option of doing the class and pool work over several weeks back in the United States or Canada, and then traveling to an exotic destination to fulfill the dive requirements in a more desirable location. Proof that the class and pool work were successfully completed must be in hand before Aruban dive shops can administer the qualifying dives, usually four dives. These dives are underwater exercises and tests that must be passed satisfactorily. All PADI-affiliated dive shops on Aruba offer a package price for this service and should be contacted prior to arrival, with all paperwork in order. A signed form from a doctor confirming the diver's fitness for the sport is also required.

Pregnant women and individuals with chronic conditions requiring daily medication, such as diabetes, high blood pressure, heart disease, asthma, epilepsy, or having had recent major surgery, are usually not eligible for any of these activities. A bad cold or congestion will also disqualify since this can result in serious damage to the sinuses or ear drums. As much as you might want to do it, be sure to inform the operators of any possible conditions, and listen to the instructor when they tell you no.

❰ JAD'S DIVE SHOP

The only dive shop located within Lago Colony next to Baby Beach, Jad's (Seroe Colorado 245E, 297/584-6070, http://jadsaruba.com, resort course $99, full certification $425) offers the best way to dive some of Aruba's most stunning reefs. No other dive operator has the advantage of their location, with boats taking divers out to more remote spots on the east side in record time. Patrons will find this PADI facility is very conscientious, and the staff personable and informative. Located on the far end of the island from major resort areas, they also do hotel pickup and return.

DIVE ARUBA

One of the island's most experienced PADI Open Water instructors, Clive Paula, operates Dive Aruba (Williamstraat 8, 297/582-7337, www.divearuba.com, Mon.-Sat., dives and classes by appointment, resort course $85, full certification $425). He runs a small, very personalized operation out of Oranjestad, taking only seven divers at a time. Dive trips are geared to certified divers, so if seeking a novice resort course, it is important to book ahead. Departing from the town harbor, his super fast boat can assure quick access to the more remote and unusual sites. Trips include hotel pickup and return.

❰ UNIQUE SPORTS OF ARUBA

One of the most respected PADI-certified scuba shops in Palm Beach is Unique Sports of Aruba (J. E. Irausquin Blvd. 81, between RIU and Radisson Resorts, 297/586-0096, www.uniquesportsaruba.com, resort courses 9:30am Mon.-Sat. $95.50, PADI certification $437.75, National Geographic $125 extra, SNUBA $55), the exclusive island agent for SNUBA. It is also a National Geographic Dive facility, with specialty courses including two additional dives. They offer eco-awareness dive training, with particular attention to techniques that insure no harm to the marine environment. A NITROX-enriched air diving course is also on the menu.

Unique Sports of Aruba runs sailing and snorkeling trips with their Cruzencat catamaran, which also feature SNUBA sessions. For those who feel more comfortable walking into the water, they offer an alternative twice daily that enters offshore at Arashi. These private sessions are for 2-4 divers. Their desk is an agent for small craft activities, such as waverunners and tubing.

ARUBA WATERSPORTS CENTER

Located between the Radisson and Occidental resorts is Aruba Watersports Center (J. E. Irausquin Boulevard 81b, 297/586-6613, www.arubawatersportcenter.com, 9am-5pm daily, resort course Mon.-Sat. $90, open water $400, bicycle rental $25), a reliable family operation

NIGHT DIVING

Aruba is the perfect place for certified divers who have never enjoyed the exhilaration of night diving. As beautiful as the underwater world is during the day, once night has fallen, it exposes a rarely seen environment. Nocturnal sea life comes out to play, unveiling new mysteries of the deep.

The deeper a diver descends during the day, the more color is lost. Bright corals and fish take on a bluish cast. The bright lights used at night expose the actual brilliant hues of sponges and corals, as can never be seen during the day. The stunning colors of various creatures that come out to feed are amazing. Diurnal fish actually get sleepy at night, so they are not so quick to dart away.

The most daunting aspect for novice night divers is keeping oriented to the dive boat or entry point. In the pitch-black waters, particularly over an extensive reef area, divers can get confused. For this reason, the Antilla is a superb choice for an inaugural nocturnal dive. It is a huge object, surrounded by interesting sea life. It is also easy to stay oriented to location and where the dive boat is tied on. The dive is not too deep, and it offers enormous diversity within a limited area. The assurance of the dive boat being close by allows night divers to relax and enjoy this fascinating experience.

Divers who have been considering giving night diving a try will never have a better opportunity. Aruba's warm waters and the comfortable air temperatures also contribute to a more optimal first night dive experience.

offering diving and all small craft activities, plus Sunfish and Beachcat boat rentals. They have two PADI-certified instructors, very capable and personable, simply known as J.T. and Jake. The complex also offers a shop on the boardwalk for beachwear and sundries, a good place to pick up watertight beach boxes, sun block, and other minor items.

Other Water Activities

UNDERWATER TOURS

One does not have to get wet to enjoy Aruba's amazing underwater environment. Family-oriented excursions provide a memorable experience for all ages and non-swimmers.

ATLANTIS SUBMARINE AND *SEAWORLD EXPLORER*

Two of the most unusual transports to tour the marine landscape are *Atlantis* Submarine and *Seaworld Explorer* (L. G. Smith Blvd., toll free 800/609-7374, 297/582-4545 De Palm office, they will connect you, www.depalmtours.com; *Atlantis:* 11am daily, 90 minutes $104 adults, $54 children, under 4 not allowed; *Seaworld Explorer:* 11am daily, $44 adults, $22 children). *Atlantis* takes passengers past drop-off reefs and a few small wrecks on the south side, reaching depths of 150 feet. The set up of the submarine requires looking out portholes that line the sides of the sub. This is thrilling for one side of the submarine, but there is little to see but the sandy bottom on the other. After the sub turns, the other side gets to see the interesting stuff. They have an impossible-to-miss ticket office and logo retail shop on the Oranjestad harbor, their embarkation point.

Seaworld Explorer is a semi-submarine, the top half stays above the surface. The underwater portion has wide picture windows all around for a panoramic view. It departs from the Pelican Pier in Palm Beach, taking passengers over the *Antilla* shipwreck and west-side reef areas. If you begin to feel a little claustrophobic down below, go up top to enjoy the wide open view of the coastline.

FAMILY FUN AT ARUBA WATERPARK

In the fall of 2012, Aruba finally opened its doors to an affordable waterpark: Aruba Waterpark (Hooiberg Z/N, 297/585-0060, www.arubavacationpark.com, 11am-7pm Tues.-Sun., $11 adults, $8 children, all-inclusive food and drinks $39 adults, $13 children, over 65 free) has a great collection of slides for all ages. There are slow, steady, and shallow slides for young ones and daredevil drops for the "take no prisoners" teenagers. Lifeguards are on duty. The high slides were ingeniously designed with a gradual nature walk to the top, rather than an exhausting climb up steep stairs.

The park boasts excellent food with a continually changing menu. Standard fare of BBQ and hamburgers is always available, but the chef usually cooks up a variety of local dishes.

Planted in the midst of the Aruba countryside, with stunning views of the surrounding landscape, the waterpark is located inland. It is not that hard to find: Just head for the Haystack mount and follow the signs.

RECREATION

SEA TREK

Sea Trek (L. G. Smith Blvd. 142, 297/582-4545, www.depalmtours.com, $47 adults, $35 children) uses hard hat helmets like divers of old, but with space-age design. This allows non-swimmers to actually walk on the ocean floor, tethered to the surface. It is only available at **De Palm Island** (Balashi Z/N, 297/585-4799, www.depalmtours.com, 9am-6pm daily, $109 adults, $83 children) and is not included in the price of a day on the island. It requires no special training to enjoy.

SAILING
RED SAIL SPORTS DINNER CRUISE

Regularly scheduled dinner cruises depart from Red Sail Sports pier (J. E. Irausquin Blvd. 348 A, 297/586-1603, www.aruba-redsail.com, 6pm-9pm Wed., $99) next to the Hyatt, once a week. This cruise takes the island fantasy dinner to a new level without being too hard on the wallet. They use their biggest boat, the *Rumba,* which is 70 feet and has a limit of only 38 passengers. The sunset trip includes a buffet dinner catered by the Hyatt culinary department, known for its quality cuisine, and an open bar.

KAYAKING
ARUBA KAYAK ADVENTURES

Aruba Kayak Adventure (Ponton 88, 297/582-5520, www.arubawavedancer.com, 8:30am-2:30pm Mon.-Sat., $99) runs memorable nature tours. Congenial, entertaining guides Rosendo or Coco take kayakers, from the novice to the experienced, through the mangrove preserves of Mangle Halto and the south side. The area is rich with biodiversity. Guests are picked up at their resorts and transported to this pristine location. There is a declared limit of 18-20 kayakers per tour, with varying routes for repeat guests. Lunch takes place at De Palm Island or Balashi Beer Gardens.

DEEP SEA FISHING

Deep sea fishing can be arranged through concierge desks, major water sports companies, or many of the tent operators in Palm Beach; all have some fishing boats in their roster. If you're serious about fishing, it is always advisable to head down to the piers to watch the boats come in and see who is catching. Talk to the crew and the anglers. An amiable captain and crew always add immeasurably to the enjoyment of the day. Several boats are moored at Hadicurari Pier, between MooMba Beach and the Marriott Surf Club in Palm Beach, or in Oranjestad Harbor. Charter rates vary greatly depending on the size of the boat and length of the trip.

Oranjestad Harbor
DRIFTWOOD FISHING CHARTERS

Enjoy your catch for dinner after fishing with Driftwood Fishing Charters (Oranjestad

© ROSALIE KLEIN

Small catamarans can be rented by the hour.

Marina, 297/592-4040, www.driftwooda-ruba.com, hours vary, $460-760). Fanatical fisherman Herby Merryweather will see to it that the catch gets cooked up for no charge at their Oranjestad restaurant that same night. He has two boats; the *Driftwood II* is available only for all-day charters. Merryweather knows where the fish are and likes to catch. In fact, he needs to catch, to provide fish for Driftwood Restaurant.

TEASER FISHING CHARTERS

A consistent winner during annual fishing contests, Teaser Fishing Charters (Oranjestad Marina, 297/593-9228, www.teasercharters.com, 8am-noon and 8am-4pm daily, $350-700) runs two Bertrams 35': *Teaser* and *Kenny's Toy*. The captain and crew love the sport and share the excitement of the catch. Regular clients cite the friendly crew and their enthusiasm for the sport, which always makes a day on the water an enjoyable experience.

Hadicurari Pier
MELINA CHARTERS

For greater convenience to Palm Beach resorts, Melina Charters (Hadicurari Pier, 297/593-1550, www.arufishing.com, flexible hours, half day: $260-300, $370-425, and $480-550) is moored close by. They offer a varied menu of deep sea, bottom, and inshore fishing, for smaller game. They will gear trips to what is running at the time or a patron's preference. The owner and captain, Piet, is a personable veteran fisherman who loves the sport and does his best to find the fish.

KITESURFING, PARASAILING, WINDSURFING, AND SURFING

All along Palm Beach are a dozen or more independent operators with tents that provide spur-of-the-moment, unscheduled activities. These could be banana boat rides, tubing, waverunners, and parasailing, usually sold in blocks of 15 minutes. Each resort has at least one vendor; prices and services are the same from one

© ROSALIE KLEIN

kitesurfing near Fisherman's Huts

to the next. At Fisherman's Huts, north of the Marriott, is Aruba's windsurfing and kitesurfing center, with kiosks and tents, where lessons can be arranged or equipment rented for those with experience.

ARUBA ACTIVE VACATIONS
Dedicated to extreme sports, Aruba Active Vacations (Fisherman's Huts, L. G. Smith Blvd. across from Bakval, 297/586-0989, www.aruba-active-vacations.com, 9am-7pm daily, windsurfing $50-135, kitesurf: $100-160, mountain biking: $25-100, landsailing safari 2.5 hours, $60) is aptly named. Owner Wim Eehlers is the president of the Aruba Windsurfing Association, which conducts the annual Aruba Hi-Winds Pro Am. He and his crew are fanatical about their activities, offering patient, expert instruction. Aruba is considered to have some of the most ideal conditions for windsurfing in the world: Calm waters and steady winds make it easy to master the sport. Discover a new obsession.

ARUBA SURF SCHOOL
Due to Aruba's calm waters, surfing does not have the thrill of the Pacific or north Atlantic coasts. There is only one operation dedicated to pursuing this activity here: Aruba Surf School (Kamay 29 F, 297/593-0229, by appt. daily, 4-hour surfing tour of best spots $95, novice lessons $85). Owner and surfing fanatic Dennis Martinez does his utmost to provide a fun day of riding the waves. He picks up guests at their resorts and takes them where the best surf is to be found that day. This will certainly be at out-of-the-way coves along the north coast. Expect an outback adventure and surfing safari experience all in one.

NATIVE DIVERS WATERSPORTS
You can always count on a friendly chat and conscientious service with Vanessa at Native Divers Watersports (Washington 16, 297/586-4763, book at the tent in front of the Marriott Surf Club, 9am-5pm daily, float rental $5/day banana boat; tube rides $15 for 15 minutes;

waverunners $60/half-hour; additional $5 per child to share with up to two small children; driver must be at least 16 years old; parasailing $55). She will be happy to arrange all sorts of family activities for playing in the waves, such as tubing, banana boat rides, parasailing, and waverunners, as well as renting out floats, at standard rates. She makes it a practice of directing clients to the most safety-conscience and reputable operators. Her tent is a hospitable place to relax and she is a fountain of information regarding activities and operators.

FUN FOR EVERYONE
Located at the north end of the Riu Palace beach is George Tromp and his tent offering

Fun for Everyone (Borancana 128, 297/640-6603, www.fun4every1.com, 9am-5pm daily, float rental $5/day, banana boat and tube rides $20/half-hour, waverunners $60/half-hour, parasailing $60, beach umbrellas $25/day, beach lounges $5/day). George is highly recommended for his friendly operation. He has four fast boats of his own to accommodate all comers. Banana boat rides offer a complete tour of the coastline from Palm Beach to the Westpunt.

He also offers beach lounge rental by the day and shade umbrellas for those who are not guests of Palm Beach resorts but wish to spend the day here. This is particularly handy for cruise ship passengers.

Land Tours

Choose from full-size air-conditioned coaches, minibus tours, or safari-type vehicles that handle large and small groups. The more unique methods, such as trikes and Harley-Davidson motorcycles, take such few numbers that they are practically private tours.

The advantages of guided tours, whether large or small, are many. Drivers and guides know the island well. Aside from getting you where you want to go with minimal wasted time, guides provide interesting and informative commentary, often seasoned with wit and folklore, making for an enjoyable interlude.

Disadvantages include the need to keep to a schedule at the expense of visitors being able to explore or savor a site for as long as they wish. This is when the smaller, personalized tours, with guides who can accommodate patrons' whims, deliver the desired experience. Aruba has a wealth of both large and small tours, allowing visitors to tour exactly as they please.

BY COACH
DE PALM TOURS
Aruba's most prolific tour operator, De Palm Tours (L. G. Smith Blvd. 142, 297/582-4545, www.depalmtours.com, 10am daily, $35

adults, $26 children), has the largest fleet of air-conditioned coaches and a wide variety of tours. Coach tours tend to visit the more easily accessible and prosaic spots, with the required shopping stop at some local suppliers. Those wishing for a token glance at the island away from the resort centers, while travelling in complete comfort, will find this just about right. Buses take up to 65 passengers.

EL TOURS
A mid-size tour operator and transport provider, EL Tours (Ir. Luymestraat 6, Pos Chiquito, toll free U.S./Canada 866/978-5913, on Aruba 297/585-6730, www.eltoursaruba.com, 9am-1:30pm daily, $35-45) uses smaller buses and takes fewer passengers. It also visits many of the standard sites, but provides an option to stop at Arashi Beach for an hour of snorkeling. Equipment is provided.

MINIBUSES
There are quite a few independent operators who take small groups of 11-15 visitors, maximum, at very reasonable prices and flexible times schedules. For large families it is easy to arrange a private tour, and most are done at

a leisurely pace, allowing personalized exploration of the various sights. Vehicles are well maintained and air-conditioned, offering an attractive alternative that is less commercial than the ordinary bus tour. These independent bus operators are spirited tour guides with a wealth of information about Aruba.

Minibus tours generally operate from in front of the cruise terminal in Oranjestad. They also pick up at hotels when groups hire the entire bus. During the low season they will also provide transport for groups, saving money on multiple taxis. Minibus tours tend to stick to the more easily accessed sites and smooth, paved roads.

XCLUSIVE TOURS & TRANSFER SERVICES

Working for over 14 years as a tour guide since he was 18, the last 5 on his own, Regmy Dubero of Xclusive Tours & Transfer Services (Rooi Kochi 30 C, 297/593-3551, www.xclusivetoursaruba.com, $25) takes his responsibility as an "ambassador of goodwill" very seriously. He makes every effort to entertain his guests while proudly showing off his homeland. Tours can be customized to explore particular areas of the island. Favorite spots on the regularly scheduled tours include Casibari Rock Formation, Bushiribana Gold Ruin, Santa Ana Church, and Alto Vista Chapel. A standard tour is two hours, but it can be extended. A menu of tours is offered and passengers can pick the route that interests them most.

BINNS TOURS

Sonny Binns (Pos Chiquito 81B, 297/568-2028, binns.tours@yahoo.com, $10/hour pp, minimum two hours) has a larger bus than most independent operators: He handles up to 28 passengers. He has set tours of three and five hours, but is fluid about time and itinerary, customizing the trip to the tastes of his guests. He is also a veteran tour guide who decided to go out on his own, which makes him a very happy fella, indeed. He visits many of the popular spots, offering a selection of sights and timed tours.

HOWARD FOLKES

After more than 24 years as a tour guide, Howard Folkes of HF Tours and Transfers (Piedra Plat 46H, 297/594-1954, http://folkestours.com, $20 pp for two-hour tours, extra time is negotiable) knows every nook and cranny of Aruba. He has two busses, one that handles 29 passengers, the other 15. Trips are customizable. Though his normal point of departure is from in front of the cruise terminal, he will pick up at hotels, even if it's not a private group. Depending on the departure point and time requirements, he will suggest a menu of easily accessible sites, such as Santa Ana Church, Alto Vista Chapel, California Lighthouse, and Casibari Rock Formation.

CARAVAN AND SPECIALTY TOURS

Caravan tours offer the best of both worlds: a chance to drive your own 4x4 or heavy duty safari-type vehicle, and a tour guide in a lead car showing the way. Most caravans take 6-10 passengers. These will usually deploy the rougher roads, which are often more direct. Excursions may last a full day with a good number of stops, as standard sights are mixed with those exciting, out-of-the-way locations. Some tour operators also offer shorter tours focusing only on off-road sights. Pick-up times at resorts are 15-30 minutes prior to tour times quoted, as guest will be transported from their hotels to a centralized departure point.

EL TOURS

Using Jeep Ramblers seating only four, the EL Tours (Ir. Luymestraat 6, Pos Chiquito, toll free U.S./Canada 866/978-5913, on Aruba 297/585-6730, www.eltoursaruba.com, 9am-5pm daily, $75 half-day, $93 full-day) safari excursions are a bit more intimate, often providing friends or family with their own car. Full-day tours include lunch at the highly recommended B-55 restaurant. Aside from 4x4 tours, EL also is a go-between for interesting alternatives such as guided hiking and mountain biking, horseback rides and Harley-Davidson tours, along with dedicated eco-tours. These

RECREATION

are customized tours, so prices and hours vary depending on size of group, length of tour, and choosing a guide or exploring on your own.

ABC TOURS

The first safari tours on Aruba were run by ABC Tours and Attractions (Schotlandstraat 61, 297/582-5600, www.abc-aruba.com, 9am-5pm daily, $99 adults, $59 children, includes lunch; 8:30am-12:30pm $79 adults, $49 children, natural pool only, no lunch). They set a standard that many still copy. Owner Marvin Kelly is always thinking innovatively and working to make the tours better. They use Land Rovers with shade canopies. In 2013, they opened their own safari-style restaurant, Waka-Waka, where they stop for a BBQ lunch. The guides compete with each other to make their tours the most interesting and fun. The heavy-duty vehicles allow them to take passengers to the more out-of-the-way spots, including Conchi, Aruba's natural pool on the north coast. Patrons do the driving while following the leader, so skill at using a standard transmission is required of at least one person in a group.

Alternate tours include the Ostrich Farm, Ayo Rock Formation, Andicuri Beach, and the Donkey Sanctuary.

◖ MADI'S MAGICAL TOURS

Madi's Magical Tours (Shete 19, 297/746-1397, http://madimagicaltours.com, Sunrise Conchi Tour 5:30am-8:30am daily, $75 adults, children half price; 4.5-hour private tours $100) are run by Madi, a fifth generation Aruban who grew up with the countryside as her backyard. She admits to being a "bruha" (a white witch) with an encyclopedic knowledge of island folklore, bush medicine, and out-of-the-way sights. She is more than just a tour guide; her tours always have the feeling of *ban keiro* ("let's go tripping"). They're like an excursion with family and friends, rather than a paid excursion.

Madi takes very small groups and tries not to tie the guests into a set schedule or routine. Tours usually go well beyond proscribed times as patrons are reluctant to depart her charming

Jeep safari tour in Aruba's outback

© ROSALIE KLEIN

company. She is quite the character, with memorable, unusual tours. Pick up and return to your hotel is provided. The safari-type vehicle puts passengers in the car with her, not relegated to the back, so all can enjoy her running commentary.

Guests can choose from a sunrise tour to Conchi, which departs before dawn. Expect some breathtaking photos as the sun rises on this dramatic area of the north coast. Madi is continually adding new, undiscovered areas to her itinerary. Madi is the person to see for a tour that specializes in the unusual.

NATURE SENSITIVE TOURS
Nature guide Eddy Croes harbors a passion for the outdoors and Aruba's environment, which he shares during his Nature Sensitive Tours (jeep tours begin with pick up at hotel, 297/585-1594 or 594-5017, http://naturesensitivetours.com, hiking tours by appt. $79, full-day jeep tours $85). He was a powerful force behind Arikok National Park becoming a protected preserve and the first to begin identifying and labeling much of the flora found there. His tours are a unique experience, focused not only on the typical sights. He offers a more thorough exploration and understanding of how the many unique outback land formations came to exist.

Eddie has a wealth of stories and folklore to impart and has become something of an Internet personality, so his tours are in demand. He now takes groups of 20 or more for hiking tours using a refitted military truck. The canvas sides of the truck do not allow passengers to view the countryside while moving between locations.

MADAGASCAR ARUBA ADVENTURE
Tourists are raving about Alfredo and his Madagascar Aruba Adventure (Caya Seyda 9, 297/746-0572, madagascar-aruba@hotmail.com, 8:30am-1pm and 2pm-6pm daily, $50 adults, $30 children). This tour, like Madi's, is singled out for the charm and enthusiasm of the owner-guide. Passengers report tours often go over the allotted time because all, including

their host, are having so much fun. A little young to be called "Papa Alfred," Alfredo is very much all about taking care of his patrons and is well informed about the island and the sights. Groups are limited to 12; his shaded safari truck is well set up for taking lots of pictures.

Motorcycles, ATVs, and Trikes
In the past few years, tour operators have realized that getting there can be half the fun when the transportation is funky.

◖ BIG TWIN HARLEY-DAVIDSON
On the western outskirts of Oranjestad is the Big Twin Harley-Davidson dealership (L. G. Smith Blvd. 106, 866/978-6525 or 297/586-8220, www.harleydavidson-aruba.com, 9am-5:30pm Mon.-Sat., $140-175 half-day rentals $175-200 full-day rentals), easily spotted by the HOGs lined up in front. If it has always been your dream to be an Easy Rider, you can rent your own or take one of their guided tours for an additional $20 per person fee, gas not included. Two on a bike is allowed. Tours are conducted with only three bikes at a time, for a very personal, interesting way to see the island, Availability is limited and it's best to reserve online prior to arrival on Aruba. Always attempting to be different, the tour includes a lunch or refreshment stop at Charlie's Bar in San Nicolas.

WATAPANA ATV TOURS
Indulge in the current craze for off-roading with Watapana ATV Tours (Schotlandstraat 50, 800/482-2140 or 297/583-5195, www.watapanaaruba.com, natural pool 9am-noon daily, island tour 2pm-5:30pm daily, $88 single rider, $99 for two). ATVs are particularly suited for those tough Aruban outback trails and great fun.

◖ TRIKES
Show off your sense of style and see the island with Trikes (L. G. Smith Blvd. 333, De Olde Molen parking lot, 297/738-7453, www.trikes-aruba.com, office hours 8am-5pm Mon.-Sat., tour times are flexible, $120 for 2, $20 extra for

© ROSALIE KLEIN

Trike tours are becoming a popular and fun way to tour the island.

a third person, $50 to drive on the trike with the guide). You will see heads turn as you pass. These motorcycle and car hybrids are very comfortable and easy to drive; a short lesson and practice precedes the actual tour. Some skill with a stick shift is helpful.

Michelangelo is a very personable guide. Tooling around in these hot-colored three-wheelers is just plain fun; be ready to be noticed. The lunch stop on the all-day tours is at Zeerover for an authentic taste of Aruba.

HORSEBACK TOURS
⬛ RANCHO DAIMARI

Still one of the best ways to see Aruba's north coast is via horseback. Rancho Daimari (J. E. Irausquin Blvd. 382 A, 297/586-6284, www.arubaranchodaimari.com, 8am and 2pm daily tours, lasting 2 hours, Andicuri Tour $65, Natural Pool $78, resort pick-up and return), just north of Arikok National Park, is one of the best situated and most experienced stables, specializing in treks to the Natural Pool.

GOLD MINE RANCH

Alternative north coast destinations via horseback are on the tour route of Gold Mine Ranch (Mativadiri 60, 297/585-9870, www.thegoldmineranch.com, tours depart 9am and 5pm daily, $65-75, private tours available). The tours make seven stops along the way, boasting to be the only ranch offering a beach trot through the waves. These tours are for capable and experienced riders exclusively. Riders are paired with a horse that matches their riding skill.

EL PASEO RANCH

Closer to Palm Beach resorts and offering horseback tours along the Malmok Coast is El Paseo Ranch (Westpunt Z/N, 297/593-1440, www.elpaseorancharuba.com, daily tours at 9am, 11am, 1pm, and 3pm, $110). This stable is one of the few that includes rides with a snorkel stop in Arashi, a good spot for novice snorklers. Excursions include drinks and snacks, snorkel equipment, vests, and instruction.

© ROSALIE KLEIN

RECREATION

Horseback riding is one of the best ways to tour the Aruban outback.

BIKES, MOPEDS, AND MOTORCYCLE RENTALS AND TOURS
PABLITO'S BIKE RENTAL

Rent your own bike from Pablito's Bike Rental (L. G. Smith Blvd. 234, 297/587-8665, $15/day) for a more athletic way to get around. At the beginning of 2013, traffic authorites designated a portion of J. E. Irausquin Boulevard, L. G. Smith Boulevard north of Palm Beach, and the Sasaki Highway for biking paths. These routes offer beautiful views of the shoreline and Caribbean for enthusiasts of the sport.

GEORGE'S CYCLE RENTAL

For more than 30 years, George's Cycle Rental (L. G. Smith Blvd. 124, 297/593-2202, www.georgecycles.com, 9am-5pm daily, mopeds $40-50/day, Yamaha motorcycles $70-100/day, ATVs $120-200/day) has been the number

one choice for mopeds and motorcycles. It is located on the highway just at the western side of Oranjestad and has a variety of vehicles for rent, from tiny mopeds to ATVs with automatic transmission and hard-top shade canopies. Special discounts are available for longer term rentals of 3 or 4 days. Resort pick-up and drop-off plus helmets are part of the service.

RANCHO NOTORIOUS

Guided mountain bike tours to Alto Vista Chapel and the California Lighthouse are conducted by Rancho Notorious (Borancana Z/N, 297/586-0508, www.ranchonotorious.com, 2.5-hour tours at 8:30am or 3pm daily, $50, 14 years or older), with pick-up and return to your resort. Biking is best done outside of midday, particularly when peddling up steep inclines at Alto Vista or California Point in Aruba's intense heat.

Hiking and Running

RUNNING AND JOGGING PATHS

Naturally pounded dirt paths border the west shore along the **J. E. Irausquin Boulevard** between Manchebo resorts and Palm Beach, providing an exhilarating backdrop for a morning jog. The same hold true along **L. G. Smith Boulevard** from the Marriott Resort to Arashi Beach. Sunsets are beautiful along these routes.

In early 2013, the first phase of what will be the Caribbean's longest linear park opened. On its route, paved jogging paths were placed bordering L. G. Smith Boulevard in Oranjestad. These provide a pleasant route along the water, safe from the busy thoroughfare.

HIKING
Arikok National Park

Aruba's largest natural preserve, Arikok National Park (San Fuego 70, 297/585-1234,

exploring the hiking paths of Arikok National Park

© ROSALIE KLEIN

www.arubanationalpark.org, 8am-4pm daily, $8, with guide $20) occupies 18 percent of the island's landmass. It was designated as a formally protected area in 2000. The park has over 20 miles of hiking trails with various degrees of difficulty. Paved and dirt paths are clearly marked, and flora and fauna are identified as well. For a flat fee rangers can be hired as guides for the entire hike.

The park is a showcase of native species and Aruba's geological formations. Various trails take visitors to the coastline or the island's greatest heights. There are paved or gravel roads paralleling many of the hiking paths, with parking areas. Routes can be reduced according to ability. All quoted distances are calculated with the visitor center at the park entrance as the start and finishing point.

Tour rangers report they will call for a vehicle to pick up hikers who feel too exhausted by the intense heat of the day. It is always advisable in Aruba's tropical heat to hike as early in the day as possible, and take plenty of bottled water along to rehydrate frequently.

CUNUCU ARIKOK TRAIL

Cunucu Arikok (3.5 km, 1.5-2 hours) leads to an authentically preserved farm with a centuries-old dwelling. It is one of the most popular of all the Arikok hikes and the easiest. Parts of the route pass by Aruba's famous Kibrahacha trees, which only blossom a few days out of the year in a burst of intense yellow flowers. Typcial desert flora, including a multitude of cactus with spiny thorns, line the trails.

SEROE JAMANOTA TRAIL

Seroe Jamanota at 617 feet high offers a remarkable panorama of the entire island from San Nicolas to Westpunt; you can see the curve of the world from its peak. There are two paths to the top. The Seroe Jamanota Trail (4.5 km, 2-2.5 hours) is the easiest and follows a gradual winding road, which is paved all the way to the summit. Visitors can also park their car at the base and walk this road to the top.

MASIDURI TRAIL
The alternate route to the top of Seroe Jamanota is for the extremely fit and is one of the physical trials used to test Dutch Marines. Masiduri (7 km, 5 hours or more) takes a more roundabout path, circling around the south side of the hill. It is required to first climb and descend Seroe Large, which is 374 feet high, before climbing the steep trail to the top of Jamanota. Park rangers describe it as a true endurance test.

SEROE ARIKOK TRAIL
Aruba's second highest point, Seroe Arikok, is 606 feet. Its trail (4.4 km, 3 hours) also offers an easy ascent by paved road to the summit. Close to the height of Jamanota, it offers an equally thrilling view.

ROOI TAMBU TRAIL
Following Rooi Tambu (5.5 km, 2-3 hours) east to the sea takes hikers directly to Dos Playa, a lovely place to sunbathe. Rangers warn about swimming here, as there are riptides and undertows. It is popular with bodyboarders. The white sands, surrounding ocher cliffs, and turquoise Caribbean present a stark contrast and make beautiful photos.

ROOI PRINS TRAIL
This trail (5.5 km, 3-4 hours) takes hikers through a dried out creek bed. Rooi Prins leads to Phantage Prins, where hikers can choose to go left to circle back to the park entrance or continue east to the expansive beach area of Boca Prins.

NATURAL POOL TRAIL
Conchi (Natural Pool; 5.5 km, 4-5 hours) can be reached via this hiking trail. It heads north to the pool, then circles back following the rugged north coast before turning west to the park entrance. Natural Pool Trail offers the widest variety off all the trails, passing through cactus and scrub, as well as the rocky coast.

Golf and Tennis

GOLF
Until 20 years ago, golfers had to make do with the funky San Nicolas Golf Club, where the greens are oiled sand and astro-turf, an interesting challenge that no one took very seriously. Fortunately, since 1990, two world-class courses have been built on Aruba, both surrounded by luxurious communities, with international tournaments conducted regularly.

TIERRA DEL SOL COUNTRY CLUB AND GOLF COURSE
The Tierra Del Sol Country Club and Golf Course (Caya di Solo 10, 297/586-0978, www.tierradelsol.com, $129 May-Dec., $159 Dec.-May) is located in Malmok, just at the northwest tip of the island. It is a specially designed 18-hole desert course by the famous Robert Trent-Jones Jr. The course is renowned for its breathtaking vistas and very challenging winds. Amenities include a pro-shop, day spa, gorgeous pool deck, tennis courts, and gourmet restaurant. Villa rental on site includes green fees, along with round-trip airport transport and use of all facilities.

DIVI LINKS
In 2004, Divi Links (J. E. Irausquin Blvd. 93, 297/581-4653, www.divigolf.com, $90 with a $39 fee for replay winter-spring; $75 with $29 replay) opened a gorgeously landscaped 9-hole course with Prince Albert of Monaco, no less, hitting the first ball. Though it is part of Divi complex, Divi Links are open to the public. They have a pro-shop, state of the art clinic, and two very appealing restaurants in their clubhouse. Dedicated golfers usually do two rounds to get in their 18 holes.

RECREATION

© ROSALIE KLEIN

Wetlands and preserves at Divi Links merge golfing and birdwatching.

When carving out the course, the designers did their utmost to preserve the natural wetlands, home to many species of birds. These pools and dramatic formations provide a very unique backdrop when doing the rounds. Thousands of birds have continued to nest here, oblivious to the intruding golfers.

TENNIS

All major resorts have tennis courts for the use of their guests. The court and lessons should be reserved in advance. Visitors have access to three independent tennis facilities, one for each of the major resort areas. They usually cater to local clientele, but are happy to accommodate guests.

EAGLE INTERNATIONAL TENNIS CLUB

Aruba's first tennis club was the Eagle International Tennis Club (Engelandstraat 12, 297/587-5806, 8am-11am and 3pm-11pm Mon.-Sat., $15/hour for a court, $45/hour with a pro, $5 equipment rental). It was part of the exclusive community established for Eagle Refinery executives. The Eagle Tennis Club is a center for the sport on the island and very popular with local players. Co-owner and on-site pro Eddy Ras says they are happy to pair up players that need an opponent or a partner.

The club is located one block inland from the town's westernmost traffic circle. They have a Morning Men's club that starts play at sun-up, and vacationers are welcome to see if they can grab a partner. The fee is a donation at the player's discretion. They have six courts and a single practice court for warm up and working on form, as well as a snack bar and refreshments at local prices. Special lights allow for nighttime play.

ARUBA RACQUET CLUB

Close to the Palm Beach and Malmok resorts is Aruba Racquet Club (Rooi Santo 21, 297/586-0215, www.arc.aw, 8am-11pm Mon.-Fri., 9am-7:30pm Sat., 10am-7pm Sun., $10/hour for a court, $60 lessons with a pro, $5 equipment rental), an elegantly designed facility with eight beautiful courts and gardens. Amenities include a very cute and inexpensive snack bar and a locally priced spa, perfect for getting a massage after a couple of hours on the courts.

PRO SPORT

Tucked away in the Tropicana Resort parking lot is Pro Sport (J. E. Irausquin Blvd. 248, 597/587-5632, r_hirchfel@hotmail.com, 8am-11am and 4pm-10pm Mon.-Fri., 8am-10am and 5pm-8pm Sat.-Sun., $8/hour for a court, $50/hour with a pro, $5 racquet rental) with a homey little clubhouse and three courts. Longtime tennis enthusiasts with passion for the sport passed it down from father to son. Pro Sport is a congenial place where some of the regulars start their day with what they claim is the best cappuccino on Aruba.

ARUBA TENNIS ACADEMY

Tennis lessons can be arranged at your resort with Aruba Tennis Academy (Aloestraat 14, 297/583-7074, www.tennisaruba.com, 8am-11am Mon.-Fri. and by appt., $10-75). The team of pros conducts regularly scheduled free clinics for Hyatt Regency, Marriott, Divi, Tamarijn, and Divi Village Resorts, on alternate days. Check with the concierge to join the morning clinics. Private lessons or a pro as a partner can be arranged by appointment. The Westin and Renaissance resorts are included in this service, as well as Boardwalk Small Hotel. Aruba Tennis Academy gives lessons to cruise ship passengers with pickup and return to the Oranjestad terminal included in the package.

BEACH TENNIS ARUBA

Considering the popularity of beach volleyball, could beach tennis be far behind? Beach Tennis Aruba (J. E. Irausquin Blvd. 230, 297/592-6421, www.beachtennisaruba.com, 8am-10pm daily, $5/hour pp) has worked hard to make their annual finals an international event. Competitors are welcome to join in the October championships. There are also weekend competitions scheduled throughout the year with new ones cropping up continually as the sport gains an enthusiastic following.

This is a sort of a super-charged version of badminton with sand. Players have to get used to the idea of no bounce, which is, of course, different than normal tennis. This is a very different kind of game, with killer shots the norm, and is very physically demanding. If you are a fan, or wish to learn, courts are located at MooMba Beach and the Sand Beach Lounge.

Skydiving and Helicopter Tours

◖ SKYDIVE ARUBA

If you have an adventurous bucket list, Skydive Aruba (Noord Z/N, 297/735-0654, http://skydivearuba.com, 8am-4pm daily, every 2 hours, by appt., $250) is a way to check off an item without all the extensive training or first-time anxiety. Jumps are strictly tandem, attached to a veteran instructor, so patrons can relax and enjoy the view. Nowhere on Aruba will you see such a vista as from 10,000 feet up; it is a once-in-a-lifetime experience. Instructors film the entire jump, which will be available for purchase on DVD to be relived over and over again (or to prove to friends that it really happened).

HELITOURS

Enviable vacation photos with a bird's-eye view are the rewards of a trip with HeliTours (Oranjestad Harbor Helipad, 297/731-9999, http://arubahelitours.com, by appt. only Mon.-Sat., $200-400 flat rate, minimum 2 passengers). Truly a thrill, helicopter tours offer an entirely new perspective of Aruba. Enjoy all the excitement of an extreme adventure with little physical exertion. It is, however, extremely noisy, and you will understand why you need those big padded headphones.

TIARA AIR ARUBA
Does Curacao have you curious? Wondering how Aruba's sister islands compare? Each has a distinctly different flavor of Dutch Caribbean and can be discovered for a day with Tiara Air Aruba (J. E. Irausquin Blvd. 330, 297/586-8822, www.tiara-air.com, Bonaire: 9:10am-9:10pmMon. and Wed., $290; Curacao: 7:15am-8:45pm Tues. and Wed., $275). Twice a week they run day trips complete with tour guides to both islands, providing an interesting change of scene and just enough adventure. Though physically similar, the three islands have great differences in development.

The tours stop for lunch, but the meal cost is not covered in the tour package. Though refreshments are included. Stops on the tours consist of the most famous sights on the respective islands and a break at one of the beaches for a cooling swim.

Spas and Yoga

Aruba has an inordinate number of day spas and *estheticas*. Every major resort boasts a spa designed to envelop guests in a soothing and luxurious environment. An extremely popular service is the couple's massage, a special treatment for two with champagne, chocolates, and other accoutrements, including a private whirlpool bath for sharing that sparkling toast.

Local facilities may not be quite as glamorous, but they are usually far more economical. Priced to a local trade of repeat guests, some are conveniently located near small guesthouses.

SPAS, MASSAGE, AND BEAUTY
OKEANOS SPA
In Oranjestad, Okeanos Spa (L. G. Smith Blvd. 82, 297/583-6000, www.okeanosspaaruba.com, 50-minute Swedish massage: $115, 2.5-hour couple's package: $440) is a luxurious, full-service spa with two outlets. The main facility is within the Marina Tower of Renaissance Resort; the other, dubbed The Cove, is out on a secluded peninsula of Renaissance Island. More than one young couple has gotten engaged after sharing a couple's session in this most romantic setting. Cove packages include a 50-minute massage, a bottle of champagne or four frothy, frozen cocktails, and a fruit platter.

Only massages are given in The Cove, no body scrubs or facials. Reflexology or hot stone options are available, as is lunch. Purchasing a treatment on the island also allows access to Renaissance Island for the day, which normally costs $75. Spa guests are not required to be guests of the resort.

The main facility in the resort is very attractive. They have a steam room and community room with snacks and refreshments. Attached to it is an outdoor terrace where you can linger on lounge chairs and enjoy a great view of the harbor.

The Marina outlet carries the full menu of services. Select from exotic body wraps and skin treatments along with salon services. You might want to try the Royal Romance package: a couple's session which includes dinner at L. G. Smith Steak and Chop House, next door.

SPA DEL SOL
The Manchebo Beach area has several facilities, beginning with Spa Del Sol (J. E. Irausquin Blvd. 55, 297/582-6145, www.spadelsol.com, most 50-minute massages are around $100, couple's massage $190) on the beach at the Manchebo Resort. These are the people who brought the first day spa to Aruba. For the full island experience, all massages are administered in a curtained palapa on the beach.

Spa Del Sol is particularly known for their pampering combination packages, which last several hours. They also include a healthful, holistic lunch. The surroundings are an exotic South Pacific environment of teak and artistic carvings from the owner's collection, acquired from his world travels.

GARRA RUFA WELLNESS FOOTSPA

Annexed to Spa Del Sol is the Garra Rufa Wellness Footspa (J. E. Irausquin Blvd. 55, 297/563-7760, 10am-2pm daily, $25 for 30 minutes), a very unique treatment. A whirlpool footbath is filled with hundreds of the famed "Dr. Fish," which spawn in natural springs in Turkey. Garra Rufa have no teeth but love to gently nibble away at dry and flaky skin. It is a surprisingly pleasant and relaxing sensation.

The footbath is sterilized five times an hour with ultraviolet rays. All feet are thoroughly examined before being immersed; only healthy footsies are allowed. The baths are set up so that you can enjoy the view of the beach and sea during treatments.

ZOIA

Perhaps the most beautiful and luxurious of day spas on the island is ZoiA (Hyatt Regency Resort, 297/586-1234, http://aruba.hyatt.com, 8:30am-8pm daily, 1-hour massage $145, couple's massage $290) just off the lobby of the Hyatt Resort. Completely renovated, renamed, and reopened in 2012, this sumptuous spa features sumptuous accoutrements. Relax in the community room with snacks, holistic drinks, and continental breakfast. There is a sauna on the premises and terraces that look out on the resort's gorgeous gardens. The menu includes a special line of products by Dinah Veeris, famous in the region for natural skin care potions made from endemic plants and herbs.

Special all-day packages are conducted in a huge, luxurious room with a private terrace. This is also the room for the couple's massage, sporting a cozy hot tub for two. Each room has a private bathroom to help maintain the mood, allowing the patron to stay within their own special environment. Complete treatments, make-up, and hair packages are offered for wedding parties, for both the bride and groom.

LARIMAR SPA

Aruba's largest spa is Larimar (Radisson Aruba Resort, 297/526-6053, www.larimarspaaruba. com, 9am-7pm daily, signature Aloe Vera/Rum 80-minute massage with hot stones $185; couple's massage $250), beachside at the Radisson resort. It is beautifully appointed and a gallery for local art. Spacious, elegant treatment rooms and a stunning community area insure the feeling of being pampered in paradise. It is located right at the beach, along the Palm Beach boardwalk.

MANDARA SPA

Mandara Spa (297/586-4710, www.mandaraspa.com, 9am-8pm daily, 50-minute massage $120, couple's massage $275) is conveniently located within the Marriott Ocean Club and services three resorts. This is also a very luxurious facility with a relaxation lounge that opens out to enclosed gardens, creating a serene environment.

MENA'S SKINCARE CENTER

Conveniently located for those staying in guesthouses around Oranjestad and Eagle Beach is Mena's Skincare Center (Tanki Leendert, 297/587-6282, 11am-7pm Tues. and Thurs., 9am-5pm Wed. and Fri., 8am-5pm Sat., 1-hour massage $54). It was Aruba's first *esthetica,* specializing in facials, body wraps, and skin treatments. Mena is a living example of the effectiveness of her procedures, as she is as youthful as when she first began sharing her skills. As a local facility, her prices are geared toward residents, with fees that are much cheaper than the usual resort spa fees. There is the usual menu of massages and facials, but the center also specializes in laser depilation and permanent eyeliner procedures ($280 for both upper and lower lids). Mena has a very clean, pleasant facility not far from the resorts. It's not quite as glamorous, but neither are the prices. Pick-up at hotels can be arranged.

MASSAGE AT HOME

Those staying in smaller guesthouses without spa facilities can enjoy a therapeutic massage,

© ROSALIE KLEIN

Enjoy daily morning yoga at Manchebo Beach.

combined with a facial if they wish, right in their rooms. Call Massage at Home (Sabana Liber 51, 297/730-6660, www.massagesaruba. com, by appt., 1-hour single massage $75, couple's massage $150), run by the skilled, certified therapist Miranda Wever. It's a great time and money saver if a spa is not nearby. Private service in the room is likely to be less costly than in-house facilities.

YOGA
PADDLE BOARD YOGA AND YOGA ON THE BEACH
Condition your body and soothe your spirit with Paddle Board Yoga and Yoga on the Beach (Vela Windsurfing, 297/593-1793, yoga@

manchebo.com, SUP yoga: 3pm Fri. and Sat., $45; beach yoga: 8am Mon.-Fri., 9:30am Sat., $15). Exercise, work on your tan, refresh your chi, and meditate while connecting with nature during SUP (Stand up Paddle Board) Yoga. Sessions are conducted by Rachel Brathen, on the waters just north of the Marriott Resort. She also does Yoga on the Beach at Manchebo Beach.

Besides the regular classes, Rachel will put a session together for a minimum of three people. Paddle board technique is first taught on the beach. Boarders then paddle to a secluded area for an hour that engages the entire body. Perfect your balance, both physically and spiritually.

SIGHTS

While Aruba is best known for its glamorous hotels and beautiful beaches, there is much more to this island's character. There are a myriad of natural and historic sights to explore beyond the beach, including intriguing museums and architecture.

The streets of Oranjestad, Aruba's capital, feature historical structures and colonial homes adjacent to new modern buildings. A fine example of this, the National Archeological Museum Aruba, comprised of renovated Dutch colonial buildings, is one of Aruba's most interesting sights.

Nature lovers will also appreciate Aruba's biodiversity. The natural flora of this semiarid environment is best observed when venturing into the Aruban outback. Island trees are like giant bonsai due to the constant northeast winds shaping them with an artist's hand into striking formations. The stark limestone cliffs and terraces of the shorelines are a sharp contrast to the lush landscapes of the tourist areas.

A trip to the California Lighthouse and on to the north coast reveals a dramatic lunar landscape. Here you are transported back to a primordial era where the geological origins of Aruba are evident. At popular sights such as Casibari and Ayo Rock Formations or the Bushiribana Gold Ruin, rock climbing is a popular activity for all ages. Scaling their heights provides a rewarding sense of adventure and some exceptional photo ops. Scattered among the caves and rock formations are pictographs and petroglyphs, coded messages from Aruba's original inhabitants. They date back thousands of years.

© ROSALIE KLEIN

HIGHLIGHTS

LOOK FOR 🔲 TO FIND RECOMMENDED SIGHTS.

🔲 **National Archaeological Museum of Aruba (NAMA):** NAMA is a unique museum with interactive experiences designed to delight all ages. Two floors of exhibits and artwork provide insights into prehistoric life on the island (page 77).

🔲 **Aruba Historical Museum:** Located within Fort Zoutman, the island's oldest structure, the Aruba Historical Museum is interesting inside and out. Tableaus of antiques recreate colonial times with lively commentary (page 77).

🔲 **Butterfly Farm:** Enjoy an inspiring encounter with nature's most glorious creatures. Bring your camera and escape to a place of utter beauty and tranquility (page 80).

🔲 **Alto Vista Chapel and Peace Labyrinth:** This wistful, humble structure on the site of Aruba's first church features a cliff side location that encourages peaceful reflection. The stunning vista and charming chapel are outstanding photo-ops (page 83).

🔲 **Philip's Animal Garden:** This refuge offers an opportunity to interact with exotic animals of over 50 different species (page 84).

🔲 **California Lighthouse:** Enjoy a 360-degree panorama of Aruba with breathtaking vistas, particularly at sunset (page 86).

🔲 **Aruba Ostrich Farm:** This private nature reserve offers a memorable encounter with the largest species of bird in the world (page 87).

🔲 **Ayo Rock Formation:** On this sacred site quartz diorite formations provide a maze of open caves and passages that lead to summits with stunning panoramic vistas (page 87).

🔲 **Arikok National Park:** Aruba's largest natural preserve provides a myriad of sights and activities for hiking enthusiasts and nature lovers (page 89).

🔲 **Conchi (Natural Pool):** At Conchi, one of Aruba's most stunning natural sites, cooled lava rock has created a dramatic spot for swimming and snorkeling (page 89).

Archaeologists have catalogued over 300 in various locations. These and other sites help visitors obtain an authentic impression of the hardships overcome to survive and persist in this harsh environment.

Interspersed among the natural and historic sites, visitors will also find unexpected family-friendly delights. Preserves such as the Butterfly Farm, the Donkey Sanctuary, and

Philip's Animal Garden are enjoyable interludes for family fun.

Aruba offers a diversity of sights that deliver interesting adventures and unique settings for photo enthusiasts. A walking tour of Oranjestad provides insight into its history. Excursions into the island's natural areas reward visitors with dramatic landscapes punctuated by remnants of a prehistoric culture.

Oranjestad

By strolling the avenues and byways of Oranjestad, you can absorb a lot about Aruba's past. The island's capital is home to the majority of Aruba's cultural and historic sites. Vacationers accustomed to sprawling cities, will find the town physically very small. The most interesting historic landmarks and statues can easily be toured by foot in a single day or less with most of the restored landmark structures clustered near the harbor. This area, adjacent to Aruba's Parliament building, has been dubbed "Historical Oranjestad."

In 1996, the Aruba Monument Bureau was established to restore and preserve landmark structures. Since then, a number of colonial buildings in Oranjestad have been returned to their original glory, providing interesting insights into the lifestyle of islanders from centuries past. There are an estimated 100 landmark buildings in Oranjestad alone, and a total of 300 scattered throughout the island. The town has 20 buildings that are protected historical sights. A number of landmarks are private homes or businesses. For example, **Kok Optica Opticians** (Wilhelminastraat 11, 297/582-7237) is located in a landmark building across from Aruba's Town Hall.

Since its inception as a colonial town dating back to the 1600s, the capital city has maintained a warren of narrow, one-way streets. Driving through them can be quite confusing for first-time visitors. There is a large parking lot directly behind the main bus terminal, which is an excellent starting point for exploring Aruba's historic and cultural roots. It is adjacent to one of Aruba's most picturesque landmark buildings, the **Eman House,** now

© ROSALIE KLEIN

Most of Aruba's restored landmark buildings are near Oranjestad's harbor.

SIGHTS

LANDMARK BUILDINGS

Reserving landmark buildings to be museums or exhibit halls is a wonderful ideal. On a small Caribbean island, however, this is not always practical. Most Oranjestad historic structures house government offices. Some are rented out to support the work of the Monument Foundation, which is the official owner of the buildings. Other historic buildings are important as sites for landmark events. For example, the **Stadhuis** (Schoolstraat 2, 297/583-4400, 9am-4pm Mon.-Fri.), or City Hall, is the site for official civil marriage services. Island law requires couples must be married first by government officials, prior to any spiritual ceremony. The same holds true for those having destination weddings here.

Aruba's City Hall is a classic example of an urban villa, dating from the turn of the 20th century. The interior has been restored to its original elegance and it is a memorable venue for a wedding ceremony. Many couples that travel to Aruba for their nuptials are pleasantly surprised.

This building was originally the Eloy Arends Manor, a wedding gift by Doctor Jacobo Eloy Maria (Loy) Arends to his beloved. Doctor Arends was considered a member of one of Aruba's "first families." At the time, tradition required the groom to present to his bride on their marriage day a suitable home. He began construction of this Caribbean manor house upon his engagement to Maria Monica Lacle in 1922. She was not permitted to set eyes on the project nor even allowed to walk on the street until its completion. During their honeymoon in 1925, Dr. Arends's sister saw to the furnishing of the mansion so he could present a fait accompli to his new bride upon their return.

The restoration of the Eloy Arends Manor in 1999 was the first major project of **Aruba's Monument Bureau** (Schelpstraat 36/39, 297/583-5938, 7:30am-noon and 1pm-4:30pm Mon.-Fri.). The bureau is located in another important landmark, the **Henriquez Building,** which is attached to the eastern end of the **National Archaeological Museum Aruba.**

Officials are not certain of the exact construction date of the Henriquez Building, but photos of Oranjestad from as early as 1890 reveal it existed at that time. The structure was originally a wealthy merchant home and was occupied until well after WWII. There are still Arubans alive who grew up in this historic abode. A visit to the bureau's office can provide an interesting glimpse of a classic merchant's house from the 1800s. Bureau staff, when they're not too busy, are happy to talk about Aruba's historic landmarks.

Stadhuis is a lovely building where all civil marriage ceremonies take place.

© ROSALIE KLEIN

© ROSALIE KLEIN

The National Archaeological Museum Aruba is housed within the historic Ecury Complex.

the offices of Aruba Investment Association (ARINA).

MUSEUMS AND HISTORICAL BUILDINGS
NATIONAL ARCHAEOLOGICAL MUSEUM ARUBA (NAMA)

The daily life and culture of Aruba's inhabitants prior to the Spanish arrival is the focus of the National Archaeological Museum Aruba (Schelpstraat 42, 297/582-8979 or 297/588-9961, www.namaruba.org, 10am-5pm Tues.-Fri., 10am-2pm Sat.-Sun., free). NAMA features permanent and temporary displays, with audio and visual programs that are entertaining and informative for all ages. In addition, a section of the museum is designated as an extensive research center for archaeology students.

NAMA exhibits are designed to immerse visitors: Sit and examine cooking utensils in an authentically reproduced *maloca,* the habitat of the Caiquetios. Youngsters especially enjoy

making their way through a darkened cave to observe glowing pictographs. The attractive displays segue into colonial times and portray the ethnic diversity of the Aruban people. Fascinating artifacts are displayed in a special environment, which is crucial to the preservation of the ancient urns, tools, and works of art.

NAMA is situated within what were once crumbling Dutch colonial buildings known as the Ecury Complex, which have now been restored to pristine condition. The buildings have a particular historic significance as the birthplace of Segundo Jorge Adalberto "Boy" Ecury, Aruba's great WWII war hero. A history of the famous Ecury family, which lived here, is represented with antique photos and documents in the welcoming foyer.

WILLEM III TOWER, FORT ZOUTMAN, AND THE ARUBA HISTORICAL MUSEUM

Before the era of luxury hotels beginning in 1959, the William III Tower, attached to Fort Zoutman (Fort Zoutmanstraat Z/N, 297/582-6099, museohistoricoarubano@yahoo.com, 9am-noon and 1:30pm-4pm Mon.-Fri., $5), was the tallest structure on Aruba. The tower was constructed in 1868 as a public clock tower and lighthouse. It was first lit on February 19, 1868, the birthday of the Dutch monarch for which it is named.

Fort Zoutman is the home of the Aruba Historical Museum. The fort grounds and museum provide a lively synopsis of island culture, history, and development. The fort is Aruba's oldest intact landmark, built in 1796. It is named for Admiral Johan Arnold Zoutman, Vice-Admiral of Holland and West Friesland. He died in 1785, having never even visited the island.

The principal exposition rooms in the museum display antiques and artifacts of Aruba's colonial years. Exhibits illustrate the manner in which the people eked out a living as fisherfolk or aloe producers, as well as the everyday utensils of home life and conservative dress. One room is dedicated to a broad overview from prehistoric times

SIGHTS

© ROSALIE KLEIN

Willem III Tower

to the present, titled *Aruba: Milestones and Challenges*. This exhibition was developed in 2001 for a royal visit.

The **Bon Bini Festival** (Fort Zoutman, 297/582-3777, 7pm-9pm Tues., $5), featuring traditional island music and dance, is conducted every Tuesday evening in the courtyard of Fort Zoutman.

BESTUURKANTOOR (GOVERNMENT HOUSE) AND PARLIAMENT BUILDINGS

Observe Aruba's government in action at the adjoined Bestuurkantoor and Parliament Buildings (L. G. Smith Blvd. 76, 297/528-4900, 8am-noon and 1:30pm-4pm Mon.-Fri., free). These historic edifices, which include the Prime Minister's office, face directly onto Oranjestad Harbor. It is here where landmark decisions have been made and royalty received. Visitors may find that they are warmly welcomed by an important dignitary, if they care to stop by and inquire on the workings of island government.

The floor of Parliament is elegant and dignified. There is a spectators' gallery to observe sessions, which are sometimes heated and dramatic. The entrance is at the side of the building.

MONUMENTS

Aruba commemorates its history and position within the Kingdom of the Netherlands with some very interesting plazas, monuments, and statues scattered along L. G. Smith Boulevard.

MARCH 18 MEMORIAL

One block east of Parliament is a lagoon that divides the town. The northwest corner of the bridge over the lagoon is the site of an attractive plaza called the March 18 Memorial, which commemorates the petition for Aruban Independence.

Central to the plaza is a statue of Cornelius Albert "Shon" Eman. "Shon" Eman headed the delegation that first officially presented the petition for Status Aparte to Queen Juliana on March 18, 1948, during roundtable talks in Holland. These talks would determine the future of all Dutch territories in the region. The names of all the 2,147 signatories of that request for Aruban independence are carved in the plates on each side of the memorial's statue.

During the March 18 celebration of 2010 an eternal flame was placed at the memorial. It was lit by Prime Minister Mike Eman, "Shon" Eman's youngest son.

This is a tranquil place, highlighting an important footnote in island history. Surrounded by a small park, it offers a pleasant place to stop and relax while enjoying the charming view of the lagoon and sea.

QUEEN WILHELMINA PLAZA

Directly across from the March 18 Memorial is Wilhelmina Park. At the heart of the park is the statue and plaza dedicated to Queen Wilhelmina, ruler of the Netherlands from 1898 until 1948. She was the great grandmother of the current Dutch monarch, King Willem-Alexander.

This was Aruba's first commemorative statue, unveiled in October of 1955. The occasion was

MEMORIAL STATUARY IN ORANJESTAD

Oranjestad has a good collection of memorial statuary. Most are surrounded by small plazas and pay homage to local personages who have had a great impact on the island.

There are some interesting statuary on both the north and south side of L. G. Smith Boulevard. On the east side of the Parliament building, facing the water, is a monument to **Jan Hendrik "Henny" Eman,** founder of the Arubaanse Volkspartij (AVP). He was the grandfather of Aruba's first Prime Minister, who is named after him. Eman initiated the movement for Aruban autonomy and independence, Status Aparte, from the other islands of the Netherlands Antilles.

A 10-minute walk east from the March 18 Monument is the statue of **Segundo Jorge Adalberto "Boy" Ecury,** Aruba's beloved WWII hero. It is located on a triangular traffic island next to a small park. Boy Ecury was attending school in Holland in 1940 during the German invasion and occupation. Boy opted to join the Dutch Resistance during WWII rather than return to safety on his home island. His younger brother Nicky also stayed, but was so young he was not allowed to go out on missions.

Boy's markedly Afro-Caribbean features were an unusual sight in Holland at the time. Having such a distinct countenance made his daring missions even more dangerous. He volunteered to derail train tracks to hinder German troop and weapon movements.

Boy was captured during an attempt to rescue some of his fellow resistance fighters. He died in front of a German firing squad at the age of 22. A feature film was made in Holland of his story, starring noted Antillean actor and director, Felix de Rooy, as his father. The film tells of his search for his son's remains after the war. Boy's body was eventually found and received a hero's welcome and burial.

The far eastern end of Oranjestad is marked by the very large Plaza Las Americas rotunda. Fronting the rotunda is Aruba's center for performing arts, the Cas di Cultura. Directly in front of the art center is a small park with a memorial to **Lloyd G. Smith.**

Smith was the first general manager of the Lago Refinery, managing the facility from the time it became fully functional through the war years, 1933-1946. His policy of concern and improvement for the island beyond the refinery's gates won him the respect and admiration of his hosts. This sentiment is an example of the very cordial relationship Aruba has maintained with the United States for nearly 100 years.

Wilhelmina Park is also the site of the **Anne Frank Memorial,** erected in 2011. The charming, rather wistful statue by Dutch artist Joep Coppens is dedicated to the concept of ethnic tolerance. Its placement was the first official project of the "Foundation Respeta bida...semper corda" (Respect life...always remember).

The bronze statue depicts Anne Frank with her hands bound, but looking towards the sky "in hope of a better world," according to the artist. It stands on a pedestal with four sides imprinted with a quote from her diary: "How wonderful it is that nobody need wait a single moment before starting to improve the world." Each side is written in one of the languages commonly spoken on Aruba: Papiamento, English, Dutch, and Spanish.

a royal visit by Wilhelmina's daughter, Queen Juliana. It is a beautifully landscaped park and a pleasant place for a break from walking and touring. The large and decorative plaza is the place for many official ceremonies and important events, most notably Koninginnedag (King's Day) on April 27, which is an impressive display of loyalty to the monarchy. Visitors to the island on this day are welcome to join the official event, which takes place in the morning.

SIGHTS

SIGHTS

RESCUING A BIT OF HISTORY

Aruba's **Besteuurkantoor (Government House)** has a special history. It was built in 1942 to serve as headquarters for the various military forces stationed on the island: American and British forces had troops stationed here to protect from German attack.

This building, rich with history, was nearly lost. The party in power from 2001 to 2009 had a plan to move all the ministries out of the old building to several new, contemporary styled offices scattered around the island. Government administration would no longer be centralized. Fortunately, Aruba's historic government house was saved from being demolished by a newly elected administration in 2009.

Prior to elections, the Besteuurkantoor sat empty and abandoned. The intention was to see this prime waterfront location leased to developers as a place for a new resort and casino. It fell into a depressing state of disrepair.

The September 2009 elections resulted in a radical change of government, with the opposing AVP party winning a record 12 seats in parliament, awarding them complete control of policy. Six weeks before his inauguration, Prime Minister Elect Michiel Godfried "Mike" Eman announced that his government would operate from the traditional historic edifice. They wished to preserve the site where queens

and other dignitaries had been received and landmark decisions and agreements enacted.

A volunteer corps of AVP party members, including newly elected parliamentarians and ministers, took to the restoration project personally. They labored day and night to restore the building. Various construction supply companies donated materials, so there was no cost to taxpayers. Islanders driving by would observe them hammering away or painting and would pull over to jump in and give a hand. It was a project that stirred the hearts of Arubans and united the community after a hard fought election.

Upon inauguration at the end of October 2009, the newly installed government began operating out of the building. It was still in the process of being refurbished. Leaky roofs and intermittent-working air-conditioning and lighting were common occurrences. Personnel kept a brave face through the extensive repairs on this landmark structure.

In 2011, the Prime Minister announced a new, modern annex to be added to the rear of the building, to which the ministers will relocate. Its official name is "The Coconut" because of its unique design. The entire area behind the Besteuurkantoor and Parliament will be turned into a park and plaza. The original building will remain.

Palm Beach, Malmok, and Noord

Palm Beach is a relatively modern district with a number of interesting sights. Not far from the busy shopping and entertainment centers are natural areas and attractions. Some, such as the Butterfly Farm, are within easy walking distance.

The area has undeveloped pockets of nature, such as wetlands known as Bubali Plas Bird Sanctuary across from the Mill Resort. A short drive at dawn provides fabulous sunrise shots from the Alto Vista Chapel. Historic sights like the Santa Ana Church are a reminder of the

deep religious faith that is a cultural anchor for many Aruban people.

◖ BUTTERFLY FARM

For an exhilarating communion with nature, stop at the Butterfly Farm (J. E. Irausquin Blvd. Z/N, 297/586-3656, www.thebutterflyfarm.com, 8:30am-4:30pm daily, $15 adults, $8 children). It is located on the land side of the beach road between the Divi Phoenix and Westin Resorts. The best time to visit the farm is early in the day as butterflies are most active in the morning.

MONUMENTS TO "THE LIBERATORS"

GILBERTO FRANCOIS "BETICO" CROES

Gilberto Francois "Betico" Croes is considered by many the final, primary instrument in the establishment of Aruba's right to self-rule within the Dutch Kingdom, or Status Aparte. Originally a member of Arubaanse Volkspartij (AVP), he founded the Moviemento di Electoral di Pueblo (MEP) in 1971. As leader of that party he became the principal negotiator and facilitator of Aruba's independence from the Netherlands Antilles, earning him the informal title of "El Liberatador."

Plaza Gilberto Francois "Betico" Croes is located one block inland from Plaza Las Americas, the huge rotunda marking the eastern end of Oranjestad. Standing directly behind the Cas di Cultura is a statue of Aruba's beloved statesman, holding the nation's flag high over his head.

Betico relentlessly pursued Status Aparte while strongly promoting the concept of Aruban national pride. In 1976 he advocated and expedited the creation and adoption of an Aruban flag and national anthem.

Despite his pivotal roll in the negotiations resulting in Aruban autonomy, Betico and his party did not earn the majority during Aruba's first independent elections. The title of Aruba's First Prime Minister was denied him.

The eve of Aruba's official independence from the Netherlands Antilles, December 31, 1985, was the inauguration of its first prime minister, Jan Hendrik "Henny" Eman. On his way to the ceremony, Betico Croes was gravely injured in a traffic accident. He lay in a coma for 11 months and then passed away on November 26, 1986. After dedicating the last 15 years of his life to Aruba's Status Aparte, he never actually witnessed the realization of that goal in practice. His birth date, January 25, was declared a national holiday.

SIMÓN BOLÍVAR

The statue of Betico Croes gazes upon what is the largest and unquestionably most impressive monument in Oranjestad. Directly across the street from the plaza, Simón Bolívar majestically salutes his admirers from his rearing stallion in the Plaza Bolivariana.

"The Great Liberator" of Latin America is immortalized in a striking sculpture donated by Aruba's expatriate population from Venezuela, Colombia, Peru, Bolivia, Ecuador, and Panama. It is here that Venezuelan and Colombian Consuls welcome fellow countrymen and countrywomen and island dignitaries to observe their respective independence days of July 5 and July 20.

July 5, 1811 was when Venezuelan independence was first called for by a revolutionary congress and, in 1813, Simón Bolívar took up the cause for an independent republic of Venezuela, instigated by Francisco de Miranda in 1810. Miranda died in exile in 1816. Through many bloody battles, Bolívar finally ousted the Spanish colonists in the famous "Battle of Carabobo" on June 24, 1821.

General Simón Bolívar, leader of the war for independence, made Venezuelan independence a reality. He also dedicated his life to fighting for the independent nations of Colombia, Peru, Ecuador, and Panama. Eventually, he founded the nation of Bolivia.

Bolívar died in Cartagena, Colombia in 1830, after a life devoted to achieving freedom from the Spanish for most of Latin America. He was buried in Colombia, but in 1942, after years of petitioning, Venezuela finally received his remains with great pomp. He now lies in state at the National Pantheon in Caracas.

SIGHTS

WHAT EXACTLY ARE *CUNUCU* HOUSES?

A *cunucu* house is considered the endemic architecture of Aruba and colonial times. The configuration of what constitutes an authentic *cunucu* house is distinctive and carries practical points. The house was built piecemeal as a family grew. The characteristic peaked roof at the center delineates the original home built for the newlyweds. As occupancy expanded with the births of numerous children, rooms were added to the front, back, and sides.

City homes of wealthier families typically had a second floor for the progeny. These usually were adorned with dormer windows. This architectural feature traditionally distinguishes the houses in the town from their country cousins. More than a dozen children to a family was quite common, and boys and girls would have separate sleeping areas.

The placement of rooms took advantage of Aruba's steady northeast winds. Sleeping rooms were placed to catch the breeze and provide cool comfort, while the west end was the cooking space. Here, the characteristic *facon*, a fireplace and chimney where meals were prepared, was situated. This practical placement allowed the wind to take the heat and cinders away from the house. Islanders have such affection for this particular architecture; many new homes are built as replicas of this colonial style.

The word *cunucu* is frequently used to describe anything considered rural, while *mondi* is the actual word for deep woods. *Cunucu* is also used to indicate something endemic to the island, such as *cunucu* house or *cunucu* dog, the local mixed breed.

Charles Croes, who has made an intense study of the Papiamento language, claims that *cunucu* does not mean "country." It was the word applied to the perimeter of sand placed around rural homes, which was smoothed out each night before bedtime. Residents examined the sand in the morning for telltale footprints, indicting unwanted visitors such as scorpions or millipedes who may have made their way into the house during the night.

Trained guides will explain everything you ever wanted to know about butterflies and moths. Did you know butterflies morph in a chrysalis while moths transform in a cocoon? The most dramatically-hued examples of both flitter about freely, feeding on fruit and flowers. There are exotic and gorgeous species from all over the world. It is possible to see one emerge from its chrysalis in one of the breeding boxes.

The Butterfly Farm is a beautiful garden filled with the type of flora on which the various species feed and breed. Relax on one of the benches provided and enjoy the classical music that plays gently in the background.

Consider visiting early in your vacation since the entry fee allows for unlimited return visits for the duration of your vacation. Operators Tony and Laurie know that one visit will often turn into several. Visitors can return every day if they like, without cost. The souvenir shop also features one of the largest collections of butterfly-themed knickknacks to be found anywhere.

SANTA ANA CHURCH

Located at the first major intersection on the Noord-Palm Beach Road beyond the Sasaki Highway (there is a traffic light to distinguish it), Santa Ana Church (Noord 16, 297/587-1409, 8am-8:30pm daily) is central to the surrounding community. It was the second church built on the island in 1776, vastly larger than the Alto Vista Chapel, Aruba's first church.

It has beautiful stained glass windows and houses an intricate and impressive hand-carved oak altar by artist Hendrik van der Geld, created in 1870. The altar won an award during an exposition of religious art in Rome the year it was built. It was donated to Santa Ana by the Antonius Church of Scheveningen in the Netherlands. The church was rebuilt twice, in 1836 and again in 1886, with major restructuring in 1916.

© ROSALIE KLEIN

Alto Vista Chapel

SIGHTS

A very interesting aspect of the church is the adjacent cemetery consisting of picturesque family crypts and vaults. Digging into Aruba's foundation of solid rock is a daunting task, so this form of burial is common. Dating back centuries, crypts are brightly painted in the Caribbean way, with epitaphs that offer a peek at local family histories.

◖ ALTO VISTA CHAPEL AND PEACE LABYRINTH

Aruba's first Catholic house of worship (sunrise-sunset daily, formal services 5:30pm Tues.) was built in 1750 on what was sacred ground to the Caquetio Indians. Spanish Padre Domingo Antonio Silvestre led the mission to bring the sparse native population into the fold of Catholicism.

This modest chapel is situated on a cliff with stunning views of Aruba's rugged north coast. The entire area exudes an air of quiet contemplation. The simple, natural setting encourages reflection on the glory of creation, no matter your personal beliefs. There is an annual march at Easter along the winding road leading to its hilltop perch. The parade of worshipers stops at each of the 13 large white crosses along the way to recite a prayer.

As larger churches closer to settlements were erected, Alto Vista Chapel fell into disuse and crumbled away. A community effort in 1952, spearheaded by Shon Kita Henriquez-Lacle, prompted the rebuilding of a new chapel on the site. This charming, spiritual place is maintained with devotion by its parishioners.

Around 2005, islander Peter Auwerda constructed a Peace Labyrinth in close proximity to the chapel. It was modeled after the Chartres Labyrinth. Visitors are encouraged to walk its 11 circuits. The turns are arranged in four quadrants, with 85 lunations around the perimeter. It is believed to promote meditation and serenity. Annually, on September 21, International Peace Day, a celebration is staged at the labyrinth with the intention of promoting world and inner peace.

To get to the chapel, turn right off the Sasaki Highway and take Noord-Palm Beach Road to

© ROSALIE KLEIN

Philip Merryweather's mission in life is to rescue and rehabilitate abused exotic animals at Philip's Animal Garden.

SIGHTS

the first traffic light. The Santa Ana Church will be across the intersection on the right. Turn left onto the Noord-Westpunt Road for about a half mile. There will be a sign to turn right for Alto Vista. Follow this road to where it ends in a T-Intersection. Turn left, and follow this road until it ends at the Alto Vista Chapel.

◖ PHILIP'S ANIMAL GARDEN

At his family home (Alto Vista 116, 297/593-5363, www.philipsanimalgarden.com, guided tours 9am-5pm daily every half hour, $10 adults, $5 children under 10), **Philip Merryweather** at the age of 12 began to create a haven for neglected and abused exotic animals. Fortunately, his parents had an exceptionally large property in a rather rural area. His passion for protecting such creatures as ocelots, monkeys, kangaroos, and macaws began when he observed how they were often neglected. By the time he rescued them they were quite a handful, traumatized and aggressive. His patience and determination to learn of their special needs and provide the proper environment contributed to their rehabilitation. Proper care and comfort of such creatures has become his mission in life.

For several years, as his shelter grew in size and diversity, he did not permit visitors or conduct tours. Philip now houses more than 350 animals from over 50 species at his reserve. A few years ago, he began conducting open house events on national holidays for island youngsters regarding the humane treatment of all animals. He hoped to make residents aware of the very special care such exotic creatures require and the serious responsibility of possessing what should be best left in the wild. Aruba has since passed stringent laws regulating the importation of exotic animals or trafficking of endangered species, which are enforced.

Philip finally decided to open his doors to the public for regular tours to finance the feeding and care of the animals. Philip's Animal Garden is a non-profit foundation with all entrance fees and donations going towards the maintenance of the facility.

PRESERVING ARUBA'S HERITAGE

One of the island's oldest homes, the Eman House, is representative of the complex work of Aruba's Monument Bureau and Monument Foundation. It was a high profile project that sparked an interest in landmark buildings, inspired by one woman's determination to ensure that Aruba's historical and cultural legacy is not lost.

The structure is a classic *cunucu* house, the popular term for the homes that typify early colonial domestic structures. The interior dates back to 1860. The building was expanded and renovated by Richard Johannes Eman van der Biest after he acquired it in 1908. One of his children married John Gerard Eman, the founder of Aruba Bank NV, the island's first financial institution.

Originally located in the middle of the town's main street, behind the main branch of Aruba Bank, it was slated to be torn down to make way for a parking lot. The Director of the Aruba Monument Bureau, Yvonne Webb-Kock, personally pleaded with the president of Aruba Bank to donate the remains of the house for preservation. He agreed to do so only if it would be moved from the existing location. The bank even donated a substantial sum for the move and restoration.

Authentic *cunucu* houses have a singular construction. The walls are extremely thick, usually more than a foot wide. They consist of large chunks of coral rock held together with the local version of adobe. Moving the building was an engineering challenge requiring innovative thinking. Webb-Kock, a certified civil engineer with a degree in interior design, admits "it was mostly guesswork." The cavalcade transporting the building in pieces to its new location drew crowds of spectators. It took hours to travel the short distance to its new home on the Weststraat, just behind the main bus terminal. Replacing crumbling sections of walls with modern materials during the reconstruction process presented new challenges, demanding constant experimentation and adaptation.

Finally, the renewed building was unveiled in 2002. It was a perfect location for Aruba's Numismatic Museum, until 2010. Unfortunately, that island institution is now defunct. In 2011, the building went through a complete refurbishment to become the headquarters of Aruba Investment Association, ARINA.

North Coast

The California Lighthouse is a demarcation point for touring in an ordinary car as opposed to venturing into what is truly 4x4 country. The dividing line is the base of the California Lighthouse mount: If traveling beyond, drivers must contend with some grueling gravel roads. A four-wheel drive is best, or an all-terrain vehicle. Sights along the way are, for the most part, natural formations providing dramatic landscape shots and backgrounds to the rare historic structure. This part of the island, to this day, is not very well settled. This is a fun day for all who enjoy an off-road adventure. North coast sights can also be approached by regular roads passing through Paradera or Santa Cruz, but then it will not be an outback adventure.

Unless otherwise specified, sights do not have regulated hours and can be visited freely without any fees. Most of these, with the exception of Black Stone Beach and Conchi, are regular stops on all bus tours of the area. The harder-to-reach locations are on the itinerary of most safari tours.

Along the north shore is a stark landscape, dramatically demonstrating Aruba's geological composition. The limestone cliffs carved by the waves and the speckled pillow basalt, created by lava bubbling up from eruptions far under the sea, are a stark contrast to resort areas.

SEROE PRETO CITY OF LIGHTS

One of Aruba's most attractive sights takes place only during the holiday season at the end of the year. Those fortunate to be on the island from early December until the first week of January can enjoy a very special treat: **Seroe Preto City of Lights** (Seroe Preto Z/N, 24 hours daily, free), an annual community effort. Volunteers build this fantastical town out of colored lights each year with a different theme. It is extensive, taking up the entire hillside. Walkways allow visitors to climb the hill and be immersed in the experience. Usually the festival includes at least one notable Aruban landmark. For impressive pictures, bring a tripod or improvise; you will need some way to keep a camera steady.

The City of Lights is only on display from the first weekend in December to Three Kings Day (January 6). It is a labor of love by the **Stichting Hunbentud Uni Seroe Preto** (United Youth Foundation of Seroe Preto). The average annual cost is $12,000 to construct the scene, not including the utility bills. The project is funded by donations and fundraising events throughout the year. The first efforts began back in 1957. These were very simple compared to the elaborate work of art the project is today.

Most nights during the week, the festival is relatively quiet and is ideal if you wish to take pictures without too many people present. During the holiday break and on weekends it is very busy. Friday and Saturday nights mean musical performances by seasonal singing groups called "Gaita" until late. There are often wagons selling snacks and refreshments as well. It is all very festive.

On the final night volunteers host a blowout farewell bash, before turning off the lights. Everyone brings food and drink and the music performances go on until dawn. The tone segues from "Silent Night" to "Don't Stop the Party" as carnival bands take over to mark the beginning of the incoming carnival season. This is a joyous, authentically Aruban holiday experience.

The first thing to capture your attention while traversing this north coast road is a proliferation of purposely placed rock piles, some quite artistic, which litter the landscape. How this practice actually began is a mystery. A number of tour guides decided it would add some spice to their tours to tell clients it was an old Amerindian tradition to pile the rocks and make a wish, ideally to return to Aruba. Each guide has their own version of the tale. Since the rock piles first began appearing about 15-20 years ago, it's unlikely that they stem from an ancient tradition. Visitors are welcome to play along with the charade; children love it.

◀ CALIFORNIA LIGHTHOUSE

The California Lighthouse (Westpunt Z/N, 24 hours daily, free) sits on the peak of Westpunt, the northwest point of the island. It is a beacon to a spot that offers some of the most stunning views of the north and west coasts, particularly at sunrise and sunset. These colorful events are dramatically played out daily over California Dunes at dawn and the coastline of Palm Beach and Arashi at dusk. It is an excellent stop for some wonderful photos. The lighthouse itself is closed to the public. There is only one road leading to the north coast which rises directly to the peak.

The lighthouse has an interesting history behind its rather typical name. The Amerindian name for the area is Sasarawechi, but the lighthouse was named for a wooden U.S. cargo ship that sunk nearby during rough seas. The remains are an established dive site in rather shallow waters.

Contrary to widespread misconception, this is *not* the ship that refused to answer the Titanic's distress call in 1912. That ship was the *S.S. Californian,* a 447-foot steel-hulled ship, which was sunk by a German torpedo in 1915. According to local oral history, the area became popular for salvaging the cargo from the ship, which would wash up on shore. Islanders began referring to the area as California Point.

© ROSALIE KLEIN

At the Ayo Rock Formation, enjoy easy rock climbing with beautiful views.

BUSHIRIBANA GOLD RUIN

Impossible to miss while traversing the north coast road is the almost medieval contours of the Bushiribana Gold Ruin (Mativaderi Z/N, on the north coast road next to the juncture leading to the Ostrich Farm, 24 hours daily, free). Built in 1874 by the Aruba Island Gold Mining Company of London, the ruins are atmospheric, weather-beaten, and appear far more ancient than they actually are. Youngsters love climbing among the terraces and surrounding rock formations. Combined with the dramatic crashing sea along the coast, the ruins and their view from its ramparts offer interesting photo ops.

This unique stone structure is a remnant of Aruba's gold rush. It all began when 12-year-old William Rasmijn first found traces of gold at Rooi Fluit in 1824 while herding his father's sheep. This discovery heralded a new era of prosperity and increased settlement for Aruba. The ruins are also a landmark for the turnoff to the Ostrich Farm, which is less than a mile inland.

◖ ARUBA OSTRICH FARM

A bit of Africa plunked down in the middle of Aruba's outback, the Aruba Ostrich Farm (Matividiri 57, 297/585-9630, www.arubaostrichfarm.com, 9:30am-3:30pm daily, $12 adults, $6 children ages 3-6) is an interesting private nature preserve. Tours are conducted every half hour.

Interacting with these huge, animated and curious birds will stay with you for some time. It is impossible to visit with them and not be entertained. Be careful with brightly colored cameras and sparkly jewelry. The birds are very attracted to such items, and the adults have *very* long necks. They will attempt to pluck them from your person. You do not want to discover personally that movies depicting the comical consequences of ostriches swallowing valuables are, indeed, based on fact. You will depart from your ostrich interlude with other interesting ostrich factoids.

Aside from a memorable and comical encounter with the largest species of bird in the world, it is a great lunch stop. Fortunately, in addition to ostrich, the restaurant offers a wide selection of dishes. If you are planning to try ostrich meat at the restaurant, it is best to save the tour for *after* lunch.

◖ AYO ROCK FORMATION

Travel back to pre-ceramic times with a stop at Ayo Rock Formation (Ayo Z/N, signs indicate turnoff on route 7A, 24 hours daily, free), where huge quartz diorite formations provide a maze of open caves and passages. They eventually lead to summits with stunning panoramic vistas. The area is easily explored. Trails have been carved out by park rangers to provide easy paths leading to the summits.

Arawak Indians sought shelter here and their shamans used this place to commune with the spirit world. There are a few particularly spectacular cave paintings in the hollowed out formations. This is Aruba's gold country, and gold dust can be seen glinting in the soil around Ayo's formations. This is an ideal rest stop with picnic tables and public bathrooms.

SIGHTS

Santa Cruz, Paradera, and Piedra Plat

These inland areas of Aruba take visitors completely into the realm of everyday island life, far removed from the tourist scene. Residential communities are dense. Scattered throughout are Aruba's impressive rock formations, such as those at Casibari, a busy stop on most tours. Travel through these barrios to reach Arikok National Park.

The Santa Philomena Church in Paradera dominates the skyline, as does the Hooiberg (Haystack Mountain). This is often mistaken as Aruba's highest point. It is a very distinctive element of the island landscape.

HOOIBERG (HAYSTACK MOUNTAIN)

The Hooiberg peak (Hooiberg Z/N, accessible from roads 4A or 7A to Santa Cruz, a sign indicates the turn leading directly to the base of the stairway, 24 hours daily, free), which means haystack in Dutch, offers a remarkable panorama of Aruba. A stairway of 563 steps challenges those who wish to test their fitness. The reward is fantastic pictures to prove you actually did it. Its positioning at the middle of the island provides a unique perspective.

The distinctive profile of the Hooiberg is one of the first things that catches your eye when arriving on Aruba, as it is front and center upon exiting the airport. It is the island's third highest point.

No roads or easy paths lead to the top of the Hooiberg. The steps are not comfortably sized or spaced, but there are some places to take a rest along the way. Attempting to climb to the top is only recommended if you are in excellent shape and good health. The vistas stretching to all points of Aruba and the mountains of Venezuela make the climb worth the effort.

CASIBARI ROCK FORMATION

The fantastical quartz diorite formations at Casibari (Casibari z/n, off of Santa Cruz-Paradera Rd., 24 hours daily, free) are lots of fun for the family. The climb can be accomplished easily by almost all ages. It is located just off the principal Santa Cruz-Paradera Road and the turnoff is clearly marked. The formations are more concentrated and organized than the sprawl of Ayo. Tunnels and byways through the rocks have been tailored and trimmed and are strung with ropes for safety. One passage through is a bit tight, allowing only one person to pass at a time, which might be a bit difficult with very small children. Surrounding the principal attraction are gardens and paths for exploring indigenous flora.

This is a stop on nearly every tour, making it a bustling place with crowds of people at most hours. Across from the entrance is a place to get a cold drink and use the lavatories. There is a little snow cone wagon by the entrance that sells authentic coconut water straight from the freshly opened coconut, an interesting and invigorating treat.

DONKEY SANCTUARY

A right turn past the entrance of the Ayo Rock Formation will take you over some rough but traversable roads that finally turn to asphalt. You will travel through an authentically rural Aruban community to Santa Lucia and the Donkey Sanctuary (Santa Lucia 4A, Donkey Distress Hotline 297/593-2933, www.arubandonkey.org, 9am-4pm Mon.-Fri., 10am-3pm Sat.-Sun., free).

Animal and nature lovers will enjoy this refuge and attractive natural park. The donkeys are intelligent, gentle, and friendly. They eagerly nibble carrot or apple pieces if you bring them a treat. Children especially enjoy getting to know the donkeys. There are always some very young donkeys on hand.

The sanctuary is a non-profit foundation, supported by donations from visitors and purchases of some very adorable souvenir items from their shop. It is through volunteer efforts that Aruba's remaining donkey population has managed to survive.

Brought to Aruba by the Spanish 500 years ago, *buricos* (donkeys) were the principal mode of transport on Aruba and an important element of the economy for centuries. They were finally abandoned for internal combustion vehicles with the advent of the Lago Refinery. When the first car was brought to Aruba and assembled in 1915, the island sported a population of around 1,400 donkeys.

Donkey owners released their donkeys into the countryside to survive as best they could. Though hardy animals, by 1970 only 20 donkeys could be counted among the wild population. The two main families living in the wild were in a serious state of distress when concerned islanders founded the nonprofit Fundacion Salba Nos Burico (Save our Donkeys) in 1997.

The Donkey Sanctuary's entrance is concealed down a dirt road turnoff with a steep dip. Watch for the sanctuary sign; it is easy to miss. The sanctuary is more easily accessible by regular car through Santa Cruz by following the first turnoff for Arikok National Park.

◖ ARIKOK NATIONAL PARK

Aruba's largest natural preserve (San Fuego 70, 297/585-1234, www.arubanationalpark.org, 8am-4pm daily, $8) occupies 18 percent of the island's landmass. The park has more than 20 miles of hiking trails with varying degrees of difficulty. There are some lovely beaches along the north shore, particularly popular for body boarding. Aruba's two highest peaks, Jamanota and Arikok, are within the park. Trails have been tailored to offer nature enthusiasts journeys through the wild. They can take anywhere from two to eight hours to complete, depending on your degree of fitness. Most major sites can also be accessed by car.

The park was designated a formally protected area in 2000. Becoming a registered foundation made it eligible for funding from the European Union (EU). Island government dedicated monies to the paving of gravel roads though the park without endangering flora and fauna. Funds from the EU allowed the construction of a formal visitor center and ranger

headquarters, where you can also gather basic information about the flora and fauna native to the area.

If driving a four-wheel drive vehicle, Arikok National Park can be reached by continuing along the road from the Donkey Sanctuary. It is also accessible over better roads via Santa Cruz, with a pass through Paradera and Piedra Plat on the way from the main resort areas.

◖ CONCHI (NATURAL POOL)

The native name for one of the north coast's most breathtaking sights, Conchi (access is within Arikok National Park, follow the road to the summit of Seroe Arikok then down its back side directly to the entrance, 24 hours daily, free), comes from the bowl shape of lava rock that comprises this dramatic coastal formation. A wall of pillow basalt protects the cove from the huge waves crashing against it, forming a calm pool for swimming and snorkeling. There are various terraces popular for climbing and jumping in the water, effecting a sort of natural water park.

Be prepared on arrival for a long climb down a stairway to the pool and what seems like an even longer climb back up. The beauty of this site is definitely worth the effort, but getting here and back is truly an adventure.

Rugged, winding roads approaching Conchi are impossible to traverse with an ordinary car. It is strongly suggested to leave the driving to an experienced guide with a reliable, tested vehicle, at least for the first visit. The other option is to arrive by horseback. **Daimari Ranch** (www.arubaranchodaimari.com) at the northern border of the park conducts a trek to the Natural Pool on a daily basis.

QUADIKAKIRI AND FONTEIN CAVES

The Quadikakiri and Fontein Caves (Arikok National Park, San Fuego 70, 297/585-1234, www.arubanationalpark.org, 8am-4pm daily, park admission $8) provide easy and safe spelunking opportunities. Both caves have quite a few authentic Amerindian pictographs and dramatic formations. These can be enjoyed without a flashlight as they are comprised of

SIGHTS

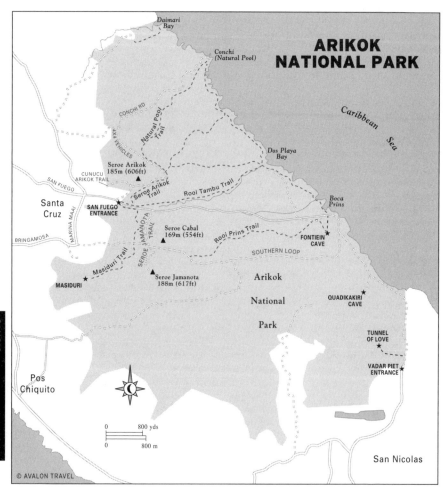

large chambers filled with light from natural openings in the ceilings. Park rangers guide visitors through the caves for no fee (though tips are appreciated). They are equipped with flashlights to illuminate some of the more interesting points.

Chambers in Quadikakiri are connected by some easily traversed passages. Some passages are only four feet high and most adults will have to bend down to walk through them. This will provide a bit of excitement and a real feel of cave exploring without any danger. A closely monitored bat population does no harm.

The caves have dramatic stalagmite and stalactite formations, some still in the process of forming. Safe paths have been laid out for those wishing to do a little exploring on their own. The more hazardous and poorly lit areas have been blocked off. Visitors are asked to respect these limitations for their own safety.

San Nicolas, Savaneta, and Pos Chiquito

Aruba's "Sunrise City," San Nicolas, has an authentic Caribbean feeling to its mains street and byways. It is best known as the site of the Lago Refinery and Colony, but has a distinct character of its own. The inhabitants are proud of their multicultural roots. In the late 1920s, many people from all corners of the Caribbean came to San Nicolas to find work at the refinery. They raised families and integrated into the community, enriching Aruba's culture by infusing it with many of their traditions.

Most visitors come to San Nicolas to explore areas such as Baby Beach, but there are also interesting sights, such as Lourdes Grotto. Heading back west towards the hotels, you will pass a number of attractive shore areas in Savaneta and Pos Chiquito.

LOURDES GROTTO

The interesting natural formations that comprise Lourdes Grotto (turn left on Pastoor Hendrikstraat at the San Nicolas YMCA where a sign indicates the turnoff, dawn-dusk daily, free) are dominated by a 700-kilo statue of the Virgin Mary. The area has an ethereal quality that inspires spiritual reflection. It is a shrine to St. Bernadette, the Lady of Lourdes, and many believe in its healing properties, like that of its namesake. The grotto is a natural formation in the rock cliffs on the road to Seroe Preto, or Black Point, clearly indicated with road signs.

Local oral history reports some islanders having a vision of the Blessed Mother at this spot. A community effort realized and

© ROSALIE KLEIN

SIGHTS

Natural limestone caves were converted into the Lourdes Grotto.

maintains this tribute with candles and fresh flowers. Each year **St. Theresita Church** (St. Theresitaplein 8, 297/584-5118) in San Nicolas organizes a pilgrimage to the site on February 11, the Feast Day of Our Lady of Lourdes, which culminates with a mass. The site was first unveiled in 1958, 150 years after St. Bernadette had her original vision.

FOOD

One of the principal reasons cited by Aruba's repeat visitors for their unflagging dedication is the superb quality and selection of restaurants. The diversity of Aruba's population is reflected in the wealth of authentic ethnic restaurants scattered around principal tourist areas. Not only can you choose a different place for dinner every night, but you can indulge in a different cuisine.

This explosion of eateries took place primarily over the last 15 years. Previously, fine dining was the ken of the hotels. There wasn't much competition from independent restaurants, and, generally, hotels were relatively pricey.

Many excellent eateries for breakfast, lunch, and dinner are now within easy walking distance of resorts. This has resulted in the hotels re-evaluating their menus in order to compete with local eateries. Patrons will find hotel dining usually priced equally to independent restaurants, with their culinary teams striving to be trendy and innovative.

A burgeoning influx of classically-trained chefs from Europe and the United States has resulted in fusion cuisine holding sway over island kitchens. This melding of regional flavors and fresh, local ingredients with Cordon Bleu cooking is producing some tantalizing original dishes touted as having Caribbean flair.

For Americans looking for familiar food, a good steak, hamburger, or pizza is never far away from major resorts. International food franchises are abundant, but so are many independent restaurants with interesting and unique menus. Quality, moderately-priced meals are readily available.

© ROSALIE KLEIN

HIGHLIGHTS

LOOK FOR ◖ TO FIND RECOMMENDED RESTAURANTS.

◖ **Smit & Dorls Coffee House:** Aruba's first coffee shop is still the most charming. Relax with a good cup of coffee and one of their complimentary cookies (page 98).

◖ **Twister Café:** The owner of this cozy Dutch pub is one of the island's top gourmet chefs. Aside from the inexpensive regular menu, Twister hosts three special nights of culinary magic the last weekend of each month (page 100).

◖ **Casa Vieja:** For budget-friendly, authentic regional cuisine Casa Vieja is your best bet. Whole fresh fish and meat platters that feed three easily, as well as Colombian "stew soups," are their specialty (page 101).

◖ **Pizza & More:** This pizza joint is not only the best deal on Aruba for pizza, they also offer great prices on excellent pasta dishes (page 102).

◖ **Yami Yami:** With good Chinese food at local prices, this is Aruba's favorite fast food (page 107).

◖ **Passions:** This beachfront restaurant is unquestionably one of the most romantic din-

ing spots on the island, with excellent food and a tranquil ambiance (page 107).

◖ **Carte Blanche:** Enjoy fine gourmet dining in a cozy, friendly place. The hosts and chef make it utterly memorable (page 112).

◖ **The Old Cunucu House:** Find authentic Aruban cuisine in this 150-year-old farmhouse, in the most charming of surroundings. They have excellent fresh fish and international specialties at extremely reasonable prices (page 114).

◖ **Amuse Bistro:** Gourmet French food with a touch of the Caribbean is how owner and chef Patrick describes his very pleasant open-air eatery in the Playa Linda Resort (page 119).

◖ **Marina Pirata:** Enjoy a dockside dinner with fish fresh off the boat at this island institution. The congenial hosts and reasonably priced menu add to the appeal (page 126).

◖ **Zeerover:** This is where to go for the very freshest of fish. It is a beautiful spot on the water with an authentic Caribbean ambiance (page 127).

Island restaurants also boast authentic Thai, Bavarian, Belgian, Indian, Filipino, Chinese, and Middle Eastern eateries run by members of the local immigrant communities. Adventurous eaters who sample local dishes, such as sate with *pinda* (peanut) sauce, *cabrito stoba* (stewed goat), *keshi yena* (filled cheese), and other recipes of the region, are generous with their praise.

Aruba is also home to a well-respected culinary institute, where graduates receive certification from the American Culinary Federation. The institute attracts students from all the Americas, producing a new generation of young

chefs who are passionate about cooking and local cuisine.

One of the most enjoyable pastimes on the island is beachside dining. The vibrant blue seas, cooling trade winds, rustling palms, and breathtaking sunsets enhance the flavor of a meal as much as any seasoning.

Romantic dinners under the stars are available in countless venues with memorable settings, even on a beautiful sailboat. Each night, dinner can be a gourmet adventure in some dazzling locale or a simple meal in cozy surroundings.

FOOD

Oranjestad

Contrary to restaurants in resort centers such as Manchebo Beach and Palm Beach, most restaurants in town are filled with islanders on their way to work in the morning or on a lunch break. In ambiance and clientele, dining in Oranjestad is a very different experience than dining at the beachside eateries in the resorts. Here, you are in native territory, and these restaurants are more reasonably priced to accommodate the locals and feature a definitive regional ambiance.

ARUBAN

CAFÉ MARYLI

A bastion of authentic *cuminda criollo* (local cuisine), Café Maryli (Caya Ernesto Petronia 72, 297/588-9781, 11am-6pm Mon.-Sat., $10-13.50) is a very clean, tiny place at the very northern border of town. It occupies the front corner of the small Heimee shopping mall.

The specialty of the house are Aruban stews and soups made from whatever is fresh and available. The menu is on a small chalkboard and changes daily. Platters usually come with pan-fried pork chops, roast chicken or ribs, and a choice of fresh fish, grilled, fried, or Creole style. Here is where to find authentic local dishes such as pan bati or funchi, usually served with fish or soup.

Most islanders order takeout as the teeny-tiny dining room offers few tables. It has a certain island charm, however, and tables open up after the lunchtime rush.

ASIAN

Sushi has become very stylish on Aruba and not only among visitors. Pacific Rim cuisine, featuring flavors from all corners of Asia and surrounding island nations, is very much coming into vogue on Aruba.

Chinese food has been the number one choice among natives for fast food since the first immigrant opened a restaurant, decades ago. The "Chinese/Dutch," restaurants, which are the most common type on Aruba, always have some Indonesian dishes on their menu. Generally, you can get tasty, filling meals at most Asian venues with prices that please the budget-conscious traveler.

ASIAN DELIGHT

Particularly busy with a takeout trade, Asian Delight (Wilminastraat 68, 297/583-7751, 11:30am-9pm Tues.-Sat., $6.25-16) is the top choice among islanders for their yummy, yummy value-priced Yami-Yami special. In addition to takeout, there is a very small dining area for eating in.

The à la carte menu also features inexpensive Chinese and Indonesian dishes with generous, family-size portions, but most customers pick up their Yami-Yami. This is a combo meal of appetizer and main course served on a bed of either Bami (lo mein) or Nasi (fried rice). Choose from mini spring rolls or three different soups (wonton, egg drop, hot and sour) as an appetizer, then select from 10 different main courses. Most are surprisingly good, in particular the chicken and fish dishes. Try the Tjap Choy, a fresh blend rich with crispy vegetables and tender chicken in mild sauce.

The regular menu is extremely diverse. Several Indonesian and Thai dishes are featured. Specialty dishes range from Japanese teriyaki chicken or "Old Fashioned" fried rice with absolutely everything.

Asian Delight is not far from L. G. Smith Boulevard. It is best reached by walking up the street on the west side of the lagoon that divides the town (aptly named Lagoonweg), which takes you directly to their door.

FUSION DELI

For something really different, try cuisine from Suriname at Fusion Deli (Caya Betico Croes 49A, 297/588-3588, 8:30am-7pm Mon.-Sat., $3.15-5.50). This country along the northern coast of Latin America also experienced the

WHAT IS ARUBAN FOOD?

Aruban food has been influenced by its history and by the diversity of cultures that inhabit the island. It has some very surprising elements. The Dutch left their mark by integrating into island cuisine traditional dishes from another former colony, Indonesia. The seasonings and mainstays of this Pacific country are very much in evidence at nearly all local restaurants and a part of most islanders' everyday diet.

Basic dishes of the Indonesian kitchen are **bami** and **nasi goreng,** which traditionally consist of leftovers and whatever is handy. Meat, chicken, and vegetables are stir-fried and mixed with lo mein noodles (*bami*) or fried rice (*nasi*). Each chef has their own recipe.

Most Asian restaurants serve a *bami* or *nasi* special, which is a sampling of Indonesian dishes with a local touch. The rice or noodles are surrounded with small servings of sate (pork, chicken, or beef mini-kebabs) with *pinda* (peanut) sauce, coconut shrimp, chicken, fish, fried sweet banana, sometimes breaded, and other traditional items.

Another holdover of colonial days is a favorite snack, **loempia,** large egg rolls, second in popularity only to **pastechi,** a regional favorite. These tender, half-moon shaped, fried pastries are filled with perhaps cheese, or chop suey, curried chicken, fish, or beef. They are not empanadas, which are made with cornmeal, also a popular item. *Pastechi* is the Aruban way to start the day, usually paired with a malta, a strong root beer.

A very unique dish to the ABC islands is **keshi yena,** or "Full Cheese." Traditionally, Edam cheese came in a large ball. It was eaten by cutting or scooping out the soft cheese and leaving the hardened rind, which was then filled with a stew of chicken, beef, or seafood. The halves were then wrapped together in foil to be baked in a slow oven. It was served whole and opened at the table by cracking it with a ritual hammer. Today, any restaurant claiming to serve local food will have this on the menu. The hours-long traditional method of preparation has been replaced by surrounding the basic stew with melted Gouda cheese, which is milder than Edam.

Aruban food could be described as peasant food, based on what could be found regionally and cheap. **Stoba** (stew) is a mainstay. It can be made of chicken (*galena*), meat (*carne*), goat (*cabrito*, tastes like lamb or perhaps a touch gamier), or *konkomber*, a sort of local squash. "Pigtail" is exactly what it indicates; nothing is wasted here!

Favorite side dishes include **pampona** (pumpkin), plantain (fried banana), or **funchi** (the local version of polenta, very firm cornmeal that can be sliced or cubed). It is often fried and served with melted cheese (you can feel your arteries hardening even as you eat it), which is a beloved treat. Another standby is **pan bati,** meaning beaten bread; it's a cornmeal pancake that is nothing like a tortilla, sort of a firm breakfast pancake.

Aruban food really shines in the assortment of fresh Caribbean fish available on most menus and fundamental to the island diet. If you have never had fish from this part of the world before, you will find it a revelation. The sweet, moist, clean taste of the local catch can convert the most ardent fish hater.

Ciguatera, a nerve toxin that is a concern when dining on species high on the food chain, such as snapper or barracuda, is not an issue here. Fish from local waters are completely safe to consume.

influences of being a Dutch colony. Indonesian dishes are a staple of their menu. Most of the plantations in Suriname, however, had many East Indian laborers, and the country has a substantial Hindu population, which has impacted the nation's cuisine.

Curried foods are typical, wrapped in large, round flat Indian breads and called roti. Fusion Deli is a center for this hearty dish, which attracts many of the office workers in town during lunch hour. Diners select from tasty, filling, and inexpensive meals of roti and Surinamese *broodjes,* Dutch for "small breads." Interesting typical drinks of coconut, ginger, or almond milk are also offered to complete this exotic experience.

TATAMI SUSHI HOUSE

A bit off the beaten track, Tatami Sushi House (L. G. Smith Blvd. 124, 297/582-9945, 11am-2:30pm and 5:30pm-10:30pm Tues.-Fri., 4pm-11pm Sat., 5:30pm-10:30pm Sun., $8.40-14.30) is a cozy place hidden at the back of a very modern building at the west edge of town. (It is called the Portofino Mall, but you will have absolutely no way of discerning that.) CMB Loan Division is in front, making it easier to find.

Tatami Sushi House offers a very nice, personalized selection of sushi made fresh to order, with some very interesting creations from the chef. There are conventional items such as California rolls as well as exotic combinations and some reasonably priced assortment platters. They have some cute Papiamento names like "Bon Bini" (Welcome), which comes with 12 pieces of sushi, or a big "Mi Dushi" (My Sweetheart) special for two. The dining room is tiny and reservations are recommended.

BEACHSIDE DINING

At the very east end of L. G. Smith Boulevard is the Surfside. This is the only part of Oranjestad that offers actual beachside dinning, aside from Renaissance Island. Three spots provide a special environment and good food. Here you will find some of the most romantic restaurants in town.

BAREFOOT

Uniquely designed, Barefoot (L. G. Smith Blvd. 1, 297/588-9824, www.barefootaruba. com, 5pm-10:30pm daily, $24.50-39.50) takes its name from the centralized dining room: a sandbox with tables, where patrons are encouraged to take off their shoes and wiggle their toes in the sand. There are also no-sand options if the sandbox is not for you.

The circular dining area is an open-air terrace looking out on one of the most appealing locales for sunset watching. Elegant gourmet cuisine from European chef-owner Gerco is

earning rave reviews. Gourmet dishes emphasize seafood, such as fresh crab cakes or seafood ragout. Preparation and presentation is elegant, but expect somewhat smaller portions in the European fashion.

NIKKY BEACH RESTAURANT AND LOUNGE

Adjacent to Barefoot, Nikky Beach (L. G. Smith Blvd. 1A, 297/582-0153, www.nikky-beacharuba.com, 9am-10pm daily for meals, bar open until 4am daily, $17-24) is not so much a restaurant as an environment. It is an all-day spot with an elegant shaded club area and a pool on the dining terrace. The beach and restaurant are lined with stylish couches and lounges. It offers service on the terrace or beach to enjoy the island ambiance. Most local patrons on the weekends linger through the day and well into the night.

Day fare includes typical lunch baguettes (the Dutch seem to have a particular affection for them) with gourmet touches, or platters of assorted local and Dutch snacks. These can be ordered for nibbling on the beach. They also have gourmet breakfast omelets with salmon and shrimp. The dinner menu is diverse, with well-prepared grouper tempura or lamb chops.

On weekends they often host some high decibel music events until the wee hours, changing this from a quiet beachside eatery into a trendy club.

PINCHOS GRILL AND BAR

A distinctive menu and memorable location marks Pinchos (L. G. Smith Blvd. 7, 297/583-2666, 5:30pm-10:30pm daily, bar open until midnight, $19-44) as one of the most romantic places to dine on Aruba. The ultra-cool ambiance and live, mellow music on weekends makes it a popular place for chic, elite business people to stop by for a relaxing cocktail.

Veteran restaurateurs Robby and Anabella Peterson realized a dream when they opened Pinchos. It is named for the skewers on which the main courses are cooked over an open, wood fire grill. Located on a dock out over the water, it is, without a doubt, one of Aruba's best spots to watch the sunset, and the decor is keyed to encourage this ambiance. There are hammocks for two, and huge throw pillows and low couches for lounging while dining at low tables (great for drinks and cuddling, but not so much fun if you have to balance your plate on your knees). They do have normal seating as well.

The restaurant is known for their distinctive dipping sauces and unique marinades. Chicken kebabs and Black Angus rum-infused blue cheese tenderloin are delicious and different, as are the jumbo shrimp and chunky fish kebabs. They also have a selection of main courses off the skewer, but *pinchos* are their claim to fame.

BREAKFAST, BRUNCH, COFFEE SHOPS, AND SWEETS

Aside from the installation of international franchises such as Starbucks and Dunkin' Donuts, Oranjestad has no end of attractive coffee shops and breakfast and lunch spots.

COFFEE BREAK

Local caffeine addicts usually choose Coffee Break (Caya Betico Croes 101A, 297/588-5569, 7am-6pm Mon.-Sat., lattes $2.80) as the place to get their morning fix and meet with friends. This is a very cute, clean, little place done in old-fashioned soda shop decor with rounded, padded stools along the counter. Comfy chairs for reading the morning paper fill one corner of the café and they have free Wi-Fi.

Coffee beans are freshly ground; imagine all those fancy coffees you know and love, priced to the local trade, in florins instead of dollars. This means about 45 percent less than what the resorts and high profile outlets charge.

Local snacks and pastries are the food fare, as well as waffles or pie of the day à la mode. They also offer elaborate, iced-coffee treats and ice cream floats.

COFFEE 4 U

Extremely popular with island intelligentsia is Coffee 4 U (L. G. Smith Blvd. 108, 297/582-2906, 7am-7pm Mon.-Fri., 8am-6pm Sat., 8am-2pm Sun., $4.50-8), located just past the gas station on the western end of town. The specialties here are Italian cappuccinos and lattes, enjoyed at a very stylish, contemporary collection of chairs and tables. Free Wi-Fi makes this a favorite meeting spot for convivial business conferences.

The menu includes pastries and light meals. Quiches comes in exotic combinations, such as spinach and feta or bacon and brie. Paninis and baguettes are also the fare, very typical for an island coffee house menu.

DELIFRANCE

Perhaps Aruba's first trendy lunch spot, Delifrance (L. G. Smith Blvd. 150, 297/588-6066, 7am-4pm Mon.-Sat., 8am-1:30pm Sun., $7.85-9.50) is still one of the most popular places for business meetings over coffee, quiche, soup of the day, or their creative sandwiches on crusty baguettes. Choose from the rustic, expansive, air-conditioned interior or the terrace overlooking this busy center. Hot or cold baguettes or freshly-made soup and salad specials are favorites. Along with the advantage of being very close to the Manchebo Beach resorts, this is one of the few local shops to feature bagels with cream cheese and lox.

DE SUIKERTUIN

Fashionable islanders love lunch at De Suikertuin (Wilhelminastraat 64, 297/582-6322, www.desuikertuin.com, 7am-5pm Mon.-Sat., $4-14). "The Sugar Garden" is aptly named. Housed in a landmark *cunucu* house, it features a beautifully landscaped patio in the backyard for outdoor dining. Or choose the quaint, air-conditioned and authentically maintained indoor rooms.

De Suikertuin offers a rather typical Dutch-European menu with Aruban touches. Try the very nice pumpkin soup, a local delicacy. Luncheon baguettes include anything from peanut butter with sprinkles (a Dutch thing) to smoked salmon with dill dressing. Other options are quiches and a changing menu of hot dishes.

DJESPIE'S PLACE

Attached to Coffee Break and sporting the same decor, but separated by a door, is the cute little snack stop, Djespie's Place (Caya Betico Croes 101, 297/588-5569, 7am-6pm Mon.-Sat., $1-4 snack or sandwich), a popular hangout with islanders. The focus is on an authentic Aruban snack menu. Quick lunch options include *pastechis* (fried pastries) and croquettes, or well stuffed sandwiches and hamburgers.

LECCA LECCA

Even if only for a sweet treat, a trip to town is not complete without a stop at Lecca Lecca (Weststraat 13, 297/288-4074, 9:30am-7pm Mon.-Sat., $2.85-8.25). This stylish snack shop is conveniently attached to the main bus terminal, for anyone seeking a refreshing break before bussing it back to their resort. Upstairs is the factory where they turn out fresh gelato and airy, light, fresh fruit sorbets, daily; leftovers at the end of the day are donated to local centers for children.

Gelato has far less fat than ice cream but is rich and satisfying. They boast 60 plus recipes made with only organic milk, fresh ingredients, and no artificial colors, flavorings, or preservatives. Try the grapefruit, passion fruit, or carrot sorbets for a complete surprise to the taste buds.

Lecca Lecca also serves fresh soups. They have their own bakery where the chef bakes paninis, quiches, and baguettes. The cappuccino and espresso served are authentic Italian coffees and get a thumbs-up from aficionados.

◖ SMIT & DORLAS COFFEE HOUSE

Aruba's first coffee shop, Smit & Dorlas Coffee House (De La Sallestraat 30-A, 297/588-4888, http://coffeehousearuba.com, 9am-6pm Mon.-Fri., 9am-2pm Sat., lattes $2.50) offers 14 fresh ground coffees from around the world and 40 loose teas, both black and herbal, in the most delightful surroundings imaginable. Styled after vintage Viennese pastry shops, it not only serves excellent coffee, but delicious paninis, a quiche of the day, and baguette sandwiches. It is also famous for their fresh made cakes, all reasonably priced. Coffee House is the

Smit & Dorlas Coffee House, Aruba's first coffee shop

© ROSALIE KLEIN

embodiment of why enjoying a cup of coffee or tea with a friend is such a treasured institution; it's the sort of place where you will want to linger.

Hot beverages are served with delicious complimentary cookies, which will entice you back for more. There is no other place on Aruba to purchase these cookies. The shop also sells unique, hard-to-find, designer coffee and teapots made for two that can be lovely gifts.

Coffee House is located not far from the main post office, which is a 10-minute walk inland from the Renaissance Resort. Take a right turn at the traffic light just past the post office, at De La Sallestraat, and find it five minutes farther along on the south side.

STARBUCKS

If you can't live without your Starbucks (Renaissance Mall and Renaissance Marketplace, 297/523-6750, 7am-10pm daily) never fear, they are here. The Renaissance mall outlet sports chic, award-winning Caribbean design, air-conditioned surroundings, and the famous Starbucks' coffees and refreshing green tea and fruit frappes. Located at the very center of the mall, next to the pier for the boat to Renaissance Island, the lounge area has deep couches for relaxing and checking your email with free Wi-Fi.

The Renaissance Marketplace Starbucks is across the main street, right on Oranjestad Harbor, a setting with a lovely view. Here you can relax on the outdoor terrace and enjoy the breeze. This is a nice place to watch the fishing boats make way early in the morning or government officials grab their caffeine fix before sessions of Parliament. Both cafés sell a collection of dedicated Starbucks Aruba logo gear, for those who take their coffee souvenirs seriously or seek a gift for the fanatic back home.

CARIBBEAN FUSION

Unadulterated, full-blown French cookery is hard to find on Aruba these days. Instead, it is considered quite fashionable to incorporate regional seasoning and indigenous fruits and vegetables to liven up the menu. Chefs are also more health conscious in their cooking style, with less emphasis on rich, heavy sauces. Passion fruit sauces and mango salsas produce exotic flavors that chefs find enchanting, and the customers seem to agree.

IGUANA JOE'S

A trendy Caribbean menu is the signature of Iguana Joe's (L. G. Smith Blvd., 297/583-9373, www.iguanajoesaruba.com, 11am-midnight Mon.-Sat., 5pm-11pm Sun., $15-20), along with some entertaining surroundings. Located on the second level of the Royal Plaza Mall, it was first in a very successful local franchise, followed by Smokey Joe's and Iguana Cantina in Palm Beach. Famous for their island potions, they also serve traditional local favorites, including *keshi yena* (filled cheese shell) and Aruban-style fresh fish. Regional specialties such as jerk chicken and jambalaya spice things up. They are also very popular for their ribs. The food is always good and they have a funky, fun decor with a great view of the harbor and boulevard, ideal for observing island life.

THE PADDOCK

A very popular hangout with young Dutch students, The Paddock (L. G. Smith Blvd. 13, 297/583-233, www.paddock-aruba.com, 9am-10:45pm, bar open until the last patron leaves, $2.50-22.25) occupies a prime spot right on the water.

Talk about funky decor! You can't miss the velociraptor hanging out on the roof, right next to the Volkswagen. As a venue that attracts poor students who come to Aruba to do their internships, it has a reasonably priced menu and an ambiance that appeals to all ages. It becomes a hangout for younger folks later at night.

Dutch baguette sandwiches are a standard here, from the local favorite cheese and pickles to paper-thin carpaccio. *Tosties* (the local version of grilled cheese), hamburgers, and sharwarma (their spelling!) are considered specialties. They have a very diverse dinner menu with emphasis on fish and seafood. Every

FOOD

Fresh seafood is a smart choice when dining out in Aruba.

Wednesday evening they offer an all-you-can-eat rib special (from 9am to closing, $13). Visit their website for an amusing hint of what to expect from this distinctly Dutch eatery.

QUE PASA

A long-time Oranjestad favorite with an eclectic menu, Que Pasa (Wilminastraat 18, 297/583-4888, www.quepasaaruba.com, 5pm-11pm daily, $18-26) features regional cuisine with European flair. Lively Caribbean decor in a landmark building showcases a great deal of original art. A second level with a terrace offers alfresco dining overlooking the street.

Loyal patrons rave about their tomato soup, very good ribs, and fresh catch of the day. An eclectic menu includes carpaccio, tuna tataki, or duck breast salad. Que Pasa is best known for its fresh specials of the day, which could be fish, steak, or something else altogether. Their exceptionally friendly staff is happy to recite the specials and offer an honest opinion.

7 WEST

Located on the north side of the harbor, 7 West (Weststraat 7, 297/588-9983, www.7-westaruba.com, 9am-4:30pm and 5pm-10:30pm daily, $7.25, $10 daily specials, $15 all-you-can-eat ribs Fri.) is often overlooked because of its second-story location. However, the appealing open-air eatery has a prime location. Terraces provide a great view, and it is priced for a local crowd. They recently redecorated and the interior is quite attractive, with rounded booths providing a cozy environment.

Lunch platters of ribs (which are excellent, tender, and tasty), fried chicken, or jerk chicken are uniformly priced. They also feature a daily lunch special: Usually (but not always) it is fresh fish, depending on Chef John Boomkamp's whim. Their signature burger is done the Dutch way, with a fried egg, bacon, Gouda cheese, and sautéed onions. They also have a children's menu. No additional service charge is added to the bill.

◖ TWISTER CAFÉ

Deep in the heart of Oranjestad, find the surprising Twister Café (Dominicanessenstraat 10, 297/583-9077, twistercafearuba10@yahoo.com, 5pm-2am Mon.-Sat., $10-18.50, culinary weekend $38.50) to enjoy an unexpected gourmet treat.

Twister has a cozy, intimate neighborhood bar ambiance, with a regular Dutch clientele. Owners Linda and Annie are congenial hosts. For over 10 years, Linda was executive sous-chef and then executive chef of what was always considered Aruba's premier gourmet restaurant, Chez Mathilde. Now that it is closed, she is completely focused on Twister. She brings her deft touch to the kitchen, at extremely reasonable prices.

The menu ranges from authentic Dutch *stampot,* a unique mix of vegetables, mashed potatoes, and meat, to Tournedos of Beef. The plat du jour could be duck breast, or whatever is fresh; they are also known for their hearty soups.

Every last weekend of the month, Annie and Linda host a special "Culinary Weekend." They devise a unique menu and seat up to 30. The five-course meal consists of soup, two appetizers, a main course, and dessert, for one very reasonable price, drinks not included. The same meal is served for three nights: Friday, Saturday, and Sunday, beginning at around 8pm. Doors open 45 minutes prior for a meet and greet. Sunday evening is strictly no smoking. If you have particular dietary concerns, they will prepare an alternate dish. It is a leisurely, congenial evening of wine and food appreciation.

Main courses for this culinary adventure could be beef Wellington; pan-seared lamb and duck breast; a combination of Chilean sea bass, salmon, and a fresh local offering; lamb three ways; or a poultry medley with ostrich and duck leg. You can expect something special and memorable since Linda has a fine reputation as an innovative and intuitive chef.

COLOMBIAN

Aruba's rapidly expanding expatriate Colombian population has resulted in a number of informal cafés with authentic cuisine. Colombians like their big meal at lunchtime, and typical dishes are *sopas,* huge bowls filled with meat or fish, tons of veggies, and some broth; it's almost a stew. The other favorite dish is a mixed meat platter, typical to Latin America; each country has their own version. These include several different cuts of beef, pork, sausage, and organ meats. If you have a taste for tongue, liver, kidney, heart, and tripe, you will be very happy with this, or you could ask them to substitute an extra piece of chicken or sausage.

◖ CASA VIEJA

Among Aruba's growing population of Colombian spots, Casa Vieja (Cumana 8, 297/588-1627, 7:30am-11pm daily, $3.50-20) is one of the most authentic. It is found on the eastern end of town by following the Caya Betico Croes. In this tiny place, food is served on a small covered patio with a thatched roof and a few garden chairs and tables. This is a

© ROSALIE KLEIN

FOOD

whole snapper at Casa Vieja

good spot for inexpensive breakfasts, which are served all day. The food is simply prepared, there is a lot to eat, and it is dead cheap.

A full selection of soups is first on the menu. Sunday is their day for sopa de mariscos (seafood soup) and the enormous mixed meat platters that can feed four. Those platters are heaped with beef, chicken, pork, thick bacon, chorizo, and whatever else is on hand. They also do an excellent fresh, whole snapper. Many from Aruba's Colombian community come here to enjoy their Sunday meal.

EL ESQUIVEL

There is a cluster of budget priced eateries in the middle of the Caya Betico Croes, the main shopping street. El Esquivel (Caya Betico Croes 49A, 297/588-0108, 9am-11pm daily, $5.50-20) is another cute little hole-in-the-wall with just a few tables doing a brisk local business.

This tiny café on a corner is rustic and popular for their *sopa di dia*. The Sunday seafood soup usually runs out by the afternoon since it is such a popular item. Mixed meat platters range from the smaller sized "Peasant" to the "Big Mixed Platter," enough for three or four people. Fish stews, or shrimp and fish platters, grilled or fried, are also nice for nonmeat eaters.

The menu has a translation of the Spanish names of dishes, but not too thorough an explanation of what you get, which may be challenging on the mixed platters. The crew tend to be a bit weak in English, but you can point at what you want.

ITALIAN

Oranjestad used to be the place to go for Italian food on Aruba. Palm Beach is now the "Little Italy" of the island, but the town still has a couple of very moderately priced finds.

CASA TUA

Casa Tua (Renaissance Marketplace, 297/583-1990, www.casatuaaruba.com, 11am-11pm daily, $12-36) was Aruba's first gourmet pizzeria. The Oranjestad outlet (there is also one in Palm Beach) has an elegant ambiance and a

terrific location by the water end of the mall. There is indoor and outdoor dining, situated so patrons can enjoy the free nightly shows at the bandstand.

Patrons rave about the pizza and reasonably priced pasta, declaring it "the best pizza in Oranjestad." Other dishes tend more towards seafood, with only a few meat dishes, but no veal.

◖ PIZZA & MORE

The best prices anywhere on Aruba for great pizza and pasta are found at Pizza & More (Caya Betico Croes 63, 297/588-2333, 10:30am-8:30pm Mon.-Sat., $3.50-14) on the main shopping street in the center of town. It is a very small, simple place right next to Maggy's Emporium. This is where locals go when they want good pizza or pasta at a fraction of what is charged by spots close to the resort areas.

There are changing specials every day. They make very good lasagna with meat, mushrooms, or spinach; seafood; chicken; or whatever is fresh. The menu includes fresh, hearty soups of the day served in a good-size bowl with crusty focaccia. There are no veal dishes or beef beyond meat sauce and meatballs. The main courses of chicken with mushrooms or curry shrimp or Scampi, served with salad and pasta, are also tasty. The restaurant also caters and delivers to your resort for no extra service charge.

MIDDLE EASTERN

A surprising number of families of Middle Eastern, particularly Lebanese, descent live on Aruba, sharing their traditional cuisine.

SULTAN

The original Middle Eastern restaurant, and still considered the best by many, is Sultan (Caya Betico Croes 229, 297/588-2598, 11am-3pm and 5:30pm-11pm Mon.-Sat., 5pm-11pm Sun., $8.85-18). It is found just a bit beyond the eastern edge of Oranjestad, on the Cumena traffic circle.

This cozy, simple place is reasonably priced. It tries to recreate a Middle Eastern ambiance in decor and atmosphere. Arabic pop videos play on a plasma screen. There is a party room in the back for groups to lounge on colorful cushions and dine while reclining. The menu declares that they are determined to make you "weak in the knees" with their authentic cuisine.

Main courses feature a mix of Middle Eastern favorites, kebabs of chicken, lamb, or tenderloin or a platter of large falafel, which is perfect for vegetarians. Shawarma is their specialty. All main courses are accompanied by ample portions of excellent hummus, tabouli salad, and saffron rice or baba ganoush and pita bread. If you have a large party, they offer an expansive sample platter of every kind of kebab and regional delicacy ($55 flat rate). Every dish comes with their homemade sauces; the creamy garlic sauce is tasty and mild, definitely worth trying. Approach the tomato-based salsa with caution: It is *super* spicy.

PERUVIAN
LA GRANJA
Always a local favorite for good BBQ chicken, La Granja (Hospitaalstraat 2, 297/583-5602, 11:30am-10pm daily, $9-17) expanded their menu to include ribs, chops, and other items, including fresh shrimp when they have it. An average meal is half a bird cooked over a wood-fired grill; this is the classic Peruvian rotisserie style. Other main courses are a full pound of steak or grilled pork. Try some of the Peruvian condiments, more like relishes, which lend a new and exciting taste to familiar poultry.

The restaurant features quick, cafeteria-style service and a rustic setting with picnic-type tables. It can be found by going inland from the far eastern end of Caya Betico Croes, where the tram rails end. The building takes up an entire corner just a block beyond Coffee Break.

PORTUGUESE
GOSTOSO
For a very long time Gostoso (Caya Ing Roland H. Lacle 12, 297/588-0053, www.gostosoaruba.com, noon-3pm and 6pm-10pm Tues.-Fri., noon-4pm and 6:30pm-10pm Sat.-Sun., $21-33) was rated Aruba's number one restaurant on the most popular review sites. As would be expected from the seafaring Portuguese people, fish and shellfish are big on the menu. The owner-operated eatery also features some Aruban dishes.

The food is excellent and they make great white sangria. Steaks are prime Black Angus beef. Particularly recommended from the menu is the Espetada Marinara, a very unique presentation of surf and turf, or order Catch of the Day in Mango Sauce, made with grouper or Chilean sea bass; portions are very generous.

This charming little place tucked away on an Oranjestad side street has one or two drawbacks. Rather poor acoustics means it gets quite noisy when filled (and it usually is). Its popularity can possibly result in a long wait for a table after 7pm. Don't have a heart attack when first perusing the menu; prices are in Aruban florins, not dollars.

SEAFOOD
Aruba is a fish and seafood lover's paradise. Clean waters guarantee a catch of the freshest and most delicate flavor. An authentic fresh catch of the day is always a treat, but make sure the restaurant actually uses a fresh, not frozen, fish.

AQUARIUS
A favorite lunch spot for island movers and shakers is Aquarius (L. G. Smith Blvd. 82, 297/583-6000 ext. 6158, 7-11am, noon-3:30pm, and 5:30pm-11:30pm Mon.-Sat., 7-11am and 5:30pm-11:30pm Sun., breakfast buffet $18, Sunday brunch $30, lunch buffet $15-20, dinner seafood buffet $39) next to the reception desk of the Renaissance Marina Tower. The restaurant has a pleasant, chic decor and an extremely friendly and accommodating staff.

It is entirely possible to find bank presidents or an important minister or parliamentarian dining at the next table or queuing up for the fabulous lunch buffet. There are two choices: cold, which consists of just the salad bar, soup of the day, dessert table, and unlimited ice tea, or full buffet, with a selection of local dishes.

FOOD

The cold is a delicious and diverse array of all you can eat fresh sushi, some gourmet cold fish dish of the day, a variety of ceviche and seasoned salads, and all the greens and accompaniments you could possibly imagine, with fresh-made dressings. The soups are always good, as is the dessert assortment, which changes daily.

Dinner adds on to the buffet a fresh fish station where patrons choose from at least a few different kinds of fish and shellfish, sautéed before their eyes and to their specifications. Try the yummy mango salsa to accompany your fish.

DELIMAR

Authentic regional cuisine from Lima, Peru distinguishes Delimar (Wilhelminastraat 4, 297/582-6139, 11am-3pm and 4:30pm-9:30pm Thurs.-Tues., $16) from other fish and seafood restaurants. Since Lima is a port town and central to the coastal region, it relies heavily on seafood, cilantro, and particular regional dried peppers for its distinctive cuisine. Delimar owners, chef Marco and his wife Lorena, have imported these directly from their homeland for an authentic flavor.

The couple is passionate about what they deliver to the table. Dishes are made to order, allowing patrons to specify the degree of spiciness they prefer, or dishes can be pretty hot. If looking for a really different style of preparing fish, this is the place. In keeping with the cuisine, their bar is stocked with Peruvian beers and some liquor from the region.

Generous portions of seafood are served as *arrisotado,* the Peruvian version of risotto; *tacutacu,* with rice and beans; or *cau-cau,* seafood only. Here is where Peruvian expatriates and families go for their Sunday lunch. It is conveniently located just behind the Renaissance Resort.

THE OLD FISHERMAN

Ask an islander where to go for fresh fish in Oranjestad and they will tell you The Old Fisherman (Havenstraat 36, 297/588-3648, http://oldfishermanaruba.com, 8am-11pm daily, $22-44). It started out as a tiny hole in the wall right on the water at the harbor, where local fishermen would drop off their catch. Food was sold only to take away. It was so popular with islanders wanting fresh fish that they moved into their present cozy surroundings with a distinctively local decor. Find them on the side street next to the bus station.

Platters of fresh fish and seafood are named for friends and family, and prepared as you like it: sautéed, breaded and fried, with creamy garlic sauce, or meunière. The signature dish here is the "Claudio Wolfe"—a whole red snapper fried, grilled, or stewed. The dining room is filled with natives, and there is always a feeling of being with a family and their friends, rather than at a commercial establishment.

STEAKHOUSES

Most steak restaurants go beyond their advertised specialty, offering fish and poultry to accommodate patrons who might be in the mood for something else. Usually, it is a mediocre offering, as beef is their thing. It's best to stick to the fine fish restaurants for seafood (which, in most cases, do an only passable steak; it works both ways) and to the steakhouses for steak.

EL GAUCHO

No conversation about Oranjestad steakhouses is complete without a mention of El Gaucho (Wilminastraat 80, 297/582-3677, www.el-gaucho-aruba.com, 11:30am-11pm daily, $37), Aruba's first and, still considered by many, foremost Argentine steakhouse, though much pricier than it used to be. There are mixed reviews on some items on the menu, such as the short ribs, but their churrasco, the Gaucho Steak, is an 18-ounce hunk of boneless sirloin that is consistently excellent. It's usually enough for more than one person to consume.

There is a kids' menu with favorites such as macaroni and cheese and hamburgers, plus a video game room to keep the little ones busy. Mariachi singers perform every night, which is very interesting if you are new to experiencing them live.

© ROSALIE KLEIN

the famous *churrasco* steak at El Gaucho in Oranjestad

L.G. SMITH'S STEAK & CHOP HOUSE

Aruba has some very fine eateries where they are fanatical about every dish being superlative. Such a restaurant is L.G. Smith's Steak & Chop House. (L. G. Smith Blvd. 82, 297/583-6000 ext. 6195, www.lgsmiths.com, 5:30pm-11pm daily, early bird special 5:30pm-7pm daily, $26-44, $79 per couple for three-course special with wine pairing).

Gourmet food and fine wine pairing is the restaurant's passion. At least once a year they bring in a celebrity chef from Europe or the United States to devise a special limited-time menu of unique and impressive dishes. Average pricing for the special menus is $44-60 per person for a three-course dinner, which includes several options. Wine pairing with each course costs an extra $30-35 total.

The regular à la carte menu specializes in certified Angus prime beef steaks, ranging from a petit filet mignon to a massive 20-ounce Porterhouse. They also have some gourmet vegetarian dishes, such as vegetable Wellington, and elegant desserts.

Located on the Renaissance Mall mezzanine level, a wall of picture windows provides a gorgeous view of the harbor. The restaurant's decor is elegant "island chic." Attached to the Crystal Casino, they have a lounge bordering the gaming area, where they serve light fare after midnight. They also work with Okeanos Spa, next door, to offer a "treatment and dinner" package.

YAMANJA WOODFIRE GRILL

Regulars rave about Yamanja Woodfire Grill (Wilminastraat 2, 297/588-4711, www.yemanja-aruba.com, 5:30pm-10:30pm Mon.-Sat., $25 and up, prix fixe menu $42.50-55), located directly behind the Renaissance Resort Marina Tower. This charming restaurant occupies a landmark building and offers indoor and outdoor dining.

Grilled meats are their specialty and the mesquite wood imparts a singular flavor. U.S.-certified Angus beef is served, which does make the à la carte menu somewhat pricey. They offer suggested wine pairings. For families and the

FOOD

© ROSALIE KLEIN

Don't skip the elegant, gourmet desserts at L.G. Smith's Steak & Chop House.

budget minded, they have a less expensive kids' menu and a three-course early bird special.

WINE AND TAPAS
CELLAR 23

As you enter Cellar 23 (Havenstraat 23, 297/583-4968, 11am-8pm Mon.-Sat., $5.20-12), you will see more than 1,000 wine labels on display. This beautifully maintained landmark building is a bodega and tapas spot, and is the retail outlet for one of the largest wine distributors on Aruba. The interior ambiance is a modern, elegant wine cellar. There is also a front terrace for dining outdoors. The owners used to have a gallery, so the walls are covered with works by local artists. This has become the trendy power lunch venue for Aruban business people.

Patrons can select a vintage (there is a 25 percent corkage charge) and arrange their own tasting session from a dozen varieties of tapas. They also offer a Happy Hour special 5pm-7pm featuring an entire bottle of the Vintage of the Day and a platter of gourmet snacks. The à la carte lunch menu is reasonably priced. Menu items range from *tosties,* the local version of grilled cheese with various additions, to seafood paella or garlic shrimp.

Eagle Beach and Manchebo Beach

Aside from resort restaurants, this area has traditionally had a paucity of eateries compared to Oranjestad and Palm Beach. There are several contributing factors, including the overall lack of the development of the area, as yet. This is quickly changing and the infusion of a tourist population is bringing more places for dining out, from gourmet to local.

Most restaurants are lined up along the beach, within the resorts, or across the Irausquin Boulevard, close by. A few interesting venues, such as Madame Janette, Pam Pam and Yami Yami for bargain priced meals, which should not be overlooked, can be found off the highway and traveling a short distance up the Bubali road. Most Restaurants in the resorts feature a mix of typical lunch fare such as hamburgers, wraps, and Caesar salads during the day, but offer a bit more innovation and romantic settings once the sun goes down.

EAGLE BEACH AND VICINITY

Aruba's southwest point, Punto Brabo, ends at Costa Linda Resort, the demarcation point between Manchebo Beach and Eagle Beach. Aside from Passions, all resorts and restaurants along J. E. Irausquin Boulevard are found on the land side of the street, across from the beach. Eagle Beach ends at Aruba's famous fofoti trees, a distinctive landmark: This is the base of the Bubali Road, which leads across the Sasaki Highway and to some interesting places to dine.

Asian
🄲 YAMI YAMI
The Bubali Commercial Center is a small commercial center on the Bubali Road. It is where you find the suburban outlet of Asian Delight, called, appropriately, Yami Yami (Bubali 69C, 297/587-0062, 11:30am-9pm Tues.-Sun., $6.25-16) after the bargain-priced meal that is a staple for many islanders.

This outlet also has a pleasant and slightly more spacious dining room than its predecessor, and a sushi bar. Made-to-order sushi combos start at $15 for a 21-piece platter. "Party Platters" are only made to go, which is useful for entertaining in your suite or for devouring outside while watching the sunset.

Beachside Dining
🄲 PASSIONS
Though actually on Eagle Beach, Passions (J. E. Irausquin Blvd. 252, 297/587-0110, www.passions-restaurant-aruba.com, beach bar 10am-11pm daily, restaurant noon-4:30pm and 6pm-9:30pm daily, $19.50-46.50) is the only shore side restaurant between Manchebo Beach and Palm Beach. It rates as one of the most romantic spots on Aruba's entire west coast, truly set apart from all the others. The location on the beachfront of the Amsterdam Manor Beach Resort lends a particular air of tranquil seclusion.

The menu is the epitome of Caribbean fusion, with emphasis on fresh fish and seafood. Dishes range from chicken breast and a variety of fish and shellfish to a surf and turf of filet mignon and lobster tail. Innovative sauces and presentation of seafood have earned this restaurant a high rating, but the real attraction is the location ambiance. For a special anniversary dinner or a marriage proposal, it is ideal. Mellow singers with a romantic repertoire are regularly featured.

Caribbean Fusion
CARAMBOLA
Martijn Haselhoef, well known to many island visitors for his years as maître d' at the famous Ventanas Del Mar, has realized his dream restaurant with Carambola (J. E. Irausquin Blvd. 64, 297/587-6695, www.carambola-aruba.com, 8:30am-10:30pm Tues.-Sun., $25-45). His exacting attention to detail and exceedingly friendly reception are his trademarks.

This is a particularly lovely spot in the

FOOD

DINING ALFRESCO

One of the great attractions of the tropics is a romantic sunset dinner on a beach or in some delightful gardens. A lovely meal under swaying palms with the cooling trade winds rustling is a fantasy come true; though, not so much when the wind nearly blows the food off your plate. Aruba is known for some particularly strong winds, and many restaurants have been designed with that in mind. Several places set up windbreaks or design the building to provide a tranquil environment.

Unfortunately, this can create another situation, with open-air dining areas getting uncomfortably warm, especially if the heat from the kitchen is blowing your way. Dress lightly, but bring a sweater if it turns out this is not the case.

Dressing lightly exacerbates the other issue with dining outdoors. There is the possibility of mosquitoes or sand fleas making a meal out of patrons, particularly around sunset, when they are active. Everyone enjoys the casual ambiance of the island and the option to dine in Bermuda shorts and light clothing. Bare legs under a table are an immediate attraction for some annoying insects, especially if there was rainfall in the previous weeks.

This is a problem all over the Caribbean, even more so on other islands where it rains a bit nearly every day. In these cases, a windy desert island such as Aruba is appreciated even more, but that is no guarantee of being entirely bug free. However, it is not usually such an issue at restaurants situated where there is a steady breeze or not much greenery.

Long pants with shoes and socks are suggested. If you wish to completely enjoy that fantasy meal with large areas of skin exposed, invest in some bug repellent, particularly in the mid to late fall.

© ROSALIE KLEIN

Seaside restaurants are ideal for romantic sunset dinners.

FOOD

Paradise Beach Villas. It is a beautiful place, with a winding staircase to a cozy mezzanine level, perfect for large groups and special occasions. There is also outdoor dining.

A diverse menu of classic dishes is punctuated with the local touch. Try peanut soup, which will surprise you, and the fresh fish. Diners have the option to customize their surf and turf: Filet mignon can be matched with a choice of shrimp, scallops, or lobster, and is priced accordingly. Another must-try is the ccc chowder (clams, crab, and conch) served in bread bowl; this is delicious and a meal by itself.

This venue is particularly known for their gourmet holiday brunches. They conduct them on holidays such as Thanksgiving, Christmas, and Mother's Day.

MADAME JANETTE

Beautiful gardens and excellent food has made Madame Janette (Cunucu Abao 37, 297/587-0184, www.madamejanette.com, 5:30pm-10pm daily, $28-45) a consistent favorite with longtime visitors. Regulars have their favorites menu items, but the interesting seasonal menus and daily specials always attract interest.

Host and partner Ramon is an island expert on obtaining the freshest of exotic and fine quality comestibles, while Karsten is a certified master chef. Together they founded the restaurant, garnering a loyal following almost immediately for their gourmet preparation and value. Even after more than a decade, reservations are still required days in advance to get a table.

Seafood specialties include bang bang shrimp, fresh catch of the day, Asian honey soy sea bass, and whole de-boned yellow tail snapper, adding a fresh twist to standard dishes. Asparagus season, showcasing those large, white stalks that are highly valued by Dutch chefs, is from mid-April to late June. This results in a continually changing menu of asparagus-based recipes.

Dress is casual and comfortable, and it is advisable to dress lightly. It can get warm because of the windbreaks. They also feature appropriate nightly entertainment.

PAM PAM CAFÉ

Traveling inland, nearly to the end of the Bubali Road, you can spy a sign to turn right to the Perle D'or Resort and Pam Pam Café (Boegoroi 11z, 297/587-/7710, 8am-10pm daily, $3-20 for the BBQ buffet), which is within the resort. Pam Pam has delightful tropical island surroundings and a Dutch-influenced menu. They keep prices down (except for the drinks) by deploying a self-service system geared to the many young Dutch students who comprise a large percentage of the Pearl D'or clientele. Place an order at the bar, get a number, and they will call it out when the food is ready. Pam Pam has a breakfast, lunch, and dinner menu, though no specific hours for when they stop serving one meal and move on to the next.

Typical Dutch baguettes dominate the breakfast and lunch menu along with inexpensive personal pizzas. Wednesdays are worth a visit for the BBQ buffet (6pm-9pm). It includes BBQ steak (sometimes chewy); chicken (drumsticks only); very good fresh made sausage; pork sate (kebabs); and superb ribs, which are definitely worth loading up on. There is a nice selection of side dishes and surprisingly good local desserts, flan and bread pudding; make sure to check them out. This is a great deal, but the exorbitant drink prices are something of a spoiler ($4 for a *very small* soft drink or juice might make you want to stick with water). A glass of wine or beer is far more reasonable.

SCREAMING EAGLE

Many veteran visitors will point to Screaming Eagle (J. E. Irausquin Blvd. 228, 297/587-8021, www.screaming-eagle.net, 6pm-11pm daily, $27.50-59) when asked what is considered one of the great bastions of gourmet cuisine on Aruba. Chef-owner Erwin Husker has a reputation for his flair in the kitchen and for producing very interesting, inventive recipes with a distinctive touch. They also charge high prices for said cuisine, which food fanatics and dedicated patrons cite as worth the experience.

A fine wine cellar and a quirky but chic decor, along with the exquisite recipes, have proven a very successful formula. Here you

FOOD

can dine lounging on bed-like couches; but there is also normal table seating for the less adventurous.

The fluid menu offers a chef's signature special of the day. Always extremely inventive and delicious, the special costs what one might pay for an entire meal. The Screaming Eagle is a spot for discerning diners with expansive budgets.

Dutch
TULIP

For a bit of Holland in Aruba, Tulip (J. E. Irausquin Blvd. 240, 297/587-0110, www.tulip-restaurant-aruba.com, 7:30am-10am, noon-4pm, and 5pm-10:30pm Wed.-Mon., $4-20) is an appealing place to find distinctly Dutch cuisine for breakfast, lunch, and dinner.

It is the resident restaurant for a small resort that was a retreat for Dutch Marines stationed on the island. Tables are set up alfresco and scattered around the terrace and very lovely gardens. Aside from Dutch classic dishes, there are some Caribbean and Indonesian flavors on the menu. Typically Dutch are the *pannenkoek,* giant crepes with fresh fruit or savory fillings; *patatja oorlog,* fries with peanut sauce; and *frikandel,* a really big, long sausage sandwich. Among the local dishes offered is a delicious *keshi yena,* the standard of stewed chicken smothered in Gouda cheese.

The dinner menu is extensive and diverse, with traditional items, such as very good potato pancakes with applesauce, served with reasonably priced lamb chops.

It is located a bit north of La Quinta Resort and screened by shrubbery; the nondescript entrance is on Irausquin Boulevard and can be easy to miss.

MANCHEBO BEACH AREA

Within this cluster of resorts just on the edge of town are some excellent restaurants, and the clubhouse at the Divi Links contains two fine places, one somewhat pricey, the other comparatively moderate, with spectacular views of the golf course and surrounding area. Divi Resort management has had a definitive hand in advancing the quality of choices now available to those staying at the low-rise resorts.

Asian
GINGER

An interesting addition to the immediate area is Ginger (Alhambra Casino and Shopping Bazaar, J. E. Irausquin Blvd. 47, 297/280-9989, 5:30pm-11pm, $11-22), a stylish venue, offering an elegant Pacific Rim menu. It is within convenient walking distance of the resorts. The Alhambra mall completed renovations at the end of 2012 and now offers a sleek, chic, entertainment center with some equally chic shops and restaurants. Ginger's decor and menu is the epitome of the new style that Divi Properties is bringing to this Eagle Beach entertainment complex.

Ginger is based on a very small chain of boutique restaurants in Holland. Dani, the executive chef, was sent there for training. The diverse menu runs the gamut from sushi and sashimi combos to wonton soup and Asian carpaccio of Kobe beef. You can enjoy main course noodle soups from Tokyo, Jakarta, and Singapore. Try the Malaysian *otak otak,* a mix of shrimp, scallops, and fish cooked and served wrapped in a banana leaf. Guests rave about the tasty and different green curry chicken.

Pacific Rim cuisine is often quite spicy. You can put out the fire with their signature ginger lemon cream dessert, a tangy, light, and frothy lemon mousse with fresh ginger sauce. It is absolutely yummy and different, worth stopping by just for the dessert even if you don't have dinner.

Beachside Dining
BUCUTI RESTAURANT

Formally known as The Pirate's Nest, Bucuti Restaurant (J. E. Irausquin Blvd. 55B, 297/583-1100 ext. 109, www.bucuti.com, 7am-10:30pm daily, lunch $8.50-20, dinner $18-35) reflects the elegant changes in the renovated shore side café. Like the resort, this restaurant is strictly adults only.

Originally one of the most distinctively designed eateries on Aruba, Bucuti Restaurant

a frothy lemon cream cocktail at Ginger

was built to look like a wrecked galleon on the shore. It has an expansive deck right on the beach with "Island Chic" decor: lounges surrounded by curtains, and a very interesting gimmick for attracting a waiter's attention.

The menu reflects the tastes of what they assume to be a more discerning patronage. Lunch items are a bit higher-priced compared to nearby beachside eateries, but there is the advantage of dining without fractious children anywhere in the vicinity.

Even the most standard offerings of wraps and sandwiches have a gourmet touch. Smoked salmon for the salmon tempura salad is not lox, but the fresh and delicate kind. Mediterranean bread bowl, a grilled chicken breast salad with kalamata olives and chick peas, is served in a crusty edible bread bowl, as is the creamy seafood chowder.

The dinner menu is not quite as inventive with steaks, seafood, and pasta, plus some vegetarian dishes. There is also a special area set aside for a romantic dinner on the beach. There are only three tables for two, with two sittings per night: 6pm and 8:50pm. The romantic dinner includes complimentary wine or champagne and three courses with appealing choices; the service charge is included in the package.

MATTHEW'S BEACHSIDE RESTAURANT

Casa Del Mar Resort had seen a number of places come and go in this charming spot by the sea. With Matthew's Beachside Restaurant (J. E. Irausquin Blvd. 51, 297/588-7300, www. matthews-aruba.com, 7:30am-10pm daily, $28-45, all you can eat ribs $23, private beach dinner for two $150) it is a win-win situation. Owner Stefan Legger and his wife Milca built their reputation with the very popular Rumba, in town, but decided to move to the beach. Loyal patrons rave about the food, staff, and that very appealing sea view.

The restaurant features a nice, but fairly standard, à la carte menu. Emphasis is on grilled shellfish, snapper, grouper, and various sizes and cuts of steak. Their specialty nights are the real attractions. All-you-can-eat spare ribs special on Tuesday is a big draw, with reservations recommended. Thursday is the Italian menu with lots of pasta dishes but also ossobuco for those who want something less basic. On Wednesday nights they liven up the Manchebo area with their wild and crazy (and we are not exaggerating) karaoke with happy hour prices until around midnight. You will be amazed at the people you see cutting loose, considering the usual clientele of the area. (Dancing on the bar top is not unheard of.)

Matthew's does special private dinners for two on the beach, which include a complimentary bottle of champagne. These should be arranged well in advance.

TORTUGA BAR & GRILL

Timeshare owners at Aruba Beach Club swear by Tortuga Bar & Grill (Pool Deck of the Aruba Beach Club, 297/582-3000, 11am-11pm daily, 2-for-1 Happy Hour 4pm-6pm daily, $15-23) for their lunch menu of standard favorites: hotdogs, burgers, and such, with special touches and ample portions. The main restaurant is on a deck overlooking the beach, but they also have shaded tables around the Aruba Beach Club (ABC) pool deck. The hotel provides mellow, live entertainment during the evening happy hour. The "drink of the day" is two for one throughout the whole day.

When ABC owners want a casual dinner and don't feel like traveling, they readily choose Tortuga Bar & Grill. It receives raves about the excellent seafood risotto: a huge portion filled with shrimp, scallops, fish, squid, and mussels, in a tomato base.

Caribbean Fusion
◖ CARTE BLANCHE

Within eight months of opening their doors in 2010, chef Dennis, the driving force behind Carte Blanche (within Bucuti & Tara Beach resort, L. G. Smith Blvd. 55B, 297/586-3339, http://carteblanchearuba.com, 7pm-11pm Tues.-Sat., $69) saw his innovative restaurant shoot to number one on Internet review sites. Together with his partner, Glenn Bonset, they attained the rarified designation with a perfect

score from over 100 reviewers. All reviewers insist the meal was one of the best they've ever had, anywhere, and worth whatever they paid.

Patrons are seated at a U-shaped counter, allowing them to chat with Dennis and Glenn as they prepare their meal and beverages. Dennis is the sort of cook who keeps pots of herb plants by the stove to pluck and crush fresh into the pot. Recipes can be adapted to fit any dietary needs (low fat, food allergies, no sugar) and substitutes are possible, if necessary. Be sure to call ahead to check the menu and inform them if you have food issues.

The five-course Chef's Surprise is a prix fixe menu, without wine pairing or cocktails. Carte Blanche also offers an à la carte menu. Both menus are fluid, changing with the season and by the day.

Reservations should be made at least 2-3 months in advance via the form on their website. Guests are required to confirm when they arrive on Aruba, or the restaurant will take someone on standby. During high season (Dec.-Apr.), they are booked up to four or five months in advance. The cozy restaurant relocated from Palm Beach to the Bucuti at the beginning of 2013.

THE FRENCH STEAKHOUSE

One of Aruba's most famous, upscale restaurants, The French Steakhouse (J. E. Irausquin Blvd. 55, 297/582-3444, www.manchebo.com, 5:30pm-10:30pm daily, $28-33, prix fixe $35), was opened by legendary hotelier and restaurateur Ike Cohen. After almost five decades, the restaurant maintains a loyal clientele who enjoy the company of a congenial waitstaff, many who have worked there almost as long as the place has been open. This doesn't mean that they are old, but that they were trained to provide the ultimate in courtesy and service, a remainder from times gone by.

Ike is gone, and chefs come and go, but the restaurant has maintained its standards, a charming garden atmosphere, and moderate pricing. Chef George Hoek, a regional culinary icon, now rules the kitchen. Classic dishes such as rack of lamb, giant T-bone steak, fresh fish, and shrimp scampi are the fare. They offer what they call a five-course menu, which is still very nice despite coffee or tea being considered a course. It does include an appetizer, soup or salad, main course, and dessert with choices such as surf and turf with a lobster tail, which is excellent. Mellow nightly entertainment on the piano provides just the right touch.

MULLIGAN'S
The lower level of The Links's clubhouse is home to Mulligan's (J. E. Irausquin Blvd. 93, 297/523-5017, www.mulligansaruba.com, 6:30am-1am daily, $6.50-28), an open-air eatery with a spectacular panorama of the golf course and surroundings. This is a more casual golfer's lounge, with very early breakfast served before the first tee time of the day. The lunch and dinner menu is reasonable; sandwiches, burgers, and pizza all have a gourmet touch. Baguettes are priced equally to most local Dutch sandwich houses. The stone-oven pizza menu has some very interesting and original recipes. Try the Asian pizza with duck and cilantro-ginger sauce or a shawarma pizza with ground lamb, for something really different.

WINDOWS ON ARUBA
Elegantly prepared food in elegant Louis XIV decor is the trademark of Windows on Aruba (J. E. Irausquin Blvd. 93, top floor of the Divi Links Clubhouse, 297/523-5017, www.windowsonaruba.com, noon-2:30pm and 6pm-10:30pm Mon.-Sat., 10:30am-2pm Sun., $28-56, Sun. brunch $42.50), with an absolutely breathtaking view. A great local jazz trio or guitarist Ivan Jansen entertain three nights a week.

One of their most popular offerings is the gourmet Sunday brunch with unlimited mimosas or champagne. Each dish is plated and made fresh. They offer an endless choice of items, such as crêpes suzette, escargot, scallops, duck breast, and smoked salmon omelets.

The regular menu focuses on fine dining. Standard items like fresh grouper, prime steaks, and lobster tail are prepared with flair. It is one of the few venues to offer classic chateaubriand

for two, a dish that is not readily available at most restaurants. To truly appreciate the restaurant's atmosphere and assets, go for an early dinner to catch the sunset.

Italian
ELLIOTI'S
The area has two connected Italian restaurants, outside of the all-inclusive resorts, with dual personalities but the same owners. Ellioti's (J. E. Irausquin Blvd. 59, 297/593-6919, 6pm-10pm Mon.-Sat.) is more elegant with a spacious, air-conditioned dining room, though most patrons prefer the outdoor deck. They are conveniently located at the juncture of the Costa Linda and Bucuti Resorts, an easy stroll from all the hotels.

For years, executive chef Jeffrey Elliot was the sous-chef of one of Aruba's most famous but now defunct Italian restaurants, Valentino's. He gets high marks from reviewers for his shrimp fra diablo and pasta sauces. Owner Adrianna is a lover of fine food, particularly Italian, and a most congenial host. Dedicated patrons are enthusiastic about the preparation, personable staff, and the pleasant ambiance of the terrace.

PIZZA BOB'S PUB
The Bucuti side of the Ellioti's restaurant complex houses Pizza Bob's Pub (J. E. Irausquin Blvd. 59, 297/588-9046, 11am-10pm daily, $17-25), which is more of a congenial hangout than just a restaurant. Pizza Bob's has a tiny dining room (nice for lunch in the heat of the day), but the action is at the outdoor patio and bar, with a giant screen for sports events. Local singers provide mellow music nightly.

Popular for their thin-crust pizza, Pizza Bob's offers some restaurant specials as well as build-your-own options. A wee bit pricier than most island pizza joints, they do offer an early bird special 5pm-7pm, when they charge the 12-inch pizza price for a 14-inch pizza. The greatest asset of both Ellioti's and Pizza Bob's is their convenience to the low-rise resorts, and in a relatively quiet area, they provide nighttime entertainment.

FOOD

Palm Beach, Malmok, and Noord

The question in Palm Beach is not "where will we find a nice place to eat?" but more, "how can we choose from the scores of options?" According to various review sites there are 86 listed restaurants within these limited borders. New eateries are opening regularly, and consequently a number are closing; it is almost like the turnover in New York City.

The main strip, J. E. Irausquin Boulevard, is packed with restaurants and shopping malls, which also contain several places to dine. It is a bustling center of neon and bright lights. Fusion and Italian cuisine tend to dominate. Not far inland, away from the heavily populated thoroughfare, are some very interesting places, with more tranquil and genuine island ambiance.

ARUBAN
◖ THE OLD CUNUCU HOUSE

Housed in a landmark colonial farmhouse dating back over 150 years, The Old Cunucu House (Palm Beach 150, 297/586-1666, www.theoldcunucuhouse.com, 11am-11pm daily, $8-26) is a charming bit of authentic Aruba. The menu features traditional island dishes along with elegant and very reasonably priced international favorites. The indoor dining room maintains the simple decor of an old time Aruban home, while the outside terrace is surrounded by charming gardens.

It is located in a cul-de-sac at the end of a side road off the Noord-Palm Beach Road. The tranquility of the spot and the picturesque surroundings give the impression of being transported back in time, away from the hustle and

steak with island sides (*funchi* and banana *hasa*) at The Old Cunucu House

© ROSALIE KLEIN

FOOD

SERVICE CHARGE

First time travelers beyond U.S. borders will likely be puzzled by the extra 10-15 percent service charge tacked on to their check, particularly if the waiter tells them emphatically that it is not a tip. In most cases, this is at least partially true; the servers usually do not receive the full amount. Most restaurants keep 7-10 percent of the service charge to cover breakage and laundering. They rarely keep it all, but that may be the case (though they wouldn't keep employees for long, if so).

The remainder is divided among all the restaurant staff including the kitchen help and maître 'd. This usually works by a point system, with the "higher ups" getting the lion's share. The lowly but conscientious bus person, who worked so hard to clear your plates and keep the water glasses filled, doesn't see much of it.

For restaurant patrons who are unaccus-tomed to an added service charge, be aware that this is a common practice in Europe, Latin America, and other parts of the world. Some island eateries have eliminated it as a draw for customers. If you are bothered by it, check websites and menus, they will usually state clearly if they add on a service charge, or ask before making reservations or being seated.

A good rule of thumb: If you have had highly satisfactory, friendly service, leave anywhere from half the service charge or more to reward their diligence. This too will go into a pot (or is supposed to) to be divided by the staff at the end of the night. Your individual servers still don't get it all, but most likely they are being paid minimum wage and depend highly on gratuities, so it will be appreciated.

This should also be kept in mind for tour guides, boat crews, and other employees of vacation activities and services.

---

bustle of the tourist scene. There is little to be heard but the rustling of the trees as you dine alfresco on the terrace.

Typical fare such as conch and *keshi yena* (filled cheese shell) and side dishes of *pan bati* (pancake), banana *hasa* (plaintains) and *funchi* (Aruban polenta) are their specialty. The fresh catch of the day, served a variety of ways including "Aruban Style," with Creole sauce, is outstanding, as is the succulent rack of lamb rosemary. They also have an appetizer plate meant to be shared, with ample samplings of several favorite Aruban snacks: *pastechi* (fried pastry), calamari, fish cake, and meatballs.

SNACKY'S

A tiny kiosk on the sidewalk outside of Paseo Herencia Mall is Snacky's (297/745-5787, 10am-10pm daily, $1-10), right next door to Le Creperie. This is the place for Aruban and regional light meals. Though there are few things heavier or more filling than an *arepa con queso*, the Venezuelan standby for breakfast and lunch. It consists of a cornmeal bun that is fried, then cut open and filled with cheese, ham, or shredded stewed meat or chicken; one of these will fill you up completely.

At Snacky's you will find typical local snack fare, such as *pastechis* (fried pastries), *cachapas* (corn pancakes), and croquettes. They are the only place in Palm Beach selling *saco*. This is Aruba's favorite late-night nibble: a paper bag with a mix of two meats (chicken, ribs, pork chop, or chorizo) plus Johnny cake (a fried flour bun), a big chunk of fried potato, and fried plantain. This is considered the ultimate island treat, with heavy emphasis on the cholesterol content. Consider it a tasty bit of insight in the Aruban diet, which you can balance out with fresh fruit shakes, called *batidos*. These are a refreshing local favorite and healthy. Snacky's is an inexpensive oasis of authentic regional food in Palm Beach.

ASIAN
DIFFERENT

Fans of authentic Chinese cuisine dine at Different (Palm Beach 29, 297/586-6134,

FOOD

11am-11pm Fri.-Wed., $6.25-16), the favorite dining spot of Aruba's more discerning expatriate Chinese population. Most cite it to be the best Asian spot on the island. It is very traditional; tables are outfitted with Lazy Susans for passing around the family-style portions. Different has surprising and enchanting surroundings. It was originally a French restaurant, built in the style of a rustic French farmhouse with gardens.

The à la carte menu is very reasonable. They also offer a very large selection on a special takeout menu, with at least 25 choices served as Arubans like it, with rice and fries, all uniformly budget priced.

It's an easy walk from all the resorts. Head up the Palm Beach Road and turn right at the second street after the Sasaki Highway; you can see their sign from the corner.

WOK AWAY

Wok Away (South Beach Center, 297/586-1099, 11:30am-midnight Sun.-Thurs., 11:30am-3am Fri.-Sat., $12) is a very cute little place, great for late night munchies. They invite patrons to "Wok In" and "build your meal"—tasty stir-fry dishes prepared to your exact specifications. This European-based franchise is not that well known, but the food is inexpensive and delicious.

Various steps allow patrons to choose their base, meats, or seafood. Choices affect final cost and, of course, flavor. Finally, patrons select from seven different sauces with mild choices, such as black bean or oyster, sweet curry, and coco, to super spicy bun-yo-tong. Everything is cooked before your eyes in the open kitchen and served in a typical takeout box. There is a small terrace with just a few tables to eat on site, and they will provide plates on request.

No corn starch or MSG is used; the sauce is not thick or sticky. Veggies are crisp and fresh. They also have some regular specials, a surf 'n turf stir-fry and the *mai-doo-dee,* consisting of chicken, shrimp, broccoli, and corn with noodles, plus a discounted Box of the Day. It is nice to know there is a place for late-night eating

that serves something other than greasy, fried foods, which is unusual in Aruba.

BARBECUE
HOLLYWOOD SMOKEHOUSE

After originally opening in San Nicolas, Hollywood Smokehouse (Noord 19-A, 297/733-3650, 7pm-10pm Wed. only, $7-21) had droves of people heading to the other side of Aruba for their "low and slow" smoked brisket, ribs, chicken, and pulled pork. Now they are conveniently located close to resort areas in Palm Beach. Take the Palm Beach-Noord Road to the Santa Ana Church.

The menu is takeout only. JC's Sports Bar is next door, where you can pick up some cheap, cold beers. The huge portions in the platters can be ordered solo or in combination and are more than enough food for two. Platters are served with three kinds of BBQ sauce, all very spicy. Pulled pork and brisket are also available as sandwiches. This is perhaps the only restaurant on Aruba serving beef brisket; if you miss your family's pot roast, try this excellent, tender, smoked version.

NEW WEI TAI

When passing New Wei Tai (Palm Beach 4, 297/586-8864, 11:30am-10pm Sun., $8) on the Palm Beach-Noord Road, any Sunday, you will see islanders lined up for their weekly BBQ special. Huge portions of either ribs or chicken or a combo of the two are piled on an enormous heap of fried rice in takeaway containers, to be consumed on the beach. If you're not given enough BBQ sauce, ask them to put on a bit more.

Most customers usually get their food to go, but you can also have it plated to eat in their air-conditioned dining room for a nominal extra charge.

BEACHSIDE DINING

Well aware that a fantasy of most couples is to dine along the shore at sunset, every resort in Palm Beach has some sort of eatery fashioned to fully exploit this romantic setting. All have open-air casual restaurants along the stretch of boardwalk running the length of the strip, so guests need only put on a little beach cover (or not) during the day. Menus are typical lunch and snack-bar fare: hamburgers, hot dogs, Caesar salads, chicken strips, with the occasional fillip of gourmet crab cakes or quesadillas, depending on the star rating of the resort. Most usually have a kids' menu and several take orders and deliver lunch to your beach lounge chair.

For dinnertime they switch to more elaborate and diverse menus. A few also set up tables right along the water's edge for a "toes in the sand" experience. These are very popular and reservations for the high-demand sunset hours should be made well in advance. Seating is usually quite limited and at a set hour (but not always) coordinated to sunset. Some offer a prix fixe three- or four-course meal.

A few resorts have the option of arranging a private dinner for two. Enjoy a dedicated waitstaff in a more secluded area of the beach for the most romantic experience imaginable. It is perfect for a marriage proposal or a special occasion (like being in Aruba). The arrangement should be made with the concierge immediately upon arrival or in advance by email.

AZULL
The Westin Resort sets up only eight tables at the water's edge for their Azull restaurant (J. E. Irausquin Blvd. 77, 297/586-4466, www.westinaruba.com, 6:15pm daily, $53 pp), one of the most reasonably priced of the beach eateries. Reservations should be made well in advance. The prix fixe meal includes a choice of soup or salad, one of six entrées (including a filet mignon and lobster tail surf and turf for an extra $10), and the house dessert, a triple chocolate concoction, plus one glass of wine. They take your appetizer and entrée selections when making reservations, for speedier service.

For landlubbers, there is a steak choice or chicken breast, but the emphasis here is seafood and local fish, with a choice of grouper, snapper, or the fresh catch of the day.

BUGALOE
At the end of the De Palm Pier is Bugaloe (J. E. Irausquin Blvd. 79, 297/586-2233, www.bugaloe.com, 8am-midnight daily, $8.50-25), an extremely popular dinner and night spot with tourists and locals. Whether you are seeking coffee and light breakfast, lunch, dinner, or late-night snacking, you will find that the view and ambiance are unmatched. The lively, friendly service make returning patrons feel like friends.

Cheeseburgers and snacks are available all day and night; main courses are mostly seafood and fish. "Crazy Mondays" is when the chef has returned from the docks with fresh fish, and the special is a good-size whole snapper at a bargain price.

FOOTPRINTS
The Hyatt Regency Resort converts their patch of beach into a restaurant called Footprints (J. E. Irausquin Blvd. 77, 297/586-1234, www.aruba.hyatt.com, 6:30pm-10pm Fri.-Wed., $72 pp), which also features a prix fixe menu. They offer a four-course menu, with 3-5 choices per course. The Hyatt chefs are particularly inventive and attentive in designing their menus. The resort's culinary department partnered with island growers to feature freshly harvested local ingredients in their dishes and established an herb garden on the hotel's grounds. There is a real effort to elevate the quality and variety of the menus and to inject an authentic touch of Aruban cuisine and offer more than standard hotel fare.

Emphasis is again on fresh, local fish, either blackened, Cajun style, or seared with stir-fry fresh vegetables. The menu also has a seafood pepper pot with shrimp, scallops, mussels, clams, and Aruban *funchi* (the standard island accompaniment to seafood, similar to Italian polenta). Dessert choices are very tempting: passion fruit crème brûlée, coconut mousse cake, or chocolate cake with fresh berries and fruit compote.

Only five tables are available and reservations are recommended well in advance.

FOOD

PRIVATE BEACHSIDE DINING IN PALM BEACH

For true romantics, a private dinner for two on a remote corner of the beach can be arranged at a few of the larger resorts. These usually include a choice of preset menus with a range of prices. Additional amenities, such as private photographers, flower arrangements, and personal musicians are available. This is the dream setting for a marriage proposal or just a special evening for eternal honeymooners. Main course choices usually include a surf and turf with lobster tail, rack of lamb, or fresh fish dish. Menus are fairly standard from one resort to the next.

Radisson calls their private affair **Dinner by Torchlight** (J.E. Irausquin Blvd. 77, 297/586-0844, www.radisson.com, $65 pp). This includes a welcome drink and a three-course meal. While there is no additional set up fee, there is a 15 percent service charge and 1.5 percent sales tax added.

Hyatt Regency wants to see you **Pampered in Paradise** (J.E. Irausquin Blvd. 85, 297/586-1234, www.aruba.hyatt.com, $80 pp) under a private palapa. They serve a four-course meal, including appetizer, soup, or salad, a choice from six gourmet main courses, and dessert. There is a 17 percent service charge for the personal waitstaff and an additional $50 setup and breakdown fee for the private arrangement.

Marriott Resort (L. G. Smith Blvd. 101, 297/586-9000, www.marriott.com, $95-135 pp without drinks) offers three different menus. The $95 meal has four courses, and the others, for $115 or $135, serve five courses. Although, you could debate whether champagne sorbet is a course. They charge a $25 setup fee and an additional service charge of 18 percent. These dinners require a dedicated service staff, so resorts usually limit it to one or two tables nightly. It is strongly advised to arrange such a special evening via email before arriving on Aruba, or check the hotel concierge for availability when you arrive. Seating times are at your convenience.

PELICAN NEST

At the north end of the beach, between the Playa Linda and Holiday Inn is the Pelican Nest (Pelican Pier, 297/586-2259, www.pelican-aruba.com, 11am-11pm Tues.-Sun., $19.50-35), featuring an open seafood grill for healthy dining. Their ceviche (fresh fish and sometimes shrimp marinated in lime juice with onions, often cilantro, and seasonings) is rated by some as the best on the island. The restaurant generally gets low marks on service, but the location is so pretty, you might just want to order another glass of wine and enjoy it... Maybe that is why the service is slow?

PURE OCEAN

Formally the Sunset Beach Bistro, Pure Ocean (J. E. Irausquin Blvd. 75, 297/586-6066, www.sunsetbeachbistro.com, 7am-11am and 5pm-11pm daily, $17.50-38), at the Divi Phoenix Resort, is famous as the first restaurant in Palm Beach to offer dining right at the water's edge.

There are a limited number of tables just at the shoreline, but ample seating elsewhere on the beach and in the open-air dining room, a covered terrace looking out on the sea. Reserve well in advance for a shore-side table.

A long-time standby with veteran visitors for more than 15 years, the restaurant reopened in early 2013 with a refreshed menu of fusion cuisine. Fresh local fish is the focus. The fish is grilled, with Aruban Creole sauce, and served on a bed of couscous, or it comes with coconut curry sauce. For landlubbers, there are plain steaks and a sprinkling of Italian dishes, such as osso buco, chicken saltimbocca, and rigatoni and meatballs.

SIMPLY FISH

At the far northern end of Palm Beach, at the Marriott Resort, is Simply Fish (L. G. Smith Blvd. 101, 297/520-6600, www.marriott.com, 6:30pm-10:30pm daily, $31-55), a venue that offers an à la carte menu as opposed to prix fixe.

This is one of the most expensive of the beachfront eateries, with a menu leaning largely to standard offerings from northern waters, such as tuna, sea bass, and halibut, not fresh local Caribbean fish. Lobster tail, on its own or paired with filet mignon is typical of the menu. The surroundings are lovely and they have a very friendly, accommodating staff.

CARIBBEAN FUSION

◖ AMUSE BISTRO

For elegant gourmet dining in Palm Beach, few restaurants can match Amuse Bistro (J. E. Irausquin Blvd. 87, 297/586-9949, www.amusearuba.com, 5:30pm-10:30pm daily, $22.50-28.50) for creative cooking and value. Patrick is a classically-trained chef with an impressive résumé. His attention to detail and stringent standards of preparation is evident in the quality of the food; he even churns his own, very rich, ice cream. Dishes are made to order, so be prepared for a leisurely meal. Despite this, devoted fans report dining here several times during their one-week stay.

The restaurant is attractively laid out in the arcade of shops and eateries that front Playa Linda Resort. Dining is alfresco and there are some cozy couches for romantic dinners. One unique and practical amenity is the option to order main courses full size or a half plate as an appetizer, and vice versa. It allows diners to have more of what they consider a good thing, or try a bit of this and that. A "half plate" is $10 less than a regular main course price.

Grilled scallops with ginger sauce and the goat cheese salad are highly recommended. Be sure to save room for dessert, as the pineapple carpaccio with cinnamon ice cream is to die for. The basic menu is rotated three times a year to offer variety in addition to the daily specials.

BARNEY'S

Those who like discovering a comfortable neighborhood hangout for a mature crowd, while at the same time a fun place for families, will really enjoy Barney's (Palm Beach 21A, 297/586-5420, www.barneysaruba.com, 5pm-10pm Tues.-Sat., $9.50-29.50). Owners Ron and Elina have a very congenial division of labor: He loves being bartender while she sees to it that everyone is well satisfied with their meal. Patrons praise their spicy firecracker shrimp and mushrooms stuffed with escargot. They offer a diverse menu, and chef Hans has a deft touch in the kitchen. Try the smoked trout filet for a real gourmet treat.

Four nights a week, the place is busy with their themed specials: Tuesday is Schnitzel Night, with a choice of chicken or pork schnitzel prepared any of five ways; Wednesday is grouper prepared any of five ways; Thursday features unlimited ribs; and Saturday is rib eye steak.

TASTE OF BELGIUM

Popular with fashionable islanders, Taste of Belgium (L. G. Smith Blvd. 95, Palm Beach Plaza, www.tasteofbelgium.aw, 297/586-6288, 7am-1am daily, $7.50-32) sports contemporary decor while exuding Old World charm. The center of the restaurant is the fireplace lounge, where friends gather for conversation, wine, and snacks or Italian lattes and pastries.

They offer a choice of Belgian continental, full English, or full American breakfasts, including fresh-squeezed orange juice. European baguettes and wraps are typical lunch fare, while the extensive dinner menu has a distinctly Belgian touch. Choices range from vegetarian herbed pasta to *slibtong* in *citroenboter* (sole meunière). Main courses are always accompanied by their famous *frites,* the best fries you will ever have, made a special, secret way. Some come just to order the fries, with a choice of all sorts of sauces; they're perfect with some Belgian beer.

They partner with the mall's cinemas to offer a three-course dinner and movie package, which can be enjoyed before or after the film.

TWO FOOLS AND A BULL

Described as a "gourmet studio," Two Fools and a Bull (Palm Beach 17, 297/586-7177, www.2foolsandabull.com, 7pm-11pm daily, $80), with its partners Fred Wanders and Paul Faas (aka Pablo Diablo), has taken a page from the Carte Blanche playbook. The menu is closer to standard French, but with fresh local ingredients.

A beautifully renovated classic landmark house is only a short distance up the Palm Beach-Noord Road from the highway. It provides an intimate environment for the curving counter surrounding the chef and host. With only 16 patrons at a seating, everyone is made to feel like a guest, rather than a customer. Start the night with a welcome drink and a "meet and greet." If you didn't come for dinner with some friends, by the end of the evening you will have a room full.

Like Carte Blanche, there is a flat rate for the five-course meal. The menu changes daily with their whims and what is fresh. A typical meal could include as appetizers terrine of fois gras, veal with apples and pickles, rouleaux of Cornish hen stuffed with sweetbreads, seafood symphony with lobster sauce, to name only a few. Chef Fred made the name of some of Aruba's top gourmet kitchens and has a wide repertoire. The main course is always three meat cuts grilled on the fire wall. A gourmet dessert concludes this delightfully decadent meal.

Suggested wine pairings for each course are posted. Two Fools is earning rave reviews and, after less than a year, has become the number two rated restaurant on Aruba.

VENTANAS DEL MAR

For almost 20 years, Ventanas Del Mar (Tierra Del Sol Country Club and Golf Course, Caya de Solo 10, 297/586-7800, www.tierradelsol. com, 7am-10pm daily, $24-38) has been considered the epitome of gourmet dining in elegant surroundings. Chef Jim Roosman has a well respected reputation. There is seating indoors or out among stunning surroundings, with an elegant dining room and terrace overlooking the gorgeous Tierra Del Sol pool deck and rolling fairways. The magnificent vistas stretching all the way to Aruba's northwest point prompted the restaurant's name, Windows on the Sea. They are famous for their corn and crab chowder (served in a fresh-baked bread bowl), which is a meal by itself. Other popular menu items are steak, red snapper, Portobello mushroom pizza, and spinach fettuccini with roasted vegetables.

FRENCH
LE CREPERIE

Gourmet treats and breakfast can be had at this tiny kiosk (on the sidewalk fronting Paseo Herencia Mall, 8:30am-1pm and 5:30pm-10:30pm daily, $3 and up) across from the Playa Linda Resort. Le Creperie offers an inexpensive alternative to resort coffee shops. Giant, made-to-order crepes, sweet or savory, are the fare. You can order them filled with berries, whip cream, or ice cream and syrups, or with melted cheese, mushrooms, ham, or other assorted fillings to make it a meal.

The basic crepe comes with powdered sugar and charges extra for each filling. The "Por Moi" house special includes three toppings, savory or sweet. They also have mochaccino and French vanilla coffee. There are a few little tables and chairs on the sidewalk to sip, sup, and watch the world; it's very European.

INDIAN
TANDOOR INDIAN GRILL HOUSE

A contribution from another expatriate group on Aruba is Tandoor Indian Grill House (South Beach Center, 297/586-0944, www. tandooraruba.com, 6pm-10:30pm Mon.-Fri., noon-3pm and 6pm-10:30pm Sat.-Sun., $16-21, weekend lunch buffet $20), the place for authentic East Indian cuisine. Dishes are prepared in a tandoor, a cylindrical clay oven, for characteristic taste and tenderness. Overall, the food is very reasonably priced.

The lunch buffet on Saturdays and Sundays provides an excellent opportunity to sample a variety of flavors and textures. The assortment includes curried shrimp, chicken, chick peas, tandoori chicken, saffron vermicelli, and a batch of vegetarian dishes along with a very simple salad bar. It is worth trying every dish to understand the range and appeal of Indian cooking.

The regular menu is extensive, a dozen

different ways of preparing lamb, chicken, or fish, offered in degrees of spiciness from extremely mild to murderously hot. The buffet is generally on the mild side. It can be spiced up with some green chili sauce and other garnishes on the salad bar, which will make you sweat. Sample the purple *ras golla* (cottage cheese balls cooked in sugar syrup) for dessert. They are very sweet, an interesting surprise and they put out the fire.

ITALIAN

Palm Beach hosts a staggering number of Italian restaurants for such a small area. Local restaurateurs are quite convinced that vacationers from the United States can't survive a week without at least one Italian dinner and are consistently proven correct, so they offer plenty of options.

Ten Italian restaurants are located within the malls on J. E. Irausquin Boulevard or adjacent, with more in the resorts. Most are uniformly overpriced for pasta and carry the standard Italian dishes on their menus. Some feature a unique, regional pasta specialty prepared for two or more: A sauce, incorporating vodka, tomato sauce, and seasoning, is tossed and flamed with the pasta, inside a giant Parmesan cheese imported from Italy. This is done at your table and is quite a show.

ANNA MARIA'S

Authentic southern Italian cuisine prepared with enthusiasm is the fare at Anna Maria's (Kamay 25-M, 297/586-2833, aranopas@hotmail.com, 6pm-10pm Mon.-Sat., $16-36), a labor of love by chefs and owners, Anna Maria and her husband Christian. He is native-born Aruban, with Sicilian grandparents, and describes his wife as "pure Napolitano."

Sharing their enthusiasm for "Italiano Autentico" cuisine became an enterprise after first feeding friends. It started with just a few tables on the charming back patio of their impressive home. In a few years it has grown to include accommodating waitstaff and a continually expanding menu.

Hot and cold appetizers include a tasty *chupe*

de camarones, a Peruvian shrimp chowder, reflecting Christian's direct parentage. Main courses are based mostly on pasta dishes, starting with fettuccini alfredo to linguini al frutti di mare (mixed seafood). Everything is made to order, so patrons relax and enjoy the surroundings while waiting for their food. You can also watch the hosts puttering around in their kitchen.

Anna Maria's is located in a residential area off the Avenida Frans Figaroa, heading north past the commercial area around the Santa Ana Church. Turn left just before Ng's market and they are a short distance down the road.

CAFÉ BACI

Within the Westin Resort is Café Baci (J. E. Irausquin Blvd. 77, 297/586-4466, www.westinaruba.com, 5:30pm-11:30pm Fri.-Wed., $12-29), which is one of the most reasonably-priced Italian restaurants for a fine-dining ambiance and a quality menu. Chef Sabastiano, direct from Sicily, is in the kitchen churning out his authentic specialties.

Among a varied menu is the special pasta in a Parmesan wheel, perfect with a very nice, "antipasto freddi," also for two. For the kids there is a selection of pizzas and pastas, which are moderately priced.

LA VISTA

If you have super-hearty eaters and a taste for buffets, La Vista (Marriott Resort, L. G. Smith Blvd. 101, 297/520-6601, 5:30pm-10:30pm daily, $40-55) offers an Italian dinner that is an excellent value for the amount of food offered. While it may seem that $40 is high for a buffet, by comparing the quality of cuisine and standard prices at most Italian restaurants on Aruba, this is a good value, with no service charge added. Wednesdays and Saturdays cost more because they include unlimited baked, whole Caribbean lobsters.

The selection includes a pasta station, pizza station, varied antipasto bar, and a representation of meat, fish, and poultry among the main courses. The method of preparation and side dishes depends on the theme of the

FOOD

night (Tuscany, northern Italian, or southern Italian style). The pasta station offers freshly tossed linguini de mare with a plentiful mix of mussels, clams, scallops, salmon, calamari, and shrimp (you can specify exactly what you want). Häagen-Dazs ice cream at the sundae station of the dessert bar is an example of the attention to quality in everything they offer.

Expect casual dining and very clean surroundings. They also have a terrace adjacent to the beach, and walls of windows for watching the sunset. The restaurant is known for its special holiday and Sunday buffet brunches, and they offer an à la carte menu. One drawback: drinks are rather overpriced, even non-alcoholic drinks.

SEAFOOD
WACKY WAHOO'S

Great fresh fish and a feeling of visiting with friends has made Wacky Wahoo's (Palm Beach 33B, 297/586-7333, http://wackywahoo.com, 5:30pm-10pm Mon.-Sat., $22-28.50) a top-rated restaurant on Aruba. Chef and owner Harald is a good friend to all the fisherfolk and an enthusiastic fisherman. This guarantees fresh fish on the table every day for his customers. A best bet in Palm Beach for fish lovers, the main course is usually caught that morning and on your plate the same day.

Harald was a master chef-in-training with Cunard Lines when he met lovely Arubiana Roxy while he was exploring Aruba during shore leave. Both the charms of the lady and Aruba brought him back. He established the reputations of a number of island restaurants before finally opening his own place, the Hadicurari Center. It became a very popular hangout on the beach for tourists and local anglers.

Circumstances brought him to their present location and now Roxy greets customers with a warm smile and loves to be creative at the bar. The restaurant is located about a 15-minute walk inland on the Noord-Palm Beach Road.

The catch of the day might be two or three different kinds of fish listed on a chalkboard, served a choice of five different ways. Wacky Wahoo's is about fish and seafood, and Harald

has devised some very interesting and diverse recipes for preparing shrimp and conch. Good quality steak and duck with very tasty sauces are options for landlubbers. They also have some really tempting desserts; try the fresh baked brownies. The dining room has limited space and reservations are strongly recommended.

STEAKHOUSES

Palm Beach has two Brazilian *churrascarias* (steakhouses with a twist) dedicated to the art of meat cooked on an open fire. Both also offer unbelievable salad bars to make any vegetarian happy. Each restaurant provides some means to control the service, with a gadget that displays a "red light" or "green light." Once you have indicated you are finished with the salad bar and are ready for the main course, congenial waiters visit your table in a continual stream offering various cuts of beef, chicken, pork, and lamb, cooked and served on giant swords. Diners give the nod or say "No" as they please. This will continue endlessly until you say "uncle."

If you wish, this can be a long evening of leisurely dining, taking a breather with a red light to rest your tummy, then continue again. Dessert is not included, but who has room? The cost is nearly what most Aruban steakhouses charge for only a main course, so if you are really hungry and like variety, either place is a great deal and the meal is always good.

There is not much difference in the main courses between the two. They have filet mignon with or without bacon, sirloin and other beef cuts, leg of lamb, chicken breasts and legs, chorizo, and pork ribs; in total, there are about 15 different choices of meat and poultry.

AMAZONIA

The first restaurant to successfully introduce Brazilian *rodízio* (steakhouse) to Aruba, Amazonia (J. E. Irausquin Blvd. 374, 297/586-4444, www.amazonia-aruba.com, 6pm-11pm Mon.-Sat., 4pm-11pm Sun., $45, $27.50 for salad bar only) has rustic charm with indoor and outdoor terrace tables and superb sangria. They certainly sport the most expansive salad bar with 52 quality items. It is easy to fill up on grilled portobello mushrooms, sushi, superb ceviche (when they have it, which is not always), soup de jour, you name it. It is hard to leave room for all the meat to come. A particularly nice touch is the whole grilled pineapple on a sword, thinly sliced like the meats; it's a great way to clear the palate.

Amazonia expanded their menu to take advantage of sharing a kitchen with Aqua Grill seafood restaurant: They added fresh fish to the menu, carved at the table. They wish to please everyone in large groups where some may not be meat eaters. On really busy days such as Sundays and holidays, however, they will not have fish; it is too difficult to serve with all the traffic.

The staff makes a big fuss for birthdays and anniversaries, so it is a nice choice for a special meal, particularly for the kids. Desserts are not included, but birthday boys and girls get one on the house.

TEXAS DE BRAZIL

Equally appealing for meat devotees is Texas de Brazil (J. E. Irausquin Blvd. 382, 297/586-4686, www.texasdebrazil.com, 6pm-10:30pm Mon.-Sat., 5pm-10:30pm Sun., $45, $25 for salad bar only). Though its salad bar is slightly smaller than Amazonia's, it has distinctive hot dishes such as seafood thermador and saffron rice, which are good alternatives to the parade of meats. Everything is quite tasty and satisfying, with some original and unique marinated salad items and a delicious seafood chowder.

Located on the second level of La Hacienda Mall, it also has an elegant cocktail lounge on one side with a lovely view. The dining room is across the way, divided by an open-air courtyard. Between the two restaurants, one might notice the beef at Texas de Brazil appears to be marginally more tender then their competition, but the chef can be a bit heavy-handed with the salt at times.

North Coast

In the north beyond the hotel area are two restaurants known for their spectacular settings and views. Restaurant owners have done their best to provide exceptional surroundings to take full advantage of the locations. For romantic sunset dinners these are favorites with many, and it is suggested to make reservations days in advance for that particularly popular time of day. There are also some surprises just a little inland, nestled within the exclusive residential communities.

CARIBBEAN FUSION
SAVANNAH LODGE

A great place to stop and relax during a day of touring, Savannah Lodge (Matividiri 57, 297/585-9630, www.arubaostrichfarm. com, 11am-4pm Mon.-Fri., 9am-4pm Sun., $3.50-22.75) at the Ostrich Farm has a charming, rustic terrace, with fabulous views of the north coast. The menu offers a wide variety of dishes, including burgers and chicken for those who find the idea of ostrich too exotic, or are a bit squeamish after just having cooed over a baby bird. There is also a nice choice of vegetarian dishes, which might also be appealing after a tour. Try the pumpkin soup, a very-filling local specialty; pepper steak; or simple snacks, like a croquette sandwich. Living up to their name, they offer some moderately priced minced beef and chicken dishes with interesting African flavors.

The ostrich meat dishes are pricey, as it is an expensive commodity. They do not serve the inhabitants of the farm but feel they should have it on the menu. Ostrich is almost indistinguishable from fine steak, but has the lowest cholesterol content of any meat or poultry you can consume, even less than chicken or turkey breast.

FOOD

ITALIAN
LA TRATTORIA EL FARO BLANCO
Right on top of the mount of the California Lighthouse is "The White Lighthouse," La Trattoria El Faro Blanco (California Lighthouse Z/N, 297/586-0786, www.aruba-latrattoria.com, 11am-3pm and 6pm-11pm daily, mini menu 3pm-6pm daily, $16-48), a misnomer for those who understand the true meaning of trattoria, as it is anything but. An utterly delightful arrangement of open-air terraces look out on the remarkable vista of the entire northwestern shore of Aruba. One can see off to nearly Oranjestad and far inland. The staff is extremely congenial and there are mixed reviews on the food, from excellent to mediocre and overpriced, but the location and atmosphere are unmatched.

Santa Cruz, Paradera, and Piedra Plat

While touring in Aruba's outback, a number of small, local snack shops can be found or a surprising quantity of international fast food franchises for a quick lunch. They usually feature an abundance of fried foods, stews, and BBQ with fries and rice, and some lettuce and tomato passing for a salad, but they are quite inexpensive and offer great value for the money. More important sights, such as Arikok National Park, Natural Bridge, and Casabari Rock Formation, have places that sell a cold drink and a *pastechi* (fried pastry) or sandwich.

ARUBAN
URATAKA CENTER
Located on the road to Arikok National Park, Urataka Center (Urataka 12, 597/585-5212, 11am-4pm daily, $2-14) is a popular, local hangout. They tout that they serve "the best pizza," but that is because pizzerias are rare for that area.

The real gems on their menu are local favorites. This is a good place to try island standards off the grill, such as a chicken wing "basket," a heaping helping of crispy, flash-fried wings without breading, or BBQ ribs. More substantial platters are pork chops or grilled chicken "a la plancha," served on a wooden plank, which is less expensive than pizza.

Urataka is a local hangout, replete with pool table and domino tables for tournaments. It gets busy on the weekends. It is a good place to stop for a cold beer and an authentic slice of island life.

CAFÉS
ARIKOK PARK COFFEE SHOP
After hiking around the park for a couple of hours, you will find that the simple fare on the terrace of the Arikok Park Coffee Shop (visitor center, main entrance Arikok National Park, 297/585-5200, 8am-4pm daily, $1.50-2.50) tastes just about right. It is a tiny little place offering local snacks, *pastechis* (fried pastries), croquettes, hotdogs, and tuna sandwiches. The seating on the deck, where you can relax with a light meal, provides an absolutely gorgeous view of the park.

HUCHADA
One of Aruba's favorite stops for fresh breads, cakes, and snacks is Huchada (Santa Cruz 328, 297/585-8302, 6am-8pm Mon.-Sat., $3-4). The specialty is stuffed sandwiches on a choice of fresh baked rolls, often still warm from the oven. The basics include ham and cheese and tuna salad, with some interesting combinations. Try one or two items from their great assortment of cakes, pastries, and cookies, boxed up to take back to the room. Essentially a bakery, Huchada has a few tables to sit and take a break.

NATURAL BRIDGE
"THIRST AID" STATION
Relaxing a moment at the "Thirst Aid" Station (9am-4pm daily, $3-6) at the Natural Bridge is nearly an island tradition. For decades, it

has provided hot and parched tour passengers with a greatly needed pit stop (fee $0.25) and reasonably-priced cold drinks, snacks, and *batidos* (fruit shakes). Sandwiches, *pastechis,* and *loempia* (egg rolls) are priced the same as most local snack shops.

San Nicolas, Savaneta, and Pos Chiquito

Aruba's eastern and south shore has yet to be greatly developed for tourism, though it has much potential, and it will come. Most places to dine are aimed and priced to islanders (with some notable exceptions) and will be very busy with a local crowd around lunchtime or on weekends.

CARIBBEAN FUSION

B-55

This terraced restaurant (Balashi 55, 297/585-2111, b55-aruba@yahoo.com, 10:30am-10pm daily, $16.80-22.50) on a hill boasts a spectacular vista of Aruba's south side and midlands. B-55 gets rave reviews from those who have stumbled upon it in their travels, giving it a "5 out of 5" rating. It's ideally located to be breezy and comfortable; you won't feel bothered by insects or tropical heat, even at the lunch hour.

Popular with islanders, it is known for good food and a very diverse menu, with excellent daily specials. Recommended choices are the "famous seafood soup" and the BBQ combo; portions are very generous. Dinners come loaded with side dishes, and fresh fish is served in a choice of seven intriguing styles. The wine list, sold by the bottle, is exceptionally reasonable.

CHARLIE'S BAR

No trip to San Nicolas is complete without a stop at the legendary Charlie's Bar (B v/d Veen Zeppenfeldstraat 56, 297/584-5806, http://charliesbararuba.com, 11:30am-9:30pm Sun.-Thurs., 11:30am-10pm Fri.-Sat., $16-30), if only for a glimpse of the highly idiosyncratic decor. It features possibly the largest collection of miscellaneous memorabilia squeezed into one spot, even the bathroom walls are filled with curiosities and original art.

Charlie's has always been famous for their generous portions of fresh shrimp, steamed or scampi, and steak sandwiches. Dishes are served with their "Honeymoon Sauce" by chef Rosalba, which they also sell by the jar.

The bar is named for its founder, the late Charlie Brouns II, an island character if there ever was one. He left an indelible mark on San Nicolas and its people, and his son keeps his memory alive in this famous local hangout, where tourists are always warmly welcomed.

COSTA RIBA

Kamini Kurvink is an expatriate from Trinidad who has realized her dream by taking over Costa Riba (Christoffelbergweg 9, San Nicolas, 297/564-2303, noon-9pm Sun.-Thurs., noon-11pm Fri.-Sat., $10.25-20), an interesting place that can't be missed on the way to The Colony and Baby Beach. The menu is diverse and regional with East Indian elements that reflect her background. The menu's artwork also reflects Kamini's good nature and philosophy; pages are filled with humorous homilies about the pleasures of fine food and drink.

A varied menu leans heavily toward seafood dishes, many of them curried. Kamini prepares excellent whole fresh snapper. For a touch of the exotic, check out the *cabrito* (goat) stew wrapped in Indian flatbread or other roti, which come with pumpkin, *chana* (an Indian chick pea garnish), and curried potato.

Kamini has been the chef-proprietor since 2011 and her enthusiasm lends a decidedly personal touch. She has garnered a dedicated following who particularly appreciate her warm,

FOOD

welcoming presence in addition to what have been described as "the best chicken wings EVAH!"

FLYING FISHBONE

If searching for the most romantic dining experience possible, Flying Fishbone (Savaneta 344, 297/584-2906, www.flyingfishbone.com, 5pm-11pm daily, $29-42.50) is a top choice for many visitors to Aruba. The restaurant was the first to establish the toes-in-the-sand concept, and it has the perfect secluded cove to make it work.

The menu has a nice diversity, from refreshing gazpacho and shrimp tempura to gourmet seafood and prime steaks. They have a delectable lobster thermador. Everything is beautifully presented and delicious, though portions tend to be small.

Sunset is considered the optimal time to fully experience the locale; reservations are recommended well ahead for that time slot. One drawback, cab fare from major hotel areas is almost the price of a dinner, and actually the same as a compact car rental for the day. If planning to rent a car, take advantage of having the transport and reserve that night for an out-of-the-way place like Flying Fishbone. It isn't hard to find, just keep following the road that runs along the water.

GENERAL STORE CAFÉ

This pleasant eatery (Savaneta 225E, 297/584-1189, 10:30am-2:30pm Mon.-Sat., $7.80-8.50) behind the hardware and home center of the same name will surprise first-time visitors. General Store Café was originally an independent eatery set up with a stylish, homey interior. The hardware store took it over to provide a congenial lunch place for its employees, but they welcome the public. Many come from around the neighborhood to enjoy the ambiance and take advantage of the bargain menu.

Food service is cafeteria style, with everything served in large takeaway foam containers. The menu is posted at the beginning of the week with menu items changing daily: Each day they offer a choice of four new main courses and a soup. Choices can be anything from fresh wahoo with white wine, beef or vegetable lasagna, or breaded shrimp. Every day there is some sort of *stoba,* a dish that is authentically Aruban. All main courses are served with mashed potatoes, vegetables, and plantains. If it's too heavy on the carbohydrates, they will gladly substitute more steamed vegetables.

Cold options include attractive, creative salads, wraps, and hero sandwiches. The staff is extremely friendly and accommodating. It is a very nice place to relax and get out of the heat after a long morning of touring.

The hardware store is on the highway, bordered by a dirt road. Turn inland at that road and find the restaurant directly behind.

RUM REEF BAR

An absolutely adorable outdoor restaurant adjacent to Jad's Dive Center, Rum Reef Bar (Seroe Colorado, 297/584-2569, 11:30am-6pm daily, $4-16) is neatly sandwiched between Baby Beach and Roger's Beach. The menu is simple: sandwiches, hamburgers, hotdogs, platters of chicken wings, and sate or grouper Aruban style, with Creole sauce. They make a nice, well-packed snack platter with calamari, hotdogs, chicken wings and nuggets, some coconut shrimp, meatballs, and fries and onion rings, meant to serve three or four while downing some cold beers. It gets very busy on the weekends with the local trade.

SEAFOOD
◖ MARINA PIRATA

One of Aruba's original "local" fish restaurants, Marina Pirata (Spaanslagoenweg 4, Pos Chiquito, 297/585-7150, 6pm-10pm daily, $31-40) offers that dining-on-a-fishing-dock charm, with a bit more elegance. Twinkling lights and hurricane lamps have prompted patrons to describe the atmosphere as "magical." A long-time favorite of veteran visitors, it is famed for its fresh fish and prompt, amiable service. This is where they brought Gloria Estefan for dinner when she wanted to eat somewhere "authentic."

Kids love feeding the fish that come right up to the dock in large schools, attracted to underwater lights.

They have a half dozen ways to sample the fresh catch of the day. It is a great place for whole red snapper and fresh Caribbean lobster. The signature dish is the Spaans Lagoen special, a seafood mix. It is prepared à la *coquille St. Jacques* in a creamy sauce ringed with cheese-crusted mashed potatoes.

Driving to Marina Pirata can be confusing because the road seems to end at nothing. The restaurant is right on the water, out of sight, down some steps leading to the water. It is clearly marked with an archway and sign, but you can't see the proper entrance from street level.

◖ ZEEROVER

Fish fanatics and shrimp lovers cannot miss a meal at Zeerover (Savaneta 270, 297/592-9080, 11:30am-8pm daily, kitchen closed Mon. but bar is open, $15). Since it's located right on a dock where a number of fishing boats are moored, don't be surprised to see your meal carried in fresh while you wait to order. Patrons stand on line at one window to order fish and a second window to order drinks.

The menu is simple: whatever fish is on hand and fresh shrimp. The attendant taking your order will show you what they have, and you pick out the fish filet, steak, or whole fish of your choice: It could be grouper, wahoo, marlin, or snapper. Shrimp can be medium or huge, or a bit of both. The selection is then weighed and tallied.

Pick out a table, either in the shade of the terrace or out on the dock. Enjoy a cold beer, and, somehow, miraculously, no matter how busy they are, the servers find you and deliver your order, fresh and hot. Everything is combined in a single basket, family style, with some plastic plates and forks (some regulars bring their own silverware). Most end up eating with their fingers, so sinks with soap and towels are distributed around the restaurant. There is always one conveniently close by.

© ROSALIE KLEIN

waterfront dining at Zeerover

Fish and shrimp are flash-fried; there is no other option for preparation. It is consistently excellent and fresh. Try the papaya pica that they will offer to bring to the table. It is a locally-produced relish that is very spicy, just a little goes a long way, but really enhances the fish.

It's popular mostly as a lunch place. Dinner is a hit-and-miss proposition: Food is served only as long as fresh fish is available. It is not unheard of for them to close the kitchen by 5pm because they have run out of fish. Even with dinner reservations, it is advised to call and confirm.

On an island of elegant restaurants, Zeerover is an authentic Caribbean fish shack, though quite a bit more comfortable and elaborate. Popular with the seafaring crowd, it's mobbed on Sundays and the wait to order can be an hour or more. Service is fine once the order is in, but choose a weekday if you don't care to stand on line for so long.

ENTERTAINMENT AND EVENTS

Whether you are a music, art, or food aficionado, enthusiastic athlete, sailor, sports spectator, fashionista, or celebrity-watcher, Aruba has something exceptional for everyone. Top Latin, jazz, soul, and classic rock groups, including superstars such as Marc Anthony, Chaka Khan, Alicia Keyes, and Crosby, Stills, and Nash, can all be found in concert at Aruba's many fine venues, and at ticket prices much lower than in the United States. Free shows are featured at most busy entertainment centers nightly and scores of special events associated with national holidays and weekly festivals amuse and enlighten while sharing traditional island culture with visitors.

It is safe for visitors to roam around principal tourist areas at night in search of amusement. Oranjestad and Palm Beach are the hubs for lounges, discos, and free entertainment. Well-lit and bustling shopping malls contain elegant or casual family eateries, late-night lounges, and stages where free shows are performed nightly. Most are set up to provide such entertainment while dining. Several shops and souvenir kiosks are open during the evening hours as well.

Almost all the large hotels have in-house casinos and cozy lounges or sport bars for relaxing and socializing after dinner. All-inclusive resorts feature organized, live entertainment nightly. Though visitors need not venture from their major resort to find entertainment, they will miss out on one of Aruba's most appealing attributes, what some dub an "all-inclusive island." Unlike many resort destinations, where vacationers often stay within the confines of

© ROSALIE KLEIN

HIGHLIGHTS

LOOK FOR (TO FIND RECOMMENDED ENTERTAINMENT AND EVENTS.

(**Fusion Wine and Piano Bar:** Elegant and chic, Fusion is a place for a discerning crowd to relax and savor fine wines paired with gourmet tapas (page 133).

(**Bugaloe:** With an authentic island atmosphere, Bugaloe is a favorite with all ages. Located out on the water, Bugaloe features great bands, and the dance floor is always filled (page 134).

(**Señor Frog's:** This Mexican restaurant by day converts to a singles' club with a sense of fun late at night. It remains one of the best places on Aruba for young people to connect (page 136).

(**Carnival:** The Carnival celebration rules Aruba from the first Saturday after New Year's Day until Ash Wednesday, with a seemingly endless lineup of parades, musical events, beauty pageants, and themed street parties (page 140).

(**Himno y Bandera Day and International Half Marathon:** Aruba's National Day, March 18, encompasses elegant protocol events, a joyous celebration of national identity and pride, and a half marathon (page 141).

(**May Day:** Imagine the camp of the Royal Dutch Marines turned into a theme park for the day (page 142)!

(**Soul Beach Music Festival:** Top R&B singers and big-name comedians converge on Aruba for Memorial Day weekend, with five days of concerts, media events, and parties (page 142).

(**Aruba Hi-Winds Pro-Am:** For over 25 years Aruba has been hosting the renowned Pro-Am windsurfing and kitesurfing competitions in the world (page 143).

(**Caribbean Sea Jazz Festival:** Columbus Day is a time for interpretive music under the stars. Local and international jazz, innovative art, and gourmet food are all served up at bargain prices (page 144).

(**New Year's Eve:** Island-wide pyrotechnics start the new year with the biggest bang heard anywhere (page 145).

their all-inclusive resorts, particularly at night, on Aruba tourists easily mix and mingle with local residents who equally enjoy the many amenities of the more populated tourist areas.

Oranjestad is the epicenter of the majority of special events on Aruba. The biggest Carnival parades, national holiday celebrations, conventions, conferences, sporting events, and most concerts are here. The beginning months of the year are filled with a seemingly unending parade of Carnival events, but Aruba really begins to "heat up" with the advent of late spring-early summer and fall with exciting events like the Soul Beach Music Festival, Caribbean Sea Jazz Festival, and sporting events such as the Aruba International Regatta and the Aruba International Pro-Am Golf Tournament. Aruba's physical attributes attract world-class athletes from around the globe to such events as the Aruba Hi-Winds Pro-Am windsurfing and kitesurfing competition in July and the International Beach Tennis Tournament in November. These are exciting days for both participants and spectators.

Nightlife

Palm Beach is a bustling center of clubs, restaurants, shows, and late-night shopping, making it easy and convenient for vacationers to enjoy an evening out. Every sort of nighttime activity is just a short stroll from any resort. Visitors staying in Oranjestad and Manchebo Beach will find convenient casinos and clubs, with most nightlife focused around the major resorts and the casinos in their area.

ORANJESTAD

Most of Oranjestad generally tends to quiet down at night, except for the few blocks along L.G. Boulevard surrounding the harbor. The Renaissance Marketplace, right on the water, is always lively with musical performers at the waterside bandstand nightly. Many of the clubs within the mall arrange their own entertainment. Outside the mall, several venues that are cozy eateries during the day turn into hot nightspots until all hours once the dinner hour is over. Most clubs line the harbor, providing lovely views and a distinct island feel.

CAFÉ CHAOS

One of Oranjestad's most popular nightspots, Café Chaos (L. G. Smith Blvd. 60, 297/588-7547, 5pm-1am Mon.-Thurs., 5pm-3am Fri.-Sat., happy hour 10pm-11pm Sat., no cover charge) has a cozy, European pub ambiance: all dark wood paneling, humorous signs, and good cold beer on draft. It is located across from Wilhelmina Park.

Café Chaos has that ability to morph from a quiet place early in the evening to a busy, raucous hangout as the night wears on. Weekends feature some of the island's top bands on their small stage. The crowd often overflows out onto to the sidewalk after the midnight hour.

CAFÉ THE PLAZA

A favorite spot to enjoy free musical performances nightly is Café The Plaza (Seaport Marketplace, 297/583-8826, www.

cafetheplaza.com, 8am-1am daily, no cover charge), a very popular hangout with most of Aruba's Dutch community. The restaurant is open for breakfast, lunch, and dinner until midnight; tables are usually pretty well filled inside and out from the lunch hour on. Patrons particularly enjoy the outdoor terrace for drinks and platters of typical Dutch snacks such as *bitterballen* or *frikendel*. This congenial spot is perfect for lingering while listening to great bands on the Renaissance Marketplace stage.

CILO CITY LOUNGE

A chic and relaxed place for a quiet drink by the harbor is Cilo City Lounge (Seaport Marketplace, 297/588-7996, www.cilo-aruba.com, 7am-1am daily) on the L. G. Smith side of the Renaissance Marketplace. It is a popular after work "meet and greet" spot for island movers and shakers, as it is located directly across from Parliament. They have live performers nightly 7pm-10pm.

GRAND CAFÉ TROPICAL

Grand Café Tropical (Seaport Marketplace, 297/582-8577, www.grandcafetropical.com, 4pm-1am Mon.-Thurs., 4pm-2am Fri.-Sat., happy hour 4pm-7pm daily, no cover charge) is a cute and cozy club where patrons are welcomed by friendly owner Evert. The bar's comfy neighborhood ambiance encourages participation in Karaoke Wednesdays and dancing to live music on weekends on the tiny dance floor. Seating is principally on the outside terrace, with a nice view of the harbor. The daily happy hour features fancy martinis for $3.

JIMMY'S PLACE

Though they just consider their establishment "a typical Dutch bar," Jimmy's Place (Windstraat 17, 297/582-2550, www.jimmys-aruba.com, 5pm-2am Mon.-Thurs., 5pm-4am Fri.-Sat., 8pm-2am Sun., no cover charge) has become the island's unofficial upscale gay and

PARTY BUSES

When looking for a happening nighttime hotspot, you want the scene to be fun and busy. However, Aruba's club crowd works during the week and usually saves their partying for Friday and Saturday nights. Commonly, locals hit the clubs following some other event or after a night shift, so places don't begin to fill up until late.

For vacationers, every night can be considered a party night, and one of the best ways to guarantee the atmosphere you seek is to sign up for one of the *paranda* tours, or party buses. Wherever you go on a party bus, you bring the party with you. They also remove the concern of locating an obscure, out-of-the-way local club or recklessly driving under the influence. Wildly painted buses pick up guests at their hotel and safely drop them back afterwards. This removes much of the anxiety of "going local" in an unknown land, while assuring a fun time.

Party buses boast congenial hosts and drivers, who are there to lend to the hilarity. The hosts are well practiced at getting the party started. One tour option is to leave earlier in the evening to enjoy a champagne toast on a secluded beach at sunset; dinner at a local restaurant follows. The rest of the evening is spent at picturesque local bars, with a drink included at each stop. More drinks can be purchased at special prices, usually only a dollar or two. Another option is to dine on your own with a pickup time later in the evening; this option is popularly known as a "Pub Crawl" and only includes the bar-hopping portion of the tour.

Two of the longest running and most respected *paranda* tours are the **Kokoo Kunuku** (Noord 28 P, 297/586-2010, www.kukookunuku.com, 6pm-midnight Mon.-Sat., $65, with dinner, Pub Krawl 9pm-12:30am Mon.-Sat., $40) and the **Banana Bus** (SchubertStraat #10, 297/593-0757, www.bananabusaruba.com, Tues.-Thurs., Pub Crawl $45 pp).

lesbian hangout. The crowd is usually a 50-50 mix of straight and gay. The polished wood tables and the lovely rear gardens are very pleasant and homey here. This spot is the most fun on the weekends when there is a live DJ. Like most of Aruba's clubs, things pick up late at night after locals get off of their shift at the resorts and restaurants.

LOCAL STORE

Oranjestad's hot spot for the younger crowd is Local Store (Weststraat 4D, 297/583-8339, 10am-1am daily, no cover charge), located above Nobel Jewelers, across from the Royal Plaza Mall. Taking advantage of the location, the club is entirely open, with a funky interior design and a giant terrace overlooking the town. Prices are geared to locals and they have early evening happy hours with cheap beer.

The club presents live music on weekends, with local bands specializing in the Caribbean sound. Expect lots of reggae music, trance, house, and reggaeton. On Mondays they offer a beer bucket and wings special while giant screens broadcast the football game.

MANCHEBO BEACH AND EAGLE BEACH

The preponderance of timeshare and condominium resorts with family clientele has kept this area relatively quiet at night. The Alhambra Casino complex, which reopened in 2012 after a complete makeover, is the center for most of the nighttime excitement. It is within easy walking distance of almost all the Manchebo Beach resorts. Free tram service to and from the center to the more distant Tamarijn or Dutch Village runs until all hours of the night. For the cluster of resorts farther north on Eagle Beach, the casinos at the Tropicana and La Cabana Resorts provide most of the entertainment.

BUSTER'S GARAGE

Fans of Buster's Garage (L. G. Smith Blvd., 297/660-4251, busterssportsaruba@aol.com,

© ROSALIE KLEIN

Alhambra Casino at Manchebo Beach, one of 12 casinos on the island

7:30am-1am Sun.-Thurs., 7:30am-2am Fri.-Sat., no cover charge) were very happy to hear they reopened at a new location, inside the Tropicana Casino. Owner Rusty is known for his hospitality and personal touch. The atmosphere has always been that of the neighborhood bar, where everyone comes to watch the big game.

They maintain three separate satellite feeds and promise, "if there is a game taking place anywhere, we'll find it." Two giant projectors and 16 plasma screens are strategically placed to catch the action from anywhere in the bar. Gaming tables nearby fill in during halftimes; try beer pong, the drinking game that keeps guests happy, win or lose. The menu offers typical bar food, including one of the biggest plates of cheesy nachos anywhere.

The dining room is detached enough from the casino that families can feel comfortable about coming with the kids for dinner. There are even video games and air hockey to keep them busy. On Wednesdays, Thursdays, and Fridays there is live music after 8pm.

◖ FUSION WINE AND PIANO BAR

A sophisticated upscale local clientele has made Fusion Wine and Piano Bar (Alhambra Shopping Bazaar, 297/280-9994, 6pm-1am Mon.-Thurs. and Sun., 6pm-2am Fri.-Sat., no cover charge) their favorite place to while away the late-night hours. They offer an extensive wine cellar and gourmet tapas menu, with live music on weekends. There are front and back open areas to enjoy the balmy Aruban evenings, along with excellent and attentive service, comfy lounges, and an elegant, tasteful ambiance.

PALM BEACH, MALMOK, AND NOORD

Unquestionably, Palm Beach is Aruba's center for nighttime excitement. It offers a wealth of evening activities, mostly within the many large malls that line J. E. Irausquin Boulevard. There are several eateries that segue into appealing cafés and popular gathering places as the night wears on. Many feature live musical

ENTERTAINMENT

© ROSALIE KLEIN

Dance the night away and learn salsa at Bugaloe or Grand Café Tropical.

performances for free. Shopping is also a prime after-dinner activity, with scores of stores and kiosks around the area offering their wares until 10pm or later.

BRICKELL BAY SAND BEACH LOUNGE
Aruba's newest and chicest open-air night club is the Brickell Bay Sand Beach Lounge (J. E. Irausquin Blvd. 370, 297/280-9967, www. arubasandbar.com, 11am-1am Sun.-Thurs., 11am-3am Fri.-Sat., no cover charge, over 21 only), right on the main Noord-Palm Beach Road bisecting J. E. Irausquin Boulevard. For those who love the shore, the beach bar feeling has been transplanted to this convenient location.

The club features a VIP section with dedicated waitstaff and a stage for live music surrounded by a dance floor. Every Sunday features live entertainment during the happy hour (4pm-7pm) with special prices on all drinks, including premium brands. Wednesdays is "Ladies Night Out" with $5 champagne

cocktails and 2-for-1 mojitos (8pm-9pm). Generally nice prices on exotic, frozen cocktails are part of the regular menu.

The light menu has typical bar food done with an elegant touch. Other amenities include two pro-sized beach tennis courts, plenty of plasma screens for catching PPV sporting events, and access to the Brickell Bay Resort pool deck, which raises this nightclub above the usual Palm Beach offering.

◖ BUGALOE
This charming eatery (Water end of the De Palm Pier, 297/586-2233, www.bugaloe.com, 9am-midnight daily, no cover charge) recommended for breakfast, lunch, and dinner turns into one of Aruba's favorite nightspots after the dinner hour. A diverse, all-ages crowd enjoys the casual atmosphere of the pier, which provides that authentic island feeling. This spot never gets steamy, smoky, or hot as you are always bathed by the trade winds. There are great live bands on Tuesdays, Wednesdays, and on the weekends, plus free salsa lessons on Wednesday nights. The music and mood is friendly and welcoming, with the dance floor filled with jolly people most of the night.

CONFESSIONS
For twenty-somethings, the hip place to be is Confessions Disco Club (J. E. Irausquin Blvd. 81, 297/586-6676, www.confessionnightclub. com, 8pm-1am Wed.-Thurs., and Sun., 9pm-3am Fri.-Sat., $6 Fri.-Sat., no cover charge Wed.-Thurs. and Sun.). This is a full-fledged disco with decor that harkens back to the days of "Saturday Night Fever"; it's a place to put on that glittery dress and spiky heels.

Confessions is tucked away behind Daniel's Steakhouse in the Gianni's Garden complex, across from the Radisson Resort. It gets busy earlier in the evening than most clubs and will fill up well before midnight.

Each night has a defining theme: Wednesday is Ladies Night with free wine and martinis until 10pm; Thursday is Gentlemen's Night with exotic dancers and beer for a $1; Friday is Latin Night (no freebies); Saturday is Crossover,

CASINOS

Aruba boasts 12 casinos. Palm Beach resorts host seven busy gaming rooms. These are within easy walking distance of each other. Manchebo Beach resorts have the **Alhambra Casino** and Shopping Bazaar, only minutes from their doors; Eagle Beach has the homey **Tropicana Casino** and **Glitz Casino** in **La Cabana Resort.** Oranjestad is serviced by Crystal and Seaport Casinos, which are part of the Renaissance resort.

All of these casinos tout a player's club with a VIP card that costs nothing to obtain, and an immediate reward of a $10 play coupon. Using the card when playing slots and table games puts credits on the member's account. Points can be redeemed for logo items, or many resorts will give credit towards dinners in their restaurants. Other services, such as spas and extra nights in the resorts, are also awarded for points. Membership also allows winnings to stay credited to an account, allowing vacationers to keep their winning safe until they are ready to leave the island.

The **Westin, Radisson, Occidental,** and **Holiday Inn Resorts** have dedicated poker rooms, where tournaments of Texas Hold 'Em are conducted nightly. Other Palm Beach Resorts with casinos are the **Marriott Hotel** proper, **Hyatt Regency,** and **Riu Palace.** All have standard table games: craps, roulette, and blackjack, as well as hundreds of slot machines accepting various levels of bets, from a penny to hundreds of dollars. The Crystal Casino has a special bank of slots that award a brand new car when hitting the big jackpot. The casino gives away around six cars a year. The casinos also host special tournaments sporadically through the week in slots and blackjack. It is best to check with the casino in your resort, as schedules change regularly. There are often special international tournaments, particularly around holidays.

Crystal and Seaport Casinos (www.arubacrystalcasinos.com) are located right by Oranjestad Harbor. Crystal is the only casino on Aruba open 24 hours a day, to date. The Seaport Casino offers an elaborate sports book gallery, with real-time broadcasting of races

and sporting events. Most casinos also host some afternoon **bingo,** which is very big with the locals; a small investment can reap a modicum of rewards. Bingo may not be for high rollers, usually populated with grandparents and retirees, but it provides a congenial break from the afternoon heat, with door prizes, drinks, and snacks.

Aruba is also known for **Caribbean Stud Poker,** where you play against the house with progressive jackpots, based on the returns from all the tables. This unique game has resulted in the surprisingly frequent big winner, sometimes well over $50,000 or $100,000. Aruba levies no taxes on winnings, but one can only transport a max of $10,000 cash when traveling. Island casinos will provide the service of keeping the money in an account for regularly returning visitors. Such wins are sometimes credited with an increase in timeshare and jewelry sales because as the saying goes, "you can't take it with you!" Well you can, with some clever planning and cooperation from many friends, depending on the size of the win.

© ROSALIE KLEIN

Seaport Casino has a beautiful vew of Oranjestad Harbor.

with celebrity DJs; and Sunday is 2-for-1 drinks with Salsa music. The club often hosts special events, sometimes with an internationally renowned visiting DJ. There is always a substantial entrance fee when they do.

DREAM BOWL

For some after-dinner family fun, Dream Bowl (L. G. Smith Blvd. 95, 297/586-0809, www. dreambowlaruba.com, 4pm-11pm Sun.-Thurs., 4pm-midnight Fri.-Sat., lanes $35/hr, up to 6 shoe rentals included) in the Palm Beach Plaza Mall offers bowling jazzed up with a stylish, modern decor. The hall is all black lights and neon-glow colors, right down to the bowling balls, for a new twist on a favorite family pastime.

Aside from six lanes there are pool and foosball tables, air hockey stations, and a complete arcade to keep young hands and minds engaged. It also sports a pizza bar, if you are in the mood for a nice, casual evening and an informal meal.

GARI & WASABI

Though actually a sushi restaurant, Gari & Wasabi (Palm Beach 6-D, 297/586-0078, www.gariandwasabi.com, 5pm-2am daily, no cover charge) is most appreciated as a "meet and eat" by its clientele. Very stylish art deco surroundings are prefect for healthy snacks along with exotic martinis. Most patrons stay on well after a late dinner or gather here after some fashionable evening event. Regular events such as ladies' night and happy hour with $1 sushi rolls and $4 mojitos and sangria attract island fashionistas. Continually changing specials are posted on their Facebook page.

GUSTO

Islanders in their mid-twenties flock to Gusto (The Village Mall, 6pm-1am Mon.-Thurs. and Sun., 6pm-3am Fri.-Sat., happy hour 9pm-11pm daily, no cover charge) directly across from Señor Frog's in The Village Mall. It is a cozy bar with a chic, casual atmosphere; dress up or down as you please.

There is a nightly happy hour with all drinks half price. Check their Facebook page for themed events on weekends with local or international celebrity DJs. The music varies between all genres of popular music, from trance, house, and hip-hop to salsa and meringue. There is no entrance fee, except for special events.

MOOMBA BEACH BAR & RESTAURANT

The distinctive and funky beachfront MooMba Beach Bar & Restaurant (J. E. Irausquin Blvd. 230, 297/586-5365, http://moombabeach.com, 8am-1am daily, happy hour 6pm-7pm daily), wedged between the Holiday Inn and Marriott Surf Club, holds a singular position for nightlife in Palm Beach as one of the most popular places for young people to connect; though it attracts all ages. On the weekends it is filled with families enjoying the beach and restaurant, as well as guests from smaller resorts who have an arrangement with MooMba to use their beach.

Its bar and outdoor lounge area embody the fantasy of island life and leisure. It is popular at all hours for events, beach tennis, and great bands on the weekends. The main bar is always busy at happy hour and well into the night. It is surrounded by shops that are open until 10pm.

◖ SEÑOR FROG'S

The Aruban outlet of the famous Señor Frog's (J. E. Irausquin Blvd. 348 A, 297/586-8900, www.senorfrogs.com, noon-1am Mon.-Thurs., noon-3am Fri.-Sat., 5pm-1am Sun., no cover charge) dominates The Village Mall. It is still one of the best places to go wild along with dinner or late night Mexican snacks. Everyone wants to go home with their signature souvenir YARD, the super tall glasses that you get to keep when you order the 28-ounce drink and then pay less for refills.

This is most definitely a young person's place for late-night fun, though it's popular with families for lunch and dinner, when the atmosphere is decidedly different. After 10pm it changes gears to become a nightspot of calculated craziness, and most definitely not a family place. For example: Spring Break Bikini

© ROSALIE KLEIN

Señor Frog's

Contest for the late crowd. It starts at midnight, with all girls dressed only in bikinis getting free shots. As you might assume, much drunken naughtiness ensues.

SKY LOUNGE
The ultra-modern seating of this open-air club (Paseo Herencia Shopping Mall, 297/583-3159, 5pm-2am daily, no cover charge) surrounds the deep pool in Paseo Herencia with comfortable curved and glowing stools on an artificially-made beach. Anywhere is a perfect setting for a quiet tête-à-tête while gazing at a star-filled sky. It's very romantic. The space age-styled bar has giant screens for catching sporting events for a different ambiance.

SOPRANOS PIANO BAR
Located at the south end of Arawak Gardens, Sopranos Piano Bar (J. E. Irausquin Blvd. 370, 297/586-9944, www.sopranospianobar. com, 5pm-2am Mon.-Thurs., 5pm-4am Fri.-Sun., two-drink minimum) features excellent local entertainers with the occasional imported

entertainer that performs for a month or so. There is a request and tips jar; the latter is required to attain the former. This is an after-dinner drinks and cigars place with cozy booths on the terrace and a very atmospheric interior. Named and styled after the famous TV show, it has a mixed crowd. The patrons set the pace, as requests and music create the mood, from mellow to swinging.

SOUTH BEACH LOUNGE
Aruba's pretty people like South Beach Lounge (Palm Beach 55, 297/586-6766, 6pm-1am daily) and Yalla Yalla, their kitchen that serves Middle Eastern meals. Here one can puff exotic tobaccos from a real hooka water pipe while snacking on equally authentic Middle Eastern "fast food," the literal translation of *yalla yalla*.

The stylish and contemporary open-air deck features various seating arrangements to suit the mood. Take a high stool around the bar to watch a sporting event or sprawl on lounge chairs. Special DJ sessions are scheduled on the weekends. The crowd is eclectic, from young people on vacation to a more mature crowd of resident fashionistas, depending on the evening's event.

ZOMBIE ROOM

Zombie Room (Palm Beach, 297/741-7045, 5pm-1am Sun.-Thurs., 5pm-3am Fri.-Sat., no cover charge) at Ratland is self-described as a tiki bar. The music and style is rockabilly, with good bands on the weekends. Combined with a retail store and tattoo parlor, the fashion is totally vintage and retro chic. Have enough to drink and you might walk out with some new ink.

The Ratland building name comes from the fleet of unusual vehicles on display at the front of the shop. A "rat" is a funky, jerry-rigged construct, consisting of chopped up parts of other cars or motorcycles. Local enthusiasts and store owners call themselves "The Rats." The shop is the continuance of the famous Underground Cycles, the center for Ed Hardy on Aruba.

Shows and Concert Venues

Aruba's primary concert venues are the Aruba Entertainment Center and Cas di Cultura, both on the western outskirts of Oranjestad. Scattered around the island are several sports arenas and community centers, which commonly host large concerts with imported and local talent.

The wider beaches are often deployed for concerts, most frequently, Nikky Beach, which annually hosts the Soul Beach Music Festival. Concerts on Aruba are not about staying planted in your seat; rather, they're about socializing, dancing, and grooving to the music. Ample refreshment booths encourage a party atmosphere.

ARAWAK GARDENS

Enjoy dinner theater at no extra cost when dining at one of the five restaurants at Arawak Gardens (J. E. Irausquin Blvd. 370, no phone, 7pm-10pm daily, no cover charge), just across from the Occidental Resort. Singers and musicians entertain, and all restaurants have outdoor terraces surrounding the gazebo where they perform. The music is usually mellow: classic rock, golden oldies, and show tunes. Visitors can dine at Salt & Pepper (Dutch-Continental cuisine and tapas), Fishes N' More (Seafood), Tango Argentine Grill (Steakhouse), and even a Burger King, with island ambiance.

CAS DI CULTURA

Aruba's Cas di Cultura (Vondellaan 2, Oranjestad, 297/582-1010, www.casdicultura. aw) is the performing arts center where classical musical concerts, dance recitals, plays, and myriad other events are staged. It has a 400-room auditorium that hosts local and imported talent.

The theater is flanked by the Rufo Wever School of Music and the Da Vinci Piano School, both of which frequently conduct concerts in the auditorium. Annual events that call the Cas di Cultura home are **Aruba Piano Festival** (www.arubapianofestival.com). It features renowned classical musicians from around the world.

The Cas di Cultura also has an exposition room where smaller events are conducted, and art or educational exhibits are displayed.

At Aruba's "House of Culture" performances are usually dedicated to classical, jazz, and island music and dance. The center has no house orchestra, and programs are entirely dependent on whichever group is renting the auditorium. There are usually shows every Friday and Saturday night, and often during the week. Upcoming performances are posted on their website.

PASEO HERENCIA SHOPPING MALL

Great for all ages is *Waltzing Waters,* a sound, water, and light show in the Paseo Herencia

© ROSALIE KLEIN

free live entertainment at the Paseo Herencia Shopping Mall

Shopping Mall (J. E. Irausquin Blvd. 382-A, 297/586-6533, http://paseoherencia.com, 7:30, 8:30, 9:30, and 10:30pm daily). The mall also features numerous special events during the year on national and international holidays. Every Monday they host a free cultural show beginning at 8pm and on Thursdays they feature the *Cirque Aruba* show, a fantasy program of tumblers and clowns.

The mall also runs a horsedrawn carriage, which will take people back to their hotel at the end of the evening; a ride along the boulevard is $30 for 25 minutes. Shetland pony rides for kids around the mall are $5 for about 5 minutes.

Festivals and Events

Within one week of the start of the New Year, Aruba begins a long calendar of special events, punctuated by ebullient parties. Weeks of Carnival happenings heat up the winter months beyond the tropical temperatures. The "low season-slow season" months are enlivened by numerous festivals, international sports competitions, and concerts to attract visitors with diverse interests. They provide additional motivation to choose Aruba as a destination.

Something exceptional is taking place nearly every month of the year, for an extra fillip to a vacation.

WEEKLY FESTIVALS
BON BINI FESTIVAL
The long-running Bon Bini Festival (Fort Zoutman, 297/582-3777, 7pm-9pm Tues., $5) features authentic insight into traditional island culture, music, and dance. Music is performed

on regional instruments such as the "caha di orgal" (an organ grinder), the wiri, and steelpan. Enthusiastic young dancers in native costume perform. There are also booths for inexpensive local art, handicrafts, and snacks.

Performers change from one week to the next, so there is no predicting the program. Count on either folkloric or carnival dancers. This is a pleasant way to spend two hours, and a nice way to segue into having dinner at one of Oranjestad's excellent restaurants.

CARUBBIAN FESTIVAL
Established in 2011, the Carubbian Festival (Bernardstraat, San Nicolas, 297/582-3777, 6pm-10pm Thurs., $64 adults, $32 children, purchase voucher at De Palm desks) is a celebration of the multicultural heritage that is particular to San Nicolas. Every Thursday night the main street of the town is converted into an elaborate street fair. Three stages have music throughout, but the big action is on the main stage. Acts change weekly, but the grand finale is always a rousing Carnival show with audience participation. Vouchers provide prime seating and table service for drinks. A Pan-Caribbean menu reflects the many nationalities that made San Nicolas their home when the refinery first opened. Three generations later, their cultural traditions and diversity carry on.

A standard package includes a choice of meal, transportation by bus to and from San Nicolas, and a drink. More tickets for drinks can be purchased at the festival. There are some very interesting regional beverages, most non-alcoholic, with purported natural, healthful properties. They are worth trying for the unique experience. Many booths are on hand selling local arts and crafts, as well as logo souvenirs.

JANUARY AND FEBRUARY
◀ CARNIVAL
Carnival events (multiple venues, parades free, musical contest and election $5.50) start the Saturday after New Year's Day (unless New Year's Day falls on Thurs., Fri. or Sat., then they will wait another week) and can last 4-10 weeks depending on the advent of Ash Wednesday. A full calendar with times, description of events, locations, and parade routes can be found in English on www.visitaruba.com.

For islanders, Carnival is the most anticipated event of the year, beginning with a nighttime parade through Oranjestad called the *Fakkeloptocht,* Dutch for Torch Parade. Carnival events will occur most weekends until the arrival of Ash Wednesday, except for the final week when they are nearly every night. Music contests, queen elections, and parades, parades, parades, day and night. This is a chance to sample local, original music composed each year just for Carnival. Live bands are vital to the parades, moving along in specially designed trailers, while thousands of participants garbed in sumptuous costumes dance alongside. Each group is judged for their artistic floats and exotic road pieces.

The major parades after the Torch Parade are Balloon Parade (San Nicolas), Children's Parade (San Nicolas and Oranjestad), Youth Parade and Tivoli Lighting Parade (Oranjestad), Jouvert Morning (San Nicolas), Grand Final Parades (San Nicolas and Oranjestad), and finally, the Burning of Momo (Aruba Entertainment Center, Oranjestad).

At the Aruba Entertainment Center, Carnival queens are selected during extravagant pageants in four age categories, from child to a mature Mrs. Carnival. Two of the biggest events are musical contests, the selection of the Tumba King or Queen and the Roadmarch and Calypso King or Queen (San Nicolas).

The party ends at the stroke of midnight on commencement of Ash Wednesday with the burning of an effigy of Rey (King) Momo, a pagan figure who rules over revelers and the dark of night.

The ritual commencement of the new Carnival is announced annually on November 11, at 11 minutes after 11am. The same evening, an inaugural event will be conducted, usually at a venue close to most resorts, to initiate island visitors into the traditions and

© ROSALIE KLEIN

Noted Aruban dancer Alydia Wever performs in an authentic costume on Himno y Bandera Day.

ceremony of remembrance is followed by a cultural night of speeches, musical performances, and folkloric dance.

MARCH
◖ HIMNO Y BANDERA DAY AND INTERNATIONAL HALF MARATHON

Aruba's National Day, March 18, or Himno y Bandera Day, begins before dawn with an International Half Marathon starting in San Nicolas and ending in Oranjestad. This has traditionally attracted runners from Latin America, the United States, and Europe, with cash awards and trophies. Their day of celebration continues with festive events and an elaborate street fair and national show at night in the Plaza Betico Croes; entrance is free. This is the best place and time to buy Aruba souvenirs, as the fair features authentic, locally-made handicrafts. It is remarkable how many ways Aruba's attractive flag can be incorporated into alluring garments and jewelry; you name it, you'll find it here.

RADISSON GOLF CLASSIC

This annual charity tournament played at **Tierra Del Sol Golf Course** (Caya di Solo 10, 297/586-0978, www.tierradelsol.com) raises funds for international and local foundations. Monies raised go to help street kids, abused women, and at least one foundation dedicated to helping cancer victims.

WENTE/PAPIAMENTO GOLF TOURNAMENT

The famous California Wente Vineyards partners with local restaurant Papiamento for a weekend of golf and gourmet food, all for a good cause. Proceeds go to a different Aruba foundation each year. Events are punctuated by a welcome reception in Papiamento Restaurant's elegant gardens. Unlimited Wente vintages flow throughout the weekend (wine tastings along the greens are actually a part of the competition).

Arion Wine Company (Ponton 38 Q,

excitement of Carnival, Aruban style. It varies from one year to the next.

Aside from the official activities, many resorts will schedule "jump-ups" for their guests. These are open-air festivities with usually one of the more popular Carnival bands, beer stands, and lively entertainment.

A shorter Carnival season means more frequent events; none are sacrificed due to lack of time. Aruba's Carnival is rated as second only to Brazil. If your vacation preference is a time of unbridled indulgence, this is the time to visit Aruba. Many come every year just to enjoy the spectacle.

BETICO DAY

The first official national holiday of the year is January 25, "Betico Day" (Plaza Betico Croes, behind the Cas di Cultura, 5pm-10pm), in memory of "El Liberatador," Gilberto Francois "Betico" Croes. A solemn

297/594-3326, www.arionwinecompany.com) sponsors the event and handles registration. Eric Wente, head of the famous wine-making family, plays host for the weekend. The first prize is a trip to the Wente Vineyards in the Livermore Valley, with a weekend of golf on their famous course.

APRIL
KING'S DAY
The month ends with the most important Dutch holiday of the year, King's Day on April 27. It is a time for revelry and activities of all kinds. Visitors are welcome to observe the protocol ceremony honoring the monarch, at Wilhelmina Park beginning at 10am in the morning. All through the day there are flea markets, car club and Harley-Davidson motorcades, kite competitions, and open houses at all island museums.

MAY
◖ MAY DAY
The month starts the best way possible, with a holiday. On May 1, International May Day, the Royal Dutch Marines open their camp in Savaneta (turn off for the camp from Hwy. 1A is clearly marked, 9am-6pm) and turn it into a giant theme park. The day is filled with the island's best flea market, inexpensive food stands, musical performances, boat rides, and aerial and sea-based demonstrations of marines in battle. It's a great way to mix and mingle and observe island life; all proceeds from the day are donated to a local charity.

◖ SOUL BEACH MUSIC FESTIVAL
The Soul Beach Music Festival (multiple venues, www.soulbeach.net, combo package for all parties and VIP concert seating $365), founded by comedian and film actor Sinbad, has a home on Aruba. It is a Memorial Day weekend tradition for thousands. Five days of media events along with beach and after parties culminate in three concerts by chart topping R&B, hip-hop, and soul performers. One night is dedicated to the hottest comedians of the moment. Alumni include Jamie Foxx, Jennifer Hudson,

Toni Braxton, R. Kelly, L. L. Cool J, and Mike Epps; expect to see top talents for a fraction of the price it would cost in the United States. Packages and charter flights can be arranged through their website.

JUNE
ARUBA WINE, FOOD & ART FESTIVAL
Every other year, on even years, is the Aruba Wine, Food, & Art Festival (Westin Aruba Resort, J. E. Irausquin Blvd. 77, 297/586-4466, www.westinaruba.com, $35-125). Three days are dedicated to the finer things in life: gourmet food, fine wines, wonderful art, and music. Events include a "Best Chef" competition with diners actually deciding the result. They cast their vote after enjoying a fabulous four-course meal of dishes created by competing chefs. The meal includes wines that the chefs paired to their dishes. The grand finale of the weekend is an elegant black-tie dinner prepared by a visiting celebrity chef, in which the chef matches the dishes to five kinds of Moët and Chandon champagnes.

ARUBA INTERNATIONAL PIANO FESTIVAL
Lovers of classical music will be in heaven during the Aruba International Piano Festival (Cas di Cultura, Vondellan 2, 297/588-9926, www.arubapianofestival.com, $14). Famed classical musicians from around the world perform nightly for a week of concerts in homage to the great composers. Taking part in the Crescendo Competition for Young Musicians or sitting in on the master classes is free.

ARUBA INTERNATIONAL TRIATHLON
The month ends with the Aruba International Triathlon (contact IBISA at idefre@setarnet.aw, 297/585-4987), which consists of a 1.5k swim, 40k bike race, and 10k run, with cash prizes and trophies for the winners. The main event begins at Eagle Beach across from the MVC-Club, next to the Tulip restaurant. It starts with a two-loop 1.5k swim, then a 40k bike segment (eight loops along Irausquin

© ROSALIE KLEIN

The annual Aruba International Regatta is a fun event with daily sailing races and parties.

Blvd. from Costa Linda Resort to Divi Phoenix Resort), and ends with a five-loop run along the same bike course. Around 400 athletes from Aruba, the United States, Europe, and Latin America compete in the triathlon.

JULY
◀ ARUBA HI-WINDS PRO-AM

One of the most respected amateur windsurfing and kitesurfing competitions in the world is the annual Aruba Hi-Winds Pro-Am (Fisherman's Huts, L. G. Smith Blvd., Malmok, www.hi-windsaruba.com, no fee for spectators). Expect to meet some of the greatest names in windsurfing in the region, including the PWA Women's World Champion in Freestyle Windsurfing since 2008, Sarah Quita-Offringa, a native Aruban. She often lends her presence to the event in which she first competed and which holds a special place in her heart.

The entire week is punctuated with beach parties, fashion shows, and breathtaking demonstrations of athletic prowess, include the celebrated nighttime aerial kitesurfing display.

Spectators are welcome to join the fun, where cheap, icy cold beer never stops flowing.

AUGUST AND SEPTEMBER
ARUBA INTERNATIONAL REGATTA

Aruba's premier all-class sailing event is the Aruba International Regatta (Surfside Beach, http://aruba-regatta.com). It is a great weekend for sailing enthusiasts, with everyone from windsurfers through cruising class competing. One day is dedicated to the "Round Aruba" race, the only race that circumnavigates the island, a challenge for all sailors.

ARUBA INTERNATIONAL PRO-AM GOLD TOURNAMENT

At the end of August or beginning of September, golf fanatics can join or watch the Aruba Pro-Am (Tierra Del Sol Country Club and Golf Course, Malmokweg z/n, 297/586-0978, www.tierradelsol.com), attracting golf pros and players from around the world. The 36-hole tournament guarantees one highly respected pro mentoring each four-person team.

ENDING THE YEAR ON ARUBA

As New Year's Eve approaches, the fact that fireworks are the required method of bidding farewell to the old and greeting the new becomes impossible to ignore. The fireworks go on sale just after Christmas, and the nightly displays don't stop until everyone runs out of rockets.

This is particularly noticeable on the last business days of the year. Tradition demands that businesses set off a *pagara*, a roll of various-sized firecrackers that can number anywhere from 5,000 to 5,000,000. The most famous is the one set in Oranjestad by Meta-Corp, usually stretching the entire length of the Renaissance properties and beyond. It holds up traffic for nearly an hour and takes about 20 minutes to expend. It is believed that *pagaras* chase away any ill will or *fuku* (FOO-KOO, this is really the name for the bad vibes). The business establishment or home is now cleansed for the coming year.

At the stroke of midnight on New Year's Eve, homes and restaurants set off their *pagaras*. The New Year starts with Aruba enveloped in a fog of firework smoke. Resounding through the night is the noise of hundreds of millions of firecrackers exploding simultaneously. Bring your earplugs!

The event encompasses three days of competing on the Tierra Del Sol course for great prizes and beautiful trophies. The weekend includes elegant evening events and organized activities for non-golfers.

OCTOBER
C CARIBBEAN SEA JAZZ FESTIVAL

The Caribbean Sea Jazz Festival (Renaissance Marketplace and Convention Center, 297/588-0211, www.caribbeanseajazz.com, $50) has become a destination for many on Columbus Day weekend. This is two nights of great music, gourmet food for pennies, and original art created just for the event on exhibition and for sale. International stars join renowned regional performers under the stars. CSJF has welcomed David Sanborn, Chaka Khan, Oscar D'Leon, Angie Stone, and Candy Dulfer, to name only a few. The party starts well in advance with the featured artists performing free warm-up events at local venues.

NOVEMBER
ARUBA INTERNATIONAL BEACH TENNIS TOURNAMENT

Whether a fanatical player or a spectator, find the world's top seeded players and all levels of competition at the Aruba International Beach Tennis Tournament (J. E. Irausquin Blvd. 230, 297/592-6427, www.beachtennisaruba.com, mid-Nov.). International sports journalists credit Sjoerd de Vries, founder of Beach Tennis Aruba, as the premier promoter of the sport in the Americas.

Professional players from around the globe converge on Eagle Beach for the playoff rounds, but the finals could be at any of a number of venues guaranteed to provide an exciting night for spectators. One year the courtyard of The Village Shopping Mall was filled with sand and converted into a court.

Athletic tournaments on Aruba always provide a congenial, party atmosphere for competitors and the audience, along with exciting sporting action.

DECEMBER

During Christmas and New Year's, Aruba is packed not only for the escape from winter's worst but also for the great excitement of the season; Aruba has its own lively traditions, music, and events associated with the season.

Check www.aruba.com for the calendar of special events, as the ever-changing schedule features new festivals, sporting meets, and concerts; one-time happenings are regularly added to the calendar.

SINTERKLAAS FEAST DAY

Aruba's loving observance of Dutch traditions is never more evident than on the Festival of Sinterklaas (takes place all over the island, Dec. 5). This beloved figure was the precursor for Santa Claus, based on a very real person. He arrives on Aruba 2-3 weeks prior to his feast day, greeted at the port by thousands of children and parents.

On December 5, the eve of his actual feast day, the stately gentleman will be seen everywhere, including at many resorts, accompanied by his gaily dressed *swarte pieten* (Moorish for "elves") distributing toys and sweets to both island and vacationing children. It is a fun occasion for all ages.

HOLIDAY SHOPPING IN ORANJESTAD

The capital's merchant association members (MAMBO, Caya G. F. "Betico" Croes, 10am-6pm every Sat. until Christmas) turn Oranjestad's "Caya Grande" into a festive holiday celebration on the weekends. All through the day there is entertainment from seasonal local singing groups called *gaita*, performing a lively regional music of the same name.

At the beginning of the month, there is a visit from Sinterklaas, prior to his feast day, and after that, Santa Claus holds court with young children at various venues.

ARUBA DANDE FESTIVAL

Another beloved holiday tradition is the local version of caroling, which is focused on the New Year. The annual Dande Festival (changing venues, various community centers, www.visitaruba.com, begins at 8pm on a weekend between Christmas and New Year's, free) is a competition, lasting almost until dawn, to select the next Dande King or Queen. Many resorts host Dande exhibitions for their guests around this time.

Traditionally, the New Year's "serenade" of Dande is performed by roaming minstrels who travel from home to home. Deploying "inside information" from an informant in the household, they usually personalize the song's lyrics to the lives and foibles of the residents in a most humorous manner. An important part of the ritual is the passing of the hat and a small monetary reward from each family member for their entertainment.

During the Dande Festival, lyrics are far more topical and sometimes contain political and social commentary. Most often they deliver a message of enjoying life and of good wishes for the coming year.

◖ NEW YEAR'S EVE

Those who think watching a ball drop while freezing is the epitome of New Year's Eve excitement have yet to experience the change of year on Aruba. As midnight approaches, a frenzy of fireworks can be seen and heard everywhere. At the stroke of midnight, the sky fills with pyrotechnics from every neighborhood, after which the professional display begin!

The streets of Oranjestad are usually filled with spectators for a magnificent display sponsored by the Renaissance Resort, over the harbor, officially welcoming the New Year.

Vacationers find that nearly every resort on Aruba hosts a special dinner for their guests to celebrate the year's changeover. Many restaurants also stage special evenings lasting until midnight, with champagne included.

Hotels also stage fireworks displays for their guests. Most notable are those staged by the Divi and Tamarijn Beach Resorts by the Manchebo Beach and Eagle Beach area; Hyatt Regency Resort in Palm Beach; and Renaissance Resort in Oranjestad.

SHOPS

When traveling to an exotic destination, it is natural to wish to return with a unique memento or a great bargain. There are many shopping centers in Aruba that offer a variety of options, with signature designer stores, countless jewelry shops, souvenir and handicrafts shops, and flea markets.

For souvenirs, some of the best buys are at the open-air markets. A small group of native artisans produces interesting handicrafts and original paintings and watercolors. These can be found for sale at various festivals conducted by the resorts. Crafts such as macramé and appliqué are more the ken of Latin American cultures. Many attractive items from these countries, such as hand-woven hammocks and embroidered garments, are a common item at various open-air markets.

The smaller jewelry stores are known to perform their "calculator dance" when a shopper inquires about a particular piece. Being knowledgeable about gemstones and having a taste for bargaining certainly helps in attaining some remarkable discounts, but it requires patience and determination. This practice is not particularly Aruban, but it is something that has come into vogue since 2002.

European perfumes and high-end cosmetics and skincare products are comparatively good buys, as are wines from Europe and Latin America. Canadians report that famous brands of U.S.-produced cosmetics and skincare products are as much as 25 percent less than what they pay at home.

Hard liquor is discounted at the duty-free shops at the airport, but not beyond, except

© ROSALIE KLEIN

HIGHLIGHTS

LOOK FOR ◖ TO FIND RECOMMENDED SHOPS.

◖ **Mopa-Mopa:** The Quillasinga people of Colombia still produce the beautiful handicrafts sold here in the same manner that their ancestors did in centuries past (page 149).

◖ **Gandelman Jewelers:** A respected regional family operation, Gandelman is the exclusive agent for Rolex and Patek Phillippe on Aruba (page 151).

◖ **Queen's Jewelers:** Shop where Dutch royalty choose to shop. Environmentally and socially conscientiously mined diamonds are a part of Queen's Jewelers diverse and elegant collection (page 151).

◖ **Renaissance Mall:** If designer labels are your obsession, then this is the place to indulge. The greatest concentration of top American, European, and Latin designer shops is found in these elegant corridors (page 152).

◖ **Super Food:** Food shopping can be gift shopping for lovers of Dutch cheeses. Aruba's most popular market is distinctly Dutch and the quality of their products is exacting (page 156).

◖ **Terrafuse:** Don't go on a hunt for that unique souvenir, make it yourself at Terrafuse's glass art classes (page 156)!

◖ **Aruhiba:** This store has the largest and most diverse selections of Cuban, Honduran, and Dominican cigars on Aruba. Aficionados, however, should stop by to try Aruba's own homegrown and rolled brand, which cost far less (page 157).

◖ **Caribbean Queen:** This sparkling boutique showcases handcrafted jewelry and accessories by local artisans, each of them a queen of their craft (page 157).

◖ **Kristie's Jewels:** With a truly elegant and eclectic collection of fine Italian jewelry in Palm Beach, Kristie's is a perfect spot for luxury nighttime shopping (page 160).

◖ **Paseo Herencia Shopping Mall:** This lively shopping center has a variety of restaurants and shops, and offers free entertainment (page 161).

SHOPS

for the locally bottled Ron Superior Rum. This is best to buy on your way in or your way out of the island. Smokers also declare cigarettes on Aruba cost much less than in the United States. Dutch cheeses are an excellent buy, and, as long as they are uncut and sealed in the original rind, they can be brought back into the United States. The best places to buy these are at the supermarkets.

Cigar lovers will be thrilled to know that Cuban cigars of every brand are widely sold here. Aruba has it own brand, Arubhiba, made of locally grown tobaccos, which can be taken back to the United States without fear of confiscation. Another locally manufactured item is Aruba Aloe sunblock, skin- and haircare products.

Tons of tee and polo shirts with all sorts of Aruba logos, suited to all ages, are displayed anywhere and everywhere, from street stalls to hotel newsstands. These inexpensive items make good gifts.

Well-known names such as Louis Vuitton, Coach, Gucci, Mario Hernandez, Mont Blanc, Salvatore Ferragamo, Ralph Lauren, and Tommy Hilfiger all have dedicated outlets either in Oranjestad or Palm Beach. Aruba, however, is not a true duty-free port. European designer goods are marginally discounted over what they would cost in the United States. Other items, especially electronics like cameras, mobile devices, and video games, are uniformly more expensive.

Oranjestad is best known for daytime shopping. Until 2006, it had Aruba's only shopping center. Since then, "mall fever" struck Palm Beach. One multi-purpose mall after another has cropped up, with a plethora of goods, restaurants, and activities. Shops at the Palm Beach malls usually open in the late afternoon hours. Mindful that most visitors prefer to spend their days on the beach, they offer the convenience of nighttime shopping often accompanied by entertainment.

Oranjestad

Downtown Oranjestad is Aruba's daytime shopping destination. Stores in town open their doors anywhere between 8:30am-10am and close between 6:30pm-8pm. There was a time, not so long ago, when almost all stores closed for an extended two-hour siesta. Modern times and more competition have eliminated such island practices completely, a boon for fanatical shoppers. There are only a few die-hard "local" shops that don't remain open all day. Nearly all shops are closed on Sundays, except for a very few that open when a cruise ship is in port.

The area around the cruise terminal could rightfully be dubbed the local "diamond district." One store after another boasts well-known names of fine quality jewelry and gemstones. Several are internationally affiliated, with service outlets in the United States. A few have their own on-site artisans creating original pieces.

Most stores and malls are clustered around the harbor. Within their halls are name brand designer shops, complemented by attractive cafés and stylish surroundings. Caya G. F. Betico Croes has always been considered the town's main shopping street. One half has high-end stores with well-known brands, but the eastern end is mostly dedicated to local shops with low-end goods. It now sports tram service to and from the cruise terminal to facilitate exploring the vendors that line the avenue.

Caya G. F. Betico Croes, the main shopping street in Oranjestad's downtown area

© ROSALIE KLEIN

ART, HANDICRAFTS, AND SOUVENIRS

Aruba's history is such that traditional native crafts practiced by their Amerindian population are long lost. Many of the people who have come to live here kept the connection with their homeland and brought with them several of the native handicrafts still practiced in Venezuela, Colombia, and other Latin countries. Most can be found at flea markets and souvenir shops.

Aruba does have an active and talented community of artists and painters, whose works can be found for sale at a number of surprising venues.

HENDRIK SCHOUTEN STUDIO

Transplanted Dutch artist Hendrik Schouten (L. G. Smith Blvd. 82, 297/585-3374, www. hendrikaruba.exto.org, 2:30pm-6pm Mon., 2:30pm-7pm Fri., 10:30am-5pm Sat.) performs his craft before visitors' eyes in his Renaissance Marketplace studio. He has an imaginative way with portraiture and an arresting artistic style. He is quite prolific, and there is enormous demand for his work. If you are interested in original art, it's worthwhile to stop by his studio.

◖ MOPA-MOPA

Aficionados of genuine, artfully crafted handiwork should not leave Aruba without visiting the Mopa-Mopa shop (Renaissance Marketplace, L. G. Smith Blvd. 82, 297/588-7297, www.mopamopa.com, 10am-6pm Mon.-Sat.). Though not produced on Aruba, these unique works of art are arresting and beautiful.

Mopa-Mopa is an ancient craft, produced by the Quillasinga tribe of Colombia. It is a complex process handed down through the generations. It is still done as it was before the Spanish came to the New World. The buds of the Mopa-Mopa tree, a bush that grows in Putumayo province in the Amazon basin, are boiled to produce a resin. Color is added through natural dyes from plants. The artisans then chew the resin to soften it, so it can be stretched and cut into intricate designs. Most work conveys the Quillasinga culture, with natural subjects, such as flora and fauna,

ceremonial masks, or stories of their everyday life. The results are items anyone would be proud to own and display. This traditional Colombian craft is not readily found outside its home country.

POST ARUBA

A visit to Aruba's post office or central bank is not usually at the top of most souvenir shopping lists. These are two places, however, where ideal gifts and mementos can be found for stamp or coin collectors. Post Aruba (Irausquinplein 9 Oranjestad, 297/528-7678, www.postaruba.com, 7:30am-noon and 1pm-4:30pm Mon.-Fri.) headquarters in Oranjestad has a philately desk. Collectors find beautiful first-day-of-issue ensembles of commemorative stamps. The post office issues 10-12 commemorative collections annually. Each is created from original artwork by local artists who also design the special envelope and cancellation stamp, which is standard to a first-day ensemble.

STICHTING INSTITUTO ARTESANO AURBANO

Promenade Restaurant (L. G. Smith Blvd. 160, 297/583-8899, 5pm-10pm Tues.-Sun.) hosts the work of artists of the Stichting Instituto Artesano Aurbano (S.I.A.A.). This is a very convivial symbiotic relationship: The restaurant has lovely artwork on its wall, while island artists are attractively showcased. Patrons are welcome to make an offer on any work that appeals to them and the restaurant management will handle the sale.

UNOCA GALLERY

The government-funded foundation that supports cultural projects, UNOCA (Stadionweg 21, 297/583-5681, www.unocaruba.org, 8:30am-noon and 1:30pm-5pm Mon.-Fri.), has a permanent collection, but also hosts temporary shows with the work for sale. Aruba's most respected native artists have an excellent venue for showing their work. Art collectors, who are interested in exploring Aruba's artistic past and present, will be enlightened, and perhaps find a worthwhile piece.

SHOPS

SOUVENIRS WITH A SOCIAL CONSCIENCE

Environmentally-minded shoppers who seek something truly unique to the island should stop by the **Mad Hatter store** (J. E. Irausquin Blvd. 348, 297/586-0401, 5pm-11pm daily) and look for products by **Do Good Aruba** (297/600-8321, www.dogoodaruba.com). Their diverse selection of recycled objects that would have been tossed in landfill have been transformed into attractive ensembles.

Founders of Do Good Aruba noticed the incredible production of waste from wine and beer bottles by Aruba's many clubs and restaurants. They recruited several of them into this environmentally-aware enterprise. By reducing Aruba's production of waste from glass they are providing a community service.

Many of the original bottles are remarkably artful. Seeing them being tossed away was sad. Their inventory spans a vast array of colors and sizes, which have been recycled into shot glasses, beer glasses, tumblers, vases, and candleholders. They are all engraved with the company logo "Upcycled in Aruba with Love." Substantial orders, with a few days notice, can have a personalized message. Purchases will be properly packed for safe transport while traveling.

Each month, this minimal-profit company donates a large share of its earnings to a local foundation that is dedicated to a worthy cause.

Do Good Aruba has the high ambition of demonstrating to other entrepreneurs that "going green" can be profitable and that companies should also have a social conscience.

© ROSALIE KLEIN

Do Good Aruba Foundation sells souvenirs made from recycled materials.

CLOTHING AND FASHION
LA LINDA DEPARTMENT STORE

The invasion of designer brand shops has transformed many islanders into walking fashion plates. They are thoroughly informed in the trendiest names in garments and accessories. Yet, the island has shops that Arubans always turn to first for every day needs, which have a special place in the community. La Linda Department Store (Caya G. F. Betico Croes 3, 297/585-2120, 9am-6:30pm Mon.-Sat.) is such an island institution.

It started out as a tiny notions store back before WWII, carrying "a bit of this and a bit of that." This family business, for decades one of the largest stores on the island, still has the same philosophy. Consumer demand has expanded enormously, and so has their inventory. If misdirected luggage has left one or more family members without a change of clothes, a quick fix can be found here for any size and gender. It is one of the few stores on Aruba to stock tall and big man clothing, as well as stylish plus sizes for women.

La Linda is an anything and everything store. Find beachwear to formal clothing, beach toys to bicycles, brand name athletic shoes, or blow dryers and reading glasses, all moderately priced.

JEWELRY STORES

A concentration of fine quality jewelry stores radiate out from the cruise ship terminal. It is possible to spend an entire morning, or longer, examining the inventory of several shops to find that special piece. Be prepared to perhaps spend another hour bargaining for it. The practice of haggling over prices is not a practice of the finer stores. Shoppers who know their gems and understand current trends in the market can do well.

◖ GANDELMAN JEWELERS

One of the best known names for fine quality designer goods and watches is Gandelman (Renaissance Mall, L. G. Smith Blvd. 82, 297/529-9900, http://gandelman.net, 10am-8pm Mon.-Sat.; branch stores in Hyatt Regency and Marriott Resort 9am-midnight Mon.-Sat.). For generations, this has been where residents of Curacao and Aruba shop for fine quality jewelry. It is a successful family business with a superlative reputation.

Gandelman is the exclusive agent for Rolex, Cartier, Patek Philippe, Carrera y Carrera, Bvlgari, Breguet, and David Yurman. They also have the largest collection of Baccarat jewelry and giftware. Famous names in luxury accessories are discounted by 5-20 percent over U.S. retail prices.

NOBLE JEWELERS

Nash, the owner of Noble Jewelers (Westraat 4, 297/583-8780, nash@setarnet.aw, 9am-6pm Mon.-Sat.), is an icon of the jewelry trade on Aruba. He has a clientele that returns annually and swears by the quality, price, and service of his store. Noble is the exclusive dealership for Hearts on Fire diamonds in Oranjestad. The brilliant stones are particularly known for the exceptional quality and fire, due to their unique, multi-faceted cut. Noble is also very community-minded, annually providing the volunteer foundation Friends of the Handicapped with their most important fundraising raffle prizes.

◖ QUEEN'S JEWELERS

The news media has put a spotlight on the "blood diamond," so named for deplorable practices and conditions of the large mines in several countries, and conscientious individuals are now concerned about the provenance of their gems. Queen's Jewelers (L. G. Smith Blvd. 15, 297/583-1786, www.queens.jewelry.com, 9am-6:30pm Mon.-Sat.) carries **Canadia** (www.canadia.com) diamonds and jewelry, which are certified for humane practices in the mining of their gems. Stones come from the Ekati mines, which operate in strict accordance with Canadian labor laws. They invest to improve the community surrounding the mines. Each diamond is laser inscribed and registered with an ID number.

The shop has an eclectic and varied collection. When former Queen Beatrix of Holland arrived on Aruba in 2011 for a royal visit, she stopped by Queen's Jewelers before checking into her hotel. The Queen's mother and Her Royal Highness Queen Maxima purchased two pieces.

PERFUME AND COSMETICS

Still one of the traditionally great buys of the Caribbean, European perfumes can be found at shops in all main tourist areas. Prices are exactly the same on the island as at the airport. There is no need to wait until departure to purchase that favorite fragrance, or to discover a new one. Exclusive brands of skincare products, such as La Prairie, are also discounted compared to U.S. rates.

DUFRY

One of the best known names internationally for duty-free scents and cosmetics is Dufry (Caya G. F. Betico Croes 29, 297/582-2790, www.dufry.com, 9am-6pm Mon.-Sat.). They have three stores in Oranjestad and two at the airport. An enthusiastic crew of cosmetics

SHOPS

artists is always ready to provide patrons with a new look and to advise on skin care.

MAGGY'S EMPORIUM

Since 1955, Maggy's Emporium (Caya G. F. Betico Croes 59, 297/582-2113, www.maggysaruba.aw, 9am-6pm Mon.-Sat.) has been Aruba's place to shop for the finest in cosmetics and fragrances. A fully-trained staff of enthusiastic makeup experts awaits patrons, ready to provide the latest tips on makeup trends and new scents.

Annually, during the first week in June, the shop conducts a weeklong beauty festival. This entails workshops with visiting specialists from top cosmetic companies. Sessions are usually free with the purchase of a package that includes a choice of items. Glamorous bachelorette parties end the day here with wine, hors d'oeuvres, and exotic cocktails.

PENHA

A well-established name in the Dutch Caribbean, Penha (Caya G. F. Betico Croes 11, 297/582-4160, www.jlpenha.com, 9am-6pm Mon.-Sat.) has a full selection of the most sought-after fragrances and famous brand name cosmetics. They are also the exclusive agents for Karen Kane resort wear and MAC cosmetics in Aruba. Their dedicated MAC boutique maintains a staff of expert cosmeticians ready to do hair and makeup for weddings and special occasions.

SHOPPING MALLS

AVENTURA MALL

Overlooking the town square behind the Renaissance Resort is Aventura Mall (Havenstraat 4, 597/582-5454, 10am-8pm Mon.-Sat.). It is the base of operations of Aruba's Benetton stores. They have separate outlets for women's and children's fashions. Also found here are Sun Specs designer sunglasses, Tous, XOXO, and San Marina, for European shoes and accessories.

◖ RENAISSANCE MALL

Aruba's greatest concentration of signature designer stores are in Renaissance Mall (L. G. Smith Blvd. 82, 297/582-4622, www.shoprenaissancearuba.com, 10am-8pm Mon.-Sat.), an enclosed mall in the Renaissance Resort. The shops here feature designer name brands, such as Louis Vuitton, Adolfo Dominguez, Custo Barcelona, Gucci, Furla, Ermenegildo Zegna, Vilebrequin, Faïonnable, Aldo, EPK, Diesel, with Apriori, Samoon, Erfo, Joseph Ribkoff, Hammer, Hammerle, and Gottex, sold in the Entre Nous/Eva Boutique.

The mall has Aruba Aloe and Dufry outlets. Yves Rocher is a famous, moderately-priced European line of scents and skincare. Scattered among the clothing shops are fine quality jewelers Chopard Boutique, Colombian Emeralds, Gandelman, and Jewelry Warehouse. Cigar Emporium sells Cuban cigars and the most diverse and unique collection of decorative lighters to be found on Aruba.

The mall is the ground floor of the Renaissance Marina Tower. Hotel restaurants offer excellent choices for dining. The focal point of the mall is a Starbucks that won awards as the most beautifully designed outlet in the Caribbean.

RENAISSANCE MARKETPLACE

Though it is home to a number of shops, the open-air mall Renaissance Marketplace (L. G. Smith Blvd. 82, 297/582-4622, www.shoprenaissancearuba.com, stores 10am-8pm Mon.-Sat., restaurants and clubs 10am-1am daily) is best known for its restaurants and nightlife. The shops here carry more standard souvenir stock. Adjacent to the water, a row of dining spots, including Cilo, Hung Paradise, Sushi-Ya, Spanglish, and The Dutch Pancake House, offer harbor views for breakfast, lunch, and dinner. Plaza Café, Casa Tua, Grand Café Tropical, and Cuba's Cooking provide dinner and entertainment until the wee hours of the night.

Interspersed among the restaurants and clubs are some interesting shops, including a **Mopa-Mopa** store (297/588-7297, www.mopamopa.com, 10am-6pm Mon.-Sat.), which specializes in unique handicrafts from Colombia. Rage is famous for its sterling silver jewelry. Their

© ROSALIE KLEIN

Renaissance Mall

collection includes a huge selection of stylish studs for a piercing anywhere on the body. Champagne has an attractive collection of costume jewelry and moderately-priced accessories. City Fashion outfits men and women with tropical resort wear. Souvenirs and sundries can be found at Captain Cook's, open until late at night. **Hendrik Schouten** (297/585-3374, www.hendrikaruba.exto.org, 2:30pm-6pm Mon., 2:30pm-7pm Fri., 10:30am-5pm Sat.) has a corner store-art studio, where he gives art lessons. Aruba's original movie theater, The Cinemas, Oranjestad, is in this mall, showing first-run films.

ROYAL PLAZA MALL
Aruba's first giant, multi-service mall was Royal Plaza Mall (L. G. Smith Blvd. 94, 297/588-0351, 10am-6:30pm Mon.-Sat.). Architecturally, it is a frothy confection dominating the boulevard and harbor. The first thing to catch the attention of arriving cruise ship passengers is its ornate facade and the sun glinting off its golden dome. Three stories contain dozens of shops, plus restaurants and nightclubs that overlook the harbor.

The tiers surround a large courtyard populated with kiosks selling bargain-priced knick-knacks. Among the 50 shops and eateries are respected jewelers such as Shiva's, Pearl Gems, Little Switzerland, Royal Jewels & Diamonds, and My Time and Spare Time watch stores.

Dufry (297/582-2790, www.dufry.com, 9am-6pm Mon.-Sat.) is famous for fine cosmetics and perfumes. Bula Surf Shop is Aruba's center for the most popular names in surfing gear, sandals, sunglasses, and board shorts. Among their souvenir and resort wear stores are Fantasea, Little Holland, Yellow Submarine, Souvenir Outlet and More, Bob the Fish, Del Sol, Shipwreck, Beach n' Wear, and Alcy's Boutique. The mall is home to a cigar store, Casa Del Hubano.

SUPERMARKETS
Most of Aruba does their supermarket shopping on the western end of Oranjestad. Circumstance has resulted in Aruba's major

SHOPS

markets setting up business right next to each other. The convenience of their proximity allows shoppers to go from one place to the next to check off all the items on their shopping list, as it is rare for one market to have everything you need. This is simply an aspect of island life.

Supermarket shopping on Aruba is quite an interesting experience. Expect a diversity of goods from around the world, most likely goods that you do not see in most U.S. markets. Some may lament the paucity or expense of the American brands. This is to be expected, as all items are imported, with freight and taxes added on to the cost. Compensating for the additional prices is the opportunity to sample how the rest of the world eats, and their equivalents to standard U.S. goods.

The mélange that is the Aruban community is evident in the diversity of comestibles carried by most markets. Products direct from China, India, Indonesia, and the Philippines are standard stock to service the expatriate communities. Goods that one would normally have to seek out in specialty shops in the United States are normally found on most island supermarket shelves.

One drawback of island life is the highly anticipated weekly shipment of fruits and vegetables, dairy products, and other fresh items. Shopping the day before they arrive is very disappointing, as it is difficult to find fresh milk, lettuce, and other standard items. If arriving on a weekend and staying in a place where you plan to cook, it's best to stock up immediately.

KONG HING SUPERCENTER

A well-stocked, clean market is Kong Hing Supercenter (L. G. Smith Blvd. 152, 597/588-9889, 8am-8pm Mon.-Sat., 8am-1pm Sun.) on the western outskirts of Oranjestad. On the premises are a bakery, fresh meat, and a fish department, and they have the best roast chickens of all the markets.

LING & SONS/ALBERT HEIJN

At the time of this writing, one of Aruba's best known markets, Ling & Sons (IItaliestraat 26, 297/588-7718, www.lingandsons.com, 8am-8pm Mon.-Sat., 8am-1pm Sun.) announced it had been purchased by the Albert Heijn franchise. Albert Heijn is one of the largest market chains in Europe, known for quality goods. Ling & Sons has always been considered one of the finest for its fresh specialty salads department, bakery, fresh meats and produce, and a diversity of inventory. It is highly likely it will be enhanced by becoming an Albert Heijn, with one of the most tried and true brands in Europe a principal product of the store.

Eagle Beach and Manchebo Beach

Because of the easy access by foot to all of Oranjestad shopping, this area has remained more resort- and beach-oriented. The Alhambra Shopping Bazaar has a few interesting shops but there is not much else. Local stores can be found on the Bubali Road once you cross the Sasaki Highway. Most resorts have newsstands with small sundry and souvenir shops attached. A very few facilities, such as the Divi, Tamarijn, and Casa Del Mar, have arcades with resort wear, jewelry, and perfume outlets.

ART, HANDICRAFTS, AND SOUVENIRS
THE CENTRAL BANK OF ARUBA

Aruba's financial agency, the Central Bank of Aruba (J. E. Irausquin Blvd. 8, 297/525-2141, www.cbaruba.org. 8am-noon and 1pm-4pm Mon.-Fri.) not only regulates the island's commerce, but is the agent for stunning commemorative coin collections. The proofs are high quality silver or gold limited issues. Special collections celebrate a diversity of events, beginning with Status Aparte

FLEA MARKETS

Though weekend flea markets are a Dutch tradition, it is the influx of immigrants from the Caribbean and Latin America that are largely responsible for their proliferation on Aruba. Since 2000 flea markets have come to dominate some shopping areas, and are always popular for bargain souvenirs. These amalgams of street stalls offer inexpensive resort wear and accessories, tee shirts, and decorative gewgaws, at the cheapest prices.

Upon exiting the cruise terminal, visitors are presented with a cluster of individual stalls: **The Terminal Flea Market** (directly across the street from the terminal, 10am-6:30pm Mon.-Sat.). Another flea market lines the **waterfront along L. G. Smith Boulevard** (8am-6:30pm Mon.-Sat.), which was traditionally the fruit and fish market in decades past.

Tourist Go Flea Market (L.G. Smith Blvd. 144, 297/592-2424, 8am-8pm Sat.-Sun.) is so well established, they even have a Facebook page. Dozens of stalls, with authentic regional crafts, inexpensive Aruba logo gear, and even fresh BBQ, set up on the weekends. The parking lot of the local paint factory takes on a whole new personality. An easy walk from the Manchebo Beach resorts, and right next to the major supermarkets, it is one of the best spots for browsing for all sorts of unexpected goodies.

Nighttime bargain hunters enjoy trawling the numerous kiosks that open at sunset along **J. E. Irausquin Boulevard in Palm Beach.** They operate seven days a week and offer inexpensive but stylish sunglasses, handicrafts, tee shirts, handmade costume jewelry, and attractive accessories of every stripe. **The Village Mall** hosts a flea market in their courtyard (7pm-10pm daily) with a very festive ambiance.

and Aruba having its own money. Among the coin issues that are not sold out is one dedicated to the Royal Visit in 2011. Aruba's 25th anniversary of Status Aparte is available in both silver and gold proofs. They are minted in Holland and beautifully boxed for display or gift giving.

MANA AT LA CABANA RESORT

La Cabana Beach Resort in Eagle Beach decided to show their support for the local art community by turning their main lobby and mezzanine into a giant art gallery. **Movimiento Arte Aruba Nobo** (MANA; J.E. Irausquin Blvd. 250, 297/594-2233, 24 hours daily) is the curator for the exhibits that change every three months. Aruba's top artists are challenged to create fresh works around particular themes. The works can be viewed at any time of the day or night, but to arrange a purchase, call the contact number (297/594-2233, 1pm-6pm daily).

SHOPPING MALLS
ALHAMBRA SHOPPING BAZAAR

Two years of renovations completed in 2012 unveiled a sleek, stylish center for shopping and dining in the low-rise areas. Alhambra Shopping Bazaar (J. E. Irausquin Blvd. 47, 297/583-5000, shops 10am-10pm daily, dining and entertainment 7am-2am daily) has an outlet of The Lazy Lizard for tasteful knick-knacks and resort wear. There is an Aruba Aloe outlet for sun protection products. Dedicated logo shops sell Divi-branded clothing and accessories or there's an official Aruba shop, with their distinctive graphic. Dahler & Co. features elegant fashions from macramé beach covers to sequined gowns. There is a Diamonds International jewelers and R. Glass outlet for elegant accessories.

The Market, a very well outfitted mini-market, has an excellent wine selection. An expansive, charming dining patio is surrounded by a budget-priced food court with Little Caesar's

Pizzeria, Dunkin' Donuts, Subway, and a Baskin Robbins.

SUPERMARKETS
◖ SUPER FOOD

Aruba's first building designed to be totally energy self-sufficient through renewable sources is Super Food (Sasaki Hwy. z/n, 297/588-6040, http://superfoodaruba.com, 8am-8pm Mon.-Sat., 8am-1pm Sun.). It is impossible to miss, located on the Sasaki Highway and Bubali Road intersection, directly across from the Tropicana Resort. More of a mall than a market, it has always been regarded as Aruba's Dutch grocery, known for its inventory from Holland. It is considered to have the best deli departments, as well as exceptional produce and an excellent bakery.

The new store is clean and beautiful. The arcade of shops surrounding it contains a Sun Specs outlet, a fresh fish store, and a very attractive and reasonably priced eatery. It also sports other services, such as a small branch of Aruba Bank and an ATM.

Palm Beach, Malmok, and Noord

Palm Beach after dark has been enlivened by a phenomenon that only materialized since 2006: nighttime shopping. Prior to then, it was unheard of on Aruba. Savvy entrepreneurs figured out that most vacationers would rather spend their day indulging in other activities, or laying on the beach, rather than shopping, and it has proven to be very successful. In the evenings, most malls host special events, and dining venues offer free entertainment to make nighttime shopping even more attractive.

ART, HANDICRAFTS, AND SOUVENIRS
POST ARUBA

Post Aruba (Palm Beach Plaza, 297/528-7678, www.postaruba.com, 8am-4pm Mon.-Sat.) is conveniently located near the major resorts. This branch also sells commemorative stamps, plus another very special item that is only at this branch: personalized Aruba stamps. Bring your camera's memory card with some exciting pictures of the family and have them digitally inserted into one of seven design choices of artful, useable stamps. Beautifully illustrated stamps feature Aruba's most famous landmarks. Imagine a rendering of Alto Vista Chapel with a photo of your family actually at the chapel, integrated into the design of the stamp. Sold in sheets of six, they can be used to send postcards out to friends and family anywhere in the world.

◖ TERRAFUSE

Make your own Aruba mementos at Terrafuse Studios (Turibana 14, 297/592-2978, www.arubaglassceramics.com, 3pm-6pm Tues., 9am-noon Thurs., $85 pp). They offer a singular experience for the crafty: classes in the art of glass bead-making. Participants learn a new skill along with personally creating a very unique and individual souvenir. Returning students receive a discount on the class fee.

Ciro and Marian Abath are internationally recognized artists. Ciro's work greets island visitors at the airport in the "Water" exhibit. Both he and his wife traveled the world and studied with masters of glass art. Their studio is on the grounds of their quaint and lovingly maintained *cunucu* house. Not far from the hotels, it is found along the way to the Alto Vista Chapel.

Workshops in glass bead-making are conducted twice a week. Special arrangements can be made for groups of 4-6. You will also be treated to a demonstration of glass-blowing in their studio. They use imported Moretti glass from Italy. This saves you the trouble and time of traveling to Venice to see this craft in action! Ciro and Marian have a boutique on the premises with an exquisite collection of their original glass pieces. One-of-a-kind mementos from Aruba can be found here. A taxi ride to the studio is $7; they will provide transportation back to your resort.

WESTIN ART GALLERY

One of Aruba's top hotels set a standard for showcasing local artistic talent by reserving space to create the elegant Westin Art Gallery (L. G. Smith Blvd. 77, 297/740-2678, 24 hours daily, sales rep on premises 3pm-6pmTues., Thurs., and Sat.). This is one of the most beautiful galleries to ever open its doors. Collections change every two months, and all works are for sale. Books of art by various artists not on display are available for perusal. If something on the walls is not quite to your taste, they have a large stable of renowned island artists working in several different styles.

CIGARS
◖ ARUHIBA

Cigar aficionados recommend Aruba's own Aruhiba (L. G. Smith Blvd. 330, 297/585-7833, www.aruhibacigars.com, 9am-6:30pm Mon.-Sat., 9:30am-4pm Sun.) for a good buy and a pleasant surprise. The cigars are cultivated and rolled on island, with no chemicals used to hurry the fermentation process. Aruhiba produces 16 different cigars of varying length, strength, thickness, and price. Cigar lovers report they are a very enjoyable smoke. Lack of import and shipping costs make them a bargain compared to imported stogies from Cuba, Honduras, and the Dominican Republic. A diverse selection of cigars from the entire Caribbean is also offered in their shop, which has one of the largest inventories of such stores on Aruba. Find it among the cluster of kiosks next to the Olde Molen. Interested parties are invited to tour their cigar factory in Moko by appointment.

CUBAN CIGARS

The simple, direct name of Cuban Cigars (J. E. Irausquin Blvd. 348, 297/594-2256, JJ1@ Hotmail.com, 4:30pm-10:30pm daily) is deceptive, as they carry Aruhiba and cigars from

Honduras. The tiny shop is located just at the street front of The Village mall, for after dinner cigar shopping. They have a somewhat smaller inventory than Aruhiba.

CLOTHING AND FASHION

Palm Beach fashion shops tend to focus on resort clothes and swimwear. There are several shops with beautiful items that customers can put on to wear immediately on the beach. Among them are some haute couture stores with exotic European fashion for those who like to make a statement in their dress.

BACI DI ROMA

The owner of Baci da Roma (Paseo Herencia Shopping Mall, J. E. Irausquin Blvd. 382-A, 297/586-7986, bacidaroma.aruba@yahoo.com, 10am-10pm Mon.-Sat., 5pm-10pm Sun.), or "Roman Kisses," could be a model for her elegant collection. In fact, she once was, so she knows her stuff when ordering inventory. Fine quality English couture from Traffic People and Paradise are suitable for Aruba's tropical surroundings or an elegant cocktail party back home. The timeless styling with trendy touches at reasonable prices will undoubtedly make you fall in love with something in this store.

◖ CARIBBEAN QUEEN

Bring on the bling is the motto of Caribbean Queen (Palm Beach Plaza, L. G. Smith Blvd. 95, 297/586-8737, 10am-10pm Mon.-Sat., 5pm-10pm Sun.). It's a most unusual accessory store for the woman who wants to rule any room she enters. Every item in this shop makes a distinctive statement, from crystal barrettes and earrings, adorable flowery leather sandals, to lizard-skin luggage ensembles.

Each month the shop features one-of-a-kind work by a local female artisan, their "Caribbean Queen of the Month." It could be a collection of costume jewelry made with Elizabeth van Brede's handcrafted porcelain beads and pendants. Look over the unusual clutches and belts made from recycled inner tubes by Carina Molina. (They are far more impressive than you might think!) These creative, original

SHOPS

ARUBA ALOE

Since the late 1800s, Aruba has been considered one of the world's top producers of aloe vera products. The extract from this cactus has proven to have remarkable healing properties; it was always favored as a pure, natural product for treating burns and irritated skin. The world lost interest in aloe in the 1950s, but a resurgence of interest in holistic healing and skincare has again prompted a thriving industry.

The **Aruba Aloe Museum and Factory** (Pitastraat 115, 297/588-3222, www.arubaaloe. com, 9am-5pm Mon.-Fri.) in Hato welcomes tour groups and individuals for a history of aloe on the island. In 2000 it acquired a new owner and completed renovation of the field and factory. Their R&D department developed a prescription-strength product that has been tested and praised by burn wards across Europe.

Aruba Aloe produces several lines with varying scents and strength of concentration.

There are sunblocks, after-sun soothing gels and creams, body and face lotions, and haircare products. They have 10 stores scattered about the island, including one at the airport next to the departure lounges. Store hours depend on location. Oranjestad stores are open during the day. Palm Beach and Eagle Beach outlets stay open until 10pm.

Aruba Aloe outlets are located at:

· Alhambra Shopping Mall
· Arawak Gardens
· Aruba International Airport Reina Beatrix
· Cruise Ship Terminal
· Divi Village Resort Lobby
· La Cabana Hotel Lobby
· Palm Beach Plaza
· Paseo Herencia Shopping Mall
· Renaissance Mall

works are the central theme of the store, but there are lots of other unique items to catch a shopper's eye.

KAPRICHO

This is a great place for both genders to perk up a vacation wardrobe. Kapricho (Paseo Herencia Shopping Mall, J. E. Irausquin Blvd. 382-A, 297/586-6510, Kapricho@setarnet.aw, 10am-10pm Mon.-Sat., 5pm-10pm Sun.) has a beautiful selection of resort wear and accessories for women as well as an exceptionally attractive collection for men. They feature soft, comfortable shirts from Tommy Bahama and Tori Richards, which have the tropical look without being too flowery or garish.

MAD HATTER

Be fashionably adorned from top to toes after a visit to Mad Hatter (J. E. Irausquin Blvd. 348, 297/586-0401, 5pm-11pm daily). They claim to have the largest and most diverse hat

selection in the Caribbean. Protect neck and shoulders stylishly with their great floppy straw hats, which go perfectly with beachwear. They are the exclusive agents on Aruba for the Carlos Santana signature hat collection. Their inventory includes handcrafted clutches and casual jewelry, but this is where shopping goes straight to your head.

JEWELERS

Palm Beach does not quite have the concentration of jewelers as Oranjestad. There are more than enough scattered among the various shopping centers and hotels to provide excellent variety and range of quality. Frequently, they are situated close to casinos. They know big winners need an outlet for those big cash payoffs that are hard to transport back home. Colombian Emeralds, Gandelman Jewelers, and Little Switzerland, well known regional franchises, can be found in the major hotels.

DIAMOND SHOPPING

THE FOUR C'S

It is vital while looking for the best deal in diamonds to know the "Four C's" of gemstones: clarity, color, cut, and carat. In these politically correct times, country may also be a consideration. Most consumers usually have another "C"—cost—in mind.

Carat refers to weight or size, and cut refers to the fashion in which the stonecutter has tried to best enhance the natural virtues of the gem. Multiple facets and the depth of the cut affect the brilliance and scintillation. When a round or pear shape diamond is well cut, light enters through the flat part of the stone then travels to the angled underside. Here, it is reflected repeatedly before bouncing back out to the observer's eye. This light is the scintillation, the flashing, fiery effect that makes diamonds so mesmerizing. A stone of a high carat may be poorly proportioned and heavily "discounted." This gives a false impression of a great deal. The brilliant fire that dazzles is the measure of a quality stone.

Color and clarity are the two other most important variables. Diamonds are graded against a white background. Grade is calculated by the hue of the stone compared to a set of master stones graded by the Gemological Institute of America (GIA). There is a wide range of color designations, starting with the purest white and the alphabetic letter D. Color variations work their way down the alphabet, all the way to the Z, which is the deepest yellow of colors, referred to as canary yellow diamonds. Jewelry fashions change to also deploy champagne, chocolate, and black diamonds, their value dictated by current trends. The diamonds most used in multi-stone pieces are the "near colorless" categories G and H.

A very important factor that will make a simple, one-carat stone cost thousands more than a gem three times the size is clarity. Vendor are impressed by patrons who understand what grades of clarity signify. It is a description of the stone while still in the rough, uncut stage.

FLAWS

- **FL**—Flawless, the rarest and most valuable of diamonds.

- **IF**—Internally flawless, with only external flaws while in the rough stage.

- **I1-I3**—You can see flaws with the naked eye.

- **SI1-SI2**—Slight Inclusion: You can easily see flaws with a 10X microscope.

- **VS1-VS2**—Very Slight Inclusion: You need not be an expert to see flaws with a 10X microscope, but it takes a long time (more than about 10 seconds).

- **VVS1-VVS2**—Very, Very Slight Inclusion: Only an expert can detect flaws with a 10X microscope.

There are wide varieties of flaws; many do not affect the integrity of the gem. A diamond need not be flawless to be gorgeous. Flaws can be crystal growth, which sometimes looks like a diamond within the diamond. The extent of the flaw and how it detracts from the beauty of the diamond affects its investment value. Buyers beware of I1-I3 level diamonds.

HUMANE PRACTICES

The term "blood diamond" refers to gems that are mined under repressive regimes with forced labor. African countries in political upheaval are known for this. Famous personalities have endorsed certain brands of diamonds as humane. These stones may be more expensive, but the people that work the mines have humane conditions, with all labor law benefits. These diamond companies have invested and bettered the communities near the mines, providing schools and scholarships. These gems are engraved with a microscopic logo to prove their pedigree.

GEMANI JEWELERS

Another well-respected family operation, Gemani Jewelers (J. E. Irausquin Blvd. 382, 297/588-4242, www.gemani.com, 5pm-10pm daily) is the area dealer for Chopard, Charriol, Corum, Raymond Weil, Mikimoto Pearls, and other quality designer lines. Exceptionally friendly, welcome, and courteous service is their trademark. They also carry some rare stones, such as alexandrite.

JEWELS IN PARADISE

An intimate shop in Palm Beach Plaza, Jewels in Paradise (L. G. Smith Blvd. 95, 297/586-7433, jewelsinparadisearuba@setarnet.aw), has an owner Dinesh who takes pride in carrying unique, one-of-a-kind items. He also has a varied collection of jewels, priced to any budget. Find silver and semi-precious stone pieces or a seven-carat emerald pendant; the selection is that diverse. Whether your taste runs to simple and delicate Italian design, or something from their "Maharani" Collection, inspired by traditional East Indian fashion, you can find something interesting here.

◖ KRISTIE'S JEWELS

A cozy family operation dedicated to quality, Kristie's (J. E. Irausquin Blvd. 382A, 297/586-0598, kristiesjewels@gmail.com, 5pm-10pm daily) is the Palm Beach agent for Hearts on Fire diamonds. The collection consists of unique items designed and manufactured in Italy. Their elegant store offers a tasteful, attractive selection. As agents for Silverado charms, they have an "I Love Aruba" charm with a divi tree crafted exclusively for their collection.

SHOPPING MALLS

The Palm Beach area holds Aruba's greatest concentration of malls, and a concentrated dose it is. Shopping, dining, and entertainment are all contained in bustling beehives spread over a half mile of J. E. Irausquin Boulevard. The promenade attracts islanders and tourists equally. Shopping hours uniformly end at 10pm, but clubs and cafés stay open until at least 1am, and 2am or later on Friday and Saturday nights.

ARAWAK GARDENS

Though principally a dining and entertainment center, Arawak Gardens (J. E. Irausquin Blvd. 370, shopping 5pm-11pm daily, dining and nightlife 11am-2am daily) hosts a plethora of cozy shops and kiosks with a diverse selection of souvenir items. Piles of tee shirts, beach covers in bright colors, and Aruba logo gear of every stripe, are found in the various venues.

DE OLDE MOLEN

Visitors can't help noticing a most unusual sight when they first enter the modern area of Palm Beach: An authentic Dutch windmill over 200 years old is an arresting sight. De Olde Molen foundation (L. G. Smith Blvd 330, 8am-2am daily) is the site of a strip of nightspots, and the grounds have a number of kiosks. They include **Prima Casa Real Estate,** the official **Aruhiba outlet** for Aruban-made cigars, and **Trikes Tours** and **Tiara Air Tours,** for arranging day trips to Curacao and Bonaire.

The windmill was originally built in 1804. It was used in Friesland for dredging water out of the sub-sea level lands. After being damaged by a storm in 1878, it was disassembled and rebuilt in Holland. There it was used as a grain mill, but fell into disuse after new storm damage in 1929. A Dutchman with dreams of living in the tropics purchased what remained in 1960. It was finally rebuilt on Aruba over a two-story foundation.

PALM BEACH PLAZA

The physically largest shopping center in the area, and the newest, is Palm Beach Plaza (L. G. Smith Blvd. 85, 297/586-0045, www.palmbeachplaza.com, shops 10am-10pm, dining and nightlife 7pm-2am). The three floors have 32 stores, a movie theater, bowling alley, children's care center, food court, several restaurants, cozy bars, and family entertainment.

Unique to Palm Beach Plaza is Skechers, Salvatore Farragamo, Mont Blanc, and Lalique outlets. Jewelry stores include Shiva's, Monarch

Palm Beach malls like Paseo Herencia also offer dining and entertainment.

Jewels, Rage Silver, Jewels in Paradise, and My Time, for budget-priced time pieces. Fashionistas will love Benetton and Totto clothing and accessories, Panache, Giordano, and Caribbean Queen.

San Marino and Basinger are the places for elegant shoes, while Goofy Gecko and Art Fusion provide those unusual souvenirs you seek. The mall also has outlets of Post Aruba and Western Union.

◖ PASEO HERENCIA SHOPPING MALL

The first major mall in Palm Beach, Paseo Herencia (J. E. Irausquin Blvd. 382-A, 297/586-6533, http://paseoherencia.com, shops 10am-10pm daily, dining and nightlife noon-2am daily) offers several unique shops. Most notable about this mall is its community spirit, with walls and corridors filled with island information. Displays showcase important moments in Aruba's history and internationally famous Arubans, and impart insight into island culture.

Among the 50 vendors in the mall is the fashionable shop Baci di Roma. For European couture, DGL specializes in Diesel, Gaastra, and Villebrequin. Havana Nines, Mia Boutique, and Kapricho carry elegant tropical clothing. Here is the only Hunkemoller on Aruba, the European version of Victoria's Secret. La Langosta and Agua Bendita sell exclusive lines of Latin designer swimwear. Mario Fernandez is one of the most respected names in leather designer goods. Wenger store is the official agent for their famous culinary accessories and 15-51-item utility penknives of the highest quality.

Jewelers include Kristie's, Little Switzerland, Pandora Boutique, ARZU, Pearl Gems, Times Square, and Sparkles. They offer a range from handcrafted costume jewelry to top-of-the-line precious gemstones. A two-story Maggy's Emporium has a complete menu of spa treatments and salon services, along with all popular brands of scents and cosmetics. Be sure to check out Happy Monkey, because the world can never have too many plush monkeys. There is also a handy kiosk, "First Aid," with scores of over-the-counter remedies normally sold in drugstores. The Palm Beach outlet for Mopa Mopa crafts is also here in a shop called The Mask. This is also the home to The Cinemas, Aruba's largest movie multiplex.

SOUTH BEACH CENTRE

South Beach Centre (J. E. Irausquin Blvd. 55, shops 10am-10pm daily, dining and nightlife noon-2am daily) occupies a very large complex at the corner of J. E. Irausquin Boulevard and the Noord-Palm Beach Road. Just look for the giant Hard Rock Café neon guitar and you are there. This is an amalgam of local and international eateries, with a few shops and a spa interspersed between them. Most shopping is done at the kiosks, which line the sidewalk. They offer all sorts of bargain-priced souvenirs.

Formal shops include a Lazy Lizard, for some stylish resort wear and amusing gifts. Island Treasures stocks inexpensive beach bags, sandals, wraps, and other typical tropical gear in

© ROSALIE KLEIN

SHOPS

flowery prints. They also have the South Beach Mini-Market for sundry items.

THE VILLAGE

A standout from the standard Miami Beach architecture of the area is The Village (J. E. Irausquin Blvd. 348, shops 5pm-10pm daily, dining and nightlife 7am-2am daily), modeled to look like a community of classic Aruban *cunucu* houses. This is a happening place for all ages. Aside from the massive flea market occupying the main courtyard at night, The Village is lined with several attractive stores. Mad Hatter stocks very interesting accessories and original handcrafted beadwork is found at Oma Bohemian Store.

Señor Frog's and Gusto are favorite places for the club crowd, with a highly diverse ambiance. Papillion gourmet restaurant is right next to 5 Burgers Aruba.

North Coast

Aruba's traditional wilderness offers little shopping outside of a few of the tourist sites. Most carry typical tourist items, like flowery beach covers and souvenir tee shirts. The shops of the Donkey Sanctuary and Ostrich Farm offer some very unique mementos and giftware.

GIFTS AND SOUVENIRS
AFRICAN ART BOUTIQUE
AT OSTRICH FARM

After taking a tour of the Aruba Ostrich Farm, make sure to visit the farm's unique African Art Boutique (Matividiri 57, 297/585-9630, www.arubaostrichfarm.com, 9:30am-5pm daily) for a peek at their surprising collection. Home fashion, furniture, original carvings, kitchen linens, and the like are distinctive and extremely attractive. It isn't necessary to travel half way around the world to obtain some authentic African art. Another unique item is the artwork made from hollowed out ostrich eggs. Collectors of the unusual will find these hand-painted creations most intriguing.

DONKEY SANCTUARY

In addition to an entertaining encounter with some charming residents, the Donkey Sanctuary (Santa Lucia 4A, Donkey Distress Hotline 297/593-2933, www.arubandonkey.org, 9am-4pm Mon.-Fri., 10am-3pm Sat.-Sun.) has a shop of unique crafts and gifts, which support their work. The collection of donkey paraphernalia is quite large, may of them custom-made crafts and original paintings donated by top island artists. All proceeds assist in the care and feeding of the denizens of the sanctuary.

SALES TAX

Aruba has a 1.5 percent sales tax, which is actually a turnover tax called "Belasting op Bedrijfsomzetten" or BBO. It was introduced in January of 2007 and lowered from 3 percent to 1.5 percent in 2010.

Certain enterprises and goods are exempt, such as the medical profession and prescription drugs. Commercial enterprises, particularly supermarkets, apply the sales tax. Other venues, such as jewelers, which cater specifically to tourists, absorb the tax expense or build it into the cost of goods, rather than add it on to a purchase.

CUSTOMS ALLOWANCES AND RESTRICTIONS

Travelers returning to the United States are required to declare the following on a CBP form in U.S. currency:

- Items purchased.
- Items received as gifts.
- Items bought in duty-free shops, on the ship, or on the plane.
- Repairs or alterations to any items taken abroad and then brought back, even if the alterations were performed free of charge.
- Items brought home for someone else.
- Items intended to sell or use in a business, including merchandise taken out of the United States.

To avoid being charged duty upon return, it is advised that costly electronic items that are less than six months old be registered upon departure from the United States.

EXEMPTIONS

Travelers returning from Aruba have an $800 standard duty-free exemption. It will be applied in the following instances:

- Items for personal or household use or intended to be given as gifts.
- Items declared to CBP. If not declaring an item that should have been, there is possible fortitude or penalties.
- Items classified as accompanying baggage, returning with the traveler. Mailed items do not qualify.
- Purchases of fine art, such as original paintings or sculpture, are duty-free.

Exemptions are applicable on a cumulative basis. Frequent travelers must take into account items declared 30 days or less prior to their present return. Items declared on previous journeys less than 30 days past will be deducted from the $800 exemption.

Two liters of alcoholic beverages, as long as one was produced in a U.S. Insular Possession (e.g., Puerto Rico), are allowed when combined with liquors distilled and bottled in the Caribbean basin or Andean countries. Otherwise, the limit is one liter. Travelers carrying alcohol must be over 21 and returning to a state that has no restrictions on its import. Normally, no more than 200 cigarettes and 100 cigars are exempt, if they are within the $800 allotment ceiling. The same double allowance for liquor can be applied to cigarettes and cigars, when half that allowance is purchased in a U.S. Insular Possession.

Travelers might avoid duties for a total of over $800 in goods depending on circumstances and the items. If a piece of fine jewelry costing $700 is received as a gift, while other miscellaneous goods were purchased, the official may waive duty, even if the total exceeds $800.

Cruise ship passengers who have stopped in multiple Caribbean basin or Andean countries may receive an allowance of $1,600 as duty-free purchases. This is applicable if one of the ports of purchase was a U.S. Insular Possession such as Puerto Rico or the U.S. Virgin Islands. Duty free purchases from the Caribbean basin or Andean countries are limited to $800. An additional $800 in duty-free purchases will be allowed from the Insular Possession for a total of $1,600. A number of cruises stopping in Aruba embark from Puerto Rico. This regulation allows travelers additional purchases from the embarkation point. It is essential to retain receipts on all purchases.

PROHIBITED ITEMS

- Cuban Cigars
- Live Birds of any kind—exotic, domestic, or wild (they may carry a strain of Avian Flu)
- Live fish, marine animals, and mollusks
- Meats, fruits, vegetables, plants, seeds, animals, and plant and animal products (including soup or soup products)
- Prescription drugs

Some items, such as cooked foods, may be exempt. A full declaration of nature and origin should be made to a customs officer. Travelers departing Aruba will be passing through customs prior to their return flight. If you purchased fruit (unsealed), local snacks, or sandwiches to eat on the plane, be sure to inform the customs officers.

Santa Cruz, Paradera, and Piedra Plat

The best of Aruba's shopping is focused in the commercial areas of Oranjestad and Palm Beach that serve both tourists and residents. The dedicated residential areas of Santa Cruz, Paradera, and Piedra Plat have some souvenir shops offering logo shirts and tropical pattern resort wear attached to such sights as the Casabari Rock Formation. Their inventory is the same as similar shops found within the popular tourist areas.

The most unique shop here is the Rococo Plaza, which is a must-visit for collectors and those that enjoy antique hunting.

ANTIQUES
ROCOCO PLAZA

Aruba's only antique center is Rococo Plaza (Tanki Leendert 158-G, 297/741-5640, http://antiquesaruba.com, 9am-1pm and 3:30pm-5:30pm Mon.-Fri., 9am-1pm Sat.), which can be spotted from afar by its unique dual-tower entrance. While touring some of the standard sights, you are bound to pass by Rococo Plaza. It is on the way to Arikok National Park, and worth a stop for antique enthusiasts. The store is enormous. Allow some time to peruse the 20 rooms of curios from diverse eras. Most of the inventory is imported from Europe, and there are some truly fascinating items. Collectors will have a field day.

Expect to find vintage cameras and photos, standup pianos, art deco sconces, and authentic Louis Quinze furniture. Naturally, some chaff surrounds the gems. Though there is quite a lot to work through, many unique treasures await those with a penchant for collecting.

© ROSALIE KLEIN

The distinctive towers of Rococo Plaza are easy to find.

ACCOMMODATIONS

One of Aruba's greatest attractions are the glamorous, elegant resorts that line the shore along Palm Beach, Eagle Beach, and Manchebo Beach. When the first resorts were built along the shore, the original pioneers of Aruba's tourism industry had a personal vision of ambiance that would best suit each area. They set the tone for subsequent projects, with each resort designed to create an atmosphere to meet the particular desires and expectations of their guests. There are large, bustling, full-service resorts with casinos and clubs for nighttime excitement, or small, tranquil getaways for those that seek to escape from their workaday world and fully relax.

Most of these options are usually members of the Aruba Hotel and Tourism Authority (AHATA). AHATA member resorts offer excellent service, quality accommodations, and are sincerely concerned about the satisfaction of their guests. They maintain a standard that the Aruba Tourism Authority (ATA) endorses. Many travel agents have inspected these facilities as well and are very comfortable recommending them.

Whether choosing a large, full-service resort or one of the smaller guesthouses, a consistent element is the famed hospitality of the region. When veteran visitors explain the reasons they return to Aruba annually, they list the reliable weather and beautiful beaches, but the sincere welcome they receive from resort staff and island residents is paramount.

In the 1960s, when the island was first trying to build its tourist market, Aruban families actually welcomed vacationers into their homes

© ROSALIE KLEIN

HIGHLIGHTS

LOOK FOR **((** TO FIND RECOMMENDED ACCOMMODATIONS.

((**Wonders Boutique Hotel:** This extremely attractive, elegant guesthouse is convenient to the best shopping, dining, and entertainment in Oranjestad (page 170).

((**Renaissance Resort:** Oranjestad's only full-service resort has excellent restaurants, a beautiful spa, and all the amenities for far less money than the resorts in Palm Beach (page 170).

((**Divi Dutch Village:** Offering everything for golfers and their non-golfing families, these apartments surround the lush Divi Links golf course and one of the most gorgeous pool decks on Aruba (page 171).

((**Pearl:** Not far from the beach, this hidden gem is a great value for families, with two blocks of spacious duplex townhouses, each with their own large pool (page 173).

((**Aruba Beach Front:** Luxuriate in your own beachfront home for a week in an exclusive neighborhood, or share a place for a very affordable rate. This small guesthouse is an interesting alternative to the big hotels (page 177).

((**Boardwalk Hotel Aruba:** This tranquil oasis has only 13 spacious casitas surrounded by lush gardens. It is a beautiful, clean facility with homey touches and personality (page 178).

((**Villa Bougainvillea:** Staying at spacious apartments attached to a private home with a pool and individual terraces, you will feel like a guest, not a customer (page 180).

((**Aruba Beach Chalets:** These beautiful duplex townhouse apartments, situated directly on the water are absolutely perfect for an isolated getaway, with beach access and great snorkeling (page 184).

for no charge when the few existing resorts were filled. This demonstration of authentic hospitality inspired the mission and values behind the chain of Divi Resorts, one of the largest and most popular local franchises on Aruba.

Smaller lodgings like guesthouses and apartment complexes are great for visitors who want to be truly immersed in the local environment of Aruba, away from the tourist scene. A number of guesthouses and vacation apartment complexes scattered around the island also boast hospitable staff and quality rooms (though usually not a large number of rooms). There is often a very homey environment at these establishments that allows guests to get to know the owners and feel like they are staying in someone's home. Guesthouses, in most cases, require walking some distance to a beach. A rare few actually abut the sea. Renting a car is almost always necessary if you stay in this type of accommodation. However, some guesthouse owners assist with arranging a car rental by making reservations and taking guests to the rental office or having the car

delivered. They can also procure discounts on weekly rates.

For such a small island, Aruba has a great number of accommodations to suit all tastes. Whether choosing escape or excitement for your island vacation, you can find a resort or area that fits the mood. Though very different in ambiance, the main tourist areas of Palm Beach, Manchebo Beach, Eagle Beach, and Oranjestad are in such close proximity to each other that their particular amenities are easily accessible to vacationers wishing a change of scene for the day or evening. Resort staff readily welcome visitors who are not guests of their resort to sample their shops, restaurants, and casinos.

CHOOSING AN ACCOMMODATION

Aruba's capital **Oranjestad** is mostly populated with guesthouses and smaller apartments. It has two AHATA members, Renaissance and Talk of the Town. The lesser expensive accommodations are within a similar price range, but some rent only by the week and not by the day. A few are converted homes that are exceptionally charming.

Generally, accommodations in Oranjestad are far less expensive than the principal shorefront areas of Palm Beach, Manchebo Beach, and Eagle Beach.

Staying in the island's capital imparts an authentic feeling for island life, with restaurants geared and priced for locals, just minutes from your door. Most of Aruba's historical sights are within easy walking distance. For fans of Carnival events, these are the ideal accommodations for easily taking in the parades and many of the nighttime festivities.

What the accommodations in Oranjestad generally lack is the immediate access to the beach and sea that some consider an essential aspect of a Caribbean vacation. However, there are a few public beaches within easy walking distance of most guesthouses. Renaissance Resort has compensated by creating a beach for their guests, or offering access to a private island by regularly scheduled boat transport, with beautiful, tranquil beaches.

The first resorts built on **Manchebo Beach** were very small enterprises, only 20 rooms each, with casual, "barefoot elegance" their trademark ambiance. For decades, Manchebo has been the center of timesharing on Aruba. **Eagle Beach** has become a focus for condominium development. Many of the facilities offer their unoccupied units for rent. Families seeking spacious accommodations that allow them to cook find this appealing, as do those vacationers who want to be away from the hustle and bustle of the very large Palm Beach resorts. These resorts do not have long lines waiting for beach towels, lounge chairs, or a palapa for shade, which the large Palm Beach resorts often require guests to reserve. On weekdays, the nearby undeveloped beach areas are empty; though they can get busy with islanders on the weekends.

Timeshare rooms are usually a touch more luxurious and larger than the standard hotel room, as they were built to be sold, not rented. All come with either a full kitchen or a very well equipped kitchenette, nice for families that prefer to eat in and save money for a couple of meals out. Most rooms have at least one separate bedroom and a sofa bed in the living room to accommodate a family of four comfortably.

Palm Beach is a mile-long strip of glamorous, high-rise resorts, bustling with activity both day and night. Palm Beach is where the greatest concentration of mega-resorts are found, each offering every sort of amenity and service imaginable and consisting of 300 rooms or more. These glitzy, elaborate facilities are designed to meet guests' needs and desires without them ever having to leave the premises. They offer myriad dining choices and cocktail lounges, spas, shopping arcades, casinos, shows, game rooms for the kids, access to beautiful beaches and stunning pool decks, and exceptional catering and event departments for weddings and conventions.

The major Palm Beach resorts may vary slightly from one to the next, perhaps some are a bit more exclusive (or exclusively priced) in amenities and accoutrements, but all pretty much conform to a certain standard. Most operate under some large, international, corporate hospitality brand, which usually carries with it an adhesion to the star system of rating, and, to some extent, the corporate guarantee of satisfaction.

If your taste runs to quiet little guesthouses far from the madding crowd, with a more personal touch and usually a relationship with the owner, then look beyond Palm Beach proper to the adjacent **Malmok.**

Aruba's hinterlands of **Santa Cruz** and **Savaneta** offer a scattering of guesthouses, with one on the southern shore boasting a bit of private beach. They generally offer very personal service, vastly reduced rates over the western shore resorts, and some surprising amenities, such as an on-site spa, breakfast included, or exceptionally attractive pool decks. They are almost all set up as apartments, uniformly outfitted with kitchens and extra beds or sofa beds to easily accommodate four or more.

ACCOMMODATIONS

Oranjestad

A stay in the island's capital immerses vacationers in island life, history, and activities. Scores of restaurants and shops are close by, but beaches require a bit of travel. Smaller guesthouses tend to be mostly inhabited by a business trade, rather than tourists.

$50-100
ARUBA HARMONY
Situated in Ponton, an area bordering north Oranjestad, Aruba Harmony Apartments (Palmitastraat 9, 297/592-7661, www.aruba-harmony.com, $79 studios, $179 two-bedroom suites) is secreted away in an upscale neighborhood, surrounded by attractive homes. Ten rooms circle the courtyard, which has a small pool. There is an abundance of picnic tables and comfortable deck chairs for dining outdoors, and all rooms are equipped with full kitchens. The clientele is largely European.

A unique aspect: The place gets its name from owner-operator Barbara Arends's enthusiasm for the practice of feng shui. The rooms and their placement take this into account, designed to be beneficial to your chi. Barbara also offers special packages that include treatments in the on-site spa, which are attuned to an individual's Chinese zodiac sign and horoscope. They are intended to create harmony and balance. Less expensive European spa treatments are also an option.

Activities packages in conjunction with scuba and deep sea fishing operators can also be arranged, along with ecotours. When making reservations, send flight and arrival time and you will be greeted at the airport.

ARUBIANA APARTMENTS
A pleasant but plain collection of 15 apartments close to the airport, Arubiana Apartments (Stadionweg 4B, 297/587-7700, www.aru-biana-apartments.com, $620/week) rent by the week only. They are just a short walk from Nikky Beach and the main part of town. The exterior is rather utilitarian, with no sort of grounds or pool. Rooms are spacious and attractively decorated.

The apartments include a living room, separate bedroom, fully-equipped kitchen, free Wi-Fi, and a mobile phone to use during your stay. They also offer services such as doing laundry (no ironing) and a pre-arrival shopping service to fill the cupboard for those who prefer to cook in. The apartments can sleep a family of four comfortably. They tend to attract a business and Latin clientele.

$100-200
ARUBA SURFSIDE MARINA
A very clean, modern facility, Aruba Surfside Marina (L. G. Smith Blvd. 7, 297/583-0300, www.arubasurfsidemarina.com, $145, minimum of four nights) has only a few rooms. The upper level holds three studios plus two suites with all terraces being oceanfront. Each unit comes with fridge, microwave, coffeemaker, and utensils. The first floor is entirely for meeting and conference rooms, so it does get some traffic for events and business presentations on a daily basis, and is popular with business travelers. Room rates include a continental breakfast for two served on the room's balcony.

The expansive courtyard makes it a popular place for local weddings and other catered events; there is a gazebo, gardens, and a beautiful view of the sea and shore, but no pool. There is immediate access to a very quiet, semi-secluded beach area. This is a good spot if planning a destination wedding and wishing to be away from the tourist crowds. The management is well versed in arranging wedding events, as this is their specialty.

CAMACURI APARTMENTS
The description of Camacuri Apartments (Avenida Milio J. Croes 46B, 297/582-6805, www.camacuriapartmentsaruba.com, studios

ALTERNATIVE ACCOMMODATIONS

Families on a budget or groups of friends looking to save may wish to explore the option of renting a house while on Aruba. There are quite a few new, gated communities offering condominiums, townhouses, and villas while owners are off island. Aside from these communities, there are also quite a few freestanding homes available for at least a week at a time. If you prefer privacy and are looking for an island hideaway, the cost and logistics of renting a home are ideal. Many are only minutes from the beach. Nearly all have swimming pools.

Prices vary from as little as $650 per week for a comfortable one- or two-bedroom home to as high as $10,000 for some of the luxurious mansions within the Tierra Del Sol Country Club and Golf Course. Minimum one-week rentals are required, and long-term rentals of a month or more obviously have better rates. Rental homes are usually equipped with all appliances, including TVs, and other conveniences, such as linens and tableware.

Here are four reliable brokers for villa rentals:

· **Aruba Happy Rentals** (P.O Box 5403 Oranjestad, 297/592-08287, http://aruba-happyrentals.com)

· **Aruba Palms Realtors** (J. E. Irausquin Blvd. 370, 297/566-0339 or 877/586-8962, www.arubapalmsrealtors.com)

· **Aruba Villa Rentals** (Salina Cerca 35E, 297/586-429, www.ArubaVillaRentals.com)

· **Prima Casa Real Estate** (J. E. Irausquin Blvd. 330, 297/583-3350, http://aruba-realty.com)

$111/night, $695/week) as "a hideaway" is right on the money. They have 39 apartments tucked away behind houses bordering a field and a major stadium. Camacuri is only found by turning down a dirt road, across from the Aruba Entertainment Center. There is no indication of where to go, but once you know, it is easy to find. It does offer a surprising, tranquil oasis, just on the eastern outskirts of town, with sprawling gardens and a nice pool.

Spread out over an extensive patch of land, it has a main area of rooms around a courtyard, as well as scattered, two-story casitas with suites. The largest, top-of-the-line suite has a master bedroom in a loft with its own separate bathroom. All come equipped with kitchens, even the studios. The main part of town is perhaps a 15-minute walk away; for grocery shopping, a small market is nearby, nestled in an extensive commercial area.

TALK OF THE TOWN

Not quite a guesthouse or a major resort, Talk of the Town (L. G. Smith Blvd. 2, 297/582-3380, www.tottaruba.com, $199, includes buffet breakfast) features a bit of history. The original resort of seven rooms was Aruba's first tourist hotel with pool deck, restaurant, ocean view, and meeting rooms. Those first rooms date back to 1943 when the resort was opened as The Coral Strand; the rooms are now the budget section of the resort.

Compared to Aruba's mega-resorts, this is a simple facility. The majority of the resort consists of 59 newly-refurbished, attractive, and clean rooms. A section of one- and two-bedroom apartments is aimed at long-term guests and families. The apartments are not fancy, but spacious and pleasant, with large, fully-equipped kitchens and giant plasma TVs.

An Olympic-style pool and the adjacent Moonlight Grill are the heart of the resort. A moderately priced menu offers fresh fish and local dishes along with hamburgers and hotdogs. The resort has an arrangement with nearby Nikky Beach for the use of their lounge chairs.

Talk of the Town attracts a regular business crowd since it is in town and close to the airport. It is also a favorite place at Carnival time for islanders to rent a room to watch all the major parades from the terraces.

ACCOMMODATIONS

WONDERS BOUTIQUE HOTEL

Wonders Boutique Hotel (Emmastraat 63, 297/593-4032, www.wondersaruba.com, $119) is an exceedingly charming alternative to formal resorts and is perfect for those seeking something out of the ordinary. It is fairly new and very well maintained. It only has eight, large, air-conditioned studio rooms, with very spacious bathrooms. Each room comes with a well-stocked and reasonably priced mini-bar and a coffeemaker.

Formally a very large, two-story home, the hotel is extensively decorated with original art. Though the pool is small, just big enough for a cooling dip, the entire back courtyard is delightful with lush gardens. There is a BBQ and a well-equipped shared kitchen available for guests. The management also offers breakfast on the premises, not included with the price of the room and a little bit pricey compared to a café priced for locals.

The clientele are mixed, though usually with a European flavor. The hotel is only a short walk to a number of fine coffee shops and principal attractions. The owner provides round-trip transport to and from the airport and a ride to Eagle Beach or Palm Beach, if needed.

If you really wish to feel a part of island life, this is a very good place to be; it is rated superb by reviewers on a number of websites. Host Gaston is trying to do something special here, and he is succeeding!

OVER $200

RENAISSANCE RESORT

Oranjestad has one full-service resort, the Renaissance (L. G. Smith Blvd. 82, 297/583-6000 or toll free in U.S. 800/421-8188, www.marriott.com, Marina Tower $288.60, Beach Tower $351.60), which dominates the harbor and L. G. Smith Boulevard. Though operating under the Renaissance name, this is the only major resort wholly owned by a local, family-owned company. Incorporated into the resort properties are two elegant shopping malls, two casinos, a convention center, a helipad, Oranjestad Harbor, and—offshore—_Renaissance Island. The two sections of the resort are well separated by L. G Smith Boulevard and the Renaissance Marketplace, but both have views of Oranjestad Harbor. A free tram transports guests between them.

The Marina Tower fronts the harbor on L. G. Smith Boulevard and is the adults-only section. The lobby and mall on which it sits are filled with designer name signature stores. The general ambiance is described as "island chic." The clientele is diverse; though on weekends it is decidedly wealthy South Americans enjoying a couple of days of shopping and play. Central to the mall is the dock for the ferries to Renaissance Island. The pool deck is on the mezzanine level and overlooks the harbor and L. G. Smith Boulevard. Guests at the Marina Tower lack the convenience of being able to easily access their room once out on the island, and the pool area is rather public.

Beach Tower has one- and two-bedroom suites, as the complex was originally planned and sold as timeshares. It has its very own attractive lagoon, huge free-form pool deck, and artificially-constructed beach. Each section of the resort has a dedicated concierge, activities desk, and car rental service.

Renaissance Island was developed to service the original Marina Toweer, and is a beautiful facility with a restaurant and spa, watersports operator, plus three separate beaches (including a secluded adults-only section for topless sunbathing). It is quite popular for elegant, catered affairs and weddings. The island is accessed by speedboats departing from two locations around every 15 minutes. Day passes are sold to non-hotel guests at the concierge desks, which include lunch, a drink, and a choice of water activity equipment. Unlimited use of the island is included for all guests.

This is a resort with high standards, a smoke-free policy, and the added benefit of being in town. It offers the opportunity to get more of the feel of the island and its culture.

Eagle Beach and Manchebo Beach

Dominating much of the Manchebo Beach area are the resorts run by Divi Properties. This concern also runs The Links golf course, with surrounding condos and timeshares, and the Alhambra Shopping Bazaar. Each resort has a distinctive personality.

The Divi Properties all started when a lawyer from upstate New York, Wally Wiggins, brought his family on vacation to Aruba in 1965. This began a decades-long love affair with Aruba. Wally built the first Divi resort because he wanted to have a place to stay on the beach and zoning laws would not allow a private home. They started with 20 rooms, as a permit would allow no less. It opened the same day as Neil Armstrong walked on the moon. One small step for Mr. Wiggins, family, and friends became a giant step for Aruba's tourism.

$100-200

QUALITY APARTMENTS

Many timeshare owners elect to extend their stay at Quality Apartments (Schotlandstraat 70, 297/582-0697, www.arubaqualityapartments.com, starting at $125). This family-run facility has a nice pool, plus large, comfortable, and very clean rooms. There are studios with loft bedrooms and one-bedroom suites. The entire facility has 73 units; it is located on a fairly busy commercial thoroughfare, but most rooms are set back from the street and quiet. It is not far from major supermarkets and shopping.

Amenities include a multi-machine laundromat, fitness room, free Wi-Fi in all rooms, plus a computer station for guests who don't like to travel with their toys. Over the years, guests have left behind their books, resulting in an extensive lending library of ideal beach reading, in several languages.

TROPICANA RESORT & CASINO

Tropicana Resort & Casino (J. E. Irausquin Blvd. 248, 297/587-9000, www.troparuba.com, $126 for a one-bedroom suite, service

charge and tax included) was originally built as an annex to the La Cabana Resort. This very large facility (over 360 rooms) changed hands a few times, but was acquired in 2011 by the Tropicana hospitality chain of Atlantic City. The rooms are in the process of being renovated; until completion, bargain rates are in effect.

The complex is wrapped around a very attractive pool deck with two large free form pools. One pool has a waterfall and the other attracts most of the kids with one of the best waterslides on Aruba, which also has a swim-up bar. Whirlpools and kids' pools are separate. It is a long walk to the beach.

There are no real grounds beyond the pool deck to speak of, nor lush landscaping, but you can't beat the bargain rate. Rooms were timeshares, so they have full kitchens and are spacious; though they are showing their age a bit. Since Tropicana was built as an addition to La Cabana, not much was originally invested in the lobby or guest lounge; these were left to the main resort. (La Cabana Resort is now completely separate). New management has seen the community areas attractively renovated. Affiliated casino, tennis courts, and restaurant are located in the vast parking lot. They have a small snack bar around the pool, Dunkin' Donuts and Baskin Robbins on the premises, and a mini-market.

$200-300

◖ DIVI DUTCH VILLAGE

The huge, rambling facility of Divi Dutch Village (J. E. Irausquin Blvd. 93, 297/583-5000 or 800/367-3484, www.dividutchvillage.com, Dutch Village $187, Divi Village $236, Divi Golf Village $278.57 for up to four in a room) is ideal for golfers and their families who want other activities. The closer to the course, the more expensive the rooms, but also more luxurious and newer buildings.

Dutch Village is adjacent to the Tamarijn

EXTENDED STAYS

Travelers planning to stay more than the automatically allotted 30 days may need to file a form with **DIMAS** (Wilhelminastraat 31-33, Oranjestad, 297/522-1500, www.dimasaruba.com, 7:30am-11:30am and 2:30pm-4pm Mon.-Thurs.), the Department of Immigration. Officers at the airport issue a visitor's visa for one month; anyone planning to stay longer should inform the officer while passing through immigration. Traveling as a tourist allows visitors to stay in Aruba a total of 180 days out of a year without a work or residence permit.

Upon entry at the airport an extension of a stay for more than 30 days but not exceeding 180 days can be obtained immediately by the nationals of the Kingdom of the Netherlands or its territories and independent entities, United States, Canada, United Kingdom, Ireland, and The Schengen Territory. Those with property on Aruba, such as a house, condominium, apartment, and timeshare, can immediately apply to extend their stay. They should be prepared to show proof of ownership.

The migration officer can grant up to 90 days if satisfied that the visitor has sufficient funds to cover an extended stay. All tourists applying for an extension beyond 30 days are required to have valid travel insurance (medical and liability) for the duration of the extended stay.

Those wishing to extend their stay beyond that indicated by a migration officer on the Embarkation-Debarkation form (ED-Card) can file an application for an extension of stay at the DIMAS offices. There is no filing fee for a tourist extension application. Required forms can be downloaded from their website. Applicants should have copies made of all filled out forms prior to applying.

The following documents must be presented:
· Original application form for extension of tourist stay.
· Copy of the profile page and all the written and stamped pages of the petitioner's passport, valid for at least another three months from when the extension is applied for.
· Copy of Embarkation-Debarkation form (ED-Card).
· Copy of a valid return ticket.
· Copy of valid travel insurance (medical and liability) for the duration of the extended stay.

If the petitioner is not staying at their own private residence or a hotel, they need to present a declaration of guarantee from a resident of Aruba who will accept liability for expenses incurred during the petitioner's stay. Anyone planning to stay longer than 180 days in Aruba will need a residence permit and will not be considered a tourist.

---

on the water side of J. E. Irausquin Boulevard, which also allows direct access to the beach. The buildings are spread out and arranged around three separate swimming pools, with lush gardens. These are the oldest units in the complex, but newly refurbished and redecorated. The top two floors are duplexes with master bedrooms and private baths on the upper level. All the rooms have individual hot tubs on the terraces.

Divi Village is newer and across the road from the beach. The pool deck looks out on the main thoroughfare. It is the tennis center for the resort complex and closer to the golf course, but with better beach access and is the "in-between" phase.

The final section of Divi Village is adjacent to Divi Links golf course. These apartments are set far back from the main road and beach. To compensate, there is the Infiniti pool, one of the most sumptuous and expansive pool decks on Aruba, directly overlooking the fairway. These buildings are also closer to the clubhouse, an attractive facility with two fine restaurants, Mulligan's and Windows on Aruba.

Being timeshares, Divi Dutch Village has a generally mature crowd, with lots of grandchildren around during peak holiday weeks.

© ROSALIE KLEIN

Divi Dutch Villiage

PARADISE BEACH VILLAS

Another attractive, intimate timeshare, renting per night, is Paradise Beach Villas (J. E. Irausquin Blvd. 64, 297/587-4000, www. paradisebeachvillas-aruba.com, studios $182, one-bedroom suites $312, taxes and service charge included). Situated on the south side of La Cabana Resort, this small, attractive complex has something of a history. The developers went bankrupt and the facility would have been abandoned, but the owners rallied together to purchase it and salvage their investment. This lends it a decided "community" ambiance. Rooms are rented out, but the general clientele are long-term repeat visitors who have a tangible stake in the facility.

This is also a family-oriented resort and there is a palpable relationship between staff and guests. The rooms are spacious and nicely appointed. They have an excellent on-site restaurant, Carambola, which offers discounted rates for those staying at the resort. Guests must cross J. E. Irausquin Boulevard to access the beach.

◖ PEARL

Luxurious but very reasonably priced accommodations are found at Pearl (J. E. Irausquin Blvd. 232A, 297/594-5000 or toll free in U.S. 866/978-7473, www.arubapearl.com, starting at $200, $10 for each additional person, children under 3 are free), a condominium complex that regularly rents out at a nightly rate. Prices go up as they fill up.

Located in a cul-de-sac at the juncture of Manchebo Beach and Eagle Beach, the facility has 25 identical two-bedroom duplex townhouses, with everything a family needs. There are two spacious bedrooms upstairs, each with their own bathroom, and a half-bath on the first level. The townhouse has a beautifully appointed kitchen, living room, and terrace, with high quality furniture and fixtures. Balconies overlook the two rather utilitarian pool decks, which are rarely crowded.

Conference and fitness rooms are situated off the lobby. They keep two BBQs by the large shade palapa at the main pool and an ice machine with bags of ice, to fill coolers for the beach. The concierges in the lobby assists with tours, car rentals, and more; they are very amenable and eager to please. Daily maid service is included, which is rare for a condo complex. This is a very quiet place with Eagle Beach only five minutes away on foot.

$300-400
AMSTERDAM MANOR BEACH RESORT
The noticeably unique architecture of Amsterdam Manor Beach Resort (J. E. Irausquin Blvd. 252, 297/527-1100 or 800/969-2310, www.amsterdammanor.com, standard studios $305) exterior captures one's attention. It is a bit of Bavaria in Aruba, looking something like a medieval turreted castle, yet cozy at the same time. The rooms were originally done in a very heavy, European old-country design, but have recently been redecorated for a much more sleek, modern look, and the results are very attractive.

There is a tiny pool deck but the beach is easily accessed by crossing the road. With few rooms but a long stretch of beach, the resort is never crowded. It has an excellent, romantic restaurant on the beach, called Passions.

This resort is Green Globe Certified and award winning for its eco-friendly practices, including being non-smoking throughout.

ARUBA BEACH CLUB AND CASA DEL MAR
Though physically connected and appearing as one large resort with contrasting architecture, Aruba Beach Club and Cas Del Mar (J. E. Irausquin Blvd. 53, Aruba Beach Club 297/582-3000, Casa Del Mar 297/582-7000, www.arubabeachclub.info, www.casadelmararuba.com, one-bedroom suites $325) are two separate corporate entities, each with their own general manager, reception, and expansive pool decks. (This all has to do with tax structures.) They also have separate activities directors, guest lounges, and waterfront restaurants, but share tennis courts and other facilities. Each has pleasant and reasonably priced beachfront restaurants, which are independently owned.

Lounge chairs and pool decks can be used interchangeably by all guests. A separate section away from the beach is called the Ambassador Suites. This area has a small pool and lower rates.

Aruba Beach Club (ABC) was the island's first timeshare facility, opening its doors in 1979. It has a very devoted clientele, many of them staying for months during the winter, a real "home away from home." Most bought in during the groundbreaking, and now are vacationing with their grandchildren. Both ABC and Casa Del Mar (CDM) have creative, energetic activity directors who specialize in keeping kids entertained. They often moonlight as babysitters. There is daily bingo and other such pastimes. Families will find they soon feel connected to an extended "Aruba family."

CDM has a more contemporary pool deck, but both have plain, rectangular pools, not the free-form works of art that is standard now. If you need to be near the action and nightlife, or around other singles, you might prefer staying somewhere else.

MANCHEBO BEACH RESORT
The Manchebo Beach Resort is a cozy, full-service resort with a superior beachfront (J. E. Irausquin Blvd. 55, toll free 888/673-8036, 297/582-3444, www.manchebo.com, $310 plus 20.5 percent taxes). It opened within months of the Divi Resort in 1969 and is a reflection of that time, with an informal, open-air lobby. There are only two stories, and all rooms have an ocean view. The rooms and grounds were renovated and refreshed in 2011.

Sitting right on the island's southwest point, it has the widest beach on Aruba. This is where Spa Del Sol has an attractive facility. Massages are done in curtained kiosks on the beach. Yoga on the beach sessions are also conducted daily in the shade of the spa.

The resort is an institution for much of its clientele. It is a mix of mature American and European crowds who have been staying here for years. The lobby leads directly to an equally informal open-air restaurant, which at night becomes Ike's Place. The poolside bar has a stunning view and is where most end up around sunset for happy hour. The deck is small and an extension of the restaurant, with an appealing set-up for dining. When Ike Cohen opened the resort, he installed one of the island's most famous gourmet restaurants, the French Steakhouse, which is still a great value. Chamber music recitals are hosted here once a month on Sunday mornings.

$400-500

BUCUTI & TARA BEACH

For a truly tranquil getaway, this owner-operated boutique resort, Bucuti & Tara Beach (L. G. Smith Blvd. 55B, 297/583-1100, www.bucuti.com, $448-513) is adults only. The 104 rooms are divided between two sections: the original Bucuti standard rooms with balcony and the 40 suites of the Tara, which are more luxurious and spacious accommodations. All Tara rooms have a direct ocean view. Room prices are on a modified European Plan, which includes a gourmet, full American buffet breakfast; all room taxes and service charges; plus no extra fee for local calls, which usually cost around $5+ everywhere else. Each room is provided with their own Lenovo netbook upon check-in. Skype is installed to use for e-mailing or chatting with the folks at home at no additional cost. There is free Wi-Fi throughout the resort. A unique perk to the Tara suites is a huge bathroom, with a cable television screen set up in a section of the equally huge mirror. If you can't stand to miss a minute of a show or a big game for a pit stop, you don't have to.

Guests are greeted with a complimentary champagne toast. A gift souvenir water bottle, in keeping with their strict environmental care policy, is part of the welcome. Bottles can be refilled at various water stations on the beach. The resort and its owner, Ewald Biemans, have been cited internationally several times for their pioneering sustainability policies.

Bucuti & Tara Beach has two gourmet, adult-only restaurants. The staff is vigilant about service and making sure the sense of quiet seclusion is maintained. Guests are given a red flag to hold up if they wish to order food or drinks while on the beach. Servers will not interrupt reading or dozing to take an order. The resort also has a mini branch of Intermezzo Spa offering a full menu of massages and skin treatments, and an air-conditioned fitness room. The pool is very small, but the resort is on the widest beach on Aruba.

COSTA LINDA

Costa Linda (J. E. Irausquin Blvd. 59, 297/583-8000 or 888/858-0845, www.costalinda-aruba.com, two-bedroom suites $378-589) was the last timeshare resort built by Sun Development, the founders of timesharing in Aruba, and one of the most luxurious of the four facilities they left in their wake. All units are very spacious and beautifully-appointed two- or three-bedroom suites. The ocean-end rooms have enormous patios for outdoor entertaining, with their own gas BBQs and whirlpool tubs.

This very large facility has one of the widest beachfronts on Aruba. The attractive free-form pool deck has an adjacent restaurant. It is family-oriented and quiet at night, but Alhambra Shopping Bazaar is just outside the door and past the parking lot.

OASIS LUXURY CONDOMINIUMS

A spanking new complex, Oasis Luxury Condominiums (J. E. Irausquin Blvd. 242, 297/733-4685 or toll free in Aruba 954/609-1297, http://oasisrentalsaruba.com, $405 and up, cleaning service and tax included) is only a five-minute walk from Eagle Beach. This exceedingly charming little complex has only 35 units, each deserving of the term "luxury." All have been sold, but 20 are available to rent. They are beautifully decorated and appointed two-bedroom, two-bath apartments with terraces overlooking the pool or sea, or both.

There is a dedicated concierge to assist in reservations and car rentals. The attractive pool deck has wheelchair access to the pool. This is a lovely, quiet place that has yet to be discovered.

OVER $500

Two sister resorts, Divi and Tamarijn, were built on the same concept: two-story casitas with terraces or patios facing directly out to the sea. They are separated by a small stretch of sand, and guests can use the restaurants and bars interchangeably, along with fitness rooms, tennis courts, and more. Frequent tram service takes guests between the two, at all hours of the day and night.

DIVI MEGA ALL-INCLUSIVE

Divi Mega All-Inclusive (J. E. Irausquin Blvd. 45, 297/525-5200 or 800/554-2008, www. diviaruba.com, $550 garden view, $625 ocean view), which opened back in 1969, is a long, rambling resort with rooms directly on the beach or in a new section set back within lush gardens. Along with its sister resort, the newer Tamarijn, they are generally considered "honeymoon hotels."

The rooms are not large; all first-floor rooms have direct access to the beach. The resort turned all-inclusive in the late 1990s. Since many of their loyal patrons spent their honeymoons at the Divi 25 or 40 years ago, they are now no longer a clientele comprised of only newlyweds, but of all ages and quite diverse. They have formed very congenial groups who usually gather during happy hour (which at an all-inclusive, is all day) at the famous Bunker Bar at the Tamarijn, which hangs out over the water. The success of the first Divi Resort resulted in expansion and in the Tamarijn, which shares grounds with the Dutch Village timeshares.

The original of the two resorts, Divi, has recently undergone complete renovations. The community areas are elegant. A chic, stunning, contemporary pool deck abuts the beach, and the lobby has an Internet center and shops. There is nightly entertainment, and family-oriented amenities and organized activities are offered daily.

Aside from the family-type buffet center near the beach, the resort is home to the famous Red Parrot Restaurant, featuring fresh fish and international cuisine. The themed restaurants require advance reservations. For an all-inclusive facility, the quality of cuisine and variety is way above par.

TAMARIJN BEACH RESORT

The Divi's sister resort, Tamarijn Beach Resort (J. E. Irausquin Blvd. 41, 297/525-5200 or 800/554-2008, www.tamarijnaruba.com, $500 ocean view), is located just south of the Divi and a little closer to Oranjestad. It has also undergone a complete renovations, with an atmosphere described as island chic.

Adjacent to the Divi Dutch Village timeshares, the grounds boast some very lush, beautiful landscaping on the land side of the beach. The resort's Overlook Bar and Bunker Bar offer some of the most beautiful views of the Caribbean at sunset. Guests from both resorts like to gather at either spot at day's end.

The rooms of "the Tam" are small, but provide the feeling of the beach being a part of the accommodations, as terraces and patios open to the very beautiful, tranquil shorefront.

There are no elevators, so individuals with physical disabilities should specify that they require a ground floor room when making reservations.

Most of the themed restaurants shared by the two resorts are within the Tamarijn. They include Paparazzi, for Italian cuisine; Fusion, for Pacific Rim; Palm Grill, for fresh stir-fried dishes; as well as an all-day stone oven pizza bar for snacking and meals from early in the day until late at night. Themed restaurants only serve dinner and reservations are required well in advance. The Cunucu Terrace, adjacent to the pool deck, serves breakfast, lunch, and dinner buffets, and is the spot for nightly entertainment.

Palm Beach, Malmok, and Noord

Since Palm Beach boasts the greatest concentration of accommodations and activities, it may likely be a vacationer's default choice, particularly if selecting a package through a travel agency or wholesaler, which tend to work mostly with the AHATA member resorts. During holiday time many will only accept reservations for a minimum of 10 days that include both Christmas and New Year's. Bookings often are required more than a year in advance.

Beginning from the Eagle Beach approach, these giant hotels line up along a boardwalk that has been laid out from the southernmost end of Palm Beach to Marriott Complex and is a popular spot for a morning run or walk. It also allows easy access to the various restaurants, casinos, and shops within the resorts.

$100-200

◖ ARUBA BEACH FRONT

A rare find has just come on the market: Aruba Beach Front (exclusive agent Aruba Villa Rentals, Salina Cerca 35E, Bakval 20, 297/586-4290, www.arubavillarentals.com, $875-1015/week, $50 cleaning fee) is a beautifully outfitted private home right on the water in Malmok, Aruba's most exclusive residential neighborhood. The backyard pool deck has direct access to Arashi Beach. The owner began a new policy at the end of 2012 to rent out individual guest rooms rather than the entire house. Spacious upper level digs have stunning ocean views and all rooms have large, private bathrooms. Community areas include a spacious, fully-equipped kitchen; living room; patio with BBQ and dining area; plus washing machine and dryer on the upper level.

Lower level "basement" rooms open directly to the pool deck. There are no windows in the individual rooms, but each has its own bathroom. The connecting community area is wide open, all windows and light. Each room has a secure entrance, a safe, air-conditioning, and cable TV. More amenities, such as individual refrigerators in each room, are being implemented. One of only two guesthouses in the area directly on the beach, this is a cozy alternative to a hotel room. There is more than ample parking spaces to accommodate rented cars for all guests.

ARUBA BEACH VILLAS

A complex of 31 rooms facing the beach in Malmok, Aruba Beach Villas (L. G. Smith Blvd. 482, 297/586-1072 or toll free in U.S. 800/320-9998, www.arubabeachvillas.com, studio suites $168) is a favorite destination for dedicated windsurfers. It is perfectly located to pursue this sport. Aruba Sailboard Vacations and Fiberworx board shop are attached, convenient for equipment and spare parts, waxes, and more. Aruba Sailboard works with the Villas and, during high season, room rates include unlimited equipment rental. (During off season rooms are half price, but no equipment included in the rates.) Initial lessons are not free, however. Those really interested in spending a vacation learning the sport must dedicate several hours to mastering it.

The owner, Phil, is an expatriate American who never wanted to leave Aruba, and is very happy to be a host. Rooms are rustic, but quite spacious, with big closets and bathrooms in each, even the studios, and all have fully-equipped kitchens. The oceanfront rooms have wooden decks for enjoying the view, and the beach is just across the road. There is a small pool in the back. Less expensive rooms are simple and bare bones, suited for people who will be out on the water most of the time. A charming, open-air community area faces the sea and is a popular place to kick back and talk windsurfing with other fanatics.

BANANAS APARTMENTS

A popular spot with Europeans and families, Bananas Apartments (Malmokweg 19,

HOT WATER

Visitors staying in guesthouses and alternative accommodations might be taken aback when they first see only one faucet in most sinks and showers. Since forever, the island has relied on the tropical sun to heat the water, and it does a fine job. When taking a shower anytime from around noon till sunset, the water gets surprisingly warm and produces a very comfortable shower; though, at times, it's perhaps even too hot. It all depends on the weather, which is usually reliable. First thing in the morning is the time to grab a cold shower, for those who need it.

Major resorts understand that their guests expect hot water at any hour of the day and night, and they have hot water heaters to provide it. Unfortunately, what comes out of the cold-water tap is the same sun-heated water the rest of the island is using, so there is no cold water to temper the hot. Running the cold-water tap will not result in the water getting colder, it will likely get warmer. Keep this in mind when stepping into the shower or filling a bathtub. Be sure to check first to avoid scalding temperatures. If you are fanatical about cold drinking water, find the ice machine down the hall, when you arrive.

297/586-2858, www.bananas-resort.com, studio apartments $700/week, extra person $15/night, children under 6 free) is just a short distance down the Malmokweg, which runs perpendicular to the beach road. All rooms have fully-equipped kitchens. Cleaning service and fresh towels daily are included, with oversize beach towels distributed by the pool.

Converted from two adjacent houses, each section has a small pool and one whirlpool spa. The older section has a sprawling backyard and lovely gardens with shade trees. The newer section has an open, paved pool deck and is still in the process of becoming as homey as the original. Don't balk at taking an "older" room: They have more charm and nice big wooden picnic tables on the patios for family meals.

◖ BOARDWALK HOTEL ARUBA

The first of the Malmok off-the-beach resorts is Boardwalk Hotel Aruba (Bakval 20, 297/586-6654, www.boardwalkaruba.com, one-bedroom suites start at $148, $15 pp for more than four guests, children under 12 free), where one really has a sense of being in a tropical paradise.

Formally known as Boardwalk Retreat, a very appropriate name, this is a lovely, tranquil place where 13 casitas are surrounded by lush gardens. It is removed enough but still in close proximity to all the Palm Beach action, including the Marriott Casino, just across the road.

Rooms are spacious, sleeping four comfortably, with high ceilings, large closets, dressing rooms, and fully-equipped kitchens. Each has its own patio or terrace with an individual BBQ grill that housekeepers keep clean. Generally, the rooms are spotless.

There is a small pool and whirlpool, and they have arrangements for guests to use the lounge chairs at MooMba Beach Bar, located between the Holiday Inn and Marriott Surf Club. Shuttle service to the beach is provided along with individual coolers for ice and refreshments.

The owners, twin sisters Kimberly and Stephanie Rooijakkers, took over in 2011 and their enthusiasm for Aruba and their charming facility is infectious. They are also pet-friendly; expect their adorable long-haired daschund to greet you in the lobby.

BRICKELL BAY BEACH CLUB & SPA

Being close to, but not on the beach, makes Brickell Bay Beach Club & Spa (J. E. Irausquin Blvd. 370, 297/586-0900 or toll free in U.S. and Canada 866/332-3590, www.brickellbayaruba.com, $165) a good value. It is in the heart of Palm Beach and a perfect spot for young people who are interested in the nighttime action.

RESORT TRIPPING

The major resorts, with the exception of the all-inclusive hotels, welcome non-guests to their premises to use their restaurants, spas, casinos, and shops. This particularly applies to Palm Beach, where resorts are in close proximity to each other. Vacationers can easily walk from one to the next, either on the beach boardwalk or the boulevard promenade. Walking the strip is a favorite nighttime activity. A preference for the ambiance of a certain casino or poker room can easily be indulged, as can seeing a show at another resort, usually only minutes away on foot. Pool decks, however, are for the use of guests of the resort only.

Since Riu and Occidental are all inclusive, they screen those trying to enter from their pool decks for identifying bracelets. Nonguests are turned away. Visitors are welcome through their main entrances if they wish to use their casinos. Inquire at their concierge desks about day passes to fully sample the facility.

An unimpressive exterior and lobby mask pleasant and recently renovated rooms. A spacious and attractive pool deck with bar is where the Orchid Day Spa is located. Patrons can enjoy a pool view while getting a massage, facial, manicure, or pedicure at comparatively reasonable rates. Only 98 rooms guarantee that the pool never gets crowded, and they have just added on an expansive and glamorous bar and nightspot called SandBeach Bar, with beach tennis courts. In addition, lounge chairs on the Occidental beach are available for guests.

Tomato Charlie's Pizzeria and Italian restaurant is attached, with a terrace dining room looking over the thoroughfare à la European café style. They serve breakfast, lunch, and dinner; the food is affordable and pretty decent, with room service provided as well.

Amenities include free Wi-Fi in all rooms. Up to two children under the age of 12 stay free of charge with two adults; complimentary continental breakfast is served in the room. Bills must be paid at the end of the stay in local currency. An on-site money exchange is available, though you will likely get a better rate from a bank or an islander wishing to buy dollars.

CARIBBEAN PALM VILLAGE

About a mile inland along the Noord-Palm Beach Road is Caribbean Palm Village (43-E Palm Beach Rd., 297/526-2700, www.cpvr.com, $174 studio), originally built as a timeshare complex. Aside from the studio rooms they have very spacious one- and two-bedrooms suites, broken up into seven sections with two attractive pool decks. There is a community lounge and fitness center, and an independent restaurant, Sweet Peppers, serving breakfast, lunch, and dinner; guests receive a discount in the restaurant. Community BBQ and picnic areas and a day spa are part of the complex as well.

The resort is across the street from Santa Ana Church and smack dab in the middle of a commercial area, with a supermarket, department store, and drugstore next door. In addition to having every convenience at hand, there is a busy, bustling center beyond the resort's walls. However, the pool areas within the resort are tranquil.

DEL RAY APARTMENTS

North of the Santa Ana Church in Noord is a turnoff where Del Ray Apartments (Kamay 3D, 297/586-3309, www.delreyaruba.com, two-bedroom units $145) is located, just a bit off the beaten track, but only minutes from the beach by car. One dozen comfortable, clean apartments surround the simple but large pool deck and playground. This is one of the best values in the area. They have an arrangement with MooMba Beach for lounge chairs for their guests. It is a nice little mom-and-pop operation, with a largely European and Latin clientele. It's close to shopping and only five doors away from Anna Maria's Italian restaurant.

VILLA BOUGAINVILLEA

Staying at Villa Bougainvillea (Malmokweg 4, 297/526-1055, www.villabougainvilleaaruba. com, $129-139 for up to four) is a unique experience indelibly stamped with the character of hostess Rona. It is located nearly at the main sea road and is a short walk from Boca Catalina, a nice beach.

Three utterly charming apartments attached to the proprietor's home give patrons the feeling of being a guest rather than just a tenant. Each apartment has its own entrance and a key to the gate for security. The rooms are very spacious rooms, decorated with fine and eclectic taste, creating a unique ambiance. They also each have a mini-kitchen. Bathrooms have tubs as well as showers, which is unusual at most budget places.

Each room has a little terrace and looks out on a charming backyard with a pool and BBQ. "When the spirit moves her," Rona will cook up a storm of gourmet snacks and mix a pitcher of sangria to treat her guests to a little "get acquainted happy hour."

Four good-sized *cunucu* dogs (the local mixed breed, which were rescued) have the run of the house and property. They warm up to renters quickly, but if you choose to stay here, you should be completely comfortable with dogs.

$200-300

THE MILL RESORT

Located across the street from the beachfront resorts, the Mill Resort (J. E. Irausquin Blvd. 330, 297/526-7700 or toll-free in U.S. and Canada 800/992-2015, www.millresort.com, $280) is right next to the area's signature landmark, for which it was named. Rather unique, it is a sprawling facility in the low-rise mode and was a concept ahead of its time. It was intended to be a condominium complex, with exceptionally large three-bedroom units that could be divided into separate apartments by

closing the doors. Now they have divided them into studios, junior suites, and royal accommodations, each with either full or mini-kitchens. Royal suites have a private whirlpool bath in the middle of the room. Families can combine junior or royal suites with a studio for the kids, with its own bathroom. Up to two children ages 12 and under stay free in the same room with parents.

Two-hundred rooms surround a very spacious and attractive pool deck with three free-form pools, a restaurant, and a bar. The bar is very popular with locals on Friday evenings when they have a special happy hour and usually a live band. Shuttle service to the beach is provided and they have a hut just south of the Westin where they distribute lounges chairs. There is a mini-market on the premises as well as a spa, the Intermezzo Day Spa, which was renovated to quite luxurious standards in 2012.

PLAYA LINDA BEACH RESORT

More than just hotel rooms are the accommodations at Playa Linda Beach Resort (J. E. Irausquin Blvd. 87, 297/586-6100, www.play-alinda.com, studios or one-bedroom units $200), the first and certainly the coziest, but also one of the most luxurious, timeshare resorts on Aruba. It won awards for design when it first opened, in a spot that is considered a prime location.

It hosts a number of shops, restaurants, and a mini-market both on the street side and on the beach boardwalk. They also have a very nice day spa, fitness room, tennis courts, and a beautiful pool deck with waterfall and whirlpool. The overall ambiance is most definitely family-oriented. Most guests have owned timeshares here for years. They are veteran visitors with lots of good advice about the island.

An independent Playa Linda online bulletin board on their website has entire sections dedicated to those looking for tradeoffs or rentals, and another for those offering them, where great discounts can be found. Since the average maintenance fee for the top-of-the-line rooms is around $900 per week for owners, substantial money can be saved by finding someone looking to rent out directly.

A dispatch office for an ambulance service and EMT center that services the area is headquartered in the parking lot. Someone with a chronic condition may wish to take this into account. It is also somewhat indicative of their generally mature clientele.

$300-400

DIVI PHOENIX BEACH RESORT

The checkered past of Divi Phoenix Beach Resort (J. E. Irausquin Blvd. 75, 297/586-6066, www.diviresorts.com, $359-369) and a number of incarnations have resulted in two sections of disparate configurations and price. Divi Properties acquired a failed project, restoring and enhancing the original plan. Hence, the name Phoenix, as it was rescued by a respected hospitality franchise to rise from the ashes.

They parlayed this coup into a very popular resort, where the rooms are all suites with fully-equipped kitchens, a step up from your average hotel room, especially in the new section. The original resort has a cozy, simple pool deck, and one of the first restaurants to actually provide the "toes in the sand" waterfront dining experience at Pure Ocean.

In 2008, the sumptuous new section opened. It now houses the main lobby and a luxurious free-form pool; all rooms have spacious balconies facing out over the pool or with ocean views. The pool-side restaurant and bar is also beachfront, with a swim-up bar. Naturally, the newer, more luxurious area has the higher-priced rooms.

Divi Phoenix totals 214 suites; those available for rental are mostly studios (the bedroom can be closed off with accordion doors and living rooms have sofa beds) or one-bedroom units, nice for families.

The resort has a mini-market, additional casual sandwich spot, business center, concierge and car rental desks, on-site day spa, and a very friendly, accommodating staff. It is slightly set apart from the strip of resorts, so there is a more tranquil ambiance around the beach.

ACCOMMODATIONS

© ROSALIE KLEIN

Divi Phoenix Beach Resort's swim-up bar

TIMESHARE AND CONDOMINIUM RESORTS

Timeshare rooms are a hybrid of hotels and condominiums, usually with the amenities of housekeeping and easy beachfront access. They provide concierge desks, activities coordinators, plus homey touches such as laundry rooms and mini-markets.

Families with young children often find these facilities ideal. They allow privacy for parents as well as meals in the room. With young, sometimes fussy eaters, not having to spend on costly restaurants is a worthwhile savings.

It isn't easy trading a timeshare at another location for one on Aruba, particularly during busy holiday weeks. Each timeshare has a rental office with quite a few listings, though many owners prefer to rent direct and keep the commission. Direct listings can be found on the numerous Aruba bulletin boards online or via classified ads in Aruba's English-language newspapers.

Popular online forums with listings can be found on www.aruba.com, www.visitaruba.com, http://aruba-travelguide.com, http://arubabound.com, and http://aruba-bb.com.

There are also individual bulletin boards from the various timeshare resorts. If someone has not already listed a timeshare unit for sale or available for rent in the timeframe you seek, join the bulletin board and post what you are looking for, include the particular weeks and locations you desire. There are also a number of independent travel brokers specializing in renting out timeshares.

The spate of new condo resorts on Aruba promises even more luxurious digs for fantastic rates. Condo owners wish to earn back or make money on their investment by renting it out. Often their owners use them for only a few weeks a year, much less than a hotel room is used.

A website dedicated entirely to connecting directly with owners of timeshares and condominiums is **Vacations Rentals by Owners** (www.vrbo.com). Listings are by owners eager to rent their property and willing to pay to list their properties, so bargains can often be found on this site. There are hundreds of listings offering a wealth of options.

OCEAN 105

Ocean 105 (L. G. Smith Blvd. 105, toll-free in U.S. 866/978-6986, www.ocean105.com, one-bedroom units $328) is one of two Malmok guesthouses actually on the water, with direct access to the beach. It is adjacent to Boca Catalina, which is popular with islanders on the weekend. Guests have a small patch of beach to call their own. Ocean 105 is also bordered by two nice snorkel spots for beginners, with easy shore access. A number of sailboats stop in the bay daily with charter trips.

The two-story guesthouse has only four apartments: a single one-bedroom and three two-bedroom units, which are very spacious and elegantly decorated. (The owner also has a chic, contemporary furniture shop.) There are sofa beds in the living rooms, fully-equipped kitchens, and terraces or patios that hang out over the sea, but there is no pool. Maid service is provided twice a week.

RADISSON RESORT, CASINO & SPA

Aruba's first major resort, and still one of the most elegant and attractive hotels, is Radisson Resort, Casino & Spa (J. E. Irausquin Blvd. 81, 297/586-6555 or toll-free in U.S. and Canada 800/850-5270, www.radisson.com, $318 plus taxes). In 1999, Radisson took over what had been the famous Aruba Caribbean, maintaining the elaborate ballroom and meeting rooms that make it very popular with conferences and conventions.

Rooms in the main section may be older, but they are well maintained with rather unconventional room dimensions. If you are offered a room in the "old section," take it, as they are very spacious, with high ceilings and huge dressing rooms and closets. It is a throwback to the day when people came to the island and wore gowns and tuxedos at night. (Former James Bond actor, Roger Moore, used to stay here regularly.)

The Westin Aruba Resort in Palm Beach is the only major resort that is pet-friendly.

Two additional sections of more pedestrian design were added over the years. In the past four years the hotel has undergone millions of dollars of renovations and refurbishments. One of the most notable additions of the changeover was the complete sculpturing of the pool deck to create the feeling of sitting on the beach. It is one of the most gorgeous pool areas on Aruba, with lushly landscaped paths. This area is home to one of Aruba's most interesting unofficial attractions, Victor, the Birdman, who cares for the exotic birds around the gardens.

Radisson also features a special "Plaza Club"

on the upper floors with more elaborate rooms and suites, a personal concierge and complimentary continental breakfast, afternoon tea, and happy hour, with snacks and drinks included. There is an in-house casino and their detached Larimar Day Spa, next to the beach, is the largest and one of the most luxurious on Aruba.

OVER $500
WESTIN ARUBA RESORT

Animal lovers need not leave their companions behind, Westin Aruba Resort (J. E. Irausquin Blvd. 77, 297/586-4466 or toll-free in U.S. 800/937-8461, www.westinaruba.com, $590) is Aruba's only major pet-friendly resort. This includes various amenities for guests and their companions, including a "Heavenly Dog Bed" and a surprise gift on arrival. There is a menu of dog foods and treats, and dog-sitting and walking services, if you want a night out without the fur baby.

Westin Resort began as the Concord in 1979, one of the most glamorous new resorts the island had ever seen. It came under the Westin Flag at the end of 2006. Complete renovations resulted in a chic, contemporary lobby and certain Westin trademark policies, including making it the first completely smoke-free resort on Aruba. The hotel has 481 rooms, of which 200 are either oceanfront or ocean-view and quite spacious with large bathrooms.

Hotel amenities include an in-house casino, day spa, banquet rooms, fitness and video game rooms, shopping arcade, and activities coordinators. There are nine eateries within the resort, indoors and out, and an exceptionally conscientious culinary staff.

ACCOMMODATIONS

Santa Cruz, Paradera, and Piedra Plat

Beyond the principal tourist areas, accommodations are few and far between. Aruba's government encourages tourism projects in these currently undeveloped areas, but investors are still focused on Aruba's west coast and beachfront.

$100-200
CUNUCU VILLAS

Lia Lopez is the sweet, friendly host at Cunucu Villas (Santa Cruz 23, 297/585-1616, www.cunucuvillasaruba.com, one-bedroom suites $100, for two adults and two children, $20/night for each extra person). She has 12 identical units on two levels. The upper rooms have a very nice view of the surrounding countryside. Set back on a dirt road at the end of a residential street, Cunucu Villas has an attractive pool deck with a community BBQ and large picnic tables under a shaded terrace. Rooms have simple decor and full kitchens.

Despite its rather out-of-the-way location, it is only a 10-minute walk to Huchada Bakery, and Santa Cruz's principal commercial area is a bit farther on. This is also the closest lodging to Arikok National Park.

PARADERA PARK APARTMENTS

Providing quicker access to Arikok National Park for dedicated hikers and nature buffs is Paradera Park Apartments (Paradera 203, 297/582-3289, www.paraderapark-aruba.com, $105 d, $20/night for each extra person), a very friendly, family-run operation with a dedicated following. They get a surprising number of long-term guests who have been vacationing on Aruba for years, as the accommodations are clean, attractive, and the owners are quite personable.

Paradera Park Apartments make up a small complex of studios and one- and two-bedroom suites, tucked away down a side street in what is a purely residential area. The turnoffs to get here are clearly marked. There is also one duplex suite with the bedroom and master bath on the second level. All rooms include full kitchens. The focus of the complex is a small pool with an attractive deck and garden and a community center.

San Nicolas, Savaneta, and Pos Chiquito

It is rare to find accommodations in Aruba's more rural areas, which are either deserted stretches of scrub or a national park, enjoyable for a day of exploring. However, more small guesthouses are situated on or near the scattered coves of Savaneta and Pos Chiquito, where there is close access to some lovely beaches that see very little traffic.

These primarily residential areas have some attractive and relatively inexpensive facilities. Some are particularly aimed for those who really want to get away from it all. Most provide an apartment setting, targeting budget travelers and including full kitchens, as restaurants and cafés are few and far between. If seeking a sense of being isolated on a tropical island, these places certainly deliver, but renting a car is definitely required.

OVER $100
◖ ARUBA BEACH CHALETS

The absolutely beautiful duplex apartments, Aruba Beach Chalets (Savaneta 187 B, 297/586-3350, www.aruba-beach-chalets.com, $200/

Waterfront villas for rent in Savaneta have spectacular views from the terrace.

© ROSALIE KLEIN

night, $3,000/month for a three-bedroom town-house), are great for families and for longer stays than one week. The spacious living room area and kitchen open directly onto your own patch of waterfront, with a charming back terrace for enjoying the view. These are privately-owned condos of which five are for rent. The eastern corner has an extra studio apartment attached (maybe for a nanny?) and is even more spacious and luxuriously decorated, with its own private pool; it is naturally a bit more expensive.

The logistics of the building and landscaping have pretty much created a private waterfront. For those who are looking for privacy and attractive accommodations, this will do it. It is "not far" from a few nice eateries, according to their website, but in reality, it is not that close either.

Maid service is extra; plus there is an additional fee of $125 tacked on by the resort as a cleaning fee to prepare the room for the next tenant. Laundry pickup with next day return is also available; there are no washing machines in the rooms.

CLUB ARIAS BED AND BREAKFAST

The rather surreal, idiosyncratic facade of Club Arias Bed and Breakfast (Savaneta 123-K, 297/593-3408 or in U.S. 917/508-7210, www. clubarias.com, $200 and up, includes breakfast) disguises a charming courtyard with surprisingly large pools and attractive gardens. The courtyard is the focal point, surrounded by 10 very spacious rooms, each uniquely decorated with original art and knickknacks.

Each room has its own kitchenette, and one unit has a full kitchen. But the community area sports a cozy open-air restaurant where Cordon Bleu-graduate chef Gabriel prepares gourmet omelets for the breakfast part of the bed-and-breakfast. Breakfast is served 7:30am-10:30am and Gabriel is available for private dinners on request. You do not need to stay at the resort to order breakfast, but it is only free for guests of the resort. Residence at Club Arias, named for its owner from NY, Arias Schwarz, also includes high tea with fresh pastries at 4pm.

It is located directly on the main highway that runs the length from Oranjestad to San

Rooms surround the pool deck at Club Arias Bed and Breakfast.

Nicolas, a very busy thoroughfare. But it's set back a sufficient distance for quiet, particularly the back rooms.

VISTALMAR

One of Aruba's first out-of-the-way apartment and resort facilities, Vistalmar Apartments (Bucutiweg 28, 297/582-8579, www.arubatravelinfo.com, $124/night, $749/week) has garnered a dedicated clientele. There is no beach to speak of, but there is a private dock along one of the prettiest sections of the south shore. It is very close to two yacht clubs, which is nice for dedicated deep sea fishing fanatics.

The rooms have fully-equipped kitchens and terraces looking right out on the sea and the sunsets. Breakfast is provided on arrival day, with the understanding that the cupboard is likely empty, and fresh bread is delivered daily. The owners provide airport shuttle service on arrival and departure days. Other amenities include snorkel gear, coolers, and bicycles. A car rental can be arranged as part of the package for an additional $120 a week.

BACKGROUND

A phrase from the chorus of Aruba's national anthem, "Aruba Dushi Tera" ("Sweet Land Aruba"), describes their island nation as *Nos baranca tan stima* (Our beloved rock). This simple phrase conveys the distinct self-awareness among Arubans for their desert island in the Caribbean, as well as a great affection for their landscape.

Aruba is, socially and economically, an anomaly within the region. A tranquil oasis in an area with a long history of political turmoil and violent revolution, the island attained independence from the other Dutch Caribbean islands through peaceful negotiation. Since 1986 and Status Aparte, it has proven to be a nation well suited to self-determination.

Perhaps the fact that conquistadors did not detect any rich minerals spared Aruba from their unwanted attention. After the original native population was deported to be slaves in the mines of Hispaniola, Amerindians seeking haven from warring tribes on the mainland repopulated Aruba. Prior to recorded history, Aruba was a refuge for many different groups wishing to escape the violence or class restrictions of their societies. Blessed with reliable weather, it has generally been spared from the destructive force of hurricanes.

The description "One Happy Island" is apt. It is a small island where the inhabitants understand the need to get along. The past and its legacy are treasured, while at the same time Arubans look to the future and discuss ideas like sustainability. The sense of community is strong, and government sponsored barrio dialogs solicit input.

© ROSALIE KLEIN

Arubans have enormous pride in their flag, national anthem, and, particularly, their distinctive language, Papiamento. Education is highly prized; youth are strongly encouraged to advance and earn degrees. This is significant in that Aruba has a recorded 85 percent voter turnout during elections; experts consider an educated and informed voter an important factor. According to a 2010 World Bank report, the literacy rate of females ages 15-24 years old was 99.47 percent.

The climate always inhibited the proliferation of plantations and therefore Island society did not rely on slavery to maintain its economic stability. Arubans worked their own land and reaped the meager rewards. They were forced to be inventive to construct their homes and feed their families, taking advantage of every way possible to use what was naturally available.

Aruba also had the advantage of becoming far more technically advanced than many other islands. An American presence in the early 20th century and the establishment of the Lago Refinery took the island in a new direction. This influence introduced modern conveniences and a masterful water and power delivery system. Those who have traveled the region extensively attest to the high standard of living on Aruba compared to the rest of the Caribbean and Latin and Central America. Also, as a result, there was a population expansion and an increase in cultural diversity. Thousands of workers from other parts of the Caribbean and the rest of the globe, migrated to work at the refinery, and eventually settled on the island permanently.

The Land

Cadushi cactus are a common sight on the island.

Aruba is a relatively flat island with three major peaks: Seroe Jamanota, 188 meters (617 ft.); Seroe Arikok, 184 meters (606 ft.); and Hooiberg, 165 meters (541 ft.). Constant winds continuously buffet the island from the northeast, traveling thousands of miles across open sea. Combined with the geological makeup, Aruba's north coast is a lunar landscape of limestone outcroppings along the shore. These are interspersed with quartz rock and pillow basalt. All were formed when undersea volcanoes initially created the submerged landmasses that would become the ABC islands of Aruba, Bonaire, and Curacao. Along the north coast, heavy waves dramatically crash and spume, occasionally broken by small coves and beaches.

The land resembles an elongated triangle. The south shore is dotted with small beaches, mangrove formations, and limestone cliffs. The western or leeward side is home to the miles-long stretch of beaches that so attract visitors and real estate developers. These areas from Palm Beach south have been exclusively zoned for tourism.

Located north of the equator at 12°32'28"N

and 69°57'30"W, Aruba is 19 miles (31 km) long and 6 miles (9.65 km) wide at its widest point. Approximately 72 square miles (116 km), the island is divided into seven zoning districts, each containing multiple barrios. The closest major landmass is the Paraguaná Peninsula of Venezuela, 12 miles (19 km) south; Caracas is 42 miles (68 km) from Aruba. Sister islands of Curacao and Bonaire are 55 miles (88 km) and 64 miles (103 km) east, along the 12° latitude line. Aruba is the physically smallest of the ABC Islands, but it has a population of 107,000 compared to only 15,000 living on Bonaire, which is 111 square miles (179 km) in size. Curacao, at 171 square miles (275 km), is the largest of the three and has a population of 141,766. It takes only 20 minutes to travel from Aruba to Curacao by prop plane, but the sea voyage is a challenging 15 hours through very rough waters.

GEOLOGY

Studies propose the initial undersea landmasses were formed around 95 million years ago, finally making their way to the surface through tectonic activity around 30 million years later. Aruba was formed from three kinds of rock: igneous, which is a cooling and solidification of magma; metamorphic, a rock formed from a previously produced rock; and sedimentary, resulting from the continual deposit and hardening of other rocks.

The fantastical pillow lava formations found primarily around the north coast confirm the underwater accretion of the land. After the original volcanic eruptions, a continuation of the magma flow over the rock, a process called plutonism, created layers. The majority of the island's landscape, named the Aruba Lava Formation, is a part of a huge geologic formation called a batholith. Of this, only a minor portion has been exposed after weathering, erosion, and being pushed up by the earth's movement.

The carved limestone cliffs populating coves along the shoreline are the most recently accumulated rock. Close examination of the terraces reveal a wealth of interesting marine fossils and coral impressions.

WEATHER

One of Aruba's great assets is the reliable weather: a sunny 82-92°F year round. Its proximity to the equator defines it as a tropical island, but constant breezes and sea currents keep the temperature comfortable. The sea is surprisingly cooler than expected. Temperatures are ideal for coral growth and a proliferation of colorful fish life.

Aruba is considered to be south of the Hurricane Belt and therefore rarely subject to the devastating storms for which the Caribbean is known. Usually, Aruba's weather, if it is an issue at all, is most unstable from around mid or late August until the end of November. This is a time when named storms are more likely to form in the Gulf of Mexico. Each year, weather pundits predict an increased number of storms of greater strength for the Atlantic, Caribbean, and Gulf regions. The records show it is very rare for them to approach Aruba. For the most part, they turn north from the gulf as they make their way across the Atlantic from Africa.

There is the occasional weather front that behaves utterly contrary to what is expected. Hurricanes Dean, Ivan, and Francis are examples of some systems that are so huge and powerful, even Aruba experienced heavy seas and hard rains, just from the ripple effects. Sometimes storms far away will produce small occlusions that can result in rough waters or occasional squalls. It is unheard of for travel plans to the island to be cancelled because of weather on Aruba.

The most common effect of the big storms is for Aruba's ever-present wind to die down. There is no predicting this well in advance. The year 2012 proved to be breezy and dry, contradicting the concept that long, hot, windless storm seasons might be a trend.

© ROSALIE KLEIN

Limestone terraces create fantastical formations.

Environmental Issues

OVERDEVELOPMENT AND POPULATION

Aruba faces the conundrum of many Caribbean islands: progressing economically and technologically into the 21st century, while attempting to maintain its cultural identity. Unbridled construction and development may create jobs and business opportunities, but at what cost to the physical aspects that define the island's character and support its economy through tourism?

This has now become a concern for not only the government and dedicated groups, but the average citizen. Islanders are dismayed to see developers callously bulldozing acres of land, which are habitats for countless endemic species of flora and fauna. Aside from some cases of completely unwarranted waste, other projects beg the question: Does the island really need another shopping mall or upscale housing

complex? There is already an overabundance of both. This is another dilemma, as property owners wish to generate profit from undeveloped land, which may have been in the family for generations. Legislation requiring environmental studies and prohibiting threats to endemic, endangered species are not in place to curb these actions. Exacerbating ideas of sustainability is Aruba's enormous success with tourism as its primary financial pillar.

For decades Aruba has been a golden land of opportunity within the Caribbean, attracting immigrants from other islands as well as Latin and Central America. The rapidly burgeoning population on a physically small piece of rock naturally created stresses on various systems and the infrastructure, despite the native population readily accepting and integrating these various groups socially.

Aruba's advanced system of water

distribution, and an attractive social and educational system under the Dutch, provides benefits and support many could not find in their homelands. Much of this came with the Lago Refinery, along with especially skilled labor that more than tripled the island population when it first opened.

For the quarter of a century since Status Aparte, immigrants could always count on jobs in tourism, construction, and menial positions. When Aruba achieved Status Aparte in 1986, the population was estimated at 72,000. The 2010 census counts over 107,000 legal residents. The demands on the infrastructure, the loss of natural lands cleared for all the needed housing, as well as the boom in development of tourism venues has caused great concern among environmental groups. Add to that the further strain created by a visiting population of more than 1.5 million per year, and the waste this produces on a land of very limited area to store it.

TRASH AND RECYCLING

Unfortunately, the region is still generally well behind the times compared to the United States, Canada, and Europe in regards to recycling, or a general attitude towards maintaining their environment and the proper disposal of litter and mass waste. Severe strictures to inhibit illegal dumping have been enacted. Many are very sensitive to this situation; hence hard legislation was enacted in 2012 to address the issue. It is encouraging that travel executives who regularly visit Caribbean nations in their business report that they find Aruba far cleaner than most other destinations in the region.

Aruba maintains an official landfill on the south shore at Parkietenbos, where the trash is burned. There is regular weekly collection conducted in almost all communities, as well as private operators for businesses and hotels that require more frequent service. However, large items and appliances or large quantities of debris from yards are not carted away by the public service.

Collaborating with private waste haulage services, various foundations and companies have organized a number of island-wide cleanups. There are at least three beach cleaning efforts annually sponsored by various concerns where hundreds, sometimes thousands, of volunteers participate; tourists are welcome to join in.

Until the summer of 2012, some individuals owning unused parcels of land had turned them into dumps for profit; it was announced that this is now forbidden, without exception. To fully enforce the closure of all unauthorized dumps, teams of inspectors have the power to issue heavy fines or arrest when warnings are ignored. The landfill eliminated any charge for dropping off large amounts of refuse. Unfortunately, a public recycling plant constructed by a U.S. concern to produce "Fluff" is not performing as promised and is under investigation.

Plans are in place and projects have begun for systems of recycling, along with educational programs, both public and private. Some local entrepreneurs are building centers for collection and sorting of recyclable refuse, which is shipped to plants. Incentive programs have taken place for the public to turn in their waste and win prizes. Concerned interests tour the schools giving lectures along with contests for students to collect recyclable waste, conditioning the next generation to what is necessary for a sustainable Aruba.

AIR POLLUTION

A glance at a chart compiled by the U.S. Department of Energy's Carbon Dioxide Information Analysis Center (CDIAC) in 2008, based on information gathered by the United Nations Statistics Division, reveals Aruba as #9 in the world regarding carbon dioxide emissions in metric tons of CO_2 *per capita*. This is among 214 nations. Without question, the operation of the refinery in San Nicolas is directly related to this standing. Figures show the now defunct Netherlands Antilles, which was dissolved in 2010, was rated the #4 country with the most CO_2 emissions *per capita* in the world, likely due to the huge Shell refinery in Curacao. The Valero refinery has been idle since April of 2012, which should prove beneficial to Aruba's emission rating. They announced in September that the facility would be turned into a transshipment station, with no plans to restart the refinery at any time.

The CDIAC chart tracks emissions from 1990 to 2008, and there are sharp declines in the years when Aruba's refinery was inactive; improvement of Aruba's status can be expected since the refinery stopped running in 2012. Despite the refinery's emissions, and that of WEB's power producing plant at Balashi, along with the burning of trash at the landfill on the south side, visitors have always found Aruba's air delightfully fresh, for the most part only carrying the scent of clean salt seas.

It is possible that when planning these facilities, the engineers kept in mind the prevailing northeasterly wind, which push all the fumes away from the island immediately. Even when frolicking at Baby Beach or Roger's Beach, in the very shadow of the refinery, the emissions could be seen, but not smelled.

RENEWABLE ENERGY

WEB, Aruba's other great source of CO_2 emissions, is also working, in conjunction with the government, to reduce and possibly eliminate entirely the island's dependence on oil for power and water. The primary concern is not necessarily the environment but the practicalities of a very turbulent and speculative oil commodity market, driving prices up to a point where the average islander cannot afford to pay their electric bills. Purification of the air will of course be a very positive outcome of reducing Aruba's oil use to produce electricity.

Other renewable energy technologies are being pursued. In 2009, the Vader Piet Wind Farm, consisting of 10 giant wind turbines, began operating on the far northeast coast of Aruba. It was the hope of the government and the company running the wind farm to establish a second at Urirama, near the Alto Vista Chapel, but this is meeting with strong resistance from nearby residents; the situation has created a stalemate.

A project is already underway to build a giant solar gathering field in the parking lot of Aruba's airport, which will also act as shade for the cars. Import taxes on materials and equipment to harness clean energy sources have been drastically reduced, encouraging residents to find alternatives to the energy produced by WEB. WEB has switched over to reverse osmosis water purification, which requires far less energy. They started a program in 2011 called "Save Together with Us," which encouraged consumers to be frugal in their energy consumption. Items that reduced water and electricity consumption were distributed as gift bags to all low-income neighborhoods.

The declared goal of island administrators is to make Aruba completely oil independent by 2020. They have been vigilant in reaching out to every possible international organization in the realization of this goal. In 2012, the Carbon War Room, founded by Sir Richard Branson, officially endorsed and affirmed their support to make Aruba the first completely oil independent nation in the world. This is a process that will require not only installing new forms of harnessing energy from low emission-producing sources, but also a change of wasteful energy habits on the part of residents.

TNO, a Dutch energy think-tank, established its first Caribbean branch in Aruba in 2011. They connect scientists, technology, and stakeholders to devise plans that will assist various communities in fulfilling their energy needs. In October of 2012 they broke ground on a Smart Community, the centrally-located community of Kibaima. This experimental community will consist of 20 homes and operate solely on renewable energy sources. TNO describes Aruba as "the perfect springboard for markets in the United States and South America." Their involvement in this project and Aruba's goals will hopefully stimulate interest by private companies from Europe in investing in the Caribbean and Latin energy markets. TNO's stance, and that of the Aruban government, is that investment and business in renewable technologies can provide opportunities for jobs, profit, and an improved quality of life for the entire region.

Islanders are being encouraged to refit their families with electric or hybrid cars. Some entities, such as Divi Properties Aruba, are actually awarding small electric cars to those who purchased condominiums. Aruba's power distributor, ELMAR, is conducting programs to promote the import and purchase of electric cars and the construction of solar energy structures to house and charge them. Duties on electric automobiles have been reduced from the usual 40 percent for gas burning vehicles to only 2 percent, to further encourage consumers to make the change.

LITTER ON BEACHES

Efforts continue to make individuals and large concerns, such as resorts, aware of the multiple consequences of plastic cups, plates, and straws, as well as foam containers to Aruba's environment. Some are proposing that only reusable glasses, dishes, and silverware be used anywhere near the beach.

It is very common for resorts to provide meal and drink service to their guests on the beach in disposable foam containers, with plastic cutlery, and drinks in plastic cups. If these are not disposed of immediately and properly, the trade winds will likely blow them about. Not only is it unsightly litter, but far worse, it can end up in the sea, where they can become deadly.

Various marine life, particularly turtles, feed on jellyfish; plastic and foam cups and the plastic rings that hold together a six pack of cans, can easily be mistaken for their favorite food. This often results in a turtle choking to death. This is a far more common occurrence than most would imagine and a serious threat to a number of species. The cups and foam debris accumulate under the water and litter the marine environment. The same holds true on sailing cruises when drinks are served; care must be taken so that the cups are not blown overboard. Paper goods are at least biodegradable, but these should also be disposed of quickly and properly, especially newspapers, which do tend to get blown about.

Conscientious guests at resorts should not hesitate to speak up if a facility does not provide a sufficient number of conveniently located waste disposal units. If trash bins are filled up beyond capacity before the end of the day and there is spillover, bring it to the management's attention; they will respond. Aruba's resorts, like Bucuti & Tara Beach and Amsterdam Manor, have made great strides in the past five years to become green certified. Many are reverting back to glass and silverware. Visitors can help encourage this practice by selecting green-certified resorts.

Volunteer Programs
ARUBA REEF CARE PROJECT
What began as an underwater reef cleaning effort by some young diving enthusiasts is now the long-standing Aruba Reef Care Project (297/740-0797, castroperez@gmail.com), which polices both the shore and marine environment. Volunteers sign up with a number of dive operators to use either scuba or snorkeling gear to clean under the water, while hundreds take to all the island beaches to remove refuse. (This event took place over the July 4 weekend for more than a decade, but in 2012 the event moved to September.) Volunteers are rewarded with a congenial party (this is Aruba, after all) and lunch afterwards, plus a raffle for many great prizes donated by local concerns (dinners for two, weekend stays at resorts, and so on) and an attractive certificate.

COASTAL ZONE CLEAN-UP
Since 2002, the Aruba Hotel and Tourism Association (AHATA) Environmental Committee has conducted their Costal Zone Clean-Up (297/582-2607, vanessa@ahata.com) in November. They also target every beach and award prizes for groups that collect the most refuse.

PROJECT AWARE
Every April, Red Sail Sports conducts Project Aware (297/586 1603, info@redsailaruba.com). Red Sail rewards its volunteers with a sailing cruise on one of their large catamarans, to wind down after a morning of

SAVING ARUBA'S TURTLES

Every year during the months of March-November there may be sections of beach cordoned off, particularly around Eagle Beach. This is to protect the eggs and hatchlings of Aruba's local and migrating sea turtle population, which mate and nest here during these months.

Four species in particular are the concern of **TurtugAruba** (hotline 297/592-9393, http://turtugaruba.org), the local foundation that works to protect the island's turtle population. The green sea turtle and the hawksbill are native to Aruban waters and can be seen year-round while snorkeling and diving, though the hawksbill is considered a critically endangered species.

Leatherbacks and loggerheads normally feed and live in far distant oceans, usually in the North Atlantic, but will travel thousands of miles to return to the same waters to mate where they first entered the sea. The females lay their eggs on the same beaches where they hatched years before. Most often they do this under cover of night, a remarkable sight.

Once the eggs are laid and buried, mom returns to the sea and the hatchlings brave survival to adulthood on their own. So many things, including human actions, are a threat to newly-born turtles. Driving on the beach is discouraged for this reason.

TortugAruba asks that observers report, but do not disturb, a female laying her eggs. The area will be cordoned off to protect the nest and monitored during the two-month gestational period. Volunteers maintain a vigil for when the young turtles emerge, helping them make it to the sea safely.

a baby leatherback turtle

© ROSALIE KLEIN

strenuous garbage collecting. Their effort is on a smaller scale, focusing on a particular beach needing attention.

GARNIER ANNUAL BEACH CLEANUP
Aruba's newest effort, Garnier Annual Beach Cleanup in May (297/582-5672, lizayra.

polak@curapharm.com) also does a "surgical strike" on certain beach fronts vulnerable to incoming tides that dump garbage tossed overboard by passing ships, mostly tankers. Certain beaches along the north coast need regular policing because of this. The amount that can accumulate in a short time is alarming.

Flora and Fauna

FLORA
Trees
A combination of year-long tropical temperatures with little rainfall produces a wild plant population leaning heavily towards succulents, thorny flowering plants, and trees. They sport an abundance of prickles from microscopic to inches long as natural protection to being eaten by roaming herbivores. Hiking trips into the Aruban countryside require care to avoid them.

Island trees are best known by their charming names in Papiamento. **Kwihi** are prolific and valued for their wood. When being felled to build lots for houses, whole trunks often end up as arresting tables, maintaining their original configurations. Kwihi are practically weeds, germinating easily in the slightest bit of soil, with huge thorns to protect the young green plants. They finally grow into majestic shade trees.

Watapana, or **divi** trees *(caesalpinia coriaria)*, when full grown, almost resemble what artists try to accomplish with bonsai; the continual northeast wind bends and carves them to lean over in dramatic, gnarled formations. Common advice for those who decide to go out exploring the outback on their own and eventually get lost: Just follow the direction in which the Divi trees point and you will always end up back in Oranjestad.

Another tree that is abundant and green year-round is the aptly named **Crown of Thorns** *(acacia tortuosa)*, called *hubada* by islanders; it is good to give these a wide berth. They produce an appealing yellow ball of a flower, but keep their long, painful spikes even when full grown.

Vacationers fortunate to be visiting in May or June might be rewarded the rare sight of the **kibrahacha** *(tabebuia billbergii)*, commonly known as yellow poui, in bloom. This only happens for a few days a year and, during that time, only when there have been some showers, which will trigger a flurried attempt at seeding and pollinating. The normal foliage of the hills around Arikok National Park or the Hooiberg turns into a riot of brilliant yellow blooms, which disappears in less than a week. The tree gets its local name from the extreme hardness of the wood; it literally translates as "break the hatchet" *(kibra* means "break" and *hacha* means "hatchet").

Fruits
A number of regional wild fruit trees are scattered across the landscape, producing an impressive harvest in wetter years. **Sea Grape** *(coccoloba swartzii)* are a sweet snack and provide welcome shade alongside many beaches. The **West Indian Cherry** *(malpighia emarginata)*, locally known as *chimarucu*, is sometimes sold in the markets. Cultivated in gardens or growing wild are **kenepa** *(Melicoccus bijugatus)*, also known as "Spanish Lime." This is a regional tree that produces clusters of green skinned fruit the size of a litchi. Inside is a large seed coated with a delicious pulp that is a favorite treat, eaten by sucking on the seed and a tasty and non-fattening way to stop smoking!

Aruba has an endless variety of cactus and prickly flowers growing wild or cultivated, not the least of which is aloe vera. The most common endemic varieties are the towering *cadushi*,

THE ARUBAN ORCHID

Aruba does have a specific strain of the orchid *Brassavola nodesa*, which is native to the region. It originates in Venezuela, where it is referred to as *Dama de Noche* (Lady of the Night) because it emits a noticeably sweet, somewhat citrus scent from sunset to sunrise. Aruba has a cactus that had already claimed that name by producing beautiful white blooms only at dark. Local orchid aficionados refer to the Aruban strain of orchid as the far earthier *Puta Chiquito* (Little Prostitute).

During the 1940s, Esso executive Russ Ewing, who lived in the colony, harbored a passion for orchids. He produced a unique hybrid by cross-pollinating the hardy Aruban *Brassavola nodesa* with the Venezuelan *encyclia cordigera*. The result was larger than both. He registered this new species with the Royal Horticultural Society of the United Kingdom as *brassoepidendrum arubiana* on January 1, 1950. The common name is the "Aruba Good Friend."

The **Aruba Orchid Society** (sociedaddiorquidiaaruba@yahoo.com) has existed for almost 40 years and is very active. They recruit members and stimulate interest in cultivating orchids with regular shows. They have published some how-to books on growing orchids in Papiamento.

---

better known as **candle cactus** *(stenocereus griseus)*. It produces a deep red, tasty fruit, attracting birds who manage to avoid the proliferation of thorns.

Showing off a very delicate yellow flower is the "tuna" or **prickly pear** *(opuntia wentiana),* which will also eventually produce a sweet fruit of many seeds. The comical *bushi,* or **Turk's Cap cactus** *(melocactus macracantthos),* have brilliant neon-pink flowers sprouting from their white, spongy centers. These become tart, equally bright pink fruit, shaped like a small pepper to attract lizards and birds.

Flowers

Among the many wild flowering plants, one of the most noticeable is *Passiflora* or **Passion Flower,** known in Papiamento as *shoshoro.* The bulbous pods open into a delicate purple flower with green stigmas. It is a tenacious vine, often twining around other plants.

A garden left to grow naturally will eventually produce an abundance of typical dessert foliage, scrub, and cacti. Though brilliantly hued tropical flowers, such as dewdrops, azaleas, hibiscus, frangipani, flamboyan, and begonias, are imported, they are commonly seen decorating landscaped resort gardens and most homes. Recycling waste water from septic tanks is a common practice to maintain these gardens.

FAUNA
Insects

Being a tropical climate, insects of every type are found in abundance. Desert denizens, such as scorpions and millipedes, are common to the outlying areas, but have a distinct distaste for well populated neighborhoods, and the chance of seeing one around a resort is highly unlikely.

During a 2003 study of the ABC islands (Aruba, Bonaire, and Curacao), 29 species of butterflies were collected on Aruba with **Lycaenidae, Pieridae,** and **Hesperiidae** being the most common families found. **Monarch butterflies** *(danaus plexippus)* are seen everywhere, as milkweed, their chosen plant for laying their eggs, grows abundantly. Known as the athletes of the insect world, they travel thousands of miles, often "hitching" rides on boats at sea. It is likely that Aruba was a welcome rest stop along the way to Latin America, where they established a home. Butterflies are a tasty treat for most birds, but monarchs are foul and poisonous because of the caterpillars feeding on the milkweed. They display their dramatic colors without fear of being eaten.

Birds

Aruba is an important rest stop and haven for many migrating species. Over the centuries, several have stayed and made Aruba their home. Two brilliantly colorful species common to Aruba are the native *Prikichi* (**Caribbean Brown-throated parakeet**) and the **Trupial.**

The **Yellow Oriole** is a cousin of the Trupial, and amidst the ABC islands has earned the name *Trupial Kachù*. On Aruba it is better known as a *Gonzalito*.

Aruba's more common predatory birds, **eagles, falcons,** and **hawks,** are best known by their charming local names such as *Caracara, Falki, and Kini Kini.*

Common to the Caribbean is the **Tropical Mockingbird** *(Chuchubi).* This dramatically marked gray bird nests on rooftops and ferociously defends its home against all intruders. It wakes the neighborhood with its beautiful song. The **Bananaquit,** a bold, tiny bird that loves sweets, is called *Barica Geil,* meaning "Yellow Belly" for obvious reasons.

The **Brown Pelican** is common to all three ABC islands, but researchers find Aruba is where it has been confirmed with certainty that pelicans breed. During breeding season the hind neck plumage turns dark, reddish-brown. It remains white during other times or in the winter.

Wetlands are home to herons, egrets, cormorants, and ducks of various species. The yellow feet of the **Snowy Egret** has earned it the name "The Lady with the Golden Slippers," which helps to differentiate it from a Great Egret.

Though **flamingoes** are usually associated with Bonaire, a thriving flock can be found on the Flamingo Beach of Renaissance Island. They are very accommodating about posing for photographs. The characteristic deep salmon color is a result of their diet; a particular brine shrimp is a favorite. They also eat small marine snails and the larvae of pesky flies and mosquitoes, making it a worthwhile creature to preserve and protect, not only for its beauty.

Reptiles

As one would expect from a desert climate, the island is home to a wide variety of lizards *(lagadishi),* from tiny geckos to iguanas of all sizes. It is not uncommon to find birds and lizards gathered at the edges of outdoor restaurants ready for crumbs and bits of fruit or bread tossed their way.

Iguanas *(Iguana iguana)* are plentiful and can be seen around hotel gardens, particularly rock formations. While adolescent they maintain a brilliant jade green hue. As they grow they begin to develop the characteristic striped tail. Eventually, they fade to dusky, camouflage colors.

The **Aruban whiptail lizard** *(Cnemidophorus arubensis)* or *Kododo Blauw* is an endemic species named for the striking aqua coloration shown by the mature male; females and the young are varying shades of brown.

Visitors to Arikok National Park will see a display of the **cascabel** *(Crotalus durissus unicolor),* Aruba's endemic and endangered rattlesnake, and the santanero, the Aruban **cat-eyed snake** **(***Leptodeira bakeri).* Only the cascabel is venomous and rarely seen outside of the wilds. The **santanero** can be found anywhere, even in domestic gardens, but is absolutely harmless; both snakes help to control vermin.

ARUBA'S NATIONAL BIRD: THE SHOCO

An endemic species of the American Burrowing Owl, the Shoco, was declared Aruba's National Symbol in 2011. Studies have shown that of the three ABC islands (Aruba, Bonaire, and Curacao), Aruba is the only one graced with this amusing, tiny creature. Their large, golden eyes are a particularly beautiful, distinctive feature.

A pair of them will usually be found protecting their nest, which is a hole in the ground. When they anticipate the possibility of being disturbed, one will fly off to draw attention away from the nest.

Being a ground-dwelling bird, their habitats are extremely vulnerable to boa constrictors and the ill effects of bulldozing and construction. Bird protection lobbyists hope that their national symbol status will provide the impetus for laws protecting their nests.

© ROSALIE KLEIN

the cascabel, Aruba's endangered rattlesnake

INVASIVE BOA CONSTRICTORS ON ARUBA

Aside from Aruban companies finally promoting recycling, an aspect of another environmental issue is being looked upon as an opportunity. A predator threatening indigenous mammals and birdlife is the boa constrictor. How it was introduced into the Aruban landscape is a matter for debate. Many point to the practice of buying the snakes as an interesting pet while young, than letting them go into the wild. It is also proposed that the very young boas were nestled among bunches of bananas and other fruit brought into the island by small boats from Venezuela.

However they arrived, their intrusive presence was noticed around 1990 as they began consuming not only vermin but threatened native species of birds, rabbits, lizards, and, on rare occasions, pet cats and dogs. Herpetologist Andrew Odum from the Toledo Zoological Society has taken a particular interest in the impact on the native cascabel. The largest boa

constrictor found on Aruba to date measures 2.9 meters (nearly 10 ft. long).

Boa constrictors give birth to up to 64 young snakes at any time; they are immediately viable and out hunting for food. Their preferred method is to wait in ambush for their prey, which they crush and kill. They can be found on the ground, under bushes, in trees, and on cacti. A scientific team from Texas did an extensive study as to how they are impacting the local wildlife.

The snakes are found mostly in Arikok National Park and in rural areas; one section of Arikok is reserved for the study of the snake and its habits. A Boa Task Force headed by Arikok National Park Biologist and Director Diego Marquez began a training program for the general populace, conducting regularly scheduled boa hunts on weekends. Perhaps 100 boas were caught at a time, but the task force assumes for every boa found there are at least another four in the bush. To continue to tackle this problem,

Arikok National Park acquired sponsors and placed bounties on boas.

In 2011, **Arte Sano Studios** (297/733-5232, artesano@setarnet.aw) opened a workshop producing various accessories made from boa skin. Each item is handcrafted and unique. This new industry is also a social project, teaching a trade and rehabilitating delinquent young islanders. The project is heartily endorsed by both Aruba Bird Conservation and the Boa Task Force, turning a liability into an asset by establishing an industry of singular, fine quality products made in Aruba, while diversifying the economy. They expect to produce two limited collections annually.

Marine Life

The island's tropical marine environment is an important asset, with extensive reefs in depths from 2 feet to over 200. They are populated with uncountable species of brilliant tropical fish and colorful corals, providing breathtaking experiences for thousands of vacationers annually. Colorful angelfish, triggerfish, wrasses, and parrotfish, of all varieties and hue, are in the water. Fortunately, there is no manufacturing despoiling these waters with toxic runoff.

Aruba also appears to have a minimal population of dangerous predatory fish, and shark attacks are unheard of. Barracuda are plentiful, but their fierce appearance and fictional media have imbued them with an undeserved ferocious reputation.

Divers and snorkelers should be mindful that they are much larger than any fish life they will encounter. Actually, humans are the largest and most dangerous predator around. Most fish will dart away at your approach, except in the few areas where they have become accustomed to being protected and fed. Spear fishing is illegal in Aruba and any equipment for this pastime will be confiscated at customs.

INVASIVE LIONFISH

The influx of nonnative species, like lionfish, threaten indigenous animals: Lionfish are a challenge to every island from The Bahamas,

south. They began showing up in Aruban waters around 2010. Speculation places their invasion as a result of the destruction done by Hurricane Andrew in 1992; lionfish began being spotted soon after in waters around Florida, then The Bahamas. It is suggested they escaped into the wild after homes where they were kept in aquariums were destroyed and flooded. Some lionfish hunters are firmly convinced that they were introduced by people releasing them into the wild when they became too big and troublesome to care for; they are an aggressive species that will consume every other fish in a tank.

Lionfish are native to the Indo-Pacific and Red Sea, where a natural form of control has developed. Predators such as large groupers and certain sharks consume them with regularity. The fish also do not reproduce as often or develop as quickly in their natural habitat as they do in the Caribbean's warmer waters. Their fins are distinctive, containing highly venomous spines, so there are few fish that will feed on them. They can extend the spines and stick in the throat of any fish attempting to eat them.

Lionfish are extremely prolific and ravenous, deadly predators. They have been observed literally vacuuming schools of smaller fish into their large maws, which extend for this purpose. They also hunt in packs, cooperating to drive their prey towards the waiting jaws of the larger, dominant lionfish.

Though stunningly beautiful, they are a real pest, reproducing in regional waters at an alarming rate, 2,000,000 eggs annually. Devouring the many fish that play an important role in the delicate reef environment has serious ramifications. Within a year, they can strip a reef area of nearly 80 percent of its small fish population. A number of these feed on the algae which grows on coral and are necessary for keeping the reef healthy; lionfish disrupt this entire marine cycle and the reef can die.

Various solutions have been initiated to deal with the issue, including fishing tournaments directed specifically at lionfish. Diving operations are encouraged to hunt them whenever spotted in the water, or to notify the agency charged with their control. There is a group called "Lionfish Hunters" that regularly hunts them and provides instruction on how to do it properly.

Special events conducted by the local fishing organization, Centro di Pisca Hadicurari, and the Aruba Marine Park Foundation, teach consumers how to clean and prepare lionfish for the table. They are quite tasty, despite the paltry return of edible flesh proportional to the size of the fish. It took no time for islanders to imbue lionfish soup with the magical properties of such expensive medications as Viagra, a greatly desired effect long attributed to the meat of the iguana. Perhaps now lionfish can prove useful and give that endangered species a respite from poachers seeking to liven up their weekends.

Mammals

Most mammals that are actually indigenous to the island are small desert creatures such as rodents, very tiny hares (some fit in the bowl of a standard soup spoon), and quite a few bats, found mostly but not exclusively in the caves at the eastern end of the island. The last are being closely monitored to insure that their population remains constant, as they are necessary, feeding on annoying insects and pollinating fruit plants. None of the bats are rabid; rabies does not exist on Aruba.

Aruba also has a marine mammal population of dolphins and the occasional whale pod passing by on their migratory patterns. There is an organization dedicated to monitoring and protecting them: the Aruba Marine Mammal Foundation (http://arubadolphins.wordpress.com) founded in 1998.

Aruba has a notable population of undomesticated donkeys and goats. These are remnants of a time when they were brought to the island for breeding and allowed to roam freely; they are not really native species. It is not unusual when touring through Arikok National Park and other undeveloped areas to suddenly come face to face with a family of donkeys or goats living in the wild.

History

Aruba's lack of value to Spanish conquistadors earned it the label *"Islas Inutiles"* (Useless Islands) along with Curacao and Bonaire, so records of its encounter by Europeans are somewhat sketchy. Alonso de Ojeda is credited with first spotting Curacao, and it is presumed Aruba and Bonaire, around 1499, describing them as *"islas adyacentes a la costa firme"* (islands adjacent to the mainland). Ojeda returned to Spain in June of 1501 to be appointed governor over the coastal regions of Coquibacoa and Guajira, with the "Adjacent Islands" under his administration. It appears Aruba also earned the title "Isle of the Giants," which is interesting because unearthed remains of Aruba's indigenous people reveal they were quite short by modern standards.

Historians are unsure of the actual true origins of the modern name Aruba; the discovery of gold in 1824 fuels speculation that it is an adaptation of the Spanish word for gold, *oro*. Some assert it means "Island of Shells." The lack of documentation regarding the early history of the island makes it difficult to know for certain.

EARLY HISTORY
Caquetio Indians and the Spanish Rule

The fortunes of the ABC islands (Aruba, Bonaire, Curacao) were always tied to their proximity to the mainland, whether under the rule of the local Amerindian caciques (chieftains) or the Spanish. The Paraguaná peninsula east of Lake Maracaibo was a seat of power for the caciques and during the 1500s the fate of Aruba remained closely related to what is now known as Venezuela.

A small community of Amerindians, a subgroup of the peaceful Arawak people called Caquetio, lived nomadic lives, establishing small villages along the coast and in the caves at the island's south end. It was important to be able to harvest food from the sea. Over 300 of their pictographs and a few petroglyphs (rock carvings as opposed to paintings) can still be seen. The indigenous population was eventually enslaved by the Spanish and by 1515 nearly all were transported to Hispaniola to work in the mines.

Juan Martinez De Ampues was appointed administrator of the ABC islands in 1525. Under his (relatively) benevolent administration, an agreement was made with the supreme Amerindian chieftain of Coro, called Manaure, residing in Paraguaná. This allowed the Caquetios to return to the islands and awarded them protected status; in a sense, Aruba became a reservation.

De Ampues declared slave hunting of Amerindians illegal on the ABC islands; his intentions, however, were far from altruistic. The treaty with the Manaure was that in exchange for protection, the chieftain would capture new slaves from other tribes to be sent to the mines.

Eventually, to settle his enormous debt, Charles V of Spain awarded the trade rights to the region to the Welsers, a German banking family. Their 30-year administration ending in 1559 proved particularly harsh for the indigenous people of the peninsula, prompting them to flee to the nearby islands.

Beginning in 1529, Aruba was deployed as a *rancho*. It was one great pasture for roaming goats, pigs, cows, sheep, horses, and donkeys. Most Amerindians left on the island tended the herds. This has spurred speculation as to the original flora of the island, as compared to the cacti that dominates today.

Introduction of Christianity

It was during the mid 1500s that the conversion of the Caquetios to Catholicism by missionaries began in earnest. Archaeologists have unearthed a number of remains in a communal gravesite discovered in 2002. The skeletons have all been identified as Amerindian, but the burial style is a mix of Caquetio traditions and those uniquely identifiable as Christian. Other artifacts confirm the graves dating from this period. The mixture of cultures indicates the conversion process had not yet fully taken hold, with sacred Amerindian practices still a part of the burial ritual.

Aruba's first Christian church, the Alto Vista Chapel, was built in 1750 on what was sacred ground to the Caquetio Indians. Spanish Padre Domingo Antonio Silvestre led the mission to bring the sparse native population into the fold of Catholicism.

The Dutch Conquer Aruba

Aruba's defining relationship to the Netherlands was established during the Eighty Years' War for Independence between the Dutch Republic and Spain (1568-1648). It prompted the Dutch to conquer Spanish and Portuguese colonies in the Caribbean, with direct Dutch trade beginning around 1593.

Merchants in Holland were eager to establish a Dutch trading company similar to the highly profitable Dutch East India franchise. Dutch trade in the area was restricted by a treaty until 1621. When the treaty expired, a group called the *Heren XIX* (19 Gentlemen) actively sought private investors to open trade routes. Encouraged by the Dutch Republic, they founded the West Indian Company (WIC). Many were interested in this high-risk enterprise, which included substantial financial assistance from the government.

Dutch trade in the region was also another method for Holland to interfere with their Spanish enemies, a desirable offshoot of any enterprise. They also wished to "free the natives" from religious oppression, which was a fundamental motivation behind the war. Holland defeated Spanish forces in Curacao in 1634, taking possession of all three islands.

Despite the involvement of the Dutch in the slave trade from Africa, the native population of the ABC islands was treated equally under Dutch law as colonists. It was prohibited to enslave Amerindians. Despite being equal under the law, documents prove it was not practiced. Discrimination made life harsh for the Amerindian population.

The advent of the Napoleonic Wars resulted in Aruba falling under control of England between 1799 and 1802, and again from 1804 until 1816. Very little is written about this period and the effect on island culture or tradition is undetectable. Aruba soon reverted back to Dutch control.

Slavery

It was long believed that since Aruba did not have the extensive agriculture and plantations of other islands, as well as it being sparsely populated, slave labor of imported Africans was not practiced among the colonists. Careful investigation by a new generation of historians has disproved this. Historical documents reveal an estimated 10 percent of the population during the late 1700s and early 1800s were household slaves, usually maids, nannies, cooks, gardeners, and handymen. They were fortunate to have a more lenient and closer relationship with their owners and families, and it is believed they were better treated than field hands. Aruba did not experience a slave revolt such as Curacao, home of the notorious slave markets, did in 1795. By declaration of the King of the Netherlands, all slaves were freed throughout the Kingdom and its territories in 1863. Records show Aruba had almost 500 slaves living on the island at the time.

Settlement on Aruba in the 1700s

Actual settlement in Aruba was forbidden until at least 1750. There was concern about the security of the area and Curacao, an important port and commercial center, if there was over-development and population on its sister islands. Only a few personnel of the West Indian Company (WIC), including the Lieutenant Governor, his entourage and slaves, plus about 20 soldiers, occupied the island. Aruba's status of being virtually ignored by administrators encouraged smuggling, as Aruba was a tax-free port, as well as a hideout for privateers and pirates, or "Zeerovers."

Aruba's isolation ended when Mozes Maduro, a Sephardic Jew originally from Portugal, was granted land and became the first non-Amerindian settler. The WIC deployed a system of land tenure, with land usage leased in exchange for various services or fees, but WIC continued to own the land.

Settlers coming to Aruba from around 1780 began changing the makeup of the population. According to Jan Hartog's history of Aruba, a report from the early 1800s counts the population of the island as comprised of 1,732 inhabitants. Of this, 564 were the original indigenous inhabitants, 584 freed "colored people," and 37 free "black people," along with 133 "colored slaves" and 203 "black slaves," with less than 100 white colonists. Accounts from the 1800s by an unknown Dutchman described the islands as quite unsuitable for agriculture and basically useless. Even then, however, it states that "Arubans displayed great pride and love for their island, despite the barren, infertile soil."

Decline of Amerindian Population

As the colonial influence grew, the native Amerindian population and culture declined. The death of Aruba's last full-blooded native Amerindian, Nicolass Payklaas, is reported to be in 1843. Based on the accounts of colonial Aruba by historian Father van Koolwijk, the end of the Amerindian Historic Period is pinpointed by scholars as 1860. Aruba's Colonial Era is defined from 1724 until 1924, with the establishment of the oil refineries. The departure of Esso and the first closing of the San Nicolas refinery coincide with Aruba's independence from the five other islands of the Netherlands Antilles.

STATUS APARTE—ARUBAN INDEPENDENCE

Aruba's achievement of independence from the other five islands of the Netherlands Antilles, while remaining an autonomously ruled entity within the Dutch Kingdom, is an inspiring success story. It was achieved without bloodshed or violent revolt, setting an example for other islands. Indeed, it is the Aruban model that paved the way for the same status for Curacao and San Martaan in 2010. The other islands of the Netherlands Antilles, Bonaire, Eustatius, and Saba, now called the BES islands, chose to become Dutch municipalities. Their status is more closely related to Holland than before.

The AVP and PPA

The concept of Status Aparte starts with the story of Jan Hendrik "Henny" Eman, founder of the Arubaanse Volkspartij political party (AVP). He planted and nurtured the seed of decentralization. He organized a petition to separate from the Colony of Curacao. Getting signatures was a monumental task in pre-war Aruba, often done by donkey cart traveling from home to home. The 2,147 signatures confirmed that Eman had obtained the majority support for this movement.

It was Eman's son, Albert "Shon" Eman, who first presented Aruba's formal proposal to Queen Juliana on March 18, 1948. This was during roundtable talks with Suriname and the other Dutch islands at Den Hague in Holland. The crown "took it under advisement."

These talks resulted in the Constitution of the Netherlands Antilles enacted in February 1951. On March 3, 1951, the Island Regulation of the Netherlands Antilles was issued by royal decree. Eventually, this spurred Arubans even more to seek independence from the other islands, as it was frustrating to have Aruba's economic and developmental reins in the hands of Curacao politicos.

Particularly dissatisfied by this turn of events was Juan "Juancho" Irausquin, a member of the AVP along with its founder, Henny Eman. Irausquin went on to establish the Partido Patriotico Arubano political party (PPA) and to build Aruba's first major resort in Palm Beach, the Royal Caribbean.

Henny Eman died in 1957 and his son "Shon" Eman took over leadership of the AVP. The PPA began to acquire some influence until Irausquin's death in 1962. "Shon" Eman died in 1967 and the influence of both parties waned with the founding of MEP by Gilberto Francois "Betico" Croes.

Betico Croes and the Path to Independence

The ascendancy of Betico Croes in Aruba's political arena began in 1967. He was originally a part of the AVP party, but began his own political party, *Moviemento di Electoral di Pueblo,* while taking up the banner of autonomy. He is credited with actually assigning the formal name of Status Aparte, making national identity and self-determination a priority. It was during the 1960s and 1970s, with the decline of the refinery, when Aruba began to focus more on tourism. Tourism would soon become the principal pillar of the economy. The desire to construct more hotels and acquire additional airlift was again hampered by controls from Curacao.

Aruba's acquisition of Status Aparte was not entirely without incident. The month described as *Agustus Scur* (Dark August) in 1977 was marked by civil disobedience and protest marches. Work stoppages by Elmar, which regulates and distributes electricity, brought business to a standstill. Lights were out for several nights during the summer months as a show of solidarity and a wish for Holland to respond to the will of the people. Those who were children and witnessed these events describe it as "exciting, adventurous times."

Betico Croes led the highly successful talks with Holland in 1981 and 1982, which resulted in an agreement for Aruban self rule under Dutch supervision for the first 10 years. The date set for it to be enacted was January 1, 1986, with Aruba to be fully independent from Holland in 1996.

Surprisingly, elections in 1985 resulted in Henny Eman, son of Albert, and now leader of the AVP, becoming Aruba's first prime minister. It was during his administration that Aruba's independence from Holland was renegotiated. Aruba remains an independent part of the Dutch Kingdom and islanders maintain their Dutch citizenship and passports.

ECONOMIC DEVELOPMENT
Gold and Phosphate

Aruba's economically elite families during colonial times established their fortunes through shipping and importing necessary goods. Others eked out a living farming, fishing, and by breeding horses and selling what livestock they could. Change came when gold was discovered in 1824 by 12-year-old Willem Rasmijn, while herding his father's sheep along the north coast. As with all the New World, the crown had sent surveyors to search for precious minerals nearly a century before on all the ABC islands, but nothing of consequence was discovered. The gold find at Rooi Fluit started a gold rush, increasing the population and facilitating the official designation of Oranjestad as the capital of Aruba. Some argue Aruba's first capital was Savaneta on the south side, as this was the headquarters of the Dutch Marine Commander, and it is where their camp is still located today.

Everyone who could afford a pickaxe went looking for gold, but regulations were set in place to control its sale to the government at fixed prices. This naturally encouraged many attempts to smuggle gold to more lucrative markets. Finally the government prohibited free prospecting, choosing to award mineral rights to the highest bidder. The initial rush died down after about five years, but new veins found in 1854 revived interest in the economic development of the island. Gold mining rights passed from one company to another until they finally settled with the Aruba Island Gold Mining Company of London.

The discovery of phosphate during the early 19th century provided another economic stimulus for the island. Aruba Island Gold Mining Company of London demanded the harvest rights, claiming they already had exclusive rights for the extraction of minerals. The courts denied their suit, and rights were awarded to the Aruba Island Phosphate Company Ltd. It did not fare very well, and eventually evolved into the Aruba Phosphaat Maatschappij.

The establishment of gold and phosphate industries stimulated immigration to Aruba and settlement to areas such as San Nicolas, which was virtually ignored until then. This is where the phosphate works were established. In 1833,

Aruba had a population of 2,476, which increased to 8,065 by 1893.

The collapse of the gold and phosphate industries reduced immigration to Aruba to a trickle, with an increase of only 1,000 people in 30 years by 1923. However, Aruba's fortunes changed radically with the inception of the Lago Oil Refinery.

Aloe Vera

The production of aloe also contributed to the prosperity and influx of the population in the 1800s. Introduced to the island in 1840, aloe vera thrived in Aruba's arid climate to produce a high quality extract, which was in great demand.

The aloe industry truly became profitable in 1890 when Cornelius Eman founded Aruba Aloe Balm. At one point, nearly two-thirds of the island's agricultural production was dedicated to aloe. Aruba became the world's #1 exporter of aloe products. World interest waned in the early 1950s, and Aruban production and export dropped dramatically.

New methods of manufacture and a renewed interest in the natural healing properties of aloe prompted Louis Posner to acquire the factory and fields in Hato in 2000. He replaced the old plant with a modern, attractive facility that accepts visitors for tours and provides a history of the industry.

Refinery Era

No island historian would deny that the opening of the Lago Refinery was a defining moment in Aruba's history. It brought employment, prosperity, and technology, resulting in a noticeably higher standard of living and education than other nations in the region.

ARUBA'S FORGOTTEN REFINERY

There were actually *two* refineries opening at almost the same time. Lago was preceded by two years by a collaboration of British Petroleum and Royal Dutch Shell. The Arends Petroleum Maatschappij, better known by the English translation of *Arend*—Eagle Oil Company. This was located on the western outskirts of Oranjestad, where an exclusive gated and guarded community was constructed for the management.

Eagle Oil Company occupied a vast expanse of land, from what is now Bubali, where the company's medical facility was located at Quinta Del Carmen, to the turbo rotunda now situated at the far west border of Oranjestad. It extended about a quarter mile inland. Within its borders were a social club, tennis club, private golf course, and private train lines to transport construction materials. A pier was built for the tankers where the Tamarijn Beach Resort now stands. Oranjestad Harbor had not yet been dredged and refitted for large ships. The pier was demolished in 1974.

The end of WWII reduced demand for the Eagle Refinery product, as they did not produce jet fuel. It closed its doors in 1954. The majority of employees were relocated to Shell's Curacao refinery. The land was sold back to the Aruban government, with the housing purchased by islanders to become an upscale community. The beach areas were zoned for tourism.

THE SAN NICOLAS REFINERY

The discovery of oil in Lake Maracaibo, Venezuela in 1918 would herald a complete change of lifestyle and standards for Arubans. The Venezuelan dictator, Juan Vicente Gomez, purposely generated great interest in U.S. and European oil companies to relieve the country's extreme debt. He spurred development of the industry by granting concessions and selling oil very cheaply. Those days are long gone.

An impediment to development was the fact that filling the large ocean-going tankers with crude oil at Maracaibo was simply not possible. Smaller ships called lake tankers were used. A more suitable transshipment station was sought, where the loads of the smaller tankers could be transferred to huge ocean-going vessels. In 1924, Captain Robert Rogers of the British Equatorial Oil Company began scouting out a site for such a terminal. Originally he had Curacao in mind, but the Dutch government was not cooperative, concerned about competition for their Shell refinery.

Powerful U.S. oil companies were wielding strong influence in the region at the time. They were reluctant to build refineries in Latin America because of the constant political turmoil, a situation that still exists. Aruba attracted their attention for its stable government and close proximity to the source. During negotiations, Gomez also pressured the Dutch government to concede to the construction of a facility.

San Nicolas harbor would require dredging and preparation at great cost to accommodate the big ships. The already existing remains from the phosphate industry made it very attractive to Captain Rogers. A few savvy local businessmen were also involved in convincing him of the wisdom of a facility on Aruba. They pointed out the advantage of Aruba being even closer to Maracaibo than Curacao, whose port was already well occupied from the Shell refinery. Rogers was convinced that the money saved from the extra miles of lake tankers hauling all the way to Curacao easily justified the expense of creating the deep water harbor at San Nicolas.

Within a year after the contracts were signed, British Equatorial Oil was purchased by Canadian Lago Oil & Transport. The original intention of only a transshipment terminal to a full-blown refinery took over during the planning stages. Lago Oil & Petroleum Company Limited began operations in January 1929, under General Manager Lloyd G. Smith.

The construction of the first refinery already radically affected Aruba's economy. The refineries were providing jobs locally and bringing in workers from around the world. Their operation required certain skills not found among islanders. Once construction was completed, the need for new skills and personnel resulted in an increase in island population of 7,000 new residents originating from 56 countries. In 1945, only 32 percent of the employees at the refinery were native born.

Eventually, the refinery was taken over by Rockefeller's Standard Oil of New Jersey, which became Esso, then Exxon. The refinery and adjacent residences continued to be referred to as

"Lago" and "Lago Colony," a name still used to this day.

It was the influx of immigrants and near doubling of Aruba's population that prompted the construction of one of the first modern, large-capacity water desalination plants in the world. It was accompanied by a complex and efficient clean water distribution system. Experts and engineers traveling through the region assert these advances in production and distribution to every home and business, as a key element in the higher standard of living enjoyed by Arubans over many other Caribbean nations.

WAR STORIES OF ARUBA'S FAMOUS SHIPWRECKS

The **Antilla** was a German cargo ship, one of three along with the **Heidelberg** and **Troja** moored in the neutral waters of the Aruban coast, but believed to be used to supply U-boats. Curacao harbor also had German ships hiding out from British destroyers before Holland was invaded in May of 1940, ending their policy of strict neutrality.

The *Heidelberg* and *Troja* managed to escape Aruba's waters but were unable to break through the British blockade and scuttled far out at sea, while *Antilla* returned to anchor when it encountered a British destroyer just outside the three-mile limit.

German sailors were well aware that their homeland was going to invade Holland and were given orders to either make a run for it or scuttle their ships. Seven were captured in Curacao. When Germany invaded, island authorities attempted to board the *Antilla* at night and claim her, but the captain refused to lower the gangway. The machine gun backup on shore was unable to sight the ship in the dead of night, so they came back at first light, which gave the ship's Captain Ferdinand Schmidt time to prepare.

Rather than turn her over, he ordered the sea cocks opened, which flooded the ship, while the rest of the crew set fires in many of the cabins. It eventually listed to port and sank in 60 feet of water around 750 yards off the coast

of Malmok. It became a haven for sea life and a favorite dive and snorkel spot, as it can easily be seen without scuba gear. Its large, open compartments allow scuba divers the thrill of an actual wreck penetration with no risk. The captain and crew surrendered and were placed in a temporary internment camp in Bonaire, then transported in July of 1940 to a POW camp maintained by the British in Jamaica for the remainder of WWII.

Pedernales was an Italian oil tanker under British registry, which was anchored off the harbor in San Nicolas on February 17, 1942 when it was torpedoed by a German submarine, U-156, along with the **Oranjestad**. The latter sank in very deep waters off the south side; in doing so, it became the first tanker sunk in the Western Hemisphere during WWII. This was part of a concerted effort by Axis powers to cripple Allied fuel supply routes and sources deploying seven German and Italian submarines attacking tankers and refineries on February 16, 1942. The U-Boat 156 fortunately had a malfunction of their long-range gun, so they were unable to do damage to the Eagle refinery. The same night, two other Lago tankers, the San Nicolas and Tia Juana, were torpedoed 25 miles (40 km) southwest of Punta Macolla in the Gulf of Venezuela by U-502. Four days later a torpedo ended up on Eagle Beach in an attempt to blow up the Refinery, and a team of four Dutch soldiers died trying to defuse it. The final death toll from crew members on the tankers was 47. This event prompted a greater U.S. military presence on Aruba for the remainder of the war.

The *Pedernales* was towed to dry dock where the bow and aft sections were removed and transported to a U.S shipping yard, joined with a new midsection and put back into use; it was finally retired in 1959. What remained of the wreck offshore was used by troops stationed on Aruba for target practice. Some of the giant unexploded ordinance can still be seen under the water.

Because of Aruba's highly strategic position in the war effort, it was officially under British protection for two years during the war. Troops

WHAT IS A LAGOLITE?

From 1925 until 1986, Aruba, specifically San Nicolas, was host to what was to become the world's largest refinery during WWII, operating under Esso, then Exxon, as the Lago Refinery. Adjacent to the refinery was "The Colony," a facility for the refinery executives. It was an elite and fully-equipped community with its own hospital, school, social center, restaurant, bowling alley, and bachelors' quarters as well as elegant homes for the married executives with families.

Many of the executives lived on Aruba for decades; many children were born and raised in this uniquely multicultural community, graduating from the school. They came to call themselves Lagolites. Despite the years that have passed since the refinery closed and the employees and their families now scattered to all corners of the globe, they maintain a healthy interest in Aruba and a great nostalgia

for what many consider absolute paradise, and the gift of growing up in such singular circumstances. Families originated from all around the world; a multitude of languages were spoken and cultures shared, along with that of the Aruban people.

Lagolites have recounted much of their history on a dedicated website: www.lago-colony. com. Input and scrapbooks from children of the 800 executives who resided on Aruba within the colony at some point in its 60-year history has created a rich tapestry of island life during its key developmental years. This was a fantasy existence for these privileged children, with stunning blue seas, beautiful beaches, a richly social and connected community with constant access to wonderful water activities and nature. It was an innocent time, when the arrival of the first jet on the island was a spectacular landmark event.

---

from England and the United States were stationed on the island to protect the refinery from the German wolf pack, the submarines continually attempting to sink tankers and destroy the refineries.

The end of WWII signaled the gradual decline of the refinery's place in the island's economy. Automation resulted in a drastic reduction in personnel, by more than half. Eventually, in the final decades, only around 700 employees staffed the refinery. A number of peripheral companies cropped up around San Nicolas, working as subcontractors to perform repairs and maintenance.

Farsighted island leaders, entrepreneurs and legislators had already turned their attention to Status Aparte and tourism as priorities for Aruba to advance and prosper.

TOURISM TAKES OVER

Nearly simultaneous with the realization of Status Aparte was the closing of Lago Refinery, seemingly abandoned overnight. The 60-year contracts for crude oil from Venezuela had expired. During the interim, oil concerns and Venezuela had constructed numerous refineries. There was really no great need to transport the oil to an outside facility. The refinery was getting old and the costs of improvements were not conducive to continuing operations.

By this time, tourism had quite a foothold on Aruba, with several large resorts already standing in Palm Beach and timeshares proliferating like proverbial bunnies. The first major resort, the Aruba Caribbean, now the Radisson, was built and opened in 1959 by Juancho Irausquin, a definitive force in the development of Aruba's tourism industry. Prior to that, Chaven Neme, who had built the first tourist hotel in Oranjestad, opened the tiny Basi Ruti Resort in Palm Beach, its first, where the Playa Linda Resort was erected 1985.

By 1980, quite a few large resorts altered the Palm Beach coastline. Visionary developers such as Ike Cohen, a Holocaust survivor from Holland, and Walter Wiggins, a New York lawyer, founded the Manchebo Beach Resort and Divi Hotel. These established the concept of the "low rise" at Manchebo Beach. In the late 1970s, Sun Development opened the first timeshare on Aruba in that area, heralding a highly successful industry which catered to a core of dedicated vacationers returning annually. Statistics have shown timeshare owners account for close to 40 percent of Aruba's annual visitors.

With the advent of Status Aparte and the closing of the refinery, island leaders saw tourism as Aruba's future. They offered very attractive conditions to developers, which are criticized now, as guarantees signed by the government cost Aruba millions on the failed plans. Huge projects were begun at the southern and northern ends of Palm Beach at nearly the same time; each experienced shortages of labor and materials. The numerous delays, rather symptomatic of the region, resulted in three unfinished projects declaring bankruptcy.

Despite this, Aruba's reliable climate, political stability, and the reputation of Arubans as famously cooperative and hospitable people attracted developers and the attention of important hospitality franchises. The Marriot chain was rewarded for acquiring and completing one failed project by opening the most successful resort in their stable. This prompted them to reclaim another failed project, which became the Marriott Ocean Club, and to construct the Surf Club, both timeshare operations. A Ritz-Carlton is scheduled to open at the beginning of 2014.

Ever practical, Cohen and Wiggins also realized the numerous small resorts, operating on shoestring budgets, could not afford to market individually. They formed a cooperative that was to become the Aruba Hotel and Tourism Association (AHATA). It is one of the most successful public-private collaborations in the region, working closely with Aruba's official tourism marketing entity, the Aruba Tourism Authority (ATA). The combined efforts of several knowledgeable businesspeople and legislators provided the marketing brain trust and will to see this fledgling industry become the principal pillar of the island economy that it is today.

THE REFINERY IN THE 21ST CENTURY

There is a footnote to the refinery's continuing role in Aruba's economic well-being. A number of businesses came and went since the departure of Exxon, interspersed with periods when it remained idle. Valero Corporation of Texas finally took over the facility from Coastal Oil in 2004. Valero initially invested hundreds of millions of dollars in modernizing the refinery, but circumstances resulted in stoppage of the facility in July of 2009.

This was two months prior to a crucial national election resulting in a complete change of Aruba's political landscape. All employees were kept on salary, and not long after, Valero and the new government announced a meeting of minds on the reopening of the refinery. It recommenced operations in early 2011. The continuing rise of crude oil prices precipitated the announcement of a number of closings of Valero refineries around the United States. The Aruban facility was included, which finally came to pass in March 2012. Employees were kept on salary while a solution was sought or a buyer found.

In September of 2012, Valero announced the refinery would serve as a transshipment station, downsizing the work force by 90 percent. Ironically, the facility would now fulfill the function originally planned for it.

Government and Economy

GOVERNMENT
The Parliament and Ministries

Aruba is an autonomously-ruled entity within the Dutch Kingdom. Arubans are considered Dutch citizens and carry Dutch passports. The government is comprised of a 21-seat parliament, with elections taking place every four years, one year after U.S. presidential elections. There is a president and vice-president of parliament, positions occupied by elected officials.

For a political party to be in power, they must capture an 11-seat majority or form a coalition among a few parties to hold a majority. The individual heading the dominant party of the coalition assumes the title of Prime Minister and appoints a cabinet of ministers.

The government deploys various ministries to administrate important aspects of island operations. Presently, Aruba has ministers of tourism, transport, labor, immigration, environment, infrastructure, public health, sport, technology, finance, utilities, social affairs, economic affairs, culture, education, and justice, who are selected from those who have been elected to parliament. Aruba also has ministers-plenipotentiary to Holland and the United States, which are appointed positions and serve the purpose of being ambassadors to these countries. The common practice is for the elected officials comprising the cabinet to have a number of ministries under their command; often they are inter-related, supporting each other with legislation and policies.

Dutch Representation

The island maintains strong ties with Holland. Despite a distinctly Caribbean-Latin culture, the official language of schools, business contracts, regulations, legislation and official government notifications is Dutch.

The Dutch Royal Monarch's official representative on Aruba is the governor, an appointed position lasting six years. They may serve a maximum of two terms. His Excellency, Governor Fredis Refunjol, took office in May of 2004 and is serving the second of two terms, due to expire in 2016. It is the governor who ratifies national ordinances and resolutions. Among his many duties, he alone awards decorations in the name of the monarchy, signs off on passports and visas, and considers extradition requests. His presence is required at all official functions that are related to Holland. He is charged with the swearing in of dignitaries such as ministers, members of the Common Court of Justice and the Public Prosecutor, as well as the Advisory Council, General Audit Office, and the Central Bank of Aruba. The following is stated on the Governor's official website (www.kabga.aw.en): "The Governor is inviolable, immune, and carries out his powers as a national organ under the responsibility of the Ministers of Aruba, who, in their turn, are accountable to the Parliament of Aruba."

Until April 27, 2013 Aruba counted Queen Beatrix as its monarch, preceded by her mother Queen Juliana and grandmother Queen Wilhelmina. On this date, Queen Beatrix abdicated the throne in favor of her eldest son, HRM Willem-Alexander, the first male monarch the Dutch Kingdom has had in place since 1890.

The Judiciary, Foreign Affairs, and Defense

Holland still has jurisdiction in certain fields: the judiciary, partly to maintain impartiality. Judges and prosecutors are appointed within the Dutch system. Foreign affairs is also under their control. If Holland signs a treaty with foreign entities, Aruba is bound by it. Aruban administrators do have the power to negotiate agreements for the island, which may not directly affect Holland. Thirdly, Holland is charged with Aruba's national protection, maintaining a division of the Royal Dutch Marines at the camp in Savaneta. Aruba has a subordinate branch of service at the camp, the ArubaMil.

Dutch Immigration to Aruba

For many decades, there were strictures against unfettered Dutch immigration to the island, which have been eased over the past few years. Much of this had to do with older Dutch laws, to prevent miscreants from escaping to the colonies after committing crimes or accumulating debt in Holland. However, it is a stated policy that jobs should first go to a qualified Aruban before issuing approval for bringing in someone from outside the country to fill the position. Individuals wishing to retire on the island must be able to prove they are financially independent, with no need to work.

ECONOMY

Aruba's economy is a free-enterprise system with entrepreneurship and fair trade heavily encouraged. Tourism is acknowledged as the primary pillar of the economy, accounting for 83 percent of the island's GDP. It provides employment for around 800 people.

Though tourism can be a volatile industry affected by global events, aside from small setbacks from the world financial crash of 2008 and the destruction of the World Trade Center, Aruba's tourism has seen steady growth since achieving Status Aparte. In December of 2012, the Reina Beatrix International Airport welcomed its millionth paying passenger, and cruise ship tourism broke records during that year for their number of passengers. Statistics show Aruba welcomes over 1.5 million visitors annually.

Aruba's government is mindful that dependence on tourism alone is not in the best interest of the economy, and are always seeking methods to diversify. In 2012, a contract was signed with Repsol, a Spanish energy development conglomerate. The terms allow seismic exploration for natural gas reserves in the territorial waters north of the island, with Repsol accepting all costs for developing a rig if a viable resource is discovered.

In May of 2013, Aruba hosted an international "Europe Meets the Americas" Conference, the purpose being to implement a plan for the island to become a liaison and business hub between the European Union and Latin America and Caribbean Region. It is believed that Aruba's unique multicultural makeup can provide the meeting of minds between two very different cultures, and that this can be developed into another economic pillar for the island.

It is acknowledged that Aruba is highly dependent on imports of goods. Agriculture is encouraged, and the Santa Rosa Center of Agriculture and Animal Husbandry and Fisheries has begun a regular program instructing and encouraging islanders to grow and harvest their own food. A very small commercial agricultural industry has been established, using unique methods of desert reclamation and aquaculture.

Some small manufacturing exists on the island, such as Office Systems, which is the local and regional manufacturer and distributor for Dauphin, a famed European brand of office furniture. Freezone Aruba has proved innovative in providing not only product storage but also services, increasing Aruba's export statistics over 2012.

Generally, the standard of living is high for the region, with salaries averaging around $22,000 annually and retirement pensions also one of the highest to be found in the Caribbean. The cost of consumer goods is relatively high due to import duties and shipping costs. Aruba is also one of the most highly taxed nations in the world.

The most recent Fitch rating for Aruba's economy is "stable," as of August 2012. However, this takes into account the possible reopening of the refinery by 2014, which is being pursued by the current administration. Though it continues to operate as a transshipment station, the resulting income for Aruba is marginal. The refinery only retained 10 percent of their staff.

The Fitch Report states "Aruba's ratings are underpinned by a high per capita income, strong political institutions, social stability, a long track record of macroeconomic stability, and demonstrated capacity to rein in fiscal imbalance."

People and Culture

The most beloved time of year for most Arubans is during Carnival, where weeks of revelry consumes the island's attention. Festivities on Aruba are frequent, and instigated for the simplest of reasons. The island's motto "One Happy Island" is very apropos. Though hardworking, the Aruban dominant attitude is appreciation for their good fortune to live on the island and continue celebrating life.

Arubans are also very pro-active, with strong community concerns. Service organizations such as Rotary, Kiwanis, Women's Club, Lion's Club, and Quota, to name a few, play a strong role in community events. Visiting members of organizations like Rotary are welcome to sit in on the meetings.

Aruba has over 1,000 registered foundations, many of these established in only the last decade. It is the nature of islanders, when presented with a situation that needs attention, to recruit, organize, and educate the uninformed.

POPULATION

Aruba participated in the 2010 UNESCO worldwide census. The Central Bureau of Statistics (CBS) reports from the results a population of 106,000+ officially registered residents, of which over 35 percent are immigrants. Many have been nationalized and received their Dutch passports. According to the CBS, there are 90 distinct ethnic or national groups inhabiting this little rock quite harmoniously.

Aruba has substantial East Indian, Filipino, and Chinese populations. They have integrated well into the community while maintaining many aspects of their native cultures. Each group has some sort of community organization to continue traditions among the second generation born on the island. They are the Aruba Indian Association (IAA), United Filipino Community of Aruba (UFILCOA), and the Chinese Center where classes are taught in the language and culture. The center is located in Bubali, next to the Super Food complex.

The important celebrations of these groups have been integrated into Aruban life; IAA organizes a community event for Diwali. The Honorary Consul of the Philippines to Aruba and UFILCOA conduct a protocol event annually at Wilhelmina Park for Filipino Independence Day. Aruba's Prime Minister and important dignitaries usually attend. The Lion Dance, authentically performed by the Chinese community, is a welcome part of many island celebrations. Every year, the congregation of Temple Beth Israel conducts a community First Seder for Passover. Jewish vacationers are welcome and regularly participate.

During a visit of the royal family in October of 2011, reigning monarch HRM Queen Beatrix was accompanied by then Dutch Crown Prince HRH Willem-Alexander and Crown Princess HRH Maxima, who then became King and Queen in 2013. They were treated to the first official event at Aruba's Linear Park. It was comprised of authentic performances by a dozen of Aruba's various ethnic or national groups, with offerings of native food and specialized beverages. Informative displays regarding each group's culture and history were part of the event. It was a vibrant demonstration of pride in the multicultural nature of island society. Aside from these groups, there were authentic cultural programs by expatriates from Portugal, the Dominican Republic, Venezuela, and Colombia.

RELIGION

The Spanish influence is still evident with the majority of the island being Catholic, and each district has a large church. The Dutch Protestant Church is well established, with a landmark building in Oranjestad.

There is also a synagogue, Temple Beth Israel, erected in 1962, on Adrian Lacle Boulevard 2. The Jewish cemetery in Oranjestad has historic headstones dating back centuries. The present congregation is perhaps 35 families.

© ROSALIE KLEIN

A visit from the royal family is a gala event, with a grand welcome.

San Nicolas has a large Anglican Church, and there a few Methodist and Baptist institutions on the island. Evangelicalism has had a strong influence on the community over the past 20 years. A number of Evangelical ministries have cropped up in all sorts of venues, with too many storefront churches to count.

EDUCATION

Attending school is compulsory for island children ages 5-15. Elementary schools encompass kindergarten through sixth grade. English and Spanish become a part of the curriculum of local schools from fifth grade on. Upon completion of sixth grade students are filtered into academic or vocational schools. This is based on an IQ test administered in sixth grade, their grades, and observances by their teachers and principals.

Island children begin learning Dutch in kindergarten, if they do not already use it in the home. Many of the island's schools are under the authority of a Catholic school association, SKOA, or are Protestant affiliated. Aruba has two private schools without affiliation, the Skagel, which is strictly Dutch in use of language, and the International School of Aruba (ISA), taught in English, but with a distinctly multicultural flavor to the student body. ISA deploys the Montessori method in the younger grades. They provide education from kindergarten to the equivalent of 12th grade.

Exceptional students may immediately qualify for *Brugclasse* (Bridge Class), a trial, introductory year testing their performance and ability to progress on to the higher levels of learning. Diplomas are called degrees. Attaining a HAVO degree is the equivalent of a U.S. high school diploma, thus qualifying for university. The VWO program is accelerated learning for the particularly gifted and determined. It is very academically demanding. Typically, VWO students in their freshman year at U.S. universities report finding they are already at a sophomore level of college education, or beyond.

Students graduating from elementary school who are not yet ready for an accelerated program of academics are directed towards MAVO, a four-year school. Graduates can go on to acquire their HAVO or VWO degrees. They may also elect to take professional training courses at EPI, *Educativo Professional Intermedio*.

EPI consists of four faculties which award an associates degree in technology, business administration, social work or tourism and hospitality management. The last faculty of the EPI is also the center for the renowned Aruba Culinary School, where graduates receive certification from the American Culinary Federation. This school accepts students from around the world.

EPI also receives students from Aruba's *Educativo Basico Professional* (EPB) who have gone through four years or more of dedicated vocational training. EPB classes are divided into three levels of academic accomplishment, with only the top level qualified to go on to EPI. Students can work their way up the ladder of scholastic achievement from the lowest to highest level, but that is rare.

After completing four years of the lesser levels of EPB, graduates may elect to join the work force in apprentice positions in mechanics, electrical repair, woodworking, or as beauticians and caregivers. EPB also has a highly acclaimed school of culinary training, where many of the students continue to the EPI culinary school to become certified chefs. The HORECA (HOtel, REstaurant, CAfé) program also trains youngsters for the tourism and food industry as waitstaff, bartenders, and restaurant management.

For almost 20 years Aruba has had an institution of higher learning, the University of Aruba, but with a limited curriculum awarding only law and accounting degrees. Most students travel abroad for advanced degrees, primarily in Holland, the United States, or Latin America. In the past 10 years the university has expanded its fields of studies, and faculties now include hospitality and tourism management, accounting, financing and marketing, arts and sciences (similar to liberal arts), and law. Graduates earn a bachelor's degree. The University of Aruba (www.ua.aw) readily accepts students from abroad and most will find tuition is considerably less than U.S. schools.

NOTABLE ARUBANS

Aruba has its heroes and heroines, personages who have contributed greatly to the island's advancements in education, sports, culture, and technology. Among them are some who have received worldwide attention, aside from regional recognition for their achievements.

Juan Chabaya "Padu" Lampe

Best known for his musical compositions, Juan Chabaya "Padu" Lampe was the co-author with Rufo Wever of Aruba's national anthem, "Aruba Dushi Tera." He is truly a Renaissance man, painter, musician, composer, and author. Padu made his living as a representative of ALM airlines, and contributed to the island's culture not for profit, but purely out of love of the arts. His work required that he travel extensively, and he was an unofficial ambassador of Aruba, performing to appreciative audiences and establishing good will, wherever his work took him. His enormous, diverse body of work and influence on the island population earned him the popular title of "Father of Culture."

Never charging for musical performances, his presence was considered to elevate any event. Padu gave many concerts in Venezuela, where he finally began recording LPs in the 1960s. Some won Golden Piano awards, the equivalent of a Grammy. "Padu Del Caribe" was his recording name and he still has a very loyal following in the region.

Born in 1910, he earned his nickname in honor of his *Padu*, his grandfather and namesake, who had died the same week he was born. His mother called him *Padushi* ("Sweet Little Grandfather"); the nickname stuck, and later shortened to Padu.

Padu began his love affair with the arts as a painter. While just a teenager, one of his works was selected to be shown at the 1939 World's Fair in New York as an example of Caribbean art. He authored metaphysical

© ROSALIE KLEIN

Aruban artist, composer, and author
Juan Chabaya "Padu" Lampe

treatises in English, titled "The 3rd Element" and "Harmoniology—The Art and Science of Living in Harmony with the Universal Laws." They were published in 1960 and 1978, respectively.

"Sir" Dr. Edward Cheung

Passing along the Sasaki Highway on the way to a Palm Beach resort, many may spot the Dr. Edward Cheung Center for Innovation and wonder about its namesake. When he was still a relatively young man, this native son actually sent Aruba into space!

Born and raised on Aruba by immigrant parents, Dr. Cheung went on to obtain his PhD in electrical engineering, specializing in robotics, from Yale, with a scholarship from Phillips and NASA. He joined the NASA team and in 1995 was assigned to the Hubble Space Telescope (HST) maintenance project.

His work with NASA particularly electrified his homeland when HST experienced a failure in the NICMOS cooling system that threatened to send it crashing to earth. When it became clear that a substitute system was problematic, Dr. Cheung and his team had three months to devise a solution. It was named ASCS/NCS Relay Unit Breaker Assembly, or ARUBA box. It was installed during a 2002 mission, saving the HST. It can be seen in photos taken during space missions, attached to the outside of the Hubble, the word "ARUBA" very clear.

Dr. Cheung's was one of the voices heard during broadcasts of the final mission to the telescope, when they installed his invention, the Wide Field Camera III. This revolutionary equipment is delivering images to scientists of space that were never possible before. Dr. Cheung was also part of the team present for the last manned space mission of NASA, working the "Tweet Tent" at Kennedy Space Center during the blastoff.

Dr. Cheung now heads a new division at Goddard Space Center, devising robotic means of in-space repair of satellites. The new technology extends their use and saves tens of millions of dollars in prematurely replacing equipment.

During his annual visits to his family in Aruba, Dr. Cheung has made it a regular practice to give free lectures about space and the HST. It is his stated goal to inspire young Arubans in careers in science and to continue their education to the highest levels.

In 2010, NASA was proud to report that their principal engineer was dubbed a Knight in the Order of the Netherlands Lion. This is the highest honor the monarchy bestows on a civilian subject, and it is a rare occurrence. His colleagues at NASA affectionately refer to him as "Sir Ed," though the actual title of "Sir" is not an affectation of being dubbed a knight within the Dutch system.

Sarah-Quita Offringa

An exemplary role model for island youth is Sarah-Quita Offringa, the reigning Professional Windsurfing Association's (PWA) Women's Freestyle Windsurfing World Champion since 2008. At the time she won her first world championship title she had just

WHY *HIMNO Y BANDERA?*

Aruba's **National Day** is March 18, often referred to as *Himno y Bandera*–**Anthem and Flag Day.** It is a celebration of the establishment of Aruba's self-identity, 10 years before actual autonomy was achieved. It marks the day Aruba's official flag and national anthem were first introduced.

Prior to the introduction of Aruba's own flag, a contest was held with a general invitation to all islanders to submit designs for the nation's symbol. There were more than 700 entries.

The desired concept was a simple but distinctive flag, representative of the island both culturally and physically, but easily recognizable from a distance. Typical to many flags, the symbols of stripes and stars were included in the designs and many Arubans felt the sun was important to Aruba's lifestyle and history.

The color most commonly suggested was blue, representing the clear sky and sea. Other highly popular colors were yellow to represent sunlight; white for Aruba's unique beaches; and red, symbolizing sunsets, the island's clay soil, progress, or the blood of Arubans, though none was actually shed in acquiring autonomy.

A bold and unique four-pointed star, something unheard of for flags before, was settled upon as the primary symbol. It was felt that the four points represented Aruba's four main languages: Papiamento, English, Dutch, and Spanish. While the yellow stripes, sometimes attributed to the discovery of gold that first initiated island posterity, symbolized Aruba's movement to the future and independence.

"Aruba Dushi Tera" ("Sweet Land Aruba") was first known as a popular and patriotic song composed by Juan Chabaya "Padu" Lampe and Rufo Wever, more than 20 years prior. It was immediately considered for the honor. A few couplets were added to the end by the founder of the Instituto di Cultura, composer and musician Lio Booi, before it was first performed as Aruba's national song, accompanying the raising of the flag.

---

turned 17, setting a new world record for the youngest champion ever.

Sarah-Quita, "the girl with big hair," turned the windsurfing world around when she burst upon the professional scene, going pro at the age of 12. At 15, she won her first gold medal, also setting a new PWA record for the youngest to do so.

Since claiming the title, she has never lost a single competition heat or elimination round. In 2011, she was also crowned Women's World Champion in Slalom, proving to be a double-threat on the water. For the remarkable achievement of earning two world champion titles in a single year, she was selected as a contender for the ISAF Rolex World Sailor of the Year Award.

During the 2012 PWA season, Sarah-Quita placed her studies at University in Utrecht, Holland, above defending her slalom title, but successfully retained her freestyle crown. During the slalom competition in Alacti, Turkey, she claimed the gold, leaving the field so far behind that sportscasters dubbed her "the fastest woman on the water."

Though the life of a sports champion offers fame and travel, Sarah-Quita is acutely aware of her position as a role model for young Arubans. She hopes they will be equally inspired by her achievements at university as they are by her performance in sports competition. In 2013, she successfully defended her freestyle title.

THE ARTS
Regional Music and Traditions

During national holidays, Carnival, and the end of the year seasonal celebrations, Arubans most demonstrate their idiosyncratic cultural traditions. European and regional influences that comprise what is considered authentically Aruban can best be observed in the festive music and dance performances. Ties to **Holland and Dutch traditions** are evident in the celebration of **King's Day,** and at the end of the year, when **Sinterklaas** comes to visit. Families

Sinterklaas arrives with his Swarte Pieten at the end of the year.

except for slight variations in lyrics), it doesn't end until dawn. Those who make it through this marathon musical event are truly devoted to the art form.

Carnival time produces three extremely important musical competitions: the Road March, Calypso Contest, and crowning of a Tumba king or queen. These entail several nights of concert competitions, as winners are declared in three age groups, child, youth, and adult. The costumes are an important part of the event, as well as the quality of performance and the suitability of the piece, which must be an original composition.

The winning song of the adult Road March contest will be the official theme for that year's Carnival season, performed endlessly during parades and events. This is selected by judges as the best piece to inspire participants and spectators to dance along. It is usually a classic example of Afro-Caribbean polyphonic music, making it impossible to resist shaking the hips and guaranteed to start shoulders twitching. A second song, likely more popular with the public than the judges, will also be heard just as frequently. This is dubbed the "Road Jam," an unofficial winner, as no one will ever completely agree with the judges' decision.

Tumba is the island's music most steeped in the roots of slavery and African culture, brought to Aruba and Curacao in the 1700s. It has evolved to incorporate more Latin harmonics in recent times. **Calypso** is a traditional regional music originating from Trinidad and Tobago. Songs are not only judged for their musicality, but also for their lyrics and pithy social commentary. They are usually quite humorous and topical, wry observances of human behavior based on events of the previous year.

Beyond these, islanders consider the pieces derived from more **classic European music** such as waltzes, *danzas,* and mazurkas, typical of their culture. Most folkloric dance is performed to such pieces, usually composed by well-respected artists such as Juan Chabaya "Padu" Lampe and Rufo Wever (co-authors of Aruba's national anthem, an excellent example), and Leo Booi, founder of the Aruba

look forward to *olibollen,* a typically Dutch holiday treat, and fireworks on **New Year's Eve.**

The approach of Christmas means the manifestation of **gaita** singing groups performing regularly at dozens of public events and private parties. Gaita actually originates from Maracaibo in Zulia State of Venezuela. It is very lively, upbeat music. Gaita groups usually consist of 8-12 female singers, accompanied by native instruments, such as a *cuarto,* a small guitar, and *tambora,* the goatskin drums.

End of the year is also the time for **Dande,** traditionally performed by wandering minstrels. Dande has a distinctive, repetitive chorus; the lyrics change to personalize the song to each household visited. Dande minstrels come with hat in hand, for each family member to ritualistically drop in a little *propina* for luck.

Just before the end of the year is the annual Dande competition to crown a new king or queen. It starts in the early evening and there are so many bands, and the songs are so long (with each one sounding *exactly* the same,

Institute of Culture, who also contributed to the national song.

Steelpan is another musical art form integrated into island culture, which arrived with the great migration prompted by the opening of the refinery. The Connor family is particularly noted for this, and Lee and Nico Connor carry on a tradition promulgated by their father over 50 years ago, which continues with a new generation. Steelpan music is regularly heard at many events and there are concerts dedicated to it at least once a year. It is an integral part of the Bon Bini and Carubbian festivals.

Aruba has been described as "an island of dancers," by some. Every weekend several bands perform around the island, often giving free concerts. At nearly any party or gala, the dance floor will be full, particularly when the band plays merengue. Islanders dance with complete abandon during Carnival and such events.

Performing Arts

Aruba has many centers for performing arts and concerts, and a number of galleries. **Cas di Cultura** (Vondellaan 2, 297/582-1010, www.casdicultura.aw), meaning "House of Culture," is where most dance recitals and classic concerts are staged. Located on the large traffic circle at the east end of Oranjestad, it has been Aruba's theatrical and cultural center since 1958, and is booked nearly every weekend for some sort of recital or play. It also has an exhibition room for art and educational or commemorative expositions. The main auditorium seats over 400.

Holiday time on Aruba can include indulging the family in the seasonal favorite, "The Nutcracker," staged and choreographed by former star of the Bolshoi and New York Ballet companies, and Creative Director of the New Jersey Ballet, Leonid Kozlov (www.dancearuba.com and www.leonidkozlov.com). A part-time resident of Aruba, he has brought Tchaikovsky's fairy tale classic to the island as a new holiday tradition. Performances run twice over the holiday week at the Cas di Cultura.

Private studios offer dance lessons and conduct recitals annually. Visual artists are regularly featured in shows and in a few galleries. The Cas di Cultura is home to the Rufo Wever Music School, occupying one side of the building, and the Da Vinci Academy, dedicated to classical piano, on the other. Aruba is also home to several highly respected jazz musicians, many of which teach at the Rufo Wever School. They are producing a new generation of music students who are enthusiastic about interpretive music.

Internationally known performers are brought in annually for the week-long Aruba International Piano Festival in June and the Caribbean Sea Jazz Festival over Columbus Day weekend. These are just two isolated international events; at least once a month some international talent is imported to perform.

It is perhaps in the continuing tradition of original music created for Carnival where that which can truly be called Aruban originates. Many of these fine, self-trained musicians and composers are producing the distinctive, complex, polyphonic works that are close to the hearts of islanders.

Literary and Visual Arts

UNOCA (Stadionweg 21, 297/583-5681, www.unocaruba.org, 8:30am-noon and 1:30pm-5pm Mon.-Fri.) is a foundation dedicated to the promotion and development of all the literary, visual, and performing arts. They fund publication of books, both poetry and prose, usually in Papiamento; dance recitals; art expositions; and other projects that elevate the cultural awareness of the community. Their offices double as a permanent exhibit hall for local artwork, and they also sell many of the publications they have helped publish.

There is a long-established, active community producing work in several mediums. A number of foundations are dedicated to promoting education and interest among youth. Traditional painters and primitive style held sway for years, and their work is revered. Current schools of art, however, lean much more towards the abstract, impressionistic, and particularly, the avant-garde.

The most conveniently located gallery to the resort areas is also Aruba's most active: **Westin Art Gallery** (Westin Aruba Resort, J. E. Irausquin Blvd., 297/588-2267, open 24 hours daily), just off the main lobby of the resort. They host a congenial opening of a new show every two months. At least three a year are group exhibitions, showcasing several local artists. The collections are eclectic with a wide range of styles. A gallery representative is on hand every Wednesday and Friday afternoon, or can be called to negotiate a purchase.

ESSENTIALS

Getting There

BY AIR

Reina Beatrix International Airport (Reina Beatrix Airport Z/N, 297/524-2424, www. airportaruba.com) is the official and only air entry to Aruba, whether by commercial or private flights. Visitors will be pleasantly surprised by Aruba's large, comfortable air terminal. It is not typical of most island facilities. New arrivals are greeted by air-conditioned halls, decorated with artistic environments. Local artists have created a stimulating introduction to Aruban culture. A graceful sculpture garden bids visitors farewell, as they wait on line to pass through port control at departure.

The airport has a diverse and attractive arcade of shops and restaurants for departing passengers. The arrivals area also offers some duty-free shops where discounted liquor and cigarettes can be purchased before officially stepping on Aruban soil. Those who take advantage of this should be mindful of the limits, which are two cartons of cigarettes and two liters of liquor for personal use. There is a separate terminal for private flights at the south end of the airport. It has separate Aruban immigration and ICE officials. It is modern and comfortable with several amenities.

© ROSALIE KLEIN

Commercial Airlines

The Ministry of Tourism and Transportation has authorized three regional companies, the Aruban company **Tiara Air** (Sabana Blanco 70 E, 297/528-4272, http://tiara-air.com), **Insel Air** (Reina Beatrix International Airport, 855/493-6004, 297/582-1200, www.fly-inse-lair.com), and **Aruba Airlines** (Cumena 69, 297/5823-8300, www.arubaairlines.com) to provide direct access to Aruba. Each airline, which formally only provided regional service, has acquired jumbo jets to provide direct, round-trip service to cities such as Boston, Ft. Lauderdale, and Orlando. In 2012, two more local airlines applied for permits to provide airlift from the United States.

On weekends there are additional flights to Aruba from the commercial carriers as well as several charter services from the United States and Toronto, Canada. Veteran travelers know the best prices and most relaxing travel is usually on the weekdays. Weekend planes sometimes have to wait on the tarmac for a gate to deplane passengers, particularly during peak arrival time, which is mid-afternoon. All ticket offices for commercial U.S. and Canadian airlines are located within Reina Beatrix International Airport. The following are commercial airlines that fly to Aruba:

- American Airlines: 297/582-2700, www.aa.com
- Delta: 297/588-5623, www.delta.com
- Jet Blue: 297/588-5977, www.jetblue.com
- U.S. Airways: 800/622-1015, www.usairways.com

Commercial flight schedules change from one season to the next; new carriers are continually establishing airlifts and opening gateway cities. The best source for current airline information with regularly scheduled flights is the airport's official website: www.airportaruba.com.

Being so far south in the Caribbean, it would be expected that airfares to Aruba would be higher in comparison to other destinations, but the difference is surprisingly marginal, particularly during the off-season. **American Airlines,** one of the first to begin regular service to Aruba in the 1960s, has two direct flights from their Miami hub daily, servicing feeder flights from all points in the United States. A weekend flight from Miami can range from as little as $227 in Economy Class to $526 in Business during the off-season, depending on availability. High-season tickets can go for as little as $279 for Super Economy Class on the weekends. Peak holiday rates, such as Christmas, run as high $1,001 for Economy.

Aruba's most frequent carrier is now **JetBlue,** with direct flights from New York for $652 during the off-season, or $456-801 round-trip from Boston. High season rates, which are not peak holiday weeks, range $882-1,007, from Boston, and $737 from New York, which includes all taxes and airport fees. The exception is a departure tax of $36.75, which will be charged at the ticket counter when checking in for a returning flight to the United States. This is a common practice throughout the Caribbean and Latin America.

BY SEA
Cruise Ships

It was announced in 2012 that cruise ship arrivals were expected to increase from around 315 annually to nearly 400 calls at Oranjestad Harbor in 2013-14. High season for cruising usually begins in November with as many as four ships at the pier. This tapers off in April. Some cruise lines, such as Pullmantur, schedule Aruba as a port of call year-round. Immigration procedures for arriving passengers are handled by cruise officials.

Arrival by sea is under the administration of the **Aruba Port Authority** (L. G. Smith Blvd. 23, 297/582-6633, control tower direct 297/582-1740, www.arubaports.com, 24 hours daily). A complete schedule of all ships scheduled to call in Aruba, with dates and times, can be found on their website.

In 2013, a full, year-round schedule was inaugurated by **Pullmantur** (www.pullmantur.es) for their Antillean and southern Caribbean

ARUBA'S FIRST AIRPORT

An airport was in the planning stages when the first tourist flight arrived on Aruba, a tri-engine Fokker in September of 1934. It had to land in a field in Savaneta. The airport was ready to receive flights by the following January, with the first from Curacao arriving on January 19. During the first year of operation, 2,659 passenger were transported between the two islands.

The first air-traffic control tower went into operation in 1937. Aruba's importance to Allied fuel supplies during WWII brought expansion and some modernization, initiating the construction of a new terminal. It opened in 1950, and was called the Dakota Airport until 1955. On October 22, it was re-christened Princess Beatrix Airport, with her father, HRH Prince Bernhard presiding over the ceremony. The old air terminal was converted into a fire station, allowing fire trucks to always be close at hand.

Two years later, preparations began for the extension of the runways in anticipation of large commercial jets bringing vacationers to Aruba. In 1964, the first two jets to arrive were from Pan Am. One year later, ground was broken for the addition of another terminal; it was inaugurated in 1972. When HRM Juliana abdicated the throne on April 30, 1980 and her daughter was crowned, the airport then became Reina Beatrix International Airport. The airport management was privatized and entered into a strategic cooperative agreement with Schiphol International in Amsterdam in 2004. This assured the profitable management of Aruba's airport, as well as adherence to international safety standards.

The enormous expansion and modernization of the present facility was begun in 2000 and completed in 2003. This added an entirely new terminal for non-U.S. departures, and enlargement of the gate areas. They are configured to provide a complete division of arriving and departing passengers, for increased safety and control, as well as smoothing the flow.

---

itinerary on the *Monarch*. Besides being a scheduled stop, Aruba is also a port of embarkation. This allows travelers to arrange a few days on the island before or after cruising to Curacao, Venezuela, Colombia, and Panama. A local agent for cruise companies stopping in Aruba is **S.E.L. Maduro & Sons** (Rockefellerstraat 1, 297/528-2343, 8am-noon and 1pm-5pm Mon.-Fri.), which can book passage with Aruba as the embarkation point.

Cruise lines with Aruba on their itineraries include **Royal Caribbean** (www.royalcaribbean.com), offering one week on *Adventure of the Seas,* embarking from Puerto Rico. **Holland American Line** (www.hollandamerica.com) runs two-week to one-month excursions from Ft. Lauderdale or San Diego with the *Amsterdam.* **Carnival** (www.carnival.com) has the *Freedom* and *Victory* departing from Ft. Lauderdale and Puerto Rico for eight nights. **Celebrity** (www.celebritycruises.com) has two-week charters departing from Ft. Lauderdale,

as does **Princess Cruises** (www.princess.com), which also has two-week and one-month excursions embarking from Los Angeles and Vancouver, Canada.

By Private Yacht

Aruba's Immigration and customs regulations for yachts are somewhat different than most Caribbean islands. Arriving vessels must first report to the clearing center in Baracadera Harbor on the south side of the island, a bit past the dump at Parkeitenbos. Northwest entrance to Oranjestad Harbor is 12° 31' 070° 04' W, southeast entrance is 12° 30.3' N 070° 02.' Entrance to Barcadera Harbor is 12° 28.5'N 070° 01' W.

Arrivals must first clear immigration and then customs before proceeding to their berths. Visas for the Netherlands Antilles are not valid for Aruba; a separate visa must be obtained. Pleasure yachts no less than 14 meters moored in Aruban waters, or registered at a slip, are immediately eligible to extend their stay and harbor managers recommend they do so. They must be able to show proof of ownership of the boat.

On October 1, 2012, a new regulation requiring the boat itself to be declared to customs came into effect. If the yacht stays in Aruban waters no more than 180 days, then a temporary import permit must be acquired; this does not require a deposit. If it stays longer, up to one year, a temporary import permit must be applied for with payment of a deposit (or a bank guarantee) for the value of the duties on the yacht. Any stay longer than a year will categorize the yacht as an import and duties must be paid. Once a temporary permit has expired, the yacht must leave Aruban waters for no less than 15 days before another permit can be obtained.

Aruba Ports Authority charges a port fee for yachts tied up to their docks. These fees are additional to the private slip fee. Rates are $10 per hour 8am-4pm, $15 per hour 4pm-8am, and $20 per hour on weekends and holidays. A uniformed harbor security officer collects this, in cash, while boats are tied up at the slip.

Principal harbors accepting visiting yachts are Renaissance Marina, adjacent to Oranjestad Harbor, and Bucuti and Varadero Yacht Clubs, behind the airport and next to each other. Offshore, protected anchorages are, from west to east, beginning north of the Palm Beach resorts: Arashi, Malmok, Eagle Beach, Surfside, Bucuti, Spanish Lagoon, Savaneta, and Roger's Beach. VHF channels deployed by the APA are 16 and 1.

Ship Chandlers

Located within the Seaport Marketplace, adjacent to Renaissance Marina is **East Wind Marine Services** (L. G. Smith Blvd. 5, 297/588-0260, ewms@renaissancemarina.com, 8am-6pm Mon.-Sat.), which handles the marina business. The shop provides nautical maps for the entire world, can arrange for parts and repairs, and has a diverse inventory for boaters, anglers, and casual water activities.

The exclusive agent for authentic Evinrude parts on Aruba is **Salas Marine** (Bushiri 37, 297/593-4706, john@slasamarine.com, 9am-noon and 2pm-6pm Mon.-Fri., 10am-2pm Sat.). They also carry a selection of boat accessories, but no paint. If they do not have a part in stock, they promise about one week to obtain it. Salas Marine is located not far from the harbor, on a dirt road behind the complex of large supermarkets on the west end of Oranjestad.

Getting Around

Not a very large island, Aruba is thoughtfully outfitted with connecting roads that merge into a single route stretching from the far eastern tip to the very western point. The road parallels the southern shore, often bordering the beachfront. If traveling from the major resorts to the airport, Oranjestad, San Nicolas, or the California Lighthouse, stay on the road to arrive at most destinations. There are a few major roads that will connect to it, but beyond these, a good many will be sand or dirt roads. Once beyond the city limits or main thoroughfares, addresses are by area and number, and most streets do not have a title. Principal areas with street addresses are Oranjestad, and outlying neighborhoods of Ponton, Dakota, and Eagle, and San Nicolas.

The Department of Public works and Ministry of Infrastructure have not quite mastered the art of clearly understood road signs, but signs are improving. When venturing into rural areas, you will find that maps indicate some sort of road where there is little more than a well-beaten path. This makes getting around beyond the main roads confusing.

Most major destinations and resort areas are easily reached along a few principal roads, as are several sights. Exploring the Aruban outback is another matter entirely, where landmarks are a matter of interpretation. Islanders, who are

IMPORTANT ROAD SIGNS AND REGULATIONS

Islanders are very patient with rental cars that they know contain tourists unfamiliar with the road signs and traffic laws. The license plates start with a "V" for *Verhuur,* which is Dutch for "rental." They expect visitors to drive slowly in their confusion to figure out where they need to turn, and are quite understanding and helpful.

Aruba uses standard international road signs, which may be unfamiliar. Drivers need to take note of some signs in particular. A solid red circle with a white slash means **do not enter,** and if ignored, motorists will find they are going the wrong way on a one-way street. Oranjestad in particular has several narrow, one-way streets.

A round blue sign with a white arrow indicates traffic is one way, and the driver must follow the direction indicated. This can also be seen as a square, this informs the driver they are traveling in the right direction on a one-way street.

An upside down white triangle, outlined in yellow, is a **yield** sign; a white diamond outlined in yellow indicates you are on a main thoroughfare and have right of way at upcoming intersections. If there are three parallel black slashes through the sign, it is warning that status has changed. At the upcoming intersection you forfeit right of way. There should be a yield or stop sign at the intersection.

A no-passing zone will be indicated by a picture of a red car on the left of a black car. Drivers should take note of any sign with red symbols, an indication of a prohibition of some kind.

quite familiar with their surroundings, are notoriously deficient in giving good directions. It is a common practice for them to hop in their car, or change their personal itinerary, to lead visitors to the destination.

BY BUS
Arubus (Weststraat 13, 297/588-0617, www. arubus.com, 5:40am-11:20pm Mon.-Fri., modified schedule on weekends, $2.25) is the official mass transit system. Busses are new, clean, and comfortable. The L10 route runs between Oranjestad and Palm Beach, past all resorts, passing through Manchebo Beach and Eagle beach along J. E. Irausquin Boulevard. It runs a round-trip route from the Oranjestad Bus Terminal daily, nearly every 10 minutes during the day. Frequency is reduced to 20-30 minutes or more between busses after 6pm and on Sundays. A complete schedule can be found on their website. There are clearly marked bus stops, with shelters at many, along J. E. Irausquin Boulevard. They are small yellow signs stations in front of each resort and by the hospital, which is on the route.

In 2012 a "Smartcard" system was introduced. This is for residents only. Cash is still accepted for infrequent users and visitors. Another innovation was the introduction of official mini-vans for less frequently used routes and off-hours. There is also a system of privately-owned mini-busses that pick up the slack during night hours when Arubus service is more sporadic. They are strictly controlled by the Ministry of Transport and clearly marked, charging no more than Arubus. They are perfectly legitimate to use if they come along first, rather than waiting for what looks like a more official bus. They also charge less than Arubus, only $1.50 per ride.

BY TAXI
Taxis are plentiful. Find them lined up at the airport to take arrivals without transfers to their respective resorts. The airport even has a special rest station for cabbies, and the nearest lane to the terminals is reserved for taxi pickup and drop-off. Taxi drivers are happy to give you their card so they can be summoned for further service, if required.

Every resort has a taxi stand at the entrance;

Traffic will stop for pedestrians in legal crosswalks.

hotel staff call the dispatcher if one is not immediately available. Licensed cabs are clearly marked but they do not use meters. The Ministry of Transport sets the rates. Ask hotel personnel at the front desk to see the rate chart; they should have it on hand.

Cab drivers charge extra for luggage, on Sundays, and after midnight. Taxis in Aruba are rather pricey: the average rate from the Marriott to Playa Linda (if you don't feel like doing the 10-minute walk along the beach) is $6; some might ask $9. Markets will be happy to call you a cab after grocery shopping.

Taxis have display lights on their hoods or dashboards, but they do not turn on or off when occupied or empty. It is always worth trying to flag down a cab if you need one. It is not their usual procedure, but islanders are adaptable, when need be. Don't be disheartened if they don't stop; they likely have a fare already. If in town and looking for a cab, there is a taxi stand at the entrance of either section of the Renaissance Resort. An empty cab is always waiting there.

Taxi Dispatch Services

When needing a cab, and one is not in sight, try calling **Aruba's Transfer Tour Taxi** (Pos Abao 41, 297/583-6988), **Diamond Taxi Service** (Salinja Cerca 27 A, 297/587-2300), or **Taxi Address Service** (J. E. Irausquin Blvd. 228 F, 297/588-0035). All resorts have a taxi stand, usually well populated around the dinner hours. If not, the front desk or concierge personnel will be happy to call taxi dispatcher.

CAR RENTALS

Upon exiting the airport, visitors find several car rental agencies with offices directly across from the arrivals exit. Cars rented at the airport have a 10 percent surcharge added on to the regular rental rates; however, this is likely equivalent or less to the round-trip cab fare to and from most resorts.

Several resorts host car rental agency desks and others can be found close by. Car rental rates are quite reasonable; third party liability insurance is included in the rental rate as required by law, though there is normally a

© ROSALIE KLEIN

A free tram takes passengers from the cruise terminal to Oranjestad's main sights and shopping.

$150 deductible. There are 38 car rental agencies on Aruba, many with affiliations that will be familiar. Several are associated with reliable European or Latin agencies. All must conform to stated business and safety regulations, but prices can vary. Daily rates for a compact car start at $30. The lowest rate for a weekly rental is $145 for a sub compact, which includes unlimited mileage. Every manner of driver's license is accepted.

Driving on Aruba

Traffic flows on the right-hand side of the road, the same as the United States and Canada. Speed limits are posted regularly. Top speed on a highway is 80 kilometers per hour (50 mph); in town, 40 kilometers per hour (25 mph); and in "suburban" areas, 60 kilometers per hour (37 mph).

Urban areas and busy streets are populated with zebra walks for pedestrians. Traffic regulations demand that motorists stop for a person standing on the black and white striped crossings. If making your way around town on foot, look for these walks. Use zebra walks to cross the street, rather than braving traffic in unauthorized areas.

International road signs are used. A chart of these signs is usually provided with the map from rental agencies; take the time to get acquainted with them. There are few traffic lights on the island, but those at the more important intersections on the divided Sasaki Highway can be confusing. It is important when stopped for drivers to *take note of the light directly on the near side of the road, not across the highway.* A green light on an island in the middle of the Sasaki Highway is to allow highway traffic to turn left. It is *not* an indication for traffic at intersections to cross the highway. Look to the near light to the right or left to see if it is safe to feed or cross the highway. At no time is a right turn allowed on a red light.

To ease bottlenecks, roundabouts have replaced traffic lights at many intersections. Those entering the circle are always required to yield to cars already on the circle. When crossing a four-way intersection, motorists must yield to the car on the right; it is of no consequence which car arrived first. If you have not spotted a traffic sign indicating right of way at a major intersection and are confused, look at the marks painted on the road. Arrows pointing at you indicate you must yield to the intersecting street. Boxes painted where you are stopped mean you have the right of way. Left-turning traffic must always give way to oncoming traffic, until the way is clear. Passing on the left at intersections is forbidden. Make sure the turn indicator is on.

Gas Stations

Aruba has two chains of gas stations, Valero and Texaco, for a total of nine outlets. The island is not that large and they are in sufficient numbers to avoid running out of gas. Self-service pumps do not take credit cards. Motorists must first go into the station to inform the cashier of the amount of gas required and pay. Prices are in Arubian florins, but stations happily take U.S. currency and traveler's checks in denominations of no greater than $20. The exchange rate is 1.75 Arubian florins to dollars. U.S. and Canadian credit and bank cards are accepted; a valid photo ID is required.

TRAM

Aruba has a tram that departs in front of the cruise terminal that takes visitors to downtown Oranjestad along the Caya G.F. Betico Croes. There are eight stops along the route, with attractive shaded tram stations at key locations for sightseeing and shopping. The tram operates from 10am-1pm Monday-Saturday. It runs on solar power and has a hydraulic lift for passengers in wheelchairs.

The tram is part of the Green Aruba program. It is an electric tram powered by solar energy. The purpose is to reduce auto traffic through town and carbon emissions, as well as provide a pleasant service for visitors and residents.

Visas and Officialdom

Until a few years ago, travel to Aruba required only proof of citizenship; a certified birth certificate was sufficient. Regulations were passed by the United States and Canada making it mandatory for all traveling internationally to acquire a passport. Aruba, as an independent Dutch territory, is a signatory to agreements between NATO countries with an understanding that visitors from the United States or Canada do not require any special visa for travel to the island, but a valid passport is required. Aruban Immigration officers require a return ticket to be shown before approving entry. Aruba installed the newest technology in reading passports. Though, when processing large planes filled to capacity, the new technology may slow the process of passing through immigration. It has proven quite valuable in detecting bogus passports, so it is a necessary inconvenience.

Foreign nationals residing in the United States or Canada without passports issued by these countries must be able to show valid residence permits to local immigration upon entry and departure.

Prior to arrival and passing through Aruban immigration, an Embarkation and Disembarkation form, or ED-card, must be filled in, listing residence while on Aruba and length of stay. It is distributed on the plane; some travel agents have them for their clients to fill out beforehand. It is in two parts, and both parts must be filled in. The bottom portion is retained by travelers to be surrendered upon departure. It is advised to keep this in a safe place with the passports.

Aruba does not have restrictions on traveling with foodstuffs or live animals, though it is a good idea to have a certificate showing a pet is free of rabies, as rabies does not exist on the island. The importation and trafficking in exotic and endangered animals is strictly forbidden and controlled.

When traveling by cruise ship, immigration protocols are usually handled by officers from the cruise lines, and passengers returning to the terminal after a day of touring or a visit to town need only show a personal, government-issued photo ID, such as a driver's license, and the pass they received when departing the ship.

According to immigration regulations, officers at entry points may request that a tourist be able to prove to the satisfaction of the officer they have valid reservations for an accommodation in Aruba (e.g., hotel or apartment) or they own property, either a home, condominium, apartment, timeshare apartment, or a pleasure yacht moored in Aruban waters no less than 14 meters in size.

An immigration officer can also demand that a traveler show sufficient funds to carry them through their determined stay on the island, or has the sponsorship of a relative, friend, or employer living on Aruba, who can provide this guarantee.

Aruba is one of the rare vacation destinations to have a division of the **U.S. Department of Immigration and Customs Enforcement** (ICE; Reina Beatrix Airport Z/N, 297/588-7720, www.ice.gov) within its borders. This does not affect arriving passengers. However, upon returning to the United States, travelers will pass through U.S. customs and immigration on Aruba, prior to their flight. It expedites matters when arriving back in the United States, tired after a day of travel. U.S. residents need only pick up their luggage and head home. This does mean passing through two immigration checkpoints at the end of a stay. The Aruban immigration process upon departure is perfunctory; it is wise to allow time for the double process when heading for the airport. Customs declarations are made prior to entering the gate area.

CUSTOMS REGULATIONS

Personal clothing and belongings are not charged duty upon entering Aruba, nor are electronics, computers, or cameras. Individuals over 18 years are allowed to bring in one-fifth (2 liters) of liquor and 200 cigarettes, 50 cigars, and 250 grams of tobacco.

Cats and dogs from most countries are allowed if accompanied by valid rabies and health certificates from a veterinarian. Pets from South and Central America, Cuba, Haiti, and the Dominican Republic are not allowed.

Conduct and Customs

The extreme mix of Aruba's population over the past two decades has caused social behavior to evolve from what used to be. Being a predominantly Catholic island, and somewhat conservative, the attitude of residents is tempered with tolerance for visitors and the understanding they do not know island ways. The multilingual talent of the Aruban people is famous. Though most are fluent in English, particularly those working in tourism, they appreciate an effort to pick up a word or two of the local language. A genuine interest by visitors to understand island customs and traditions will be warmly welcomed and evoke enthusiastic responses to queries.

ETTIQUETE

Arubans are very polite people and appreciate good manners. Before stating one's business, a sincere *Bon dia* (Good day) will always bring a smile and similar response, with the mindset to be of help in any way possible. After midday the greeting is *Bon tardi,* and once the sun has set, *Bon nochi. Por Fabor* and *Danki* (Please and thank you) are noticed and appreciated, not just said without thought or response.

Shopkeepers and restaurant owners may stay politely quiet when a customer enters wearing only a bathing suit, perhaps under the sheerest of cover-ups, since they are not really comfortable with the skimpy attire. Arubans are accustomed to tourists wearing shorts and tee shirts around the town, but beachwear is not considered proper while walking through Oranjestad, or beyond the resorts.

Somehow this extreme politeness is suspended once they are behind the wheel of a car on the highway or need a parking spot. Islanders will park anywhere—on sidewalks and other places that would amaze—but they do try to respect and not block driveways, at least most of the time. During Carnival and special events, anything goes. They are very good about allowing traffic to filter during commuter-hour snarls in town, or where there is roadwork; again, their innate courteousness comes into play.

CONCEPTS OF TIME

As with much of the Caribbean and Latin America, punctuality on Aruba is highly subjective. The Dutch influence of things rigorously being on time and dealing with American expectations daily has generally improved the Aruban attitude. Visitors do need to learn patience as most things are done at island pace. If planning a day tour, be sure to allow plenty of time for breakfast or select buffet style if you wish to be ready by pick up time. Dinners will usually be leisurely, but that is the purpose of such a vacation, is it not?

Tips for Travelers

WHAT TO TAKE

Aruba is decidedly casual. Typical resort wear will easily see visitors through the week. Fancy dresses and sports jackets are not required. Visitors may wish to bring some sweaters or blazers, as air-conditioned restaurants can get chilly, as can nights, when walking about in Aruba's gusty trade winds.

Sunny days of intense tropical strength require a goodly supply of sunblock. Sunglasses are always needed. A spare pair of prescription glasses is advised, but contact lenses can be easily replaced. During the fall rainy season it is a good idea to pack some mosquito repellent, particularly if you plan to do much dining alfresco. The electric current is the same as the United States; no special adapters are required. Roaming charges on cell phones can be outrageous. Phones can be rented for far less. It is not necessary to change money for local currency. U.S. dollars, traveler's checks, and credit cards are readily accepted everywhere.

TRAVELERS WITH DISABILITIES

Aruba still has a ways to go to be completely wheelchair-friendly, but they are industriously working towards this. Oranjestad is getting a facelift whereever you look, with the needs of pedestrians and those with disabilities integrated into the plans. An ambulance dispatch station has been set up at Playa Linda Resort, centrally located to all of Palm Beach. A few businesses offer transportation in vans set up to board individuals in wheelchairs.

Lite Life Medicab

Before arrival, travelers with wheelchairs can arrange for Lite Life Medicab (Hooiberg-Kavel, 297/585-9764, U.S. number 786/955-8829, info@litelifemedicab@com, 6am-9pm daily, $80 round-trip from airport) for transport to and from their hotel, or wherever needed. The company has several vehicles. Some deploy hydraulic lifts and have room for multiple wheelchairs with additional attendant seating; others are smaller vans with ramps.

VOLUNTEER TOURISM WITH FRIENDS OF THE HANDICAPPED

Rising above and beyond the call of keeping Aruba's beaches clean, is a very special group of annual visitors who have organized their own volunteer efforts on Aruba's behalf. **Friends of the Handicapped** (FOTH; Scopestraat 9, 297/582-7000, ext. 600, http://ffoth.org) was founded in 1987 by a group of timeshare owners who spend their winters on Aruba. These are people that not only dig deep into their pockets to help the less fortunate, they donate enormous time while on island to assist local foundations dedicated to those with physical and mental disabilities. FOTH has partnered with several Aruban businesses to raise well over one million dollars over the years to support the important work of almost 20 Aruban foundations.

Principal fundraising events are a Superbowl Sunday Lottery, Valentine's Day Sweetheart's Dinner Dance, and a bingo night at the end of February. During Sunday Mass at the Casa Del Mar (CDM), the plate is passed for donations to the fund.

Visiting volunteers work with the executive staff of the Casa Del Mar to continue the foundation's programs. CDM hosts the desk where squares are sold on lottery boards for the Superbowl. The Radisson Resort is the host for the Sweetheart's Dinner Dance, a delightful way to spend Valentine's Day: $90 includes a three-course dinner with wine, a happy hour with open bar prior, and dancing to a great local band. Silent auctions and raffles for fabulous prizes, donated by local concerns, also help raise funds.

FOTH usually distributes around $60,000 annually to worthwhile island foundations. All of this is done with the complete cooperation and supervision of CEDE Aruba, which secures and administrates funding for social projects.

Sadly, FOTH members are neither quite as young nor healthy as they once were. New volunteers are needed and welcome to carry on their very important work.

Posada Clinic Aruba

Individuals requiring dialysis during their stay can set up appointments with Posada Clinic Aruba (L. G. Smith Blvd. 14, 297/582-9477, posadaaruba@gmail.com, 7am-7pm Mon.-Sat.) in Oranjestad. Visiting patients are very positive about the cleanliness of the facility and the capable staff, who they describe as exceptionally friendly and accommodating. Each of the 13 dialysis stations has its own cable television. Staff serve snacks and refreshments during sessions. It is located right across from the Surfside Marina Hotel and very easy to find.

Aruba Happy Wheels

Special wheelchairs designed to enter the water and travel on sand are rented out by Aruba Happy Wheels (Palm Beach 472, 297/568-4787, adaptedhappywheels@hotmail.com, $40 for 24 hrs). A fold-up platform may also be rented to allow wheelchair access on difficult surfaces. They will deliver the equipment to resorts and they offer discounts for long-term rentals.

GAY AND LESBIAN TRAVELERS

Aruba has an active and open gay and lesbian community, and islanders are quite nonchalant about visitors' sexual orientation. There are some Caribbean islands where sodomy and homosexuality are capital crimes, but Aruba has no such discrimination.

There are frequent gay and lesbian cruises that include Aruba among their ports of call; all visitors are welcome.

TRAVELING WITH CHILDREN

Traveling with children, no matter the destination, presents some distinctive considerations and precautions. Aruba is, moreover, surrounded by the sea, which is adjacent to most resorts, along with onsite swimming pools, so water safety for children is paramount. Aruba's beaches do not have lifeguards stationed along the shores, so parents must be vigilant.

Utmost precaution with the tropical sun on juvenile skin is also a priority. Better than continually annoying a squirming child to reapply sunblock, keep a supply of old tee shirts for them to wear in the water, and dry ones on hand to change into afterwards.

The excitement of travel and the constant activity, along with tropical temperatures, usually results in overtired, cranky youngsters. Keep this in mind when making dinner plans. Aruba has many family-oriented eateries that provide children's menus.

If a child appears to be ill, medical service can be accessed 24 hours a day. Resort staff will assist in calling the doctor on duty and arranging a consultation. There are always at least two drugstores on the island providing off-hours service to fill prescriptions.

Aruba is, generally, a very family-friendly island. Children are welcome and respected, and most resorts provide a wealth of activities to keep them engaged throughout the day. They also have a roster of vetted babysitters, and parents can dine out with peace of mind. Sensitive to the needs of families, the Aruba Tourism Authority (ATA) devised the **One Cool Family** program. It is effective June 1-September 30 for kids ages 12 and under. Save cash on dining and accommodations by signing up through their website (www.aruba.com.). Then present your One Cool Family ID when reserving with participating vendors.

WOMEN TRAVELING ALONE

Despite unusual incidents that attracted enormous media attention, Aruba has always been considered a safe place for women to travel alone or with another woman. There are numerous busy, lively areas of entertainment and dining that allow women alone to walk freely and enjoy the island nightlife.

Female tourists are welcome at various clubs and nightspots; the opportunity to mix and mingle with locals is plentiful. Islanders are quite accustomed to women traveling on their own.

Health and Safety

SUN PROTECTION

Aruba is only 12° north of the equator. Those who have traveled to the tropics know that the sun here has to be taken very seriously. "I never burn" are famous last words for those hiding out in their rooms for a major portion of their vacation. Common sense and the wealth of information promulgated about skin damage from the sun have resulted in most visitors being smart about exposure and protection. Unfortunately, sunbathers who don't see any color blooming after a few days panic at the thought of not having a tan to show off on their return. Dermatologists know you don't get a great tan in three days, but a surprising number try for and expect it.

There is great debate about the strength of sun protection. Without a good base tan, SPF 15 should be considered the minimum strength to use. Limit sun exposure the first few days, and take a break during the peak midday hours.

Areas that many forget to cover, which are quite sensitive, include behind the ears and the back of the neck, and particularly the tops of feet, the instep, which tend to be turned to the sun and get maximum exposure. Commonly, while lying around the beach, everyone likes to break up the day with a relaxing walk along the shoreline. The gentle waves lap over their feet, insidiously washing away the sun protection. It is necessary to reapply after a bit of exercise.

Even if not actually sunbathing, but walking around town or touring, sun exposure is

ARUBA'S PURE WATER

Aruba began the process of producing sweet water from the sea in 1931, at one point boasting the world's largest plant. Wells and cisterns were originally deployed to obtain fresh water. **Water-en Energiebedrijf Aruba N.V., or WEB,** is Aruba's water and power producing plant, located at Balashi. Hence the term "Balashi Cocktail," meaning a drink of cold tap water.

Aruba's plant still ranks among the top 10 water desalination plants in the world. Executive engineers at WEB are credited with innovations in the field that have revolutionized the industry.

Frequent visitors often declare the water straight from the tap "the best in the world," a refreshing relief from the heavy chlorination to which most are accustomed. This has been purposefully planned by WEB engineers to insure it is exceptionally clean and refreshing for drinking and bathing. It is also very soft, so less shampoo or soap is required to work up a good lather.

Until 2008, Aruba deployed the unique practice of running the distilled seawater over coral to imbue it with phosphorous and manganese that enlivens what would otherwise be flat and tasteless, while providing necessary minerals for the body.

Originally, a steam method of distillation was deployed, but in 2008 WEB opened their first Sea Water Reverse Osmosis (SWRO) plant, which is far more energy efficient. Steam plants are steadily being retired as more SWRO plants are brought online. The first produces 44,000 metric tons daily, more than enough to meet Aruba's average daily demand. In July of 2012, a new plant with a capacity of 24,000 metric tons began operation. Combined, they make WEB the largest fresh water producer in the Caribbean.

no less fierce and protection should be worn. Use sunblock or wear shirts that cover the shoulders.

Children require special attention; particularly if constantly in and out of the water. This will wash off the protection. Often they are impatient and reapplying lotion constantly is a tedious chore. It is a good idea to have a few old tee shirts they can wear in the water to protect tender young shoulders, and a hat for that vulnerable back of the neck. Keep some dry shirts for them to change into when resting and playing on shore. Hair braiding on the beach is very popular, and makes hair easy to care for. This exposes the scalp, however, and strong sun block should be applied between the rows of braids.

ALCOHOL

Aruba's many fine restaurants entice visitors to indulge in exceptional, often rich meals, every night. The beach bars, happy hours, and exotic cocktails that taste like desserts encourage the over-consumption of alcohol. This is often at levels to which most are unaccustomed. A few days of this and it is not surprising that many visitors are afflicted with seriously upset digestion, or worse. Don't blame the local water.

Alcohol also dehydrates, contributing to possible heatstroke or exhaustion. Periodically, take a break on both food and alcohol over-consumption. Even on vacation, perhaps even more so, moderation in all things is wise. Drink plenty of water, juices, or non-alcoholic beverages.

DENGUE FEVER

Despite Aruba being a desert island, it does get rainfall, particularly in autumn, the rainy season for the region. Showers mean standing water and standing water means mosquitoes. Usually the island's strong winds keep them to a minimum, but during the late fall and early winter, mosquitos and dengue fever can be an issue. The rest of the Caribbean, which receives far more rainfall all year round, has much greater numbers for dengue fever, but it should not be discounted on Aruba. The amount of

BUSH MEDICINE

Being the islands, a deep-rooted (yes, pun intended) reliance on natural, homegrown remedies is rampant, even among the most erudite and educated islanders. Every drugstore has a shelf of herbs. The leaves and roots are for steeping to produce fresh, holistic teas. These are not in commercial packaging, but fresh, individual baggies, with a label sometimes describing its purpose. It's best to inquire with the pharmacist how to use the various items. Freshly processed lotions and potions are also sold; some have to be made to order and kept refrigerated, such as *Lotio Alba*, a mild, natural remedy for heat rash.

Most residents cultivate a few aloe plants in their garden, cutting a piece of leaf to apply the fresh juice to burns. Many believe the beneficial property of the plant goes well beyond the dermis, and will drink the juices mixed with water. It takes quite some determination and a healthy dose of honey to make it even remotely palatable. Others even nibble on the gelatinous meat inside the leaves, also hard to imagine for anyone familiar with the malodorous species that grows on Aruba.

rainfall over the season is a significant factor in dengue statistics.

Dengue virus is carried by the Aedes Aegypti mosquito, which requires clean water, not dirty, in which to lay their eggs. The mosquito has very distinctive white striping on its legs. Standing puddles are not breeding grounds for the Aedes Aegypti, but any sort of container in which rainwater can pool, provides a place for them to lay their eggs. This is another reason why controlling litter is so important.

There are four strains of dengue. Each strain can produce a general malaise, similar to flu, but with distinctive symptoms. Dengue symptoms can include severe headache; pain around the eyes, back, and joints; high fever; a rash; and possibly nausea and diarrhea. Depending on the strain, symptoms can be minor to severe. It is a virus and antibiotics are useless.

A single bout of dengue can be highly unpleasant, but is not fatal, unless, like the flu, other chronic conditions are present. Once infected with a particular strain, antibodies are manufactured in the system, and an individual will be immune to that strain for life. If bitten by a mosquito carrying a different strain, then the reaction of the two in the body can be catastrophic. Dengue often mimics flu symptoms, so do not dismiss being ill. Go see a local doctor, as they will also arrange for blood tests to confirm if infected with dengue.

Aruba's Department of Health and Office of Communicable Diseases pays very close attention to this situation. Inspectors travel from house to house and business premises searching for breeding grounds. Homeowners and landlords are warned and citations issued for non-compliance in correcting conditions favorable for mosquitoes. Each year, in the fall, they mount an information and prevention campaign.

HOSPITALS AND EMERGENCY SERVICES

Aruba has a doctor on duty outside of normal office hours. They will conduct examinations and treatment at the **Dr. Horacio E. Oduber Hospital** (Dr. Horacio E. Oduber Hospital Blvd. 1, 297/527-4000, www.arubahospital.com, 24 hours daily). A number of resorts have a local doctor they work with regularly, who will come to the resort and make "house calls" or accept visitors at their office. Inquire with the front desk. If the resort does not have a doctor, they will advise or call an ambulance if needed. Emergency room service at the hospital is $316 for examination and diagnosis; X-rays and other testing is extra.

Emergency service for visitors must be paid for in cash or by credit card. The hospital or doctor will not accept U.S. or foreign coverage. Receipts will be issued for insurance claims once you return home. The same procedure is in place for a regular policy or a travel insurance policy.

Aruba's hospital is a clean, modern facility, continually being renovated and improved. They can perform MRIs, CAT scans, and other tests. In 2010 the hospital acquired a hyperbaric chamber.

Emergency Hotline

To further expedite emergency service for all visitors and residents, Aruba established a 911 number for a 24-hour hotline. Responders dispatch police, the fire department, or ambulances to a location, as needed.

PHARMACIES

Prescriptions issued must be filled and paid for at a pharmacy or *botica*. If at night or on Sundays, prescriptions will be at the venue on duty. Pharmacies on Aruba are open 8am-8pm Monday-Saturday. Two pharmacies remain open on Sundays, holidays, and after-hours. There will be one servicing each side of the island, with the bridge at Spaanslagoen the dividing line. They change on a rotating basis. The *botica* on duty will be posted in newspapers and in the window of all pharmacies. The venue can also be obtained by calling the hospital.

The following pharmacies are close to the resort areas. All pharmacy hours are 8am-8pm Monday-Saturday.

- **Oranjestad: Botica Kibrahacha** (Havenstraat 30, 297/583-4908), located directly behind the Royal Plaza Shopping Mall

- **Eagle and Manchebo Beach: Botica diServicio Eagle** (Caya Punto Brabo 17, 297/587-9011), located next to the Dr. Horacio E. Oduber Hospital

- **Palm Beach, Malmok, and Noord: Botica Santa Anna** (Noord 41B, 297/586-2020), located right next to Caribbean Palm Villas Resort

- **Santa Cruz, Paradera, and Piedra Plat: Botica Santa Cruz** (Santa Cruz 54 A, 297/585-8776), located on the corner across from Mundo Nobo Supermarket

CRIME

According to statistics and the CIA Factbook, Aruba is one of the safest destinations in the Caribbean. Incidents of wallets and handbags forgotten at a store or market but returned intact are common. However, there is no place in the world that is utterly crime-free.

Petty Theft

As in any vacation destination, petty theft by a few active miscreants can be an issue. Petty thieves know that vacationers have extra cash, traveler's checks, cameras, and other valuable electronics or jewelry. Vacationers should be mindful of their personal belongings and valuables.

Safe and Deposit Boxes

Safes and deposit boxes are provided by nearly all accommodations. This is the place for passports and extra monies, credit cards, and bank cards. The purchase of a watertight "beach box" for cash, a credit card, or small valuables is a minor but worthwhile investment that can be worn in the water. Do not leave a bag with your watch and wallet unattended on the beach when taking a swim; this is simple common sense.

Car Theft

If driving around the island in an open car, such as a jeep, and parking in an isolated spot to take a swim, do not leave valuables in the car. Even a closed car should be kept in sight; it is always possible to break a window and open the trunk. Wear a waist pack or small backpack for exploring the caves and Arikok National Park. Individuals who victimize tourists know the places where they are most likely to leave valuables and cash behind. Carry very little and find methods, such as watertight carriers or simply sealing them in a few plastic bags, to foil their intentions while you frolic in the water. The same applies while sitting on the beach of your resort. Do not leave a beach bag filled with valuables behind. Take with you only what you need and keep it in a watertight container you can wear in the water. It is difficult for police to make a case after the fact, unless specific items are recovered and there is definitive forensic evidence.

Car theft was on the rise for a few years, particularly of the most common rental cars. The KPA (Korps Politie Aruba, www.kparuba.com) created a specialized task force and in 2010 arrested over 25 individuals in a theft and chop shop ring, which has relieved the situation to a great degree.

WOMEN'S SAFETY

Despite some notoriety and misconceptions, female visitors experience no more unpleasant encounters or attention than they would at home, and likely far less. Making safe and smart decisions about new acquaintances in bars or on the beach shouldn't change under the influences of a tropical moon and a romantic destination.

The predilection towards excessive alcohol consumption while on vacation can impair judgment. Women should be cautious about their intake. It is advised not to leave an unfinished drink in a crowded club. Finish it before going off to the bathroom or dance floor. If it was left unattended for some time, leave it and order a new drink.

Incidents of women being bothered while walking unattended at night are rare to nonexistent, but being alert or avoiding such situations is always advisable. Larger hotels post security guards day and night to prohibit intruders to the rooms. Several overt and hidden security cameras are installed at all major resorts, and along popular walkways. Stay in well-lit, populated areas.

STRAY DOGS AND CATS

It is unfortunate, but the practice of neutering domestic animals is not performed sufficiently to control the unwanted dog and cat population of Aruba. Some will take the animals to be euthanized. Others may drop animals somewhere in the hopes that a kind person will adopt them or that they will fend for themselves. This is a state of mind prevalent throughout the Caribbean and Latin and Central America. Most islands do not have a collection service to take the unwanted dogs off the streets, despite tourists finding it distressing to see them hungry or injured. Visitors need not fear that they may be rabid, as rabies does not exist on Aruba.

Animal Rights Aruba

Aruba's Tourism Authority (ATA) announced in 2012 their sponsorship of a four-pronged program run by Animal Rights Aruba (ARA; Mabon 7A, hotline 297/593-5393, www.animalrightsaruba.org) to alleviate the situation. Awareness, education, citing and fining for the mistreatment of dogs, and financing a neutering program comprise their plan. Donations are welcome to assist the foundation in their work.

Reporting of sick or injured stray animals is encouraged. An ARA volunteer will come to check the dog, but they ask callers to stay on site until help arrives, to identify the animal.

Cas Animal

Aruba's first no-kill animal refuge is the ultimate goal of Cas Animal Foundation (hotline 297/565-2130). Founder Kirsten Arndt has converted three homes into a temporary facility, while fundraising to build a proper center.

Cas Animal conducts various fundraising and awareness-raising events during the year. Tierra Del Sol hosts a gold tournament at the end of September. Dog owners are invited to invent costumes and show off their four-legged friends during the annual Carnival Doggy Pawrade. Cas Animal maintains an Animal Ambulance to pick up strays. The foundation also welcomes donations. They can be in the form of paying veterinary bills or providing bags of dog food; anything is helpful.

Another primary objective of Cas Animal is to facilitate the adoption of local mixed breeds by tourists. Quite often, one of Aruba's sweet and intelligent strays will capture the heart of a sympathetic tourist. Ms. Arndt will assist in anyway possible in obtaining inspection and treatment for the dog from a qualified vet, allowing it to pass U.S. standards for importation. She will also assist in acquiring a carrier and arranging transport. Vacationers returning to the United States or Canada with an Aruban dog or cat is a far more common occurrence than most imagine. The pets adapt well to their new environment.

Information and Services

ELECTRICITY

Adapters for electrical appliances and devices are not required for travelers from the United States and Canada. Aruba uses the same 110-120 volts AC (60 cycle). European appliances will require adapters, but it is likely that hotels can provide them. If not, they are readily available at home or hardware stores. Some facilities may not have an outlet that handles a three-pronged plug, but adapters for that situation are also on hand. It is advisable to notify your resort of your requirements before arrival to insure they have an adaptor reserved for your use.

Aruba is far less prone to power outages than in the past. Aruba's power plant, WEB, has greatly increased its output and efficiency of production. Though, a lightening storm could result in a loss of current. It is advised to unplug all appliances or devices, as the surge when the power comes back has been known to burn out anything from laptops to refrigerator motors.

BANKS, MONEY, AND FOREIGN EXCHANGE

The official currency of the island is **Arubian Florins,** officially expressed in writing as **AWG.** The term "guilders" may also be heard among locals, this is similar to saying "bucks" instead of dollars. The official exchange rate at banks is 1.77 florins to $1. This can vary on the street from 1.75-1.80, depending on the shop; it is completely arbitrary. Supermarkets usually exchange at 1.75, where prices are strictly in florins. Jewelry stores will most often exchange at 1.80, though prices are marked in dollars.

Aruba has four important banks. One is in Oranjestad and the other branches are strategically located in Palm Beach, conveniently close to some of the resorts. They are all only a short walk heading away from the water, past the Sasaki Highway.

It is not necessary to change money over to Arubian florins from U.S. dollars. Stores and restaurants readily accept dollars, traveler's checks, and U.S. and Canadian credit cards. A valid photo I.D. will be required when using credit or bank cards and traveler's checks at shops and markets. ATMs accepting MasterCard, Visa Cirrus, and Visa Plus for cash withdrawals or advances are located in every mall, casino, gas station, and major grocery store.

Cariibbean Mercantile Bank

Caribbean Mercantile Bank (CMB; Caya G. F. Croes 53, Palm Beach 4-B, 297/522-3000, www.cmbnv.com, 8am-4pm Mon.-Fri.) is a subsidiary of Maduro & Curiel Bank of Curacao, which is affiliated with The Bank of Nova Scotia. Palm Beach branch is midway between the Sasaki Highway and Santa Ana Church on the principal Palm Beach road.

Royal Bank of Canada

RBC (Italiestraat 36, 297/523-3100, www.rbtt.com, 8am-4pm Mon.-Fri.), the Caribbean chain of the Royal Bank of Canada, having taken over RBTT, a widespread regional institution. The main headquarters is very close to all Manchebo resorts, on the Sasaki Highway.

Aruba Bank

Aruba's first bank, Aruba Bank (Camacuri 12, 297/527-7777, www.arubabank.com,

A FANTASY WEDDING ON ARUBA

Destination weddings are in. The advantages are numerous (including financial advantages). A winter wedding can be conducted outdoors with clear skies, comfortable temperatures, and no coats.

For the legal ceremony, Aruba's Town Hall is picturesque with a beautiful interior. Government staffers perform the ceremonies with grace and emotional fervor. Formal papers must be submitted at least one month prior to nuptials, in Dutch. This is where the assistance of a local wedding planner is vital. They will translate the required forms, which are requested of the prospective bride and groom. Forms must be accompanied by:

- Birth certificate with the names of BOTH parents and an embossed Apostille Seal
- Copy of passport/picture ID
- Death Certificate with Apostille Seal (if applicable)
- Divorce Certificate with Apostille Seal OR Final Decree of Divorce with Apostille
- Letter of Intent to Marry
- U.S./Canada Negative Statement of Marriage or Affidavit of Single Status; must include Apostille Seal

Begin collecting the documents at least six months prior to the planned wedding date. Two witnesses are required to be present at the ceremony. (The wedding planner can provide them if necessary.)

If conducting only a spiritual ceremony on the beach, proof of marriage is required. Ministers need to see a certified copy of the wedding certificate. Several non-denominational ministers perform touching ceremonies in any location of your choice. **Diane Keijzer** (www. dianekeijzer.com) does a fine job. The Catholic Church will not perform destination weddings because of the required spiritual preparation.

Every major resort on Aruba has a dedicated wedding planner. Their services are available only if you are using the resort's facilities. Veteran independent wedding planners include:

- Aruba Fairy Tale Weddings (297/593-0045, www.arubafairytales.com)
- Aruba Weddings by Bonny (297/730-0350, www.arubaweddingsbybonny.com)
- Cayena Weddings (973/460-0284 or 212/292-4221, www.cayenaweddings.com)
- Ceremonies & Celebrations in Aruba (321/473-3856, candcaruba@yahoo.com)

A renewal of vows does not require all the above mentioned paperwork.

Aruba.com has a separate wedding section and a bridal registry, http://bridal.aruba.com, where friends and family can purchase gifts for newlyweds honeymooning on Aruba. Spa days, sailing cruises or tours, flowers, and romantic dinners can be pre-purchased to give as wedding gifts. Newlyweds-to-be should investigate the **One Cool Honeymoon** perks offered in cooperation with local resorts.

8am-4pm Mon.-Fri.) is affiliated with the regional Orco Group. The headquarters is near the airport, but they have a Palm Beach branch directly across from CMB Bank, only a short walk from Palm Beach hotels.

Banco di Caribe

Aruba's fourth major bank, Banco di Caribe (Vondellaan 31, 297/523-2000, www.bancodicaribe.com, 8am-4pm Mon.-Fri.) has many ATMs around the island, but no branches beyond their Oranjestad headquarters.

COMMUNICATIONS
Internet and Long Distance Calls

Islanders take pride in being technologically savvy and Internet-wise; social networking is very popular on Aruba. Almost all resorts and guesthouses have Wi-Fi, a majority of them for free. Major resorts offer in-house communications stations for guests to check their email and chat with the folks back home.

Calling the United States from hotels can be an expensive and often time-consuming affair. Guests often have to wait for the hotel operator to make the connection and pass it through to their rooms. There are several "Call Home" phone stations to be found around shopping centers and near resorts. These only require the swipe of a credit card, but they automatically charge $15, even when there is no answer.

Roaming charges on cell phones from home can often be outrageous. Aruba cell phone systems work on charging only for calls made, with users not charged for calls received. Renting a cell can prove an economical alternative for keeping in touch.

SETAR

Aruba's national telecommunication company, SETAR (Palm Beach z/n, 297/525-1000, http://setar.aw, 9am-5:30pm Mon.-Sat.) is the company that installs all landlines. They have a branch in Palm Beach where long distance calls can be made at minimal rates. It is located right next to Amazonia restaurant. Phones are outside the shop and available at all hours. A vending machine for phone cards is adjacent (the phone cards are needed for making calls). Their main headquarters is on the outskirts of Oranjestad.

SETAR also maintains a cell phone rental kiosk in the arrivals hall of the Reina Beatrix International Airport (9am-11am and noon-6pm Mon.-Sat.) to arrange mobile service immediately upon arrival.

INTERNET SERVICES

On the second level of Paseo Herencia Shopping Mall is the **iZone Internet Café** (J. E. Irausquin Blvd. 382-A, 297/586-7583, www.izonearuba.com, 10am-10pm Mon.-Sat., 5pm-10pm Sun., phone rental $5) with a full menu of Internet and communications services. Long distance calling booths allow for minutes to be purchased in prepaid blocks, or post paid. They have computer stations and cell phone rental. Other handy services include downloading your camera's memory card and burning the images to CD, plus fax machines and scanning and printing services for anyone doing business.

Most laptops and tablets do not necessarily connect to the Internet once beyond the server at your resort. Some resorts charge for Wi-Fi or only allow for one device. Many visitors complain about the quality of connection as well, particularly when using more than one device. Long-term vacationers at timeshare resorts have found **MIO** (Caya G. F. Betico Croes 222, 297/583-007, http://mioaruba.com, 9am-6pm Mon.-Sat., $40 for device, $40 for bandwidth) offers a viable solution. USB plug and play modems offer speedy Internet connections anyplace, without long-term contracts and are very moderately priced. The MiFi wireless device provides fast, reliable service to up to five devices simultaneously. Bandwidth can be purchased in monthly packages starting at 4GB.

MEDIA
Newspapers

Aruba is an island with a highly literate population that likes to keep informed. Despite the ascendancy of web-based news, it has several printed papers in each of the four predominant languages. Among them are three English papers, *The Morning News, Aruba Today* and *The Daily*. Each has a very individual character, presenting various aspects of world and local news. They can be found distributed for free at hotels, supermarkets, fast food franchises, and various other locations every morning.

THE MORNING NEWS

Established in March of 2010, *The Morning News* (Caya G. F. Betico Croes 111, 297/588-9517, www.themorningnewsaruba.com, Mon.-Sat., free) staff are veterans of Aruba's first English newspaper, *The News*. The paper is wide reaching in its coverage of local events, with space given to the most important international stories of the day. Island politics, human interest, new dining and shopping venues, and other news of import to Aruba, and particular tourists, is the focus of their content.

ARUBA TODAY

Aruba Today (Weststraat 22, 297/582-7800, Mon.-Sat., free) places more of a focus on international news, with a few local pages dedicated to superficial events. On Mondays, they feature an international version of *The New York Times* in an additional section.

ARUBA DAILY

Established with the visiting businessperson in mind, *Aruba Daily* (Engelandstraat 29, 297/764-6450, http://aruba-daily.com, Mon.-Sat., free) features the latest NYSE and American Exchange tables, and other financial news. Topical articles are for the most part the top international headlines with local news largely promotional.

ARUBA HERALD

Only found online is the *Aruba Herald* (297/583-2424, http://arubaherald.com), with a diversity of local news. They cover every aspect of island life that makes the Papiamento papers, from domestic disputes to lost dogs. International coverage is generally reserved to politics and top headlines.

Tourist Magazines

An inordinate number of annual tourist publications in English provide information on restaurants, services, and island happenings. They can be found freely distributed at supermarkets, hotel lobbies, restaurants, and stores. Hotels provide a hard copy of *Aruba Nights* in every room. Printed in both English and Papiamento is the bible of Aruba's Carnival: *Bacchanal.*

The English magazines available are:

• *Aruba Events*

• *Aruba Experience*

• *Aruba Nights*

• *Bacchanal*

• *Chef's Menu & Recipe*

• *Destination Aruba*

• *I Love Aruba*

• *Island Gourmet*

• *Island Temptations*

Radio and Television

Aruba has 18 FM radio stations and 3 AM stations. There are three island-based TV stations: **TeleAruba,** channel 13; **ATV,** channel 15; and **TOP TV,** channel 22; with two Venezuelan stations, picked up on channels 10 and 12. Television and radio programming is consistently in Papiamento and Spanish, with some Dutch newscasts. ATV (channel 15) has an English Lifestyle and News program for local events at 7:15pm Monday-Friday, with commentator Yentl Lieuw. All resorts are connected to SETAR Cable, or have satellite dishes to carry U.S. programming and sporting events, as do most bars and lounges.

Easy 97.9 FM radio plays a nice mix of soft listening music from the United States and the Caribbean. Commentary is practically nonexistent. It is relatively commercial-free and broadcasts 24 hours daily. **Hits 100** radio station at **100.9 FM** targets the 35+ audience with Billboard hits from the 1980s and 1990s. Other radio stations are geared to the cultural tastes of the region.

WEIGHTS AND MEASURES

Aruba uses the international metric system in all things. Fresh meats, produce, and baked goods are measured by kilo when purchased by weight. An ounce measure in metric is one-tenth of a kilo, a bit less then a quarter of a pound in English and American measurements.

A kilo is 2.2 U.S. pounds. A liter is 3.3 quarts, or less than a gallon. Prices on gas pumps in Aruba are per liter of gasoline and it is quite expensive.

Distance and speed postings on roads are in kilometers.

RESOURCES

Papiamento Phrasebook

The fluency in English of islanders requires little necessity for Papiamento in tourist venues. It is rare to find someone working at resorts, restaurants, or shops that does not speak and understand English well.

When patronizing native restaurants or shops a few phrases can be helpful, and sometimes necessary. Anyone with a good working knowledge of Spanish will also do well in these circumstances, as it is often more used by those who don't speak any English. Arubans who don't understand or speak English sufficiently seem to have no problem with Spanish. This could be credited to most of their media orientation and input coming from the more southern latitudes.

PRONUNCIATION GUIDE
Papiamento combines elements of a number of languages: Spanish, Portuguese, Dutch, and English, even the occasional French, such as *petit pois* for peas. Also, where emphasis is placed on a syllable can actually change the meaning of the world, changing from verb to adjective, and unlike English, it is frequently the last syllable where it is placed.

Consonants
Only a few consonants differ from standard English pronunciation

dj as in "join"-"djispi" is a precocious child, "djucu"-a good luck charm

g can be normal, as in "go," but is frequently soft "h" as in "hello"

j is a "y" sound, as in "year"; June and July are "Yuni" and "Yuli"

ñ as in the Spanish "ñ" for words such as "señor" or "aña"; both forms of "n" are used.

zj is a soft "j" such as "zjilea" (jelly), but rarely seen

Vowels
Standard vowel pronunciation is very different; long vowels in English are never applied.

a as in "papa"
e as in "they"
i as in "police"
o as in "blow"
u as in "dude"
u as in "buck"

The influence of Dutch can be seen in the oft-used *IJ*, the Dutch way of writing *Y* as in "ray." An example is *Tamarijn*, with the final syllable pronounced "rain."

TERMS OF ADDRESS
I *mi* or *Ami* (Example: *"Mi ta bai"*--"I am going"; "Who gets this?--"*Ami.*")

You *bo* or *Abo* (Example: *"Undo bo ta biba?"*--"Where do you live?", "Who do you love?" *"Abo"*)

he or she *e*

us or we *nos*

they *nan* (Also added to the end of words to make them plural *Mucha*--"Child"--*Muchanan*--"Children.")

IMPORTANT GREETINGS AND RESPONSES

Good Day *Bon Dia* (BonDEE-A)

Good Afternoon *Bon Tardi* (Bon TAR-dee)

Good Evening, Good Night *Bon Nochi* (Bon NO-chee)

How are you? *Con ta Bai?* (literally translates as "How does it go?")

Everything is good? *Tur cos ta bon?*

Yes, good, thank you. *Si, bon, danki.*

Good enough; ok. *Basta Bon.*

Welcome. *Bon Bini.*

Please. *Por Fabor.*

Thank you. *Danki.*

Goodbye. *Ayo.*

USEFUL PHRASES

It is a pleasure to meet you. *Ta un plaser di conocebo.*

Until next time. *Te otro biaha.*

Have a nice day *Pasa un bon dia--*

What time is it? *Cuant'or tin?*

I don't understand you. *Mi no ta comprende bo.*

Do you speak English? *Bo por papia Ingles?*

My name is... *Mi nomber ta...*

What is your name? *Con jamabo?*

How much? *Cuanto ta?*

How do you say...? *Con bo ta bisa...?*

Excuse me. *Despensa.*

I love you. *Mi stimabo.*

Help! *Yudami!*

Fire! *Candela!*

Merry Christmas and Happy New Year *Bon Pasco y Bon Aña.*

Happy Birthday *Cumpleaño Felis*

Congratulations *Pabien* or *Bon Suerte*

anthem and flag *himno y bandera*

Suggested Reading

DESCRIPTIONS AND TRAVEL

Bäcker, Jennifer, and Wodl, Josefa, photographers. *Wings Over Aruba*. Wings Global Media, 2011. The ultimate coffee table photography book of Aruba is very big, very bright, with new aerial angles of the prettiest places.

Bertsch, Werner and Croes, Charles. *Aruba, I am your Island*. Aruba: Self published, 2012. A lovely picture book from Werner Bertsch, combined with the reflective prose and poetry of Charles Croes, well-known as the storyteller of Aruba forums, comes in plain paperback or a handsome sleeve for gift giving.

Bertsch, Werner. *Aruba Tropical Mood of the Caribbean*. DeWit/Van Dorp, 2008. Werner is back with another picture book, more focused on the colors of Carnival.

Bertsch, Werner and Hiller, Linda. *Aruba Picture Book*. DeWit/Van Dorp, 2011. Werner Bertsch loves photographing Aruba. Another collection of his charming shots with captions by Hiller, this book is a smaller, budget-priced paperback.

Boland, Matt (Author) and Kock, Eva. *Aruba Tips for Travelers*. Vitae Publishing, 2005. This is a long-time resident's folksy bits of advice on what to expect when vacationing on Aruba. He clarifies all those new and funny things that make visitors scratch their heads in confusion.

Knevel, Theo. *Aruba, Ariba*. ATA Publishing, 2011. Stunning aerial photography will inspire anyone to take a helicopter tour. It provides a very interesting perspective.

Night, Sam. *Aruba: Including its History, the Alto Visto Chapel, the Ayo Rock Formations, the Quadriki Caves, Fort Zoutman, and More*. Earth Eyes Travel Guides, 2012. Culled from Wikipedia articles and images under Creative Commons licensing, the series of guides gathers popular subjects within one portable resource.

HISTORY

Bongers, Evert. *Creating One Happy Island.* Self published, 2009. This was published in commemoration of the 50th anniversary of the opening of the Aruba Caribbean Resort, considered the defining moment when tourism became an important pillar of the island's economy. It is a compendium by a few island writers, showcasing the visionary personalities that established Aruba as a tourism giant in the Caribbean.

Dijkhoff, Raymundo, A.C.F. and Linville, Marlene S. *The Marine Shell Heritage.* Aruba Archaeological Museum Press, 2004. Extrapolations are edited by the head of the museum's Scientific Department regarding the findings from shore areas and society created by being dependent on marine animals, particularly mollusks. Shells were used for everything from building to decoration and money.

Hartog, Dr. Johannes. *Aruba Picture Book. A Short History of Aruba,* DeWit/Van Dorp, 2003. A very short history, indeed. Dr. Hartog, historian and archaeologist, was one of the first to initiate digs and investigate the island's Amerindian population. The book focuses much on their time occupying the island.

Kock, Adolf (Dufi). *The Story of the German Freighter E.S. Antilla.* Self published, 2012. Long-time friend and chronicler of Lagolites and life at the colony recalls WWII. This is a very detailed description of the dramatic events leading up to the sinking of the *Antilla.*

Ridderstaat, Jorge R. *The Lago Story.* Cha Aruba, 2008. A visually beautiful and thorough accounting of Aruba's economic history prepares the reader by first painting a picture of the island's initial development from gold and phosphate. It passes through the years when the refinery was in its prime and the years of WWII, then finally onto the decline of its influence and the growth of tourism.

Versteeg, Aad H. and Rostain, Stephen. *Archeology of Aruba-The Tanki Flip Site.* Aruba Archaeological Museum Press, 1997. This book profiles Aruba's first major archeological dig and the revelation it contained.

Versteeg, Aad H. and Ruiz, Arminda C. *Reconstruction in Brasilwood Island-The Archeology & Landscape of Indian Aruba.* Aruba Archaeological Museum Press, 1995. Administrators of NAMA and archaeologist Versteeg delve into the significance of artifacts.

NATURE

De Boer, Bart, with Newton, Eric and Restall, Robin. *Birds of Aruba, Curaiao, and Bonaire.* Princeton Field Guides, 2012. This is the first comprehensive field guide to the birds of the region. This compact and portable book contains close to 1,000 color illustrations on 71 color plates, helping to identify the more than 200 species that inhabit the three islands.

Roll, Barbara. *Explorer's Guide to Aruba.* Loft Publishing, 2010. This is one author's charming way of opening Aruba to children in an entertaining manner.

MISCELLANEOUS

Croes, Robetico. *Anatomy of Demand in International Tourism: The case of Aruba.* Lap Lambert Academic Publishing, 2010. This is a must-read for tourism executives from Aruba's former Minister of Tourism, who now holds a chair at the UCF School of Hospitality Management. He examines the dynamics of a small island and the impact of international tourism, based on statistics from an extended study.

Fenzi-Thayer Sargent, Jewell. *This is the Way We Cook!* DeWit/Van Dorp, 1971. Already in its 14th printing, this is a compendium of recipes from the outstanding cooks of Aruba, Bonaire, Curacao, Saba, St. Eustatius, and San Maarten, for those who wish to try preparing some of the regional cuisine.

Viana, Carlos. *Prescriptions from Paradise.* Healing Spirit Press, 2012. Viana, holistic healer and certified in Chinese medicine, presents a compilation of more than 10 years of health columns. They are organized from A to Z and made easy to understand. His years of practice have resulted in some quite surprising insights. It is the winner of the 2012 International Book Award in Alternative Medicine from USA Book News.

Internet Resources

GENERAL INFORMATION
Aruba Online
www.arubatourism.com
This is one of the first Aruba websites to go online. It has been around since 1992, founded by a frequent visitor to the island. The site includes information and visitor reviews with links to websites. This is an impartial, basic site. Opinions are left to the visitors to rate and comment on services. Home of a long-established and popular Aruba forum, which is excellent for current information and input, the site also provides a booking engine for lodging through Travelocity and has webcams set up in various locations around Aruba.

Official Tourism Website of Aruba
www.aruba.com
Aruba's official website is very conscientious in providing complete information on every aspect of the island. It has booking engines for room reservations, activities, and dining out. There is a bridal registry allowing family and friends to purchase excursions, romantic dinners, and shopping as gifts for newlyweds that will be honeymooning on Aruba. Newly married couples can also take advantage of the "One Cool Honeymoon" special offers for discounts on lodging, dining, and activities. Other special packages include "One Cool Family."

The official tourism website also offers a downloadable app for smartphones: "The Official Aruba Travel Guide." It has several features for deploying offline for planning activities. Users can instantly review and rate attractions and services, then upload to social media when back within an Internet service area. GPS provides directions to sites and amenities from the user's location.

A very busy forum section made up of frequent visitors is an excellent place to pose queries and obtain firsthand advice.

VisitAruba
www.visitaruba.com
One of Aruba's longest established websites, since 1997, it is extremely thorough. It maintains impartiality, but has reviews by users and a busy forum. Frequent and first-time visitors are welcome to file trip reports, which can be highly informative.

Find a complete schedule of island events, including all Carnival events, and Aruba current events posted here. The site strives to stay topical and up to date, including useful links to restaurants, car rentals, current weather reports. Visitors can purchase their logo discount card for $13.95. This does not include postage or delivery to your resort on arrival, which can be arranged for a $3.95 fee. Cardholders receive discounts from over 100 island vendors for shopping, dining, accommodations, car rentals, and activities.

U.S. GOVERNMENT SITES
Center for Disease Control and Prevention
wwwnc.cdc.gov/travel/destinations/aruba.htm
Full and current information regarding any health issues on Aruba are located here. Though minimal, it will inform on recommended shots and medicines.

CIA Factbook Aruba
https://www.cia.gov/library/publications/
the-world-factbook/geos/aa.html
The go-to guide for statistical information on every aspect of Aruba: Factual and impartial, it lists everything from geographic details to the number of Internet subscribers.

U.S. Department of Agriculture
www.aphis.usda.gov
Listed here is exactly what is and isn't allowed in the way of live animals, plants, and foodstuffs, and why. It explains what diseases, fungus, or parasites are problems in certain areas, and what to watch out for.

U.S. Department of State
www.state.gov/r/pa/ei/bgn/22491.htm
Find official U.S. State Department policy and news of Aruba.

U.S. Travel and Customs Regulations
www.cbp.gov/xp/cgov/travel/vacation/kbyg
Find complete description of all taxable purchases, allowances, and exemptions, plus explanation of duties charged when bringing purchases over allowance.

ARUBA GOVERNMENT AGENCIES

Aruba Airport Authority
www.airportaruba.com
A complete guide to the Reina Beatrix International Airport includes arrival times, amenities, clearing customs, and the latest notice of restricted items and luggage allowances.

Aruba Department of Foreign Affairs
www.arubaforeignaffairs.com/afa/home.do
An interesting site for travelers to learn about consular affairs and Aruba's international treaty partners. It has information about all the various international organizations with which Aruba is aligned. Anyone interested in the extent of Aruba's international relations will find the information here.

Aruba Ports Authority
www.arubaports.com
Complete listing of all cruise schedules and port information includes shore safety regulations and communications, cargo services, and cruise statistics.

Arubus:
http://arubus.com
Official website of Aruba's mass transit system features complete bus schedules to every route on the island.

Central Bureau of Statistics
www.cbs.aw/cbs/home.do
Complete statistics on every aspect of island life: This is where the CIA Factbook gets their figures.

DIMAS in English
www.aruba.com/sigma/Entry_Req-Eng.pdf
Aruba's site for immigration: Find full information on entry requirements for visiting Aruba, as well as residency requirements and permit procedures, with downloadable forms.

Government of Aruba
www.overheid.aw/index.asp
This exact web address is the official site of the Government of Aruba in Dutch, which Google can translate to English. Every aspect of government authority is explained, and current government news is posted. The translation is somewhat stilted and amusing but informative.

Governor of Aruba
www.kabga.aw/en/index.php?page=default
This site explains the position and duties of the Queen's appointed representative in Aruba.

Korps Politie Aruba
www.kparuba.com
Official site of Aruba's Police Department: It has a history of the service, its various branches and districts, and travel advisories.

BUSINESS
Department of Economic Affairs
www.arubaeconomicaffairs.aw

Details of exactly what it takes to do business in Aruba, like investing, economic reports, acquiring a business license, economic relations, and Aruba's Freezone, are explained in downloadable forms for applying for business and investment permits.

WEATHER
Departmento Meterologico Aruba
www.meteo.aw

Aruba's official site for all weather warning and forecasts provides five-day forecasts, alerts, and live weather maps, in English, Dutch, and Papiamento.

RECREATION
Arikok National Park
www.arikoknationalpark.org

Everything you want to know about Arikok National Park is here: maps, hiking trails, park news, and information about island flora and fauna.

Aruba Cruising Guide
www.aruba-cruisingguide.com

This is one of the best sources of need-to-know facts and advice for private yachts. Made by sailors for sailors, it has everything from bottom clearances and how to handle harbor entries to best places for supplies and repairs. Find downloadable forms for customs and immigration that are especially for yachts.

IGFA International Billfishing Tournament
www.igfaoffshorechampionship.com

A world series of fishing tournaments for fanatical anglers is conducted at various locations throughout the year. Bucuti and Varadero Yacht Clubs host a qualifying event every October. Only the big fish, marlin and sailfish, qualify, with a strict "catch and release" policy; no fish are taken. This site has detailed information and sign-up forms.

TRAVEL
Cruise Critic
www.cruisecritic.com

This is the most complete site for finding and booking cruises with Aruba as a port of call.

REAL ESTATE
Casnan.com
http://casnan.com/realestate

Every real estate agent on Aruba and their listings are consolidated into this site. View houses, condos, and apartment sales and rentals on the island via agents, without the need to jump around from one website to the next.

VBRO Vacation Rentals for Aruba
www.vrbo.com/vacation-rentals/caribbean/aruba

An excellent site for renting condominiums, houses, apartments, or timeshares on Aruba, this is one of the most complete listings to be found anywhere for direct owner to renter arrangements. It allows savings on both sides on the commission.

ISLAND LIFE
The Bent Page
http://bentpage.net

Novelist Daniel Putkowski is a part-time resident of Aruba. He has written three novels with the island as the setting and keeps readers current on island happenings on his blog. He punctuates it with nice photography and the occasional video. His thoughts take him anywhere and everywhere. He has an entire section dedicated to videos of driving directions.

Lago Colony
www.lago-colony.com

This is an active site with great interaction by a dedicated group. They have the unusual bond of having been born or raised in the Lago Colony during the Esso/Exxon heyday. Posters share recollections, old photos, and current news. Interesting stories and discussions bring alive this important time in Aruba's history.

Temple Beth Israel Aruba
http://bethisrael-aruba.blogspot.com
Vistors curious about Aruba's synagogue, wishing to attend services while on vacation, or curious about a destination Bar or Bat Mizvah should visit this site.

Index

Food Index

Shops Index

Accommodations Index

Acknowledgments

I wish to thank some very kind, patient people who have been very helpful to me in completing my first full-length work. In particular, I want to thank Lucie Ericksen, the Moon graphics coordinator, who was always supportive and appreciative of my submissions, and quick to answer my queries. These little things make a big difference. Also to my editor Erin, working with her was very educational and I am certain improved my writing.

A particular word of thanks goes to my colleagues at *The Morning News* for their patience and support through the months of writing this book. Chandi, Rosalinda, Ingrid, Marline, and Yanis, I am touched by your faith in me, which you have always shown, no matter what the project.

I must also acknowledge Hubert and Randy from the Aruba Central Bureau of Statistics. If they were impatient with my continual pestering for maps, images, and information, they never showed it for a moment. Also a tip of my hat to Nico Luidens at Van Dorp, who always warmly welcomed my queries, and historian Luc Alofs for his input and lively discussions. In particular, Dr. Eduard Dresser, Professor of Philosophy at the University of Aruba and history buff, for his kind cooperation.

I suppose I should toss in my dog Rocky, who faithfully sat at my feet under my desk, no matter what hour of the day or night. I knew I could always count on him.

www.moon.com

DESTINATIONS | ACTIVITIES | BLOGS | MAPS | BOOKS

MOON.COM is ready to help plan your next trip! Filled with fresh trip ideas and strategies, author interviews, informative travel blogs, a detailed map library, and descriptions of all the Moon guidebooks, Moon.com is all you need to get out and explore the world—or even places in your own backyard. While at Moon.com, sign up for our monthly e-newsletter for updates on new releases, travel tips, and expert advice from our on-the-go Moon authors. As always, when you travel with Moon, expect an experience that is uncommon and truly unique.

KEEP UP WITH MOON ON FACEBOOK AND TWITTER
JOIN THE MOON PHOTO GROUP ON FLICKR

MAP SYMBOLS

Expressway	**(** Highlight	✗ Airfield	⚲ Golf Course
Primary Road	○ City/Town	✈ Airport	**P** Parking Area
Secondary Road	◉ State Capital	▲ Mountain	▲ Archaeological Site
Unpaved Road	⊛ National Capital	✛ Unique Natural Feature	▮ Church
Trail	★ Point of Interest		▯ Gas Station
Ferry	● Accommodation	🪶 Waterfall	Glacier
Railroad	▼ Restaurant/Bar	▲ Park	Mangrove
Pedestrian Walkway	▪ Other Location	▮ Trailhead	Reef
Stairs	⋀ Campground	✗ Skiing Area	Swamp

CONVERSION TABLES

°C = (°F – 32) / 1.8
°F = (°C x 1.8) + 32
1 inch = 2.54 centimeters (cm)
1 foot = 0.304 meters (m)
1 yard = 0.914 meters
1 mile = 1.6093 kilometers (km)
1 km = 0.6214 miles
1 fathom = 1.8288 m
1 chain = 20.1168 m
1 furlong = 201.168 m
1 acre = 0.4047 hectares
1 sq km = 100 hectares
1 sq mile = 2.59 square km
1 ounce = 28.35 grams
1 pound = 0.4536 kilograms
1 short ton = 0.90718 metric ton
1 short ton = 2,000 pounds
1 long ton = 1.016 metric tons
1 long ton = 2,240 pounds
1 metric ton = 1,000 kilograms
1 quart = 0.94635 liters
1 US gallon = 3.7854 liters
1 Imperial gallon = 4.5459 liters
1 nautical mile = 1.852 km

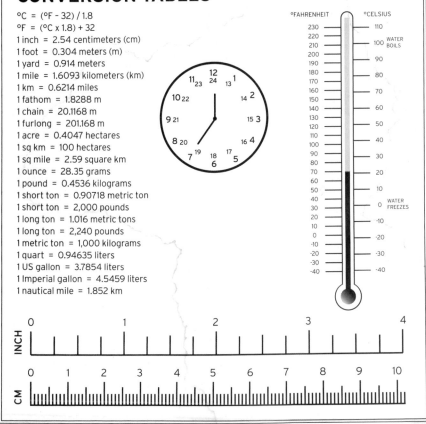

MOON ARUBA

Avalon Travel
a member of the Perseus Books Group
1700 Fourth Street
Berkeley, CA 94710, USA
www.moon.com

Editor: Erin Raber
Series Manager: Kathryn Ettinger
Copy Editor: Naomi Adler Dancis
Graphics and Production Coordinator: Lucie Ericksen
Cover Designer: Lucie Ericksen
Map Editor: Mike Morgenfeld
Cartographers: Stephanie Poulain, Mike Morgenfeld
Indexer: Greg Jewett

ISBN-13: 978-1-61238-514-3
ISSN: pending

Printing History
1st Edition – January 2014
5 4 3 2 1

Front cover photo: Palm Beach © Rosalie Klein
Title page and all interior color photos: © Rosalie Klein

Printed in Canada by Friesens

KEEPING CURRENT

If you have a favorite gem you'd like to see included in the next edition, or see anything that needs updating, clarification, or correction, please drop us a line. Send your comments via email to feedback@moon.com, or use the address above.